P9-AEU-213

Compliments of the Middle East Forum

1500 WALNUT STREET • SUITE 1050 • PHILADELPHIA PENNSYLVANIA 19102-3523
TEL: (215) 546-5406 • FAX (215) 546-5409 • E-MAIL: info@meforum.org • WEBSITE: www.meforum.org

DANCING WITH THE DEVIL

MICHAEL RUBIN

DANCING
with the
DEVIL

THE PERILS OF ENGAGING ROGUE REGIMES

Encounter Books • New York • London

First American edition published in 2014 by Encounter Books,
an activity of Encounter for Culture and Education, Inc.,
a nonprofit, tax exempt corporation.
Encounter Books website address: www.encounterbooks.com

Manufactured in the United States and printed on
acid-free paper. The paper used in this publication meets
the minimum requirements of ANSI/NISO Z39.48 1992
(R 1997) (*Permanence of Paper*).

FIRST AMERICAN EDITION

LIBRARY OF CONGRESS CATALOGING-IN-PUBLICATION DATA
Rubin, Michael, 1971–
Dancing with the devil: the perils of engaging rogue regimes/Michael Rubin.
pages cm
Includes bibliographical references and index.
ISBN 978-1-59403-723-8 (hardcover: alk. paper)—ISBN 978-1-59403-724-5 (ebook)
1. State-sponsored terrorism—Prevention. 2. Terrorism—Prevention—Political aspects.
3. Diplomacy. 4. International relations. 5. National security—United States.
6. United States—Foreign relations. I. Title.
HV6431.R85 2013
327.1'17—dc23
2013020658

CONTENTS

Introduction

PARIAHS TO PARTNERS: BRINGING ROGUES TO THE TABLE

The United States has had no shortage of enemies in its history. From Great Britain to Japan to the Soviet Union, it has fought, contained, or deterred a variety of hostile powers. Whenever possible, however, American governments prefer diplomacy to war. Historically, engagement has involved diplomats, other officials, or even presidents talking to their counterparts. During the Cold War, citizen diplomacy also became an important part of engagement. American scientists visited the Soviet Union, ping pong players traveled to China, and delegations of American Jewish activists met with Palestinian leaders. Today, diplomats view engagement as enveloping adversaries in process. Whether the adversary is the Palestine Liberation Organization, the Islamic Republic of Iran, or the Democratic People's Republic of Korea, American diplomats talk in order to set agendas, establish roadmaps, and enable more talks.

Beginning with the Clinton administration, officials have identified a category of states and nonstate actors that pose a special challenge, requiring a new concept of diplomacy. Secretary of State Madeleine Albright recognized that "dealing with the rogue states is one of the great challenges of our time . . . because they are there with the sole purpose of destroying the system." She lamented that "our friends and allies don't get it."[1] Two Clinton-era defense secretaries, William Perry and William Cohen, suggested that rogue regimes might be immune to the traditional form of deterrence that was effective during the Cold War.[2] This book examines the ways that U.S. administrations have attempted to deal with rogues; it weighs the promise and the perils of engaging rogue regimes and terrorist groups, and reflects on the policy lessons that emerge from those efforts.

What Is a Rogue?

For all the attention that presidents and the Pentagon have given to the problem of rogue regimes, there is no universal or legal definition of such a regime. The idea of "rogue regimes" has become the diplomatic equivalent of Justice Potter Stewart's quip about pornography, "I know it when I see it." Generally, we recognize a rogue when we see it. Just as few would dismiss the threat posed by terrorism to the United States simply because there is no single definition of terrorism, so the absence of an international consensus on a definition of rogue regimes does not mitigate their threat.

The concept of rogue regimes has roots in the 1970s, when political scientists used the term "pariah states" to describe isolated countries that aimed to acquire nuclear arms. Applying no value judgment to the governing ideology of such states, they singled out Taiwan and Israel as pariahs. Those countries might be pro-Western and, in Israel's case, democratic, but both sought nuclear capability because they faced hostile neighbors and were susceptible to arms embargoes.[3] In 1979, the *New York Times*, quoting intelligence officials, spoke of a "nuclear club of outcasts" comprising South Africa, Israel, and Taiwan.[4]

At the same time, a new definition of rogues was emerging, one which focused more on regime behavior than on diplomatic isolation. Television beamed stories of slaughter in Cambodia and Uganda into living rooms, transforming atrocities that policymakers might once have ignored into public obsessions. This led the *Washington Post* editorial board to articulate the difference between rogue regimes and mere dictatorships. "How does the international community deal with rogue regimes, those that under the color of national sovereignty commit unspeakable crimes against their own citizens?" the *Post* asked in 1979, naming Pol Pot and Idi Amin. As Tanzanian troops invaded Uganda, the *Post* editors applauded, saying, "It seems hypocritical to say border-crossing is never justifiable."[5] It is an enduring political irony that so many American politicians and academics today are willing to approve of force when it comes to rogues that commit atrocities against their own people, while calling for engagement with regimes that threaten U.S. national security.

In the late 1970s, terrorism also started to shape public discussion of rogue behavior. The State Department began labeling some regimes as state sponsors of terrorism in 1979. Iraq, Libya, South Yemen, and Syria were inaugural members of the club, soon joined by Cuba, Iran, North Korea, and Sudan. Nearly seventeen years before President George W. Bush would identify an "axis of evil," President Ronald Reagan spoke of "a confederation of terrorist states."[6] Parallel definitions of rogues as proliferators, human rights abusers, and terror sponsors quickly converged. U.S. officials began to describe proliferators who were also terror sponsors as rogues, outlaws, or renegades.[7] Against the backdrop of optimism about dawning freedom in the former communist bloc, lofty hope for a peace dividend, and a "new world order," the contrast between responsible states and rogues grew starker.

It was during the Clinton administration that the term "rogue" came into vogue. When Defense Secretary Les Aspin unveiled the Defense Counterproliferation Initiative in 1993, he warned that "the new nuclear danger we face is perhaps a handful of nuclear devices in the hands of rogue states or even terrorist groups."[8] Speaking the next month in Brussels, Clinton himself described Iran and Libya as "rogue states."[9] And, giving an address at Georgetown University in October

1994, Secretary of State Warren Christopher repeatedly referred to Iran and Iraq as rogue regimes.[10] In each case, the Clinton administration focused more on threats to the United States than on dangers that rogue leaders posed to their own people. Saddam was a rogue leader because he pursued nuclear weaponry and invaded Kuwait, not because he gassed Kurds and massacred Shi'ites.

It fell to Anthony Lake, Clinton's national security advisor, to define the concept precisely, although he used the slightly more diplomatic term "backlash states" as a label for Cuba, North Korea, Iran, Iraq, and Libya. "Their behavior is often aggressive and defiant," he explained. "The ties between them are growing as they seek to thwart or quarantine themselves from a global trend to which they seem incapable of adapting." They are "ruled by cliques that control power through coercion, they suppress basic human rights and promote radical ideologies." And, most important for the purposes of U.S. diplomats, Lake noted, "These nations exhibit a chronic inability to engage constructively with the outside world, and they do not function effectively in alliances—even with those like-minded."[11]

William Cohen, as defense secretary, tweaked the definition slightly to emphasize regimes that were immune to traditional deterrence. Iran's Islamic Revolution and suicide terrorism had propelled apocalyptic ide-ologies to the fore. The "mutual assured destruction" of the Cold War was predicated on the fact that no matter how antagonistic the Soviet Union was toward the United States, it was not going to risk annihilation in pursuit of its ideological goals. But if post–Cold War rogues aimed to cause destruction even if it put their own existence at risk, then traditional U.S. strategies could no longer apply.

Hence, although the fight against rogue regimes would be attached in the public mind to the George W. Bush administration with the "axis of evil" speech and the "global war on terror," it was actually Clinton's team that first explained the necessity of breaking with traditional diplo-macy, even at the cost of antagonizing friends and rivals. European allies criticized Clinton for skirting international law in his approach to rogues, while Russia criticized U.S. moves to develop a missile defense system against the backdrop of the Anti-Ballistic Missile Treaty.[12]

Critics of American policy toward rogue regimes are correct in saying that the United States has been inconsistent. The radical thinker Noam Chomsky even argued that the United States was the true rogue, and the economist Clyde V. Prestowitz Jr. has suggested that American disdain for international organizations and many treaties make it a "rogue nation."[13] Robert Litwak, a Clinton national security aide, noted the inconsistency of demonizing Cuba while treating (pre–civil war) Syria like a normal state despite its place on the State Department's terrorism list and its weapons of mass destruction programs.[14] The roots of such inconsistency lie in the desire for diplomacy. First the Clinton administration and later the first-term Obama team treated Syria benignly because the White House sought to reel it into the Middle East peace process. The effort failed spectacularly and became an illustration of the price that engagement with rogues can exact.

If there is debate over which countries are rogue, there is consensus with regard to certain regimes. The Islamic Republic of Iran broke with diplomatic norms when it took American diplomats hostage, and North Korea's reclusive communist regime has thumbed its nose at traditional diplomacy for decades. The brutality and terror sponsorship of the Libyan leader Muammar Qadhafi and the Iraqi president Saddam Hussein led both to become subject to sweeping international sanctions. Pakistan may appear to be a normal state, but the inordinate power and rogue behavior of its intelligence service places it within the definition of rogue regime. American diplomats have faced down Afghanistan's Taliban first as a government and, after 9/11, as an insurgent group. The Palestine Liberation Organization took the opposite trajectory: When American diplomats first began their dialogue, the PLO was an unrepentant terrorist group. Diplomacy led it to become a government. Other terrorist groups remain pariahs, but this has not prevented some officials from counseling engagement with them.

Why Engage?

How the United States can best handle rogue regimes is a problem that continues to confront presidents, secretaries of state, senators, and generals. Presidents have a broad menu of options ranging from diplomatic to economic to military. They have invaded and occupied, sanctioned and talked, bombed and bribed.

Each strategy has costs and benefits. The key for policymakers is to determine how to achieve goals at minimum cost. In the face of intractable foes, hard power can be tempting: Reagan bombed Libya; George H. W. Bush attacked Iraq and Panama; Clinton bombed Iraq, Afghanistan, Sudan, and Serbia, and came very close to launching airstrikes against North Korea. George W. Bush invaded both Afghanistan and Iraq. Bombing and military strikes may be effective, but the costs are high: military action is expensive, it antagonizes the international community, and it risks blowback. Every administration, for good reason, adopts the mantra that a military option against international rogues should remain on the table but as the strategy of last resort.

More often, when the White House and Congress seek to look tough, they turn to sanctions. Jimmy Carter sanctioned the Soviet Union after the invasion of Afghanistan, Reagan sanctioned Poland after the imposition of martial law, George H. W. Bush sanctioned China after the Tiananmen Square crackdown, Clinton slapped sanctions on Iran because of the Islamic Republic's support for terrorism, George W. Bush sanctioned Sudan because of Khartoum's complicity in the Darfur genocide, and Obama sanctioned Syria and Zimbabwe on account of human rights violations.

Sanctions may be symbolically satisfying and wear down rogue regimes over time, but their effectiveness—in the near term, anyway—is questionable, and they are costly to ordinary people living under the targeted regime. Reagan opposed sanctions on South Africa at least in part because black South Africans would suffer more than whites. On the other hand, when Secretary Albright was confronted with reports of Iraqi suffering under sanctions, her response was, "We think the price is worth it."[15] While tales of starving Iraqi children had been greatly exaggerated, the statement was damaging nonetheless. Perception means more than reality on the international stage, and Albright's words came to symbolize U.S. callousness. Public opinion turned against sanctions. Saddam Hussein may have been the true villain in Iraq, but it was the United States that the public condemned on the streets of London, Paris, and Berlin, as well as in the Arab Middle East. Policymakers then made narrow, targeted sanctions the economic tool of choice. But targeted sanctions elevate symbolism over effectiveness, and by avoiding discomfort they remove the potential for grassroots movements to change regime behavior. In any event, the business community often opposes sanctions, since less scrupulous Chinese, Russian, or French competitors do not hesitate to fill the gap when American companies step back.

Because of the problems inherent in other strategies, policymakers often conclude that their best option is to talk. That engagement must be a better strategy is a logical fallacy, however. Just because more coercive strategies have costs does not mean that less coercive strategies have fewer costs.

Diplomats make many arguments to advocate engaging rogues. The most basic argument is that it never hurts to talk. Within the State Department, there is a culture that treats engagement as cost-free. "We will be no worse off if we try diplomacy and fail," said Nicholas Burns, formerly the under secretary for political affairs, to the Senate Foreign Relations Committee in 2009, throwing his support behind Obama's outreach to Iran.[16] Richard Armitage, who was his boss during George W. Bush's first term, made a similar argument: "We ought to have enough confidence in our ability as diplomats to go eye to eye with people— even though we disagree in the strongest possible way—and come away without losing anything."[17]

Officials often interpret a rogue's willingness to talk as a sign that progress is possible. In 1999, for example, the State Department spokesman James B. Foley defended engagement with North Korea. "We don't meet for the sake of meeting," he said. "We believe that it is a positive sign that we and North Korea decide[d] to meet bilaterally, and we have such meetings because we believe progress can be achieved."[18] Joel S. Wit, a former State Department official and North Korea specialist, counseled the same approach early in the Obama administration. "Since Mr. Kim has said publicly that he is open to talks, the United States should do nothing to shut what may be a window of opportunity."[19] James Kelly, who led talks with North Korea for the Bush administration, argued that engagement provided the best hope. "Persistence, quiet resolve, and calmly working with allies and partners will serve U.S. interests better than loud speeches, threats or ineffective sanctions attempts," he reasoned.[20] Diplomats have likewise counseled unrestricted engagement toward Iran. "Diplomats should talk, even with our foes," explained L. Bruce Laingen, the senior diplomat held hostage in Tehran after the Khomeini revolution. "That's what we do. It doesn't make sense for us not to talk."[21]

Politicians also get involved in the game. Senator Arlen Specter was a vocal proponent of engaging rogue regimes, and he made flipping Syria his special goal. He never succeeded. After meeting one Syrian delegation in 2003, he admitted, "The only real agreement came on the utility of dialogue even in the absence of any agreement on any proposed solution."[22] But no matter: Specter saw the fact that the Syrians were talking at all as an achievement. The senator from Pennsylvania was no outlier in this regard; the belief that talk is useful as the alternative to isolation permeates American diplomacy. According to Charles Hunter, the top diplomat at the U.S. embassy in Damascus for much of 2010, "It is better to engage, discuss differences and try to overcome them, than to ignore or isolate."[23]

Keeping the door open is not the only justification for engaging rogues. Prominent politicians saw engagement as an important component of national defense in the post–Cold War world order. "Diplomacy has become more important than ever as a vital front-line defense of American interests," said Joe Biden, then the ranking Democrat on the Senate Foreign Relations Committee, in 1997.[24] Engagement was seen as a way to avoid misunderstanding and prevent rogues from stumbling into conflict. In 2003, as evidence mounted that North Korea was cheating on its international commitments to curtail its nuclear weapons program,

Biden declared, "Talking is not appeasement. It is the most effective way to tell North Korea what it must do if it wants normal relations with us. In fact, in dealing with an isolated regime and a closed-off leader, talking clearly and directly is critical if we want to avoid miscommunication and miscalculation."[25] Madeleine Albright echoed Biden's view. "Talking is the way you deliver the message that you need to have received by the other side," she told a Senate Democratic leadership news conference.[26] Direct diplomacy can certainly facilitate communication, but the question for policymakers is whether it is possible to communicate positions toward rogue regimes without formally engaging them—for example, by means of a presidential speech.

Proponents of engagement also cite amelioration of rogue behavior as a benefit of engagement, even if talks ultimately lead nowhere. Negotiations can embroil adversaries in process. In the Middle East, much of the strategic logic of engagement with Palestinians in the 1990s was to entangle the PLO so tightly in a peace process that they would be unable to extricate themselves. Nicholas Burns adopted similar logic when he suggested that "negotiation may now be the most effective way to slow down Iran's nuclear progress."[27] Leon Sigal, a former editorialist for the *New York Times*, suggested that dialogue with rogues was the best mechanism to manage their psychology. Reasoning that those states were "insecure," he said that coercion and threats of force "may give them more of a reason" to seek nuclear arms.[28]

Henry Kissinger disagreed. Recalling Cold War talks with the Soviet Union, he observed, "When talks become their own objective, they are at the mercy of the party most prepared to break them off, or at least the party that is able to give that impression."[29] Still, Kissinger favored engagement with rogues under certain circumstances. He argued that continuing the nuclear stalemate with Iran, for example, "would amount to a de facto acquiescence by the international community in letting new entrants into the nuclear club."[30]

If some diplomats use engagement as just a way to manage crisis, others believe that it offers real opportunity. In their study of the Arab-

Israeli peace process, Daniel Kurtzer, a former ambassador to both Egypt and Israel, together with Scott Lasensky, a Middle East specialist recruited into the State Department during the Obama administration, argued that diplomats can take two general approaches to reconciling with enemies: They can wait for opportunities in which to seek peace, or they can use engagement to create opportunities.[31] This was also Senator Chuck Hagel's logic when he advocated more dialogue with Iran. "Engagement creates dialogue and opportunities to identify common interests," he said.[32] The State Department spokesman P. J. Crowley described the Obama administration's Middle East peace strategy in similar terms:

> *We want to get this process started. Once we get into the process, we think that it has the potential to create a dynamic that will create some momentum. . . . We recognize that until you get into a process, it is almost impossible to make progress on these issues. So getting them started, beginning to address the specific issues at the heart of this effort, then we think that that dynamic—it will take care of itself.[33]*

Seasoned diplomats also identify more precise benefits. Ryan Crocker, a former ambassador to Iraq and Afghanistan, trumpeted the intelligence value of engagement. He advocated engaging Hezbollah in order to learn more about the organization, its personnel, and its internal divisions.[34] Likewise, Nicholas Burns argued that three decades without diplomatic relations with Iran had left Washington operating in the dark. "In the absence of diplomatic relations and the lack of a substantial American business or journalistic presence in Iran, we have no real basis to understand its government, society and people," Burns told a Senate committee.[35] Whether the intelligence gained in such diplomatic initiatives provides a net gain over sophisticated satellite pictures, phone intercepts, multibillion-dollar espionage services and broadcast media remains an open question.

The Uncertainty of Engagement

Diplomacy may provide opportunities, but it also imposes costs. Some are quite literal: diplomats often couple engagement with financial and material inducements, sometimes to the tune of billions of dollars. The results may or may not be worth the price. Had American officials not sat down to talk with North Korea's leadership in the mid-1990s, American security would be no worse; indeed, the U.S. Treasury would be wealthier, and the American strategic position would be no worse.

Aid and inducements may actually create reverse incentives and effectively reward rogues for their defiance. The United States helped bankroll a nuclear reactor for North Korea and has offered technological assistance to Iran. Bribing adversaries with incentives can contribute to a squeaky-wheel syndrome. In 2001, for example, the United States provided Mali, one of the poorest countries on earth but at the time the freest and most democratic Muslim state in the world, just $33 million in development assistance, while Lebanon, a country with one-third the population and host to numerous terrorist groups, received 50 percent more. It was not until a coup ended Mali's democracy and al-Qaeda took root in its territory that the State Department again focused on the West African country.

Successful engagement requires assessment of an adversary's sincerity, weakness, and desire. Does the rogue leader truly seek a resolution or does he merely want to delay, to give diplomats reason for hope and hold off sanctions while he pursues other aims? Arguably, Muammar Qadhafi chose to engage sincerely only in 2003, several years into his dialogue with American and British officials. Yasir Arafat, chairman of the Palestine Liberation Organization, was not sincere in his dialogue leading up to the second Camp David summit, even if some of his subordinates were. Saddam Hussein seldom approached the negotiating table with sincerity. Whenever rogues engage insincerely, they can avoid accountability, consolidate their position, rearm, and make resolutions more difficult.

Engagement does not happen in a vacuum; circumstances matter. Neither the success of Nixon's outreach to China nor Reagan's détente with the Soviet Union was inevitable. Both were the result of a confluence of events that affected the thinking of policymakers in Beijing and Moscow. Diplomatic breakthroughs occurred on the Korean Peninsula and in the Middle East after the United States' lightning victory against Saddam Hussein in 1991. The Soviet Union was gone, and rogues had few patrons. But when Iran backs Hezbollah and Pakistan supports the Taliban, engagement with either group often goes nowhere.

Calculations of strength and weakness play into the question of whether to engage. When Washington reaches an impasse with a rogue, does the threat of military force improve the chance for engagement to work, or does it set the United States down a slippery slope to war? If policymakers bluster but then back down, as Obama did after Bashar al-Assad's regime used chemical weapons against civilians in Syria, is it possible to continue engagement with credibility, or will rogue regimes conclude that America is, in the words of Osama bin Laden, merely a "paper tiger"? When rogue actors do not take American threats seriously, how might the United States restore its credibility?

Perhaps the most difficult question with regard to engagement is also the most basic: When presidents or diplomats engage, how do they measure success? It is far easier to gauge military success, and the cost of military action is also easy to calculate in terms of blood and treasure. The success of sanctions is also quantifiable: If sanctions are imposed to change behavior, compel withdrawal from territory, or force the abandonment of terrorism, it is easy to judge both success and cost in lost business. With engagement, it's trickier. Seldom does engagement lead outright to a rogue regime dismantling weapons programs or ceasing terror sponsorship. Diplomats often shy away from announcing metrics of interim success out of fear that politicians will lose patience for diplomacy if those are unmet. As important, diplomats seldom acknowledge that diplomacy can exact a cost in terms of lost momentum, lost credibility, or time that adversaries can use to develop weapons or plan terrorist attacks.

The Perils of Engagement

Talking to rogue regimes and terrorist groups makes headlines. Newspapers are far more likely to track the latest talks between American and North Korean diplomats than they are to report on the latest *tête-à-tête* between the United States and Sweden. Rogue engagement makes or breaks legacies. Had President Jimmy Carter left office after brokering peace between Egypt and Israel, he might be remembered as a brilliant foreign policy tactician. But the Iran hostage crisis sank his presidency and tarred his legacy. Clinton likewise gambled heavily on peace between Israelis and Palestinians in part to shape his legacy. Not only did his peace deal collapse, but it led to decades of further strife in the region.

Moral clarity is often the first casualty of diplomacy with rogues. Two years after the Tiananmen Square crackdown, Biden condemned George H. W. Bush's attempt to engage China. "What President Bush and Secretary Baker have been seeking to engage is the world's last major Communist regime," he said; "it is a regime marked by brutality at home and irresponsibility abroad; and it is a regime the United States should now cease to court and must no longer appease."[36]

If rogues are intractable, engagement may simply appease them. It was for this reason, at least rhetorically, that George W. Bush refused to engage rogue regimes. Speaking before Israel's Knesset on May 15, 2008, the president said:

> *Some seem to believe that we should negotiate with the terrorists and radicals, as if some ingenious argument will persuade them they have been wrong all along. We have heard this foolish delusion before. As Nazi tanks crossed into Poland in 1939, an American senator declared: "Lord, if I could only have talked to Hitler, all this might have been avoided." We have an obligation to call this what it is—the false comfort of appeasement, which has been repeatedly discredited by history.*[37]

Because diplomacy with rogue regimes has such high stakes, the decision to engage rogues often affects the way politics and policymaking work. Political appointees in the State Department serve at the pleasure of the president and their careers depend on political loyalty, so they have a stake in diplomacy's success. Career diplomats may have policy agendas just as strong as those of their political counterparts, if not stronger—though they might react with indignation to anyone who questioned their integrity. Diplomats immerse themselves in raw intelligence to decide what their superiors see or do not see. If they bury evidence of an adversary's insincerity, other officials may develop a false belief that diplomacy is succeeding. Often there is a reckoning when intelligence and reality diverge. In foreign policy, the price is paid in blood and treasure.

The State Department is especially susceptible to political manipulation. Many diplomats see engagement as their raison d'être and amplify any glimmer of hope, however contrived, into justification for new engagement. When Congress involves itself in foreign policy—making engagement conditional on a rogue's cessation of terrorism, for example—diplomats avoid findings that might be the death knell for an initiative they believe in. It is not only a problem within the State Department. As administrations become invested in high-profile diplomatic engagement, many officials face the temptation of shaping intelligence to support the initiative and manipulating the metrics by which to judge the effectiveness of their efforts.

Diplomacy can also constrain other options. As the White House pursues rapprochement, it often pressures agencies to suspend parallel policy initiatives—covert operations, military preparation, and even human rights reporting—that might upset adversaries or cause the international community to doubt the American commitment to dialogue. Clinton, for example, ordered that an FBI report fingering Iran in the 1996 Khobar Towers bombing in Saudi Arabia be recalled in order to protect the "dialogue of civilizations" that the Iranian president Mohammad Khatami was promoting. In the run-up to the 2003 Iraq War, Condoleezza Rice, the national security advisor, suspended postwar planning because she worried that preparing for conflict would mar the optics of diplomacy.

Engagement with terrorist groups brings its own unique costs. When diplomats talk to Hezbollah in Lebanon, Hamas in Palestine, or the Kurdistan Workers' Party (PKK) in Turkey, they legitimize the path to the negotiating tables that these groups have walked. The symbolism of such engagement might alter the political climate.

Even when engagement does not fail, success can be costly. As Serbs massacred Bosnians in the former Yugoslavia, Joe Biden criticized how "diplomatic intervention . . . compromised principle at every turn."[38] When Milosevic finally consented to cut a diplomatic deal, Biden was dismayed, saying he had "mixed emotions" about Milosevic's agreement to a truce. "I believe he only understands force," Biden explained. "I believe that he is the problem. I believe that, ultimately, force will have to be used. And, quite frankly, I wish we had just used this force."[39]

The struggle over when and how to engage rogue regimes is not new. Fundamentally, it is interests that determine when to engage. As Kissinger noted, "If ideology necessarily determined foreign policy, Hitler and Stalin would never have joined hands any more than Richelieu and the Sultan of Turkey would have three centuries earlier. But common geopolitical interest is a powerful bond."[40] At the same time, a cost-benefit analysis colors the assessment of interests. If one lesson can be learned from the history of engaging rogue regimes, it is that diplomacy is never a cost-free strategy. Indeed, it can often be deceptively costly to American national security.

In any case, the United States no longer has the luxury of isolation. Rogue regimes, international pariahs, and terrorists who once focused their activities thousands of miles away are developing the means to strike anywhere in the world. Talking alone will not solve the problem.

Chapter One

FROM MACHIAVELLI TO MUAMMAR

Diplomacy, like war, spans cultures and centuries. Its origins are shrouded in time. "There came a stage when the anthropoid apes inhabiting one group of caves realized that it might be profitable to reach some understanding with neighboring groups regarding the limits of their respective hunting territories," the British diplomat Harold Nicolson speculated.[1]

Both Babylonian and Pharaonic documents reveal regular exchanges of envoys with neighboring kingdoms.[2] The Chinese strategist Sun Tzu (544–496 BC) did not speak directly of diplomacy in *The Art of War*, but he suggested, "To subdue the enemy without fighting is the acme of skill."[3] Around the same time, Greek city-states exchanged ambassadors and negotiated truces, although embassies were weak, as Demosthenes noted: "Ambassadors have no battleships at their disposal, or heavy infantry, or fortresses." The Athenian orator and statesman went on to describe the disadvantage that democracies suffer in diplomacy: they seldom react as quickly as a dictatorship does.[4] Perhaps this is why the Romans preferred to conquer and impose their will, resorting to diplomacy only in order to subjugate others without the trouble of war, or to quiet frontiers while fighting elsewhere.[5]

Notions of diplomacy evolved separately in different cultures. Not every civilization shares Western assumptions about the use and value of diplomacy. In the eleventh century, the Persian vizier Nizam al-Mulk (1018–1092) described diplomacy as a cover for other activities in the *Siyasatnameh* (The Book of Government), a seminal text meant to be a manual for kings. "When kings send ambassadors to one another, their purpose is not merely the message or the letter which they communicate openly, but secretly they have a hundred other points and objects in view," the vizier wrote.[6] To this day, altruism and conflict resolution have little place in Persian notions of diplomacy. Before he was taken hostage in 1979, the American chargé d'affaires Bruce Laingen explained how Iranians negotiate. "Perhaps the single dominant aspect of the Persian psyche is an overriding egoism," he wrote, adding, "One should never assume that his side of the issue will be recognized, let alone that it will be conceded to have merits."[7]

Like Nizam al-Mulk, the Florentine statesman and writer Niccolò Machiavelli (1469–1527) maintained a skeptical view of negotiation. It was during his life that the Italian peninsula's various republics began to station resident ambassadors in rival states. Machiavelli did not write about diplomacy directly—he may not have felt it to be among the most important tools of statecraft—but he was well versed in it. His public position required him to issue instructions to Florentine diplomats, and he undertook a number of diplomatic missions himself, both within Italy and later in France and Germany. His experience may well have contributed to his famously cynical approach to international relations.[8]

While Machiavelli elevated strength of arms over the cunning of diplomats, he recognized that dialogue was a necessary delaying tactic while states consolidated their strength. "What princes have to do at the outset of their careers," he argued, "republics also must do until such time as they become powerful and rely on force alone."[9] Diplomacy was often essential to delay rather than avert war. "The Romans never had two very big wars going on at the same time," he observed. Rather, after they selected their chief military target, they would work "industriously to foster tranquility" among their other neighbors until such time as they could be confident of a military victory.[10]

The basis of modern diplomacy is the inviolability of agreements, but Machiavelli had little patience for such notions of honor. "A prudent ruler ought not to keep faith when by doing so it would be against his interests, and when the reason which made him bind himself no longer exists," he wrote.[11] Western diplomacy may have evolved far from the time of Machiavelli, but it would be naïve to assume that twenty-first-century rogues have followed the same path of development. Too often, Western engagement of rogue regimes is akin to a matchup between Machiavelli and Neville Chamberlain. In such circumstances, Chamberlain seldom wins.

Machiavelli may have de-emphasized diplomacy, but his friend Francesco Guicciardini (1483–1540), a Florentine ambassador, was more willing to engage with rival states. At the same time, Guicciardini understood that diplomacy gone sour could discredit the supporters of negotiation and invite conflict.[12] This view was challenged in the seventeenth century, when Armand Jean du Plessis (1585–1642), the Cardinal and Duke of Richelieu, advocated continuous diplomacy and suggested that negotiation could "never do harm."[13] This philosophy was wrong then, just as it is now. There is a very real cost to engagement, and a tremendous cost to continuous negotiation—diplomacy for diplomacy's sake. As Geoff Berridge, professor of international politics at the University of Leicester, and his colleagues observed in their compendium of diplomatic theory, constant engagement raises "the risk of being committed to bad agreement by corrupt, incompetent or simply exhausted ambassadors."[14]

During Richelieu's time, the Thirty Years' War provided the Dutch diplomat Hugo Grotius (1583–1645) with a backdrop for reflection in *Three Books on the Law of War and Peace*. Grotius touched on the issue of diplomacy with rogue adversaries and countered the notion, embraced by some of his peers and by many twenty-first-century proponents of engagement, that every state should receive diplomats from every other state, regardless of how distasteful their governments may be. While Grotius argued against refusing ambassadors without cause, he suggested that legitimate cause could lie in the ambassador himself, the nation sending him, or the purpose for which he was sent. There was no reason, he believed, to conduct diplomacy with representatives of "wicked" states.[15]

Through the seventeenth century and the eighteenth, across Europe, principles of diplomatic immunity and proper etiquette took shape. Wars came to be shorter as power politics displaced religious imperative. Simultaneously, European-style diplomacy began to spread into Asia, as European missions became permanent features in Persia, China, and Japan. Western states, however, did not see their diplomacy in Asia and Africa as being practiced among equals. European states were powerful, and when European diplomats grew frustrated with the slow pace or the direction of talk, they would combine diplomacy with military coercion. The era of gunboat diplomacy was born. Indeed, while the Prussian military theorist Carl von Clausewitz (1780–1831) suggested that "War is a mere continuation of policy by other means," war in the nineteenth century had become inseparable from diplomacy as the West approached the East.

Sir Ernest Satow (1843–1929), a British diplomat posted to Japan in the mid-nineteenth century, saw an advantage in gunboat diplomacy, saying: "Questions were settled promptly that, without the application of pressure on the spot, have a tendency to drag on for months and years." Still, he viewed this approach to diplomacy as "liable to abuse."[16] Impatient diplomats might call in the gunboats prematurely. Certainly, nineteenth-century gunboats, much like twenty-first-century drones, left resentment that simmered for decades.

Secret agreements and alliances were also a characteristic of diplomacy up until World War I, when the unprecedented carnage provoked popular anger at traditional diplomatic norms. Europeans and Americans alike applauded President Woodrow Wilson's call for "open covenants of peace openly arrived at."[17] Around the same time, advances in communications—first the telegraph and soon afterward the telephone and radio—diluted the autonomy of diplomats and returned power to the rulers they represented. Finally, the airplane enabled summitry.[18]

Wilsonian ideals were embraced by the young British diplomat and writer Harold Nicolson (1886–1968). With the rise of democracy, he argued, professional diplomats must be responsive to the will of elected officials.[19] Hence, in the United States, the Senate ratifies ambassadors. While Nicolson's observation might seem rational, the rogue dynamic breaks down its logic. Groups like the Palestine Liberation Organization, Hezbollah, Hamas, and the Taliban derive their authority from a willingness to use violence. When Western diplomats engage these rogues, they conduct diplomacy with agents who are not always representative of the people who inhabit the territories in question. For example, Western diplomats engaging the PLO after the outbreak of the first intifada bypassed local authority and empowered a more radical and recalcitrant terrorist organization. Likewise, a willingness to engage the Taliban disenfranchised more numerous but less violent factions within Afghanistan's Pashtun population.

Henry Kissinger—perhaps the most famous diplomat of the Cold War era, serving under Presidents Richard Nixon and Gerald Ford—believed that the behavior of states had a historical basis.[20] He argued that the twentieth century inaugurated a new kind of world system, one built upon nation-states rather than empires. "None of the most important countries which must build a new world order have had any experience with the multistate system that is emerging," he noted. "Never before has a new world order had to be assembled from so many different perceptions, or on so global a scale."[21] Kissinger warned that "History is not, of course, a cookbook offering pretested recipes" for how states should interact. "No academic discipline can take from our shoulders the burden of difficult choices."[22] Too often, diplomats who engage rogues have believed they could follow a formula, and have projected their own sense of history onto their opponents. This is a recipe for disaster.

The 1961 Vienna Convention on Diplomatic Relations, ratified by 189 different countries, codified the privileges and rights of diplomats and embassies. Diplomats won immunity and embassies became inviolate. Not every country has signed the Vienna Convention, however. States that lack full recognition are not signatories. Nor are groups fighting for statehood or some other ideological concern. Even countries that are signatories often contravene the convention. The seizure of the U.S. embassy in Tehran by Iranian revolutionaries certainly violated both its letter and its spirit. So does the terrorist targeting of an enemy's diplomats. There is no shortage of rogue actors.

Changing Attitudes on Engaging Rogues

While diplomacy has evolved over time, so too have attitudes toward engagement with rogue regimes. The twentieth century was marked by great evil, with two world wars and the rise of totalitarian regimes causing tens of millions of deaths. Since World War II, it has become a cliché to cite the experience of engaging Adolf Hitler in discussions of diplomacy with rogue regimes.

Comparisons between Hitler and today's rogues may seem cheap, but the prologue to World War II nevertheless demonstrates both the promise and the perils of diplomacy. Germans resented the burdens placed upon them by the Treaty of Versailles. After Hitler violated the disarmament provisions of the treaty in 1935, the British foreign secretary John Simon rushed to Berlin, where the two hammered out a new agreement to limit naval forces. Hitler called the signing ceremony "the happiest day of my life."[23] The reason became clear in hindsight: Britain's eagerness to negotiate convinced him that he could act with impunity. Indeed, British appeasement had become the rule rather than the exception. When Benito Mussolini declared his intention to conquer Abyssinia, the new British foreign secretary, Anthony Eden, suggested that Mussolini might satiate his imperial ambition with Ogaden only. To sweeten the loss of Abyssinia's southeastern region, Eden would offer the Ethiopian emperor a slice of British Somaliland. Appeasement failed, however. Eden's willingness to compromise on Ogaden convinced Mussolini that he would suffer no serious consequence from fulfilling his ambition.

Of course, the most famous example of failed engagement is Chamberlain's attempt to strike a deal with Hitler. Seeking to avert war, Chamberlain agreed to allow Germany to annex the Sudetenland in exchange for peace. Neither Berlin nor London paid any heed to the Czech government's objections. Returning to London, Chamberlain declared that the agreement represented "peace in our time." Six months later, German troops occupied Prague. Less than six months after that, the Nazis invaded Poland, initiating the bloodiest war in history.

To this day, opponents of engagement pillory statesmen and diplomats with analogies to Chamberlain.[24] After the Iraq Study Group led by James Baker, the former secretary of state, urged engagement with Iran, the Hollywood producer and political activist David Zucker lampooned Baker as a latter-day Chamberlain, a charge which newspapers and magazines repeated.[25]

In the view of Paul Kennedy, a historian at Yale, this treatment of Chamberlain is unfair. "When do you know that these dictators' appetites are never going to be fully sated by compromises within the existing international system?" he asked. History, after all, is replete with examples of successful compromise. Kennedy gives several, including London's settlement of the disputed Canadian border to buy peace with Washington. The deal sacrificed land that may rightfully have been British, but it also freed the British military to focus on problems in Asia and the Middle East.[26] The problem with Kennedy's analysis, however, is that it conflates rivals and rogues. British officials may not have believed Washington's positions to be correct or just, but they understood that American officials would abide by the terms of agreements once reached.

The willingness to negotiate and keep deals, even when they are not advantageous, was a major component of British strategy. Perhaps this was one reason why Winston Churchill, speaking at a White House luncheon on June 26, 1954, famously quipped, "It is better to jaw-jaw than to war-war." And, indeed, no matter how tense the rivalry between Cold War adversaries grew, engagement never ceased. Baker cited President Franklin Delano Roosevelt's engagement with Josef Stalin during World War II in disputing the claim that dialogue with enemies amounts to appeasement. "Talking to hostile states . . . is not appeasement," he said. "It is good foreign policy." Baker reasoned, "In a perfect world, we'd only work with Democracies, but the German threat justified" dealing with Stalin.[27] Roosevelt's acquiescence to Soviet designs over Eastern Europe at Yalta *was* appeasement, however, and a mistake that no subsequent U.S. president—not even Jimmy Carter—would replicate.

In July 1955, four heads of state—President Dwight D. Eisenhower; the Soviet premier, Nikolai Bulganin; the British prime minister, Sir Anthony Eden; and the French prime minister, Edgar Faure—met at their first postwar summit. The press spoke of "the spirit of Geneva." Popular enthusiasm for engagement, however, did not equate to progress. Soviet troops crushed Hungarian freedom seekers the following year, and Khrushchev threatened to use nuclear weapons against Britain and France during the Suez crisis.[28] Soviet premiers were willing to pose before the Western press, but they approached public diplomacy and engagement as tools to pursue alongside espionage, sabotage, and military coercion. This might be why John F. Kennedy, then a congressman from Massachusetts, remarked, "The barbarian may have taken the knife out of his teeth to smile, but the knife is still in his fist."[29]

Twelve years later, when President Lyndon Johnson met Alexei Kosygin, Khrushchev's successor, in Glassboro, New Jersey, the Western press was quick to evoke "the spirit of Glassboro."[30] Again, diplomacy's promise proved illusory. Little more than a year later, Soviet tanks crushed the Prague Spring and North Vietnam launched its Tet Offensive.[31]

Reaching out to enemies is not always for naught. The Egyptian president Anwar Sadat's groundbreaking visit to Israel symbolizes the power of diplomacy to bridge enmity and to solve seemingly intractable disputes peacefully. It was a bold move, but it must be understood in context: Sadat sought engagement only after trying war. Only after he failed to destroy Israel by military means did he seek to achieve more limited aims through dialogue.

An enthusiastic press extolled the romance of dialogue with enemies. Averting war is a noble aim, and diplomatic careers are made by breaking through barriers. President Nixon's trip to China is as much his legacy as Watergate. President Reagan's diplomacy with Mikhail Gorbachev figures large in his presidency. Following a summit with the Soviet premier in 1985, Reagan told Congress, "We agreed on a number of matters. We agreed to continue meeting. There's always room for movement, action, and progress when people are talking to each other instead of about each other."[32] Although the summit produced nothing concrete, it helped forge a relationship between the two men that proved pivotal in ending the Cold War.

Too often, however, proponents of engagement decontextualize triumphs such as Nixon's or Reagan's. As Kissinger explained, "Only extraordinary concern about Soviet purposes could explain the Chinese wish to sit down with the nation heretofore vilified as the archenemy."[33] Reagan pursued engagement—sometimes against the advice of trusted advisors—but he worked hard to set the right circumstances. Had it not been for a multiyear and multibillion-dollar arms buildup and the willingness to use force against Soviet proxies in Grenada, Angola, Nicaragua, and elsewhere, he could not have achieved a position of strength to enable diplomacy to succeed.

The collapse of the Soviet Union and fall of the Berlin Wall ushered in a period of unprecedented optimism. Ascending the podium at the United Nations, Mikhail Gorbachev declared, "We must look for ways to improve the international situation and build a new world, and we must do it together."[34] The political scientist Francis Fukuyama famously announced "the end of history." Rogue regimes soon spoiled the party, however. While democracy swept away the former communist regimes of Eastern Europe, North Korea stubbornly refused to get the message, but instead escalated its saber rattling and accelerated its drive to acquire nuclear weapons. Iraq's invasion of Kuwait reminded the world that Middle Eastern rogues were alive and well. Iran continued putting on weekly "Death to America" rallies. Rather than end Palestinian-Israeli violence, the Oslo Accords arguably worsened it. The Soviet Union might have exited stage left, but the curtain did not come down; instead, rogue regimes took center stage.

Both engagement and containment became strategies of choice. The Clinton administration embraced a policy of "dual containment" against Iraq and Iran, and it embargoed Libya, but meanwhile engaged the Palestine Liberation Organization, North Korea, and even the Taliban.

George W. Bush campaigned largely on domestic issues; he attacked Clinton's entanglements in Bosnia, Haiti, and Kosovo, and spoke scornfully of nation-building initiatives. The 9/11 terrorist attacks in New York and Washington forced a paradigm shift. For the first time since 1812, a foreign enemy had struck the American mainland. The 2002 National Security Strategy encapsulated the paradigm shift, fleshing out a concept not only of deterrence but also of preemption against rogue regimes and terrorist groups.

Congress and the American people united around military intervention in Afghanistan, but the Bush administration's decision to invade and occupy Iraq was far more polarizing. Although Bush entered Iraq with bipartisan support, the war turned into a political football. Critics attacked Bush's position on Iraq and his national security doctrine more broadly. The multibillion-dollar Iraq War demonstrated the cost in blood and treasure of abandoning engagement, even when it came to a brutal dictator like Saddam Hussein. Whereas Bush's policies toward rogue regimes mirrored those of his predecessors, they soon became the subject of fierce debate, particularly in the run-up to the 2008 election. On July 23, 2007, the broadcast journalist Anderson Cooper asked Senator Obama whether he would agree to meet the leaders of Iran, Syria, Venezuela, Cuba, and North Korea in his first year as president. Obama responded affirmatively, saying, "The notion that somehow not talking to countries is punishment to them . . . is ridiculous."[35]

Obama wasted no time in making engagement the central pillar of his foreign policy. "To those who cling to power through corruption and deceit and the silencing of dissent, know that you are on the wrong side of history," he declared in his inaugural address, but, he added, "We will extend a hand if you are willing to unclench your fist."

Scholars applauded Obama's approach. Professor Charles Kupchan of Georgetown University argued that engagement, often coupled with concession, was the best way to reconcile with adversaries. "Obama is on the right track in reaching out to adversaries. Long-standing rivalries tend to thaw as a result of mutual accommodation, not coercive intimidation." While Kupchan recognized that the United States might still need to isolate some "recalcitrant regimes" that refused to engage, he was optimistic. "Russia, Iran, North Korea, Cuba, and Myanmar have all demonstrated a least a modicum of interest in engagement with the United States."[36]

Kupchan, however, made a common mistake: Interest in engagement does not necessarily correlate to interest in reform, especially when the incentives gained and time wasted in diplomacy are the rogue regime's only goals. Negotiation has resolved past rivalry, but rogue regimes are not simply adversarial governments. In 1966, diplomacy may have helped Malaysia and Indonesia step back from the brink of war, but both had responsible governments that embraced diplomacy as a mechanism of conflict resolution. Conflict between North and South Korea, or for that matter the United States and the Taliban, continues not because of an absence of engagement, but rather because neither Kim Jong Un nor Mullah Omar has demonstrated a willingness to abide by the norms of international diplomacy.

Obama may have breathed new life into diplomacy with rogue regimes, but he did not end the debate about the wisdom of such a strategy, either in the United States or in Europe.

America vs. Europe

Through much of the twentieth century, partisan debates seldom shook the foundations of U.S. foreign policy, but disagreements as to diplomatic strategy often strained American relations with European allies.

American isolationism may have led to pitched battles over U.S. involvement in war, but after the sinking of the *Lusitania* and after Japan's surprise attack on Pearl Harbor, politicians united behind the president. During the Cold War, the necessity of countering Soviet designs was a bipartisan assumption. When politicians did treat national security as a political football, such as during the 1960 Nixon-Kennedy debate, it was more often to demonstrate hawkishness than to express fundamental disagreement. While conservatives lambast Jimmy Carter and liberals pillory Ronald Reagan, the two administrations maintained a common position against Soviet expansion, in favor of a strong alliance with Israel, and suspicious of Chinese intentions.

Carter may have embraced diplomacy with rogues, yet he understood that the Soviet Union had "little intrinsic interest in restraint." Western Europeans were not so certain, however. "Most European governments have the far more modest expectation that a shrewd, businesslike political and economic relationship will bolster the position of those in Eastern Europe and the Soviet Union who stress the need for economic modernization over military expansion," explained Peter Langer, a research associate at the Institute for Foreign Policy Analysis. "By treating the Kremlin as a negotiating partner, this approach will give Soviet leaders a stake in long-term détente."[37]

The Cold War revealed stark differences between the American and the European approach to diplomacy with rogue regimes and terrorists. As the *Economist* noted in 1982, "When Americans are nervous, they tend to get pugnacious. . . . They prefer strength to subtlety. When Europeans are nervous, they slide toward caution and call for patience and compromise."[38] A poll the following year found that 70 percent of the British public lacked any confidence in Reagan's judgment on diplomatic issues.[39] Vice President George H. W. Bush brushed off such skepticism when he visited Europe in February 1983. "I'm sorry," he said. "The United States is the leader of the free world and under this Administration, we are beginning once again to act like it."[40]

Likewise, European and American attitudes often differ with regard to engaging terrorist groups. American administrations of both parties tend to espouse American exceptionalism and embrace moral clarity. In *Years of Upheaval*, Kissinger ridiculed the notion of talking with terrorists. "We did not have a high incentive to advance the 'dialogue' with the PLO, as the fashionable phrase ran later," he wrote, "not because of Israeli pressures but because of our perception of the American national interest."[41] Europeans take a more pragmatic approach. While American governments refuse to negotiate with terrorists to release hostages, for example, European governments often do it with a wink and a nod.

Why should the United States and Europe approach diplomacy with terrorists and rogue regimes so differently? History is one reason. The United States may have been party to the twentieth century's great conflicts, but Europe was the battlefield. Americans in the United States sacrificed material comfort, but Europeans sacrificed their cities, farms, and homes. Another historical factor is Europe's imperial ventures, which left a moral equivalence in their wake. In 1975, the British journalist Gerald Seymour coined the phrase "One man's terrorist is another man's freedom fighter" in his novel *Harry's Game*, set during the height of the British conflict with the Irish Republican Army.

Geography is also a key. During the Cold War, while the threat of Soviet missiles hung over every American and European city, only the European populace faced the threat of Soviet tanks, artillery, and short-range missiles. It was Europe that was America's strategic depth; the relationship was not reciprocal. With the collapse of the Berlin Wall, the Soviet threat may have evaporated, but Europe's geographic challenge did not. Even in a globalized age, the Atlantic Ocean insulates the United States from chaos in the Middle East and Africa. Any instability let alone war in Libya could send tens of thousands of migrants across the Mediterranean into Europe.

Geography heightens the security threat to Europe. During the Cold War, it was far easier for Soviet-sponsored terrorist groups to operate in Europe than in the United States. Indeed, while Americans faced sporadic attacks by Puerto Rican nationalists, the Baader-Meinhof Gang terrorized Germany and the Red Brigades agitated Italy. At the height of the Palestinian terrorist campaign, the PLO and associated groups targeted airports in Italy and Austria; they hijacked or blew up planes from Great Britain, Switzerland, and France. In the first decade after the Islamic Revolution in Iran, revolutionary assassins killed eleven dissidents on French soil, sometimes hitting French citizens in the crossfire. Muammar Qadhafi retaliated against the 1986 U.S. attack on Libya by firing missiles at the Italian island of Lampedusa. Simply put, when the White House chooses violence, it is often Europe that must pick up the pieces.

Even so, the sharpest differences between European and American attitudes often boil down to trade. Many rogue regimes lie close to the European continent. Whether because of energy or exports or the fear of instability unleashing waves of refugees, European statesmen are loath to pursue any policy that could negatively affect their treasury, regardless of security costs down the road. The reason for this priority is that the U.S. taxpayer and U.S. military subsidized European defense throughout the twentieth century. Except for the British and the French, European taxpayers contributed little to the nuclear missiles, aircraft carrier battle groups, and submarines that preserved European freedom in the face of Soviet ambitions. The European public and diplomats are unaccustomed to the true cost of defense and do not understand that security's price must sometimes be paid proactively. Hence, European governments often resist imposing economic sanctions, whereas American policymakers—whether Democrat or Republican—see them as a valuable and nonviolent way to coerce rogue regimes. As of 1999, the United States had sanctioned thirty-three countries unilaterally.[42] European countries are much less likely to apply sanctions without UN direction, either on moral grounds or to penalize rogue behavior.[43]

The passage of the Helms-Burton Act in 1996 highlighted the clash between Washington and European capitals. The law extended U.S. sanctions on Cuba to foreign companies—including, of course, European companies—that traded with the communist state, and also sharpened penalties when those firms trafficked in property confiscated by Cuban authorities from U.S. citizens.

European and American public attitudes reflect the different approaches of their governments with regard to multilateralism and the application of sanctions on rogue regimes. A 1998 German Marshall Fund poll found that only 21 percent of Americans surveyed would make sanctions on Libya or Iran conditional on European participation, while 75 percent supported unilateral sanctions.[44] Sixty-one percent of Americans polled also agreed that talk with autocratic leaders should be coupled with more punitive measures.[45] Less than half of the British and French surveyed agreed with the concept of sanctions on principle, although slightly more than 56 percent of Germans supported sanctions. When the target of sanctions was Iran, support for sanctions among citizens of the three European powerhouses was even lower.[46]

It was largely in reaction to the more punitive U.S. approach to rogue regimes that Europeans promoted the concept of "critical dialogue" and "critical engagement." Previously, European governments would informally say they were involved in diplomatic engagement if they had more than one meeting with an adversary, even if there were no regular, institutionalized contacts. In the 1990s, however, the European Union began to consider itself engaged in a dialogue only with the fulfillment of three conditions: First, EU ministers or political committees had to decide formally to engage. Second, so did the other side. Third, the dialogue had to be conducted regularly.[47]

The European Union had multiple motives to engage in dialogue with rogues. Dialogues became a convenient mechanism by which outside countries could attain more structured relations with the EU.[48] Dialogues are easy to start; by 1997, the European Union was engaged in over a hundred regular dialogues.[49] This proliferation arguably diluted their importance. Once started, engagements became self-perpetuating, with careers and whole bureaucracies growing around dialogue. Amidst the moral outrage of Beijing's crackdown in Tiananmen Square in 1989, European officials froze their dialogue with China, but it was not long before they resumed it.

Because of the European enthusiasm to engage, European officials have reached out to those whom their U.S. counterparts have considered beyond rapprochement. In the early 1990s, Europeans facilitated back-channel exchanges between Israel and Lebanese Hezbollah, and also reached out to the Colombian president Ernesto Samper, whom the Clinton administration avoided because of his relationship with drug lords.

Europe's largest critical engagement project revolved around Iran.[50] Many European officials may have been sincere in their hope that they could encourage reform in Iran through dialogue and provide Tehran with economic incentives to bring its policies into conformity with the international community. Trade was a prominent concern, however. German officials especially hoped to protect an extensive trade relationship with Iran. From a strictly fiscal standpoint, sanctions can be self-defeating. When the European Union briefly worked to isolate Tehran after a German court concluded that senior Iranian officials were complicit in an assassination in Berlin, the Kremlin sought to profit. "We have good, positive cooperation with Iran, which shows a tendency to grow," said President Boris Yeltsin. The Speaker of the Russian parliament, Gennadi Seleznyov, declared, "There is no court in the world which has the authority to pass sentence on a whole nation."[51]

Many European leaders put a premium on the act of talking and refuse to acknowledge the symbolism of dialogue. On June 1, 2010, a year after the fraudulent election in Iran, accompanied by the worst unrest in thirty years, the Islamic Republic's foreign minister, Manouchehr Mottaki, visited the European Parliament in Brussels. Several European parliamentarians protested the visit. Struan Stevenson, a British conservative, called Mottaki's visit the equivalent of hosting Joachim von Ribbentrop, the

Nazi foreign minister, in the European Parliament. The president of the parliament's foreign affairs committee, Gabriele Albertini, dismissed the criticism, saying, "The choice is either to confront opinions that may be different from our own or to ignore them."[52] That dichotomy, however, ignores the costs and the complexities of engagement with rogue actors.

Chapter Two

GREAT SATAN VS. MAD MULLAHS

"The United States and Iran held their first official high-level, face-to-face talks in almost 30 years," reported the *Washington Post* in 2007. The State Department celebrated the meeting between the U.S. ambassador to Iraq, Ryan Crocker, and his Iranian counterpart; but in reality, diplomacy between the two sides was nothing new. Iran's Islamic Revolution of 1979 did not end U.S.-Iranian engagement.[1] The United States and Iran have never stopped talking. While the Obama administration sought to reinvent U.S. policy with outreach, there is little Obama proposed that did not have precedent.

How Diplomacy Prolonged the Hostage Crisis

Iran was an important Cold War ally for the United States—in Jimmy Carter's words, "an island of stability in a sea of turmoil."[2] Iran's linchpin status led successive American administrations to paper over differences with the shah. Carter, however, was unwilling to turn a blind eye to his human rights abuses.[3] Mohammad Reza Pahlavi had long been unpopular among diplomats,[4] and as Iranians took to the streets to protest his dictatorial ways, many in the State Department counseled abandoning the pro-American leader. Zbigniew Brzezinski, the national security advisor, explained that "the lower echelons at State, notably the head of the Iran Desk . . . were motivated by doctrinal dislike of the Shah and simply wanted him out of power altogether."[5] They got their wish.

On February 1, 1979, Ayatollah Ruhollah Khomeini arrived in Tehran on a chartered Air France flight and was greeted by three million Iranians. The Islamic Revolution was unprecedented in its scale: in an age before the Internet and Twitter, Khomeini mobilized fully 10 percent of the population. John Limbert, an eyewitness to the revolution, recalled how Iranians were possessed by "rage and the thirst for revenge for real or imagined grievances."[6] They projected upon Khomeini what they wished him to be. So too did Americans.

Richard Falk, a Princeton political scientist who was influential in the Carter administration, urged the White House to embrace Khomeini. "The depiction of him as fanatical, reactionary, and the bearer of crude prejudices seems certainly and happily false," Falk asserted, adding that the ayatollah's "entourage of close advisers is uniformly composed of moderate, progressive individuals . . . who share a notable record of concern with human rights."[7] It was what Carter wanted to hear, and there was no shortage of experts to tell him the same story. Richard Cottam, a diplomat and Iran scholar, reported that the ayatollah's inner circle was "afraid of the Soviet Union and desirous of relying on the U.S. for Iran's defense."[8]

Even as Khomeini launched a reign of terror, the State Department announced that it would maintain relations with the new government.[9] The American embassy went into overdrive. Because jockeying for power among Iranians was so intense, American diplomats met with any Iranian official they could. There were several months of low-key diplomacy, but revolutionary leaders stymied Carter's hope to engage at a senior level. When the president recalled William Sullivan, his ambassador in Tehran, in April 1979, Iran's revolutionary government rejected Carter's new nominee in pique over American criticism of its human rights violations.[10]

Protestors might chant anti-American slogans outside the U.S. embassy and revolutionary firing squads might work around the clock, but senior State Department officials reported that bilateral ties were improving.[11] Steven Erlanger, a young journalist who would rise to become the chief diplomatic correspondent for the *New York Times*, asserted that although the revolution was not over, "the religious phase is drawing to a close even as it is becoming formalized."[12] American diplomats in Tehran continued to speak hopefully of moderates within the revolutionary coalition.[13] The way forward seemed clear to the diplomats: they wanted to meet with Khomeini. To sit publicly with the ayatollah, they believed, would signal that Washington respected his authority.[14] L. Bruce Laingen, the senior American diplomat in Tehran, never got permission.

Brzezinski did not ask. Visiting Algiers on November 1, 1979, he met Mehdi Bazargan, revolutionary Iran's prime minister, at a reception to celebrate the Algerian independence day.[15] Brzezinski told Bazargan that the United States was open to any relationship and partnership the Islamic Republic wanted.[16] Brzezinski may have been well-meaning, but his initiative was a case study in how ill-timed diplomacy worsens relationships. Instead of grasping an outstretched hand, adversaries can respond with provocation to reinforce their ideological credentials. This is what happened in Iran.

The day after newspapers published photographs of the Brzezinski-Bazargan handshake—and the day after Erlanger filed his optimistic dispatch—protests rocked Iran, culminating in the seizure of the American embassy by outraged students.[17] Khomeini endorsed the hostage takers and their paranoid worldview, in which the United States would recruit Iranian traitors to collapse the revolution from within. "Our young people must foil these plots," he blustered.[18] Khomeini's son embraced the captors, underscoring the regime's contempt for international law.[19]

The hostage situation defined the Carter administration. Harold H. Saunders, assistant secretary of state for the Near East and South Asia, recalled internal debate about how the United States should respond:

> *The challenge facing members of the American crisis team . . . was how*
> *to bridge the gulf between the Iranian and American worlds. How*
> *could we deal with people like this? How could we make them see that it*
> *would best serve their revolutionary agenda to release our people instead*
> *of holding them? Should we hit them hard in a quick, sharp, punitive*
> *blow? Should we ignore them? Should we search out Iranian leaders*
> *who wanted the hostages freed for their own political reasons and try*
> *to find ways of maneuvering so as to make it more feasible for them to*
> *do what they wanted to do . . . ? What approach would the American*
> *people support?*[20]

The Carter administration settled on a two-track policy. First, they would maximize communications and keep the door to negotiation open; second, they would raise the cost to Iran of holding hostages.[21] Rather than keep American options open, however, the administration decided to limit them. Two days after the embassy takeover, Gary Sick, a National Security Council official, reportedly leaked word that there would be "no change in the status quo—no military alert, no movement of forces, no resort to military contingency plans."[22] Perhaps the White House believed that taking military action off the table would enable diplomacy; but by removing the threat of force, it forfeited its leverage.[23] Carter's assurances convinced the hostage takers they had nothing to fear.[24]

Carter's desire to talk to rogues broke with tried-and-true strategy. During both the Black September hostage crisis in 1970 and the Khmer Rouge's capture of the SS *Mayaguez* in 1975, the United States had quietly deployed forces to augment its leverage, even while muting its public rhetoric. Carter's aides could easily have leaked word of military preparations, but the president chose not to—a choice that undercut both diplomacy and policy options.

Compounding the difficulty of resolving the crisis were the cross-purposes of Americans and Iranians. Carter saw the hostage crisis through an American lens and accepted the captors' declared grievances at face value, even as he denounced the embassy takeover as a violation of international law. For Khomeini's followers, however, capturing the "Den of Spies" could be a tool to prevent the reconciliation that they saw as the greater threat to their nascent Islamic Republic.[25]

The hostage takers proceeded to position themselves as arbiters of the revolution's purity. The captors' spokeswoman, Masoumeh Ebtekar, explained, "Every afternoon, I and several other students spent from four to six hours writing summaries of the documents [found in the embassy]. . . . The really important ones we would expose publicly, on television."[26] Khomeini and his revolutionary courts would purge those officials whom the students exposed as talking with the Americans, even if their interaction with the embassy was routine. Bazargan became the first victim.[27]

Not surprisingly, it became increasingly difficult for the Americans to find Iranians with whom to engage. Blinded by desperation, Carter's aides hoped to find moderate revolutionaries who could sell a deal to Khomeini.[28] They discounted signs that Iranian authorities were not interested in resolving conflict. Ignorance of where power lay in Tehran compounded the problem. Khomeini was in charge, but as Secretary of State Cyrus Vance recognized, even Khomeini "was not one to row upstream" against the flow of public opinion.[29] Never mind that Khomeini helped shape public opinion. The mob mentality precluded traditional diplomacy; it is hard to negotiate with a regime that has gone rogue.

Instead of demanding that Khomeini end incitement and consolidate control as a precondition for diplomacy, Carter rushed to talk. This was understandable because of fears that the Iranians would execute hostages. Carter also believed that if he could get to Khomeini, he could temper the ayatollah's hostility toward the United States. To this end, the president asked Ramsey Clark, the former attorney general, and William Miller, a retired diplomat, to carry a letter to Tehran to ask for the hostages' release and to start a discussion about future bilateral relations. The duo were flag bearers for radicalism. Clark had met Khomeini during the ayatollah's last day in Paris and had championed his cause,[30] and Miller had described Khomeini as "a progressive force for human rights."[31] The two flew to Istanbul, but when Carter's aides announced their mission, Khomeini refused them entry and forbade any negotiation before Washington extradited the shah.[32] Clark and Miller returned to Washington, their letter undelivered. Had Carter kept his diplomacy quiet, perhaps Khomeini might have been willing to dial back the incitement and make a discreet deal to return the hostages within a month, instead of holding them for more than a year.

The administration would not take no for an answer. Soon, a delegation of congressmen left for Tehran. Rep. George Hansen, a Republican from Idaho, said that Congress might pass a resolution calling for Carter to extradite the shah in exchange for the release of some hostages. Again, the Iranians refused to negotiate. Each time Khomeini spurned Carter's outreach, he could depict himself as strong and the Americans as weak. He won before the negotiations even began. Carter may have approached diplomacy enthusiastically, but goodwill is never enough in dealing with rogue regimes. It takes two to tango.

Not every aspect of Carter's approach backfired. The president successfully rallied world opinion behind the United States. He won unanimous UN Security Council backing for a resolution seeking the hostages' immediate release, and near-unanimous support for a resolution deploring Iran's inaction.[33] Sanctions failed only because of a Soviet veto.[34] The International Court of Justice also declared the embassy seizure illegal.[35] The revolutionaries simply ignored the ruling; rogue regimes by definition care little for international institutions or world opinion.

Carter's aides justified multilateralism as a necessary precondition for successful diplomacy. Still, the seventeen days they spent courting the International Court were seventeen days in which Iranian revolutionaries could be confident that the United States would undertake no military strike that could prejudice the verdict. Rather than increase pressure on Iran, Carter's diplomatic strategy relieved it.[36] The debate over how to balance the benefit of international imprimatur with costs in terms of lost time continues to perplex diplomats. Nor did the international consensus that Carter marshaled sway Khomeini.

Carter continued to seek an intermediary even after Khomeini forbade all Iranian officials to negotiate with Americans.[37] Vance explained, "Since we could not reach the ayatollah, we had no choice but to try to work through the Revolutionary Council," even though he himself admitted that the hostage takers would not answer to the council.[38]

The Carter administration also attempted to use the United Nations to create back channels.[39] Secretary-General Kurt Waldheim tried to arrange a meeting between Vance and Iran's foreign minister, Abulhassan Bani Sadr, but failed before Bani Sadr lost his post after only two and a half weeks. Bani Sadr's precarious position did not stop him from adding to Iran's demands. In addition to the captors' calls for the return of the shah, Bani Sadr also demanded the return of the shah's assets, an end to interference in Iranian affairs, and an apology for injustices more imagined than real. No sooner did Sadegh Ghotbzadeh, a former trainer for Palestinian terrorists, assume the foreign minister's post than the Carter team reached out to him as well. "He was a contact we had to pay attention to when routes to Khomeini were rare," Harold Saunders explained.[40]

Carter considered dialogue to have no cost, but the price of desperation diplomacy was huge. Any Iranian partner had to bolster his revolutionary credentials, and so added fresh demands. The rush to engage the Iranians only deepened the crisis.

Carter's inner circle split when they heard the new demands. Some wanted to hold the revolutionaries' feet to the fire, while those in the State Department prided themselves on their cultural sensitivity and argued that any solution would require allowing Iranian leaders to claim victory.[41] Saunders explained the diplomats' logic: Even though they believed the Iranian regime should be accountable under international law, the State Department worried that Khomeini might not have the power to control the anti-American wave he had unleashed. Nor was complying with international law Khomeini's top priority; consolidating the revolution was. Any solution, Saunders and his team argued, would require the Iranians to conclude on their own that it was in their revolutionary interest to release the hostages.[42] The cost of such an approach was high: American diplomats working to preserve rather than undermine Khomeini's regime.

Circles around Khomeini took advantage of American desperation. As the hostages ended their first month in captivity, America's Iranian contacts suggested that if only the White House would be conciliatory, Iranian pragmatists might convince Khomeini to act in the same spirit. It was a strategy that appealed to Carter and prefigured the incentive packages that would characterize Western diplomacy toward Iran for more than three decades.[43]

Carter signaled openness to dialogue and would not tie his actions to Tehran's. Even with American diplomats held hostage, he refused to sever diplomatic relations. He hoped that allowing the Islamic Republic to keep its embassy in Washington would facilitate diplomacy.[44] Before its closure in April 1980, Khomeini's embassy helped plan the assassination of a former Iranian official in Bethesda, Maryland.

Carter refused to accept that incentives would not sway an ideological adversary. When his incentives failed to win Khomeini over, he augmented them, in effect making the bribery of adversaries the basis of American strategy. Thus, instead of defending a leader who stood staunchly by America during the Cold War, Carter sought to hasten the cancer-stricken shah's departure for Panama after reluctantly allowing him into the United States for medical treatment; he may also have encouraged Panamanian authorities to return the shah to Iran.[45] The gesture did not assuage Khomeini. As Peter Rodman, a former aide to Henry Kissinger, noted, "The eagerness to prove goodwill to an intransigent opponent paradoxically makes a settlement less likely."[46]

There is a logic to offering carrots rather than sticks, but there is also a drawback: the incentivizing of rogue behavior. The cost went far behind Iran, too. A willingness to reverse course under pressure and betray allies may have convinced Soviet leaders who already perceived Carter as weak and indecisive that American reaction to an invasion of Afghanistan would be slight.[47]

When the Swiss ambassador in Tehran reported that the Iranian government would assume control over the hostages so long as the U.S. government refrained from any measures to pressure Tehran, Carter played along. He delayed sanctions, alleviating pressure on a regime that was struggling to consolidate control. Khomeini took no action.[48] Even when Carter finally imposed some sanctions in April 1980, these were weak and simply confirmed the state of affairs: limiting travel to Iran for all but journalists and officials, and restricting financial transfers. His ban on importing Iranian goods was meaningless, since war and revolution had ground Iran's economy to a halt.

As the months progressed, there was one constant: Carter grasped at straws. Even though Bani Sadr had violated earlier promises, he raised White House hopes with a secret approach through a German law firm.[49] Carter maintained an almost religious belief that diplomacy could work. His diplomats counseled against any nondiplomatic strategy for fear that it would undermine diplomacy's prospects. They were more willing to condemn American actions for hindering diplomacy than to blame Iranian insincerity.[50] When Carter agreed to attempt a rescue of the hostages, Vance resigned in protest.[51]

Ten months after the embassy seizure, German intermediaries reported that a senior Iranian official was ready to talk.[52] The official was able to convince the White House that he truly represented Khomeini by foretelling demands that Khomeini would make in a speech. The speech consolidated and formalized the Iranian position: demanding noninterference by the United States in Iran's internal affairs, release of frozen assets and a return of the shah's assets, and cancellation of all U.S. claims against Iran.

The Carter administration agreed to bargain for the hostages. "It was in the national interest of the United States to negotiate with Iran for the release of the hostages, rather than to refuse to negotiate at all," wrote the legal advisor to Edmund Muskie, the secretary of state.[53] Politicians across the aisle uniformly held that there should be no negotiation with terrorists in principle, although there was no consensus when it came to the problem of rogue regimes. Alexander Haig, Reagan's first secretary of state, considered Carter's willingness to talk a bad idea.[54] Carter's decision to negotiate with Khomeini was eased by moral equivalence; many of his advisors saw merit to Iranian accusations against the United States.[55] Muskie's legal advisor went so far as to equate U.S. freezing of Iranian assets with Iran's taking of hostages.[56]

On September 13, 1980, Warren Christopher, deputy secretary of state, traveled to Bonn with his handpicked team to meet Sadegh Tabatabai, the Iranian intermediary who was also the brother of Khomeini's daughter-in-law. The State Department believed the meetings productive—when the metric is merely sitting down to talk, it is easy to claim success—but the channel soon dried up. Tabatabai stopped traveling to Bonn, and the Iranian parliament started issuing new demands. The State Department was willing to give the regime the benefit of the doubt and blamed the outbreak of the Iran-Iraq War for Tabatabai's abrupt withdrawal from talks.[57] It should not have. The Iranians frequently switch negotiators. After accepting concessions, the Iranian leadership annuls the process, reiterates its demands, and begins negotiations anew with the adversaries' concessions as the opening position.

Rather than see the war as an impediment, the State Department should have recognized it as an opportunity, for indeed that is what it was. "The blow that broke the logjam came from Saddam Hussein, not Jimmy Carter," Rodman observed.[58] Ronald Reagan's election also helped. The Iranian leadership understood Carter and knew how to exploit his weakness, but Reagan was a different matter. Iran's traditional game of increasing demands would no longer work. Events, rather than Carter's outreach, reversed the dynamic. Khomeini finally decided that further delays might cost Iran and that it was time to make a deal.

The Iranian government then cast aside the agreement reached between Christopher and Tabatabai to let international courts determine the value of the shah's assets, and instead demanded $24 billion.[59] With the costs of war piled onto the turmoil of revolution, Tehran faced financial ruin. Khomeini wanted money. The Iranian demand was blackmail; but if Carter refused to pay, Khomeini might condemn the hostages to revolutionary courts in which justice was no concern and death sentences the norm. Although American leverage was at its weakest, Carter ordered negotiations to proceed.

The price of negotiating under fire was high. Carter agreed not only to the ransom, but also to an American pledge "not to intervene, directly or indirectly, politically or militarily, in Iran's internal affairs." Even though this agreement was not a treaty and not technically binding, diplomats have cited it as reason not to pressure Iran.[60] There were also peripheral costs as a result of relying on Algeria to play the middleman. This reactionary, pro-Soviet regime was locked in a fierce border dispute with Morocco, an important American ally, and Carter's wooing of Algeria came at Morocco's expense.[61]

When the Iranian government released the hostages just minutes after Ronald Reagan took his oath of office on January 20, 1981, Carter's team trumpeted the success of their diplomacy.[62] They bragged that they had persevered, avoiding the use of force except for the failed rescue mission, and rallying the international community against Iran. Most importantly, they won the release of the hostages. Diplomacy had triumphed, they concluded.

This is debatable, however. Diplomacy prolonged the crisis to 444 days and allowed radical factions to consolidate around Khomeini. Iranian officials toyed with their American counterparts and drove up the cost of the bargain before abruptly disengaging. Carter's desperation empowered a series of anti-American intermediaries, ranging from the PLO and the Syrians, to Libyans, Cubans, and Algerians.[63] The perception of powerlessness to free the hostages eroded America's international standing and encouraged adversaries. While Carter might once have defined his brokering of the Israel-Egypt peace treaty as the central pillar of his legacy, his handling of the hostage crisis leads historians to remember his presidency as bumbling and ineffectual.[64] It was events outside the negotiating room that won the hostages their freedom.

What should Carter have done differently? Iran's negotiating behavior provides clues. Since the revolutionaries responded more to pressure than to nicety, Carter might have done more to build leverage. "Diplomacy divorced from power is futile," as Rodman observed. When Iraq invaded Iran, "suddenly the stubborn lethargy of the Iranian political system, all the internal feuding and procrastinating and jockeying for position, jelled under the pressure of *force majeure*; suddenly the economic sanctions took on a new bite as the threat of protracted war impended."[65] Carter need not have invaded Iran, but had he quietly sent troops and battle groups to the Persian Gulf, Khomeini would have noticed. At the very least, Carter might then have negotiated from a position of strength.

Carter's obsession with his own re-election also undercut diplomacy. While it was admirable that he wanted Reagan to begin with a clean slate, the more Carter's team telegraphed desperation to conclude an agreement before they left office, the more they strengthened the Iranian hand.

In the annals of the twentieth century, Carter's handling of Iran presents a paradox. Few if any U.S. presidents have been more committed to diplomacy in a crisis, and yet, by his single-minded pursuit of diplomacy, Carter froze U.S. relations with postrevolutionary Iran for nearly three decades. Hindsight is always 20/20, but had Brzezinski not pushed forward so enthusiastically in his handshake with Mehdi Bazargan, and had Carter's decisions not extended a two- or three-day crisis into a fourteen-month event, the United States and Iran might enjoy normal relations today.

The Iran-Contra Affair

The hostages' homecoming was the end of a chapter, but not the final story. The crisis left Carter's legacy in tatters, but the damage it did to Iran's image was worse. The Islamic Republic had, in world opinion, become a pariah state. Khomeini promised paradise, but he brought misery and isolation. Whereas Iranians had once seen themselves as being on track to acquire economic power and a European standard of life, it was clear by the early 1980s that Iran's trajectory had reversed.

With the hostages home, President Ronald Reagan turned his attention to the economy and to rebuilding America's military capability. Crises that define presidencies, however, are almost always unforeseen. In 1982, with terrorism resurgent, Israel invaded Lebanon to push out Palestinian guerillas. The U.S. special envoy Philip Habib brokered a deal in which Israeli forces would leave Beirut while the Palestine Liberation Organization would leave Lebanon altogether.

When Lebanon's government faltered, chaos again threatened the country. Reagan ordered U.S. Marines to join French paratroopers and Italian soldiers in the capital to shore up the government. It was a fateful decision. On October 23, 1983, an Iranian-sponsored suicide bomber drove a truck bomb into the U.S. Marine barracks, killing 241 American servicemen.

For Americans, it was the beginning of a Lebanese nightmare. Between 1984 and 1992, Iranian-backed terrorists in Lebanon kidnapped twenty-four Americans. They killed several, including William Francis Buckley, the CIA station chief in Beirut, and William R. Higgins, a Marine colonel snatched while on a UN peacekeeping mission. Most of the captives languished, while Reagan obsessively peppered his staff with questions about their condition and the possibilities for their release.[66]

It was déjà vu all over again as a hostage crisis brought relations with Iran front and center. On January 20, 1984, Secretary of State George P. Shultz designated Iran as a state sponsor of terrorism and lobbied allies to embargo arms sales to Iran, a measure designed to bite the Islamic Republic as its war with Iraq dragged on.[67]

Reagan wanted to punish Iran for its terror sponsorship, but his aides, like Carter, aimed to engage moderate regime officials. On August 31, 1984, the national security advisor, Robert McFarlane, initiated a review of U.S. policy toward Iran and asked how Washington might influence succession in Iran once the eighty-two-year-old Khomeini died. Broad strategic concerns motivated McFarlane. The original hostage crisis may have sent U.S.-Iran relations to their nadir, but the two countries' interests remained intertwined. Both Tehran and Washington wanted to support the Afghan resistance in the wake of the Soviet invasion of Afghanistan. The shah's death had rendered many Iranian demands moot, while the Algiers Accord had established an arbitration process to address other disputes.

Both the State Department and the Central Intelligence Agency informed McFarlane that they lacked influence inside Iran, so McFarlane proposed a plan to rectify this. He suggested that the United States use its allies to sell arms to Iran. The process would create relationships and, given Iran's war needs, might also develop leverage. Both the Pentagon and the State Department objected to the proposal even before Oliver North, a National Security Council aide, amended it to link the arms to the release of American hostages held by Iranian-backed groups. The proposal gained new life toward the end of 1985, soon after John Poindexter became the national security advisor. Today, the Iran-Contra affair might be remembered for the illegalities arising from its circumvention of congressional prohibitions on funding anticommunist insurgents in Nicaragua, but at its inception the initiative was about reaching out to a rogue regime.

The Reagan administration may have criticized Carter for negotiating under fire, but Reagan's team learned the difficulty of maintaining a Manichaean approach to terrorism when it faced its own hostage crisis. Whereas Reagan had faulted Carter for offering inducements to the Iranians,[68] his administration now did just that. On January 17, 1986, Reagan signed an order authorizing the sale of guided missiles to Iran through Israeli middlemen. Once Iran received the missiles, it would order Hezbollah and other proxy groups to release American hostages.

On May 15, 1986, Reagan authorized McFarlane, who had since retired, to travel to Iran for further dialogue. Ten days later, McFarlane arrived in Tehran with a few aides, carrying a Bible and a cake shaped like a key.

McFarlane's good intentions fell flat. In an intentional slight, no senior Iranian official met his plane. Years later, Hashemi Rafsanjani gloated, "Have you forgotten that Irishman McFarlane came here and our authorities were not willing to talk to him; he was stuck with our second and third rate authorities?"[69] Not only did Iranian-backed groups refuse to release any hostages, but Iranian officials piled on additional demands.[70] McFarlane's Iranian intermediaries had reverted to the same strategy they had earlier employed with Carter: they shunted responsibility to midlevel officials and then augmented their demands.

Even so, the outreach to Iran appeared successful at first glance. For fifteen months beginning in June 1985, no Americans were kidnapped in Lebanon.[71] After the release of Father Lawrence Jenco, who had been in captivity for 564 days, the Reagan administration delivered additional spare parts to Iran; but no sooner had American officials offloaded the last shipment of military equipment than kidnappers seized three more Americans.[72] The arms trade gave Iran an incentive to seize hostages.[73]

Meanwhile, neither Washington nor Tehran wanted their discussions to become public. To the Americans, ransoming hostages was anathema; to the Islamic Republic, the United States remained the Great Satan.[74]

Politics in Tehran doomed the diplomacy. Rafsanjani wanted to retain plausible deniability about his involvement in the talks so as not to fall victim to hardliners who opposed any outreach to Washington.[75] The internal Iranian debate between ideologues and pragmatists remained unresolved. The ideologues believed that export of the revolution should be Iran's key goal regardless of the international antagonism it caused and the isolation it created. Pragmatists wanted to scale back Iranian terror sponsorship in order to break Iran's isolation. Mehdi Hashemi, the head of the Office of Liberation Movements—the precursor to the Qods Force— clashed repeatedly with Rafsanjani. A week after McFarlane's secret 1986 trip to Tehran, Hashemi, the son-in-law of Khomeini's deputy Hossein Ali Montazeri, leaked word of secret talks in pamphlets distributed at the University of Tehran. Six months later, Hashemi or his immediate aides leaked word of McFarlane's meetings to a Lebanese magazine.[76] On November 4, 1986, the seventh anniversary of the embassy seizure, Rafsanjani confirmed the secret talks to the international press.[77]

Regardless of the wisdom of the arms-for-hostages scheme, the accompanying talks represented a serious attempt to reach out to Tehran. U.S. authorities trusted the Iranians to keep their silence, but Iranian officials broke their word. The resulting crisis paralyzed Reagan's second term. Whereas Reagan had a 62 percent approval rating at the start of the term, it dropped to just 46 percent with the disclosure of the Iran-Contra affair.[78] Outreach to Tehran when Iranian politics remains in flux is costly.

U.S.-Iran Engagement under George H. W. Bush

When Reagan's vice president began his own presidency, pro-Iranian terrorists held nine Americans hostage in Lebanon and tensions remained high. George H. W. Bush, a former diplomat and a realist, offered Iran an olive branch. "There are today Americans who are held against their will," he noted in his inaugural speech. "Assistance can be shown here, and will be long remembered. Goodwill begets goodwill. Good faith can be a spiral that endlessly moves on."[79] Over subsequent days, he reaffirmed his desire to improve relations. "I don't want to . . . think that the status quo has to go on forever," he said. "There was a period of time when we had excellent relations with Iran."[80]

Khomeini was blunt in response. "Iran does not need America," he declared.[81] Unlike Carter or Reagan, Bush took no for an answer and did not rush engagement; rather, he waited for the Iranian leadership to change its mind.

Change came in an unexpected way just six months into Bush's term, on June 3, 1989, when Khomeini died. The ayatollah had always seen himself as the deputy of the messiah on earth. The messiah was not yet ready to return, however, and so he needed a new deputy. Ali Khamenei, the titular president, filled the role of Supreme Leader. Journalists and diplomats saw Khamenei as a moderate, at least in comparison with Khomeini.[82] Then, on August 3, Rafsanjani became president. Speaking the next day, he suggested that "reasonable, prudent solutions" could free the hostages, and privately he told Pakistani intermediaries that U.S.

gestures might grease the process.[83] Bush felt that Rafsanjani's statement "offers hope," and State Department spokeswoman Margaret Tutwiler voiced her belief that "Iran is genuinely engaged" and that there was no reason not to expect positive results.

Bush's willingness to engage was real. He issued a national security directive saying that the United States should prepare for "a normal relationship with Iran on the basis of strict reciprocity,"[84] and he asked UN Secretary-General Javier Pérez de Cuéllar to serve as an intermediary between the national security advisor, Brent Scowcroft, and Rafsanjani.[85] Pérez de Cuéllar used Giandomenico Picco, an Italian career UN bureaucrat, as his representative.

Picco flew to Tehran and met Rafsanjani, who dismissed the idea out of hand: to talk would be to admit culpability in the hostage seizures.[86] While diplomats often embrace the notion of quiet diplomacy, the contrast between Iran's public and private postures is instructive. Rogues may express moderation publicly, but when push comes to shove, they remain rogues. Rafsanjani spoke publicly of pragmatism, and he found no shortage of useful idiots to accept his public statements uncritically.[87] Privately, he revived Iran's covert nuclear program and played a crucial role in ordering the assassinations of dissidents.

Bush was more cautious than many of diplomacy's cheerleaders in Congress who suggested that the United States offer unilateral concessions.[88] Still, Bush's engagement was not without cost. It was after Bush began his proxy talks with Tehran that Iranian officials supplied terrorists in Europe with weaponry to target Western interests, and also formed a hit squad to kill Salman Rushdie, author of *The Satanic Verses*.[89] Such actions show that engagement did nothing to ameliorate Iran's rogue behavior and may actually have made it worse. Only after he fell out of favor with his own regime did Rafsanjani acknowledge that he had responded to American goodwill with bad, on the orders of Khamenei.[90]

Just as Iraq's invasion of Iran forced Khomeini to resolve the first hostage crisis, it was Iraq's invasion of Kuwait in August 1990 that would spark a resolution of the second. Although Iranian officials had begun to

negotiate more seriously in February 1990, and even had their proxy terrorist groups release two American hostages, it was not a change of heart
about their revolutionary principles that made the difference. Instead,
it was the fact that the United States, by defeating Saddam Hussein's
army, had achieved in one hundred hours what Iran could not do in
eight years. Hezbollah quickly began releasing its Western hostages, and
the last American hostage was on his way home weeks before Christmas.
Sometimes, the best-intentioned and most careful diplomacy is ineffectual
without a demonstration of military might.

It is possible that Bush would have pressed his advantage had he won
re-election, but the electorate's anxiety about the economy changed the
plot, and Bush retired to Maine. If there was going to be any resolution
to the Iran problem, it would have to come on Bill Clinton's watch.

Clinton's Containment

President Clinton inherited a cold peace. Bilateral relations remained
frozen. As much as the Oslo Accords raised hope for Arab-Israeli peace,
Tehran's attempts to disrupt the peace process focused increasing attention
on Iranian terror sponsorship.[91] It was in this context that Martin Indyk,
Clinton's lead Middle East advisor on the National Security Council,
unveiled the dual containment policy. Because the Iranian and Iraqi
regimes were both inimical to the United States, Clinton would isolate
both. Still, the White House kept a foot in the door even as it promised
to slam it on Iran. "We do not seek confrontation but we will not normalize relations with Iran until and unless Iran's policies change across
the board," Indyk said. He welcomed dialogue. "We are willing to listen
to what Iran has to say, provided that this comes through authoritative
channels," he explained. The Clinton administration had at least learned
from Carter's and Reagan's mistakes.[92]

Iran was not interested in dialogue, though. As Tehran's terror
sponsorship and nuclear program accelerated, Clinton ratcheted up
sanctions. He issued two executive orders in 1995, the first targeting

Iran's oil industry, and the second banning most American trade with and investment in Iran.[93] The following year, he signed the Iran-Libya Sanctions Act, which empowered the United States to act against private companies investing in Iran, much to the annoyance of European states, where many of the targeted companies were based. In 1997, Clinton tightened financial restrictions to close loopholes in which companies exported American goods to Iran through third countries.[94]

The diplomacy-first crowd balked. "There seems little justification for the treatment the United States currently accords Iran because of its nuclear program," argued Zbigniew Brzezinski and Brent Scowcroft, both former national security advisors. They proposed swapping sanctions with incentives and even suggested offering preferential trade to Iran.[95] The idea of flipping rogues with trade may sound good in theory, but there is very little precedent to suggest that it has a basis in reality. Proponents of a moneyed embrace often cite China, but ignore the fact that China remains a one-party dictatorship whose military advances are increasingly challenging the United States. For all of America's diplomatic efforts, it has simply become a wealthier, more threatening dictatorship.

Mohammad Khatami's election in 1997 provided hope to diplomacy's proponents. Upon taking office, Khatami announced, "We are in favor of a dialogue between civilizations and a détente in our relations with the outside world."[96] To encourage Khatami, Clinton chose not to respond to evidence of Iranian complicity in the attack on Khobar Towers in Saudi Arabia, which killed nineteen American servicemen in June 1996.[97] Accountability became a casualty of hope.

Proponents of dialogue were euphoric. Gary Sick, a Carter aide, described Khatami as "a reformer with an outspoken commitment to civil society, social justice, the rule of law and expanded freedom." He added, "Khatami's stated goals are consistent with our interests, and there are cost-free gestures we can take to acknowledge the changed political climate and to encourage more of the same."[98] This, of course, was nonsense. In his previous incarnation as minister of culture, Khatami had censored hundreds of books. He also remained committed to anti-Israel terrorism and to Iran's nuclear program.

Khatami's call for dialogue led to a proliferation of study group reports, each urging Washington to engage Tehran with few if any preconditions. Most of these reports were naïve. The Atlantic Council, for example, recommended that Clinton might partially lift trade restrictions as "a key gesture of good faith."[99] Many Iran experts subordinated analysis to advocacy and refused to recognize Khatami's inability or unwillingness to change Iran's pursuit of nuclear weapons or its terror sponsorship.[100]

Clinton, for his part, jumped at the chance to bring Iran in from the cold. This was the stuff of which legacies were made. The secretary of state, Madeleine Albright, sent a letter to Khatami expressing a desire for dialogue. Khatami did not reply directly, but American officials interpreted subsequent statements to signal his willingness to engage.[101] In December 1997, for example, he expressed "great respect" for the "great people of the United States" and called for "a thoughtful dialogue."[102] In an interview with CNN in January 1998, he asserted, "Not only do we not harbor any ill wishes for the American people, but in fact we consider them to be a great nation." He then outlined his desire for a "dialogue of civilizations."[103]

It was music to Clinton's ears. Secretary Albright "welcomed" Khatami's call and, to show good faith, she streamlined visa procedures and offered to facilitate academic and cultural exchange.[104]

Rapprochement floundered, however; for despite Khatami's lofty rhetoric, Iranian officials refused to talk. Martin Indyk and two colleagues sought to meet the foreign minister, Kamal Kharrazi, after his speech at the Asia Society, but as soon as Kharrazi realized the American officials were waiting for him, he left.[105] If America hoped to talk, Iranian thinking went, it should first "pay the right price," which in effect was capitulation to all Iranian demands.[106] The Iranian government hinted that they would not engage in dialogue so long as sanctions and trade bans remained in place.[107] Hardline papers equated "talks and relations" with "compromise and surrender."[108] Khamenei was blunt: "We shall not show any flexibility . . . and we shall not relent." As for Khatami's idea of dialogue, the Supreme Leader clarified that "the phrase dialogue among civilizations does not mean holding talks with representatives of foreign states."[109]

Clinton refused to lift sanctions preventing investment in Iran's oil infrastructure and trade restrictions on dual-use goods. While Scowcroft criticized his obstinacy, the president's caution was prudent. Years later, Abdollah Ramezanzadeh, the Khatami government spokesman, acknowledged Tehran's insincerity. "We had one overt policy, which was one of negotiation and confidence building," he explained, "and a covert policy, which was continuation of the activities."[110] The influential Ayatollah Mohammad Taqi Mesbah-Yazdi elaborated in his memoirs: "The most advanced weapons must be produced inside our country even if our enemies don't like it."[111]

Proponents of dialogue kept trying. The State Department proposed sending a consular officer to Tehran, but the Iranian government rejected the idea, and then characterized its rebuff as a "diplomatic blow" to the Americans.[112] The State Department never created metrics by which to judge its outreach. It was easier to project goodwill onto the adversary.

Albright pursued diplomacy with Iran through the waning days of the Clinton administration. On March 17, 2000, she spoke to the American Iranian Council. After, in effect, apologizing for the American role in the 1953 coup against Prime Minister Mohammad Mosaddeq, she announced a number of unilateral American concessions: ending the import ban on Persian rugs, pistachios and caviar, three of Iran's most lucrative non-oil industries; a further relaxation of visa restrictions; and progress on releasing assets frozen during the hostage crisis. The pistachio import ban pumped tens of millions of dollars into Rafsanjani's pocket, as he had long since cornered the Iranian market.

As always, the Iranians hinted they would react positively. Hadi Nejad-Hosseinian, Iran's ambassador at the United Nations, said that Iran would be "prepared to adopt proportionate and positive measures in return."[113] But no Iranian goodwill was forthcoming. Quite the contrary: in July, the Iranian government tested a new, enhanced missile. The Supreme Leader then declared negotiations with Washington to be "an insult and treason to the Iranian people."[114] In his mind, negotiations would only boost American influence, something to be avoided at all costs.[115] Khatami asserted that the United States had not offered enough to merit a response.[116]

Ultimately, Albright's concessions did more harm than good. Kharrazi seized upon her "confessions" of regret about the overthrow of Mosaddeq to issue a demand for more apologies and also for reparations.[117] But rather than talk further, he stood Albright up during a planned one-on-one meeting at the United Nations.

As always, American cheerleaders for talks refused to take no for an answer. Instead, they echoed the Iranians' argument that Clinton had not offered enough. According to Scowcroft and Lee H. Hamilton, for example, "The U.S. sanctions are the main obstacle preventing the United States from pursuing its complete range of interests with Iran." Given the internal political squabbles in Tehran, they counseled dispensing to issue demands for a "*quid pro quo* form of reciprocity."[118] In effect, they suggested a free pass for the Islamic Republic to avoid making any concessions, and changed diplomacy from a game of chess into one of solitaire.

Proponents of engagement elevated imagery over substance. Thus, Albright announced that the United States would no longer speak of rogue regimes, but would henceforth refer to Iran, North Korea, and Libya as "states of concern."[119] Richard Haass, a prominent Republican realist, applauded Albright's new lexicon, arguing that the term "rogue" served only to limit policy options.[120] While American analysts navel-gazed, however, the Iranian press ridiculed the debate over terminology.[121]

Europe Takes the Lead

America was not alone in its dance with Khomeini. The European relationship with Iran was centuries longer and would grow to become just as traumatic. Still, Europe was not the United States. While the Carter administration debated whether to engage Khomeini in the months before the shah fell, the French government was hosting the ayatollah in Neauphle-le-Château, a small suburb of Paris. The French hoped to curry favor with the opposition that was poised to take power, but soon found their hospitality won them little consideration. Khomeini's antipathy toward the West was ideological.[122] No amount of obsequiousness would sway him.

Soon after Khomeini returned to Iran, the revolutionary authorities unleashed a wave of assassinations on French soil. The revolutionary court leader, Ayatollah Sadegh Khalkhali, vowed that the murders would "continue until all these dirty pawns of the decadent regime have been purged."[123] Iranian authorities did their best to keep their word.[124]

Subsequent events showed just how little the French government had gained through engagement. Iranian-backed terrorists bombed the French marine barracks in Beirut and the French embassy in Kuwait in 1983, and hijacked an Air France plane the following year. A Hezbollah bombing wave in Paris killed thirteen and wounded almost 250.[125] After pro-Iranian terrorists in Lebanon seized five French hostages, Prime Minister Jacques Chirac paid for their release.[126] When the French government objected to an Iranian terrorist sheltering in Iran's embassy in Paris, Islamic Revolutionary Guard Corps gunboats sprayed a French-flagged vessel with gunfire,[127] and Lebanese Hezbollah seized new French hostages. Chirac and President François Mitterrand responded by caving to every single Iranian demand, leading the *Economist* to describe the French negotiating position as "Anything else, Mr. Khomeini?"[128] Even fulfilling all Khomeini's demands was not enough. Just over a year later, Iranian assassins cut down a prominent Iranian dissident in his suburban Paris home.

Great Britain took another tack. Khomeini hated Britain deeply and infused his speeches with paranoid ravings about British malfeasance.[129] For these he found a ready audience: many Iranians shared his antipathy as a result of the British humiliation of Iran during the nineteenth and early twentieth centuries. After Khomeini came to power, revolutionary mobs set upon British property and even priests, and the Foreign Office evacuated the British embassy. Only at the end of the Iran-Iraq War did the United Kingdom again opened its embassy in Tehran. For the next several months, the two countries were content to ignore each other—until February 14, 1989, when Khomeini issued a public call for Salman Rushdie's death in response to *The Satanic Verses*, a novel which, although he never read it, Khomeini pronounced blasphemous. The Iranian government demanded that Rushdie apologize if he wanted the death sentence lifted. Rushdie complied, and Iran's leadership then declared the apology to be a confession of guilt, just as they would when Albright apologized over Mosaddeq.

The British broke diplomatic relations after Khomeini ordered Rushdie's murder, and swore not to restore them until the Iranian regime promised not to harm the novelist. But Khatami's charm offensive blinded the British just as it did the Americans. No sooner had Iranian officials promised to revoke the death sentence—thereby reaping British goodwill and a lifting of European sanctions—than Iranian security services reaffirmed the sentence. Hence, a day after the United Kingdom and Iran agreed to exchange ambassadors once again, Iranian state media labeled Rushdie an apostate, subject to death. Simply put, Iranian officials played British diplomats for fools.

While Tehran rebuffed American, French, and British attempts at rapprochement, Germany's guiding principle was trade unencumbered by politics, and so German-Iranian ties thrived. By 1987, the West German share of the Iranian market was over 25 percent.[130] In 1992, the German foreign minister, Klaus Kinkel, argued that the German approach might serve as a model. Rather than isolate Iran as the Clinton team aimed to do, the Europeans might instead try "critical dialogue,"[131] in which Europe would correlate trade with Iranian behavior on human rights and terrorism.

In practice, the critical dialogue consisted of regular meetings, but not much else. It quickly became apparent that human rights were no more than a rhetorical concern for Germany or for Europe generally.

Iranian diplomats meanwhile signaled Tehran's belief that criticism of its actions was inappropriate.

"Critical dialogue," as it turned out, only encouraged Iran's rogue behavior. On September 17, 1992, soon after Germany launched its diplomatic initiative, an Iranian cell murdered four Kurdish dissidents at the Mykonos Restaurant in Berlin. Although German police suspected that the Iranian intelligence minister, Ali Fallahian, had ordered the hit, German officials intervened to prevent his questioning during a subsequent trip to Germany, for fear that raising the topic would sabotage dialogue.[132] Instead, German officials pretended that the Iranian hit had not occurred. They even transferred high-technology computers to the Iranian intelligence service.[133]

While Berlin tried to curry favor with Tehran, it could not quash its own judiciary, which proceeded with a trial of those captured fleeing the Mykonos hit. On April 10, 1997, after hearing from 176 witnesses and reading intelligence files, a German court found a captured Iranian intelligence agent, Kazem Darrabi, as well as a Hezbollah accomplice guilty of murder, and two colleagues guilty as accessories. More importantly, the court also concluded that a committee headed by the Supreme Leader and including Rafsanjani, Fallahian, and Ali Akbar Velayati, the foreign minister, had ordered the hit.[134]

After the verdict was read, Rafsanjani threatened Germany, swearing, "They are going to suffer for it." The head of a pro-government vigilante group threatened to blow up the German embassy.[135] The European Union suspended its critical dialogue and all EU members with the exception of Greece withdrew their ambassadors from Tehran.[136] Kinkel, the German foreign minister, refused to admit defeat. "We must not break off all contact with Iran, not least because we on our part have clear demands to make," he said.[137]

Italy's prime minister, Romano Prodi, took that advice to heart and sent a trade delegation to Tehran, defying the European suspension of relations with Iran. Two months later, a consortium led by the French company Total signed a $2 billion agreement to develop Iran's oil resources. Tehran considered the deal a "moral victory" and celebrated the European slight to America.[138] For all Europe's talk about unity in foreign policy, there was always at least one European state that would break the consensus in order to profit from Iranian trade.

When critics noted that the policy of critical dialogue had not improved Iran's human rights outlook, Kinkel said that it brought Iran into compliance with the International Atomic Energy Agency (IAEA) regulations, a claim which in hindsight was naïve.[139] Khatami's election breathed new life into Europe's negotiation attempts, just as it did the American efforts. "We believe that you need to talk to people if you are to influence them," Kinkel reasoned. "If you are to influence Iran, you need to talk to them on the points where there is disagreement."[140] Like American proponents of engagement, Kinkel could never accept that dialogue might fail. Perhaps, however, he understood the *perception* of failure surrounding his critical dialogue initiative, for he rebranded it "comprehensive dialogue."

The Mykonos verdict was, for all intents and purposes, forgotten while the Iranian leaders who ordered the hit at the heart of Germany remained in their posts. The expansion of relations continued unabated, even after the European Parliament reported that Khatami's election, contrary to expectations, "did not bring about substantial democratic and political change."[141] Trade increased as political freedoms in Iran diminished.

European officials claimed their strategy was working even as the Iranian regime pushed ahead with its covert nuclear program.[142] Despite the IAEA's finding that Iran had been developing a centrifuge uranium enrichment program for eighteen years and a laser enrichment program for twelve years, Germany's foreign minister, Joschka Fischer, corralled his European Union colleagues into giving Tehran another chance.[143] The more Iran's nuclear development progressed, the more desperate the European Union grew to engage. Indeed, in the face of Iranian cheating, the foreign ministers of Germany, France, and Britain, the so-called EU3, stated that the European Union was prepared to defy U.S. pressure to isolate Tehran, continue its dialogue with Iranian authorities, and perhaps even enhance trade and access to technology.[144] So long as the Iranian regime promised to talk, European officials assumed that their strategy was effective. By making empty promises, Iranian leaders played Europe like a fiddle.

On October 21, 2003, the EU3 foreign ministers visited Tehran. They returned with an Iranian promise to suspend uranium enrichment, detail its nuclear program, list its suppliers, and sign and ratify the IAEA's additional protocol.[145] The day after the Europeans claimed victory, Iranian authorities began to backtrack. "As long as Iran thinks this suspension is beneficial, it will continue, and whenever we don't want it, we will end it," said Hassan Rouhani, the head of Iran's negotiating team.[146] Years later, Rouhani bragged that he used diplomacy with the West to run out the clock to Iranian nuclear capability. "When I was entrusted with this portfolio, we had no production in Isfahan," he noted. By the time negotiations broke off, Iran had completed not only its uranium enrichment facility, but also a heavy-water plant in Arak that could produce plutonium. Rouhani bluntly said that Tehran had offered talks to European leaders as a way of delaying UN sanctions. "The Islamic Republic acted very wisely in my view and did not allow the United States to succeed," he crowed.[147]

The European Union, however, believed their diplomacy had succeeded. When Tehran signed the Additional Protocol on December 18, 2003, European diplomats and the IAEA were ecstatic. "It's a beginning of a mainstreaming of Iran with Europe," one official said. Just as important to European officials, they believed they had proved the American approach wrong.[148]

European triumphalism was too quick. Iran signed the Additional Protocol, but refused to ratify it. Here, the devil is in the details. The IAEA enacted the Additional Protocol to close loopholes that had enabled Saddam Hussein's Iraq to develop a sophisticated covert nuclear program despite eleven clean bills of health. To entice states to sign the Additional Protocol, the IAEA offered enhanced access to nuclear technology. Once they ratified the agreement, they allowed the IAEA to conduct more robust and intrusive inspections. By signing but refusing to ratify, the Iranian government grabbed all the carrots and ignored the sticks.

Nor did it turn out that the European concept of enrichment suspension accorded with Iran's understanding. The Iranian government argued that agreement to suspend uranium enrichment did not mean agreement to suspend all "enrichment-related activities." Iranian authorities continued secretly importing nuclear equipment, even though there would have been no reason for secrecy if the equipment were for civilian purposes as they claimed when caught red-handed. It is probable that with George W. Bush in the White House, the Iranians realized they might face consequences more serious than chiding by European diplomats.[149] Only then did Rouhani agree to a full suspension.[150] Soon, however, Iran reneged on its pledge. It was typical rogue behavior. For every one step forward, Iran took two steps back. Western officials marked forward progress with concessions, and they met backsliding with a click of the tongue. Diplomats focused only on the next deal and not the bigger picture.

Meanwhile, the regime's nuclear defiance and human rights abuses both worsened. By 2004, Iranian hardline factions had rebounded. European engagement never correlated to reform. It had no impact on Iranian domestic politics except to hurt the reformists. Europeans declined to re-examine their policy: if reconciliation failed, the problem was not diplomacy but rather some outside force. Instead of blaming itself for naïveté, or blaming Iran for its insincerity, the European Union blamed the United States.[151] The mantra of diplomacy had become so strong that European leaders were unwilling to consider the possibility that offering carrots may not work.

An Axis of Evil?

Although conventional wisdom condemns Bush as hostile to diplomacy, he embraced diplomacy with the Islamic Republic more than any president since Jimmy Carter. When Bush took office, President Khatami's charm offensive was still going strong. "I want to say that the nation of Iran has no problem with the people and the nation of America," Khatami told the UN, even as he complained about American policy.[152]

When Palestinians, Egyptians, and Syrians celebrated the 9/11 terrorist attacks, ordinary Iranians held candlelight vigils. Pro-engagement politicians like Joe Biden, then chairman of the Senate Committee on Foreign Relations, seized upon the show of solidarity as evidence that Iran was ripe for diplomacy after more than three decades of enmity.[153] Never mind that the 9/11 hijackers had received Iranian assistance.[154] More important, while the Iranian people mourned, Iran's leaders gloated. Mehdi Karrubi, a reformist politician, blamed "Zionists in Israel" for the attacks, and the state-controlled press promoted wild conspiracy theories.[155] According to *Kayhan*, widely seen as the voice of the Supreme Leader, "The super-terrorist had a taste of its own bitter medicine."[156]

Like many U.S. politicians, Biden assumed that he could triumph over Iranian recalcitrance with his powers of persuasion. "I am prepared to receive members of the Iranian Majlis whenever its members would like to visit. If Iranian parliamentarians believe that's too sensitive, I'm prepared to meet them elsewhere," he told the American Iranian Council, adding, "We must also be willing to hold discussions with Iran to develop creative solutions as we did in North Korea."[157] Biden lacked the perspective to understand that engagement with North Korea had failed.

Tehran had already closed its door to such overtures. Iranian parliamentarians ruled out engagement until Congress first dropped all sanctions.[158] "We shall put in his place anyone who would try . . . to extend the hand of friendship to the most blood-thirsty enemy of this land," a *Kayhan* editorial declared.[159]

Both Democrats and Republicans sought to transform the 9/11 tragedy into an opportunity to renew diplomacy. When Bush decided to oust the Taliban regime, a mutual enemy to the United States and Iran, Tehran agreed to assist. Iranian diplomats worked closely with their American counterparts to form the new Afghan government during the

2001 Bonn Conference. Some American diplomats hailed this as a sign that Tehran had changed course.[160] More likely, Tehran aimed to extend its influence throughout all of Afghanistan.

Proponents of engagement accepted Iranian altruism on faith and criticized the White House for not sharing their own goodwill. James Dobbins, a U.S. diplomat serving in Afghanistan, blasted the White House for turning down Iran's offer to help train Afghan security forces. Dobbins simply could not conceive the insincerity of Iranian diplomats with whom he had established friendly rapport.[161] Like the proverbial blind man describing an elephant, the diplomat did not see the whole picture. Dobbins counseled cooperation even as Tehran dispatched an officer of the Qods Force, an elite Revolutionary Guards unit specializing in the export of revolution, to be its consul in Herat.[162]

Rather than bolster Afghanistan's central government, the Iranian regime worked to weaken it.[163] Tehran sent operatives under the cover of schoolteachers and aid workers. In March 2002, Afghan commanders intercepted twelve Iranian agents organizing armed insurrection.[164] Tehran also facilitated the escape of al-Qaeda terrorists from Afghanistan.[165] The Iranian government was glad to reap the benefits of conference participation, but its actions were diametrically opposed to its commitments.

Within the Bush administration, the top Middle East aides, Zalmay Khalilzad and William Burns, favored engagement and, like Biden, suggested that diplomats might sit down with reformists even if hardliners were recalcitrant.[166] Both replicated the mistakes of their predecessors by conflating rhetoric with sincerity. Most Iranians had already given up on Khatami, but the president—like Mikhail Gorbachev in the waning days of the Soviet Union—retained the admiration of diplomats even as his domestic popularity hemorrhaged.

Placing a bet on the reformers was never wise. While women and students may have wanted serious change in Iranian society, reformists like Khatami were in fact wedded to the system. As Laura Secor observed in the *New Yorker*, "Iran's reform movement, for all its courage, was the loyal opposition in a fascist state. It sought not to dismantle or secularize the Islamic Republic . . . but to improve it."[167]

Within the White House, a new strategy took shape. Rather than rely on official talks, the administration would reach out to the Iranian people.[168] Simultaneously, Bush would criticize the regime. This strategy reached its peak on January 29, 2002, when Bush, during his State of the Union address, placed Iran along with Iraq, North Korea, and their "terrorist allies" in an "axis of evil." He explained, "By seeking weapons of mass destruction, these regimes pose a grave and growing danger."[169]

Bush described Iran as he saw it and refused to paper over its behavior to facilitate talks. Former officials chided him for having a diplomatic tin ear. In doing so, they played into Iranian hands, as the regime seized upon American criticisms of Bush to deflect responsibility from their own nuclear research and terror sponsorship.[170] Bush merely shrugged off the diplomats' objections. After revelations surfaced about Iran's secret enrichment program, he quipped, "all of the sudden, there weren't so many complaints about including Iran in the axis of evil."[171]

While the Western press criticized Bush for alleged hostility toward diplomacy with Iran, the opposite was actually true. In fact, the United States sought secret talks with Iran as war with Iraq became imminent.[172] The Supreme Leader forced Iran's deputy foreign minister, Sadegh Kharazi, to resign after secret talks in Cyprus were revealed.[173] It is unlikely that Kharazi had gone rogue, as the Iranian press suggested.[174] The excuse, however, would enable the Iranian regime to walk away after determining what was in the American hand and then pocketing the proffered concessions. In its enthusiasm to engage, the Bush team had replicated Carter's mistakes.

Meanwhile, the State Department objected to White House efforts to emphasize outreach to the Iranian people over direct diplomacy. Secretary Colin Powell argued that Khatami's election had bestowed democratic credentials upon Iran,[175] a point his deputy Richard Armitage reinforced. "I would note there's one dramatic difference between Iran and the other two axes of evil, and that would be its democracy," Armitage said.[176]

Unable to win White House blessing for a strategy that would legitimize the regime, proponents of normalizing relations between Washington and Tehran heaped opprobrium upon those who urged caution.[177] Some opponents of the White House strategy alleged that Bush, arrogant against the backdrop of the Iraq War, rejected an Iranian grand bargain in 2003 to settle everything from terror sponsorship to nuclear ambitions. The offer was a fraud, crafted by a Swiss ambassador frustrated at the U.S.-Iran stalemate, and was privately dismissed as nonsense by Iranian officials.[178] Advocates of diplomacy, however, took the bait.[179] John Limbert, a former hostage and author of a book about how to negotiate with Iran, embraced the fake memo to argue that the United States and Iran were equally insincere.[180] Few mentioned the fact that Bush made his own offer the following year.[181]

In truth, when the Swiss ambassador presented the fraudulent offer to Washington, American and Iranian officials were already at the table. As the British foreign secretary, Jack Straw, met his Iranian counterpart in Paris, Khalilzad sat down in Geneva with Mohammad Javad Zarif, Iran's UN ambassador.

Not all talks build confidence; sometimes they do the opposite. American officials quickly learned that Iran would not honor its agreements. Iranian diplomats, for example, promised noninterference in Iraq, yet the Revolutionary Guards smuggled money, men, and weapons into Iraq.[182] After the Iranian foreign ministry publicized a U.S. request for cooperation in Iraq, an Iranian newspaper asserted that Iran "can make this country [Iraq] a devouring swamp for the States in the region" and suggested that American outreach proved Iranian strength. "They have been obliged to accept the reality that Iran is one of the undeniable powers, and a country which has an important role in the political calculations of the region."[183]

That was strike one for diplomacy's advocates. Strike two was Iran's accelerating nuclear program. While diplomats counseled lifting sanctions to ease diplomacy, Iran designed a facility to house 50,000 centrifuges and hid from the IAEA a ton of uranium hexafluoride imported from

China.[184] What Tehran had done with the uranium it processed, it refused to say.

Strike three was Iran's bad faith on terrorism. In the wake of 9/11, the Islamic Republic protected and assisted several hundred al-Qaeda operatives, even as it sought credit for turning over low-level functionaries.[185] Tehran suggested a trade of al-Qaeda operatives for Mujahedin al-Khalq members in Iraq, but the latter, as persons protected by the Geneva Convention, were not America's to trade. The Bush administration informed Iran that the White House would hold it responsible for any terrorism planned by al-Qaeda on Iranian soil.

Even for diplomacy's cheerleaders, evidence of the regime's insincerity was too obvious to miss. Either the reformers were treating their American counterparts as useful idiots, or the reformers did not have enough power to commit the regime to agreements. It was not in the State Department's nature to consider the first possibility, but it could not ignore the second. In a July 2003 radio interview, Powell admitted, "The best thing we can do right now is not get in the middle of this family fight too deeply."[186] The Bush team had repeated the mistakes of the Carter and Reagan administrations, but it had not yet learned the lesson.

Military commanders conduct endless studies of past battles and work for several weeks alongside those they will replace, but America's senior diplomats have no such mechanism to transmit accumulated knowledge. American diplomacy is Sisyphean, as new secretaries endlessly repeat the missteps of their predecessors. If during his first term Bush had welcomed broad debate within his administration about diplomacy's wisdom, by 2005 the debate had ended and skeptics of outreach were purged or retired. The State Department doubled down on negotiations even as the stakes skyrocketed.

Whereas Powell stumbled over whom to engage, Condoleezza Rice's team swept such concerns aside. In order to support Europe's diplomacy toward Iran, she added new incentives to their pot. "This is most assuredly giving the Europeans a stronger hand, not rewarding the Iranians," she explained.[187] Someone should have told that to the Iranians. They scoffed at Rice's offer to provide them with much-needed spare parts for their civilian air fleet as well as World Trade Organization membership to entice them to the table.[188]

Tehran then announced it would end its moratorium on uranium enrichment. In response, rather than show Tehran that its backtracking would cost the Islamic Republic dearly, the European Union offered a deal modeled on the one that Bill Clinton offered to North Korea a decade earlier: The West would assist Iran's peaceful nuclear program in exchange for Tehran's commitment to cease enrichment and halt construction of its plutonium-producing heavy-water reactor.

Unfortunately for Europe, Iran replicated North Korea's strategy: blackmail for cash and technology. Like the North Koreans, Iranian officials had learned to ignore threats, knowing that rewards were just around the corner. The IAEA, after months of foot dragging to give diplomats time to head off a crisis, found the Islamic Republic in violation of its nuclear safeguards agreement. Iran responded with defiance, breaking seals that international monitors had placed on its once-secret Natanz enrichment facility.

The Iranian gamble paid off: European diplomats offered even more incentives. The European Union foreign policy chief, Javier Solana, promised Iran "a generous package, a bold package" including nuclear technology, economic concessions, and possibly even security cooperation. In exchange, he demanded only that Iran once again halt sensitive nuclear activities.[189] Again, Iran resisted.

European officials blamed America. They could not imagine that their outreach would not work.[190] Diplomats were more willing to believe Iran's manufactured grievances than consider for a moment that the regime might be insincere. European officials lobbied their American counterparts furiously, arguing that it was Bush's intransigence, and not the assumptions underlying European diplomacy, that had caused engagement to fail.

For the State Department, revitalizing its partnership with Europe became a higher priority than holding firm on issues that caused the rift in the first place. Accordingly, it counseled surrender, at least to Europe. On May 31, 2006, Rice announced that the United States would not only talk with Tehran, but also enhance its incentive package. All she asked was that Iran suspend enrichment for the duration of talks.[191] Rice insisted that she would be no pushover. Should Iran refuse, she promised severe consequences.[192] In a conference call accompanying the announcement, however, her advisors could name none of those consequences. The Iranians noticed. The olive branch convinced them that America was a paper tiger.

The Iranian government responded with defiance. After months of silence, President Mahmoud Ahmadinejad inaugurated a facility capable of producing plutonium for weaponry in the western city of Arak. Coming less than a month after the Security Council demanded a one-month suspension of Iran's uranium enrichment, this action was deliberately provocative. The fact that Iran had spent two years building the plant while diplomats scurried to engage was even more telling.

On September 15, 2006, the European Union dropped its demand that Iran comply with IAEA and Security Council demands for enrichment suspension. Javier Solana commented, "We are really making progress: never before have we had a level of engagement, and a level of discussions . . . as we have now." In hindsight, the Islamic Republic was increasing its centrifuge capacity from 164 to 3,000.[193] For diplomats, getting Iran to the table had become the top objective, more important even than holding Iran to its commitments. Talking trumped behavior as the metric of progress.[194] In Pentagon terms, this would be the equivalent of judging battle by focusing on the shooting rather than victory.

Iranian officials reverted to tactics harking back to the hostage crisis. Talks proceeded, even though Iran's top negotiator could not confirm the Supreme Leader's compliance with the Iranian team's commitments.[195]

Not surprisingly, talks failed.[196] The following spring, Ahmadinejad stood at Natanz and announced, "Our country joined the club of nuclear nations." Two years later, the State Department's Iran point man lamented that "Iran walked away and missed a rare opportunity to pursue a better relationship with the United States."[197] From an Iranian perspective, there was no failure. Iran's leadership had engaged insincerely as a diversion while pressing forward in its nuclear ambitions. Finally, on November 30, 2007, its negotiator announced that Iran would take all past proposals for compromise off the table.[198] Iran had refined its nuclear abilities during its engagement with the European Union and had created a new reality.

Western officials responded like a drunk who concludes from a hangover that he needs more beer: by loosening demands and adding more incentives. Germany freed Kazem Darrabi, the mastermind of the Mykonos murders.[199] Rice joined other Security Council foreign ministers to offer Iran a nuclear reactor, nuclear fuel, normalization of trade, and civil aircraft upgrades.[200]

Rice meanwhile sought to move ahead with bilateral talks. Conflict in Iraq and Afghanistan provided ready topics, but efforts to win Iranian cooperation were costly. Rice's outreach led Tehran to believe that America was on the ropes, so Iranian authorities not only increased their support for militias operating in Iraq, but also began to ship weaponry to the Taliban.[201] In the same year that Rice offered incentives, explosively formed projectile attacks by Iranian-backed militias in Iraq increased 150 percent. Tehran clearly wanted to see if it might receive a higher reward for ending more violence.[202] Diplomats deny it hurts to talk, but hundreds of American servicemen paid the price.

While journalists and diplomats celebrated Americans and Iranians sitting together openly after so many years, they missed the symbolism inherent in the choice of envoys: Ryan Crocker, a career diplomat, represented the United States, while Hassan Kazemi Qomi, a Qods Force operative, represented Tehran. For the United States, dialogue was a means to resolve conflict, but for Iran, it provided cover for the export of revolutionary goals and support of terrorism.

American diplomats saw dialogue as a breakthrough, but it was a mirage. Qomi waved off evidence and denied Iranian complicity in Iraqi militia attacks. Dialogue did far less to reduce violence than to diminish the U.S. military's willingness to capture Iranian personnel involved in training terrorists. With almost religious zeal, proponents of dialogue denied Iranian wrongdoing, for admitting it would acknowledge the shortcomings of diplomacy and could delay talks for years.[203] Ironically, Iranian analysts were less dismissive of the notion that their military was in cahoots with the Taliban. "It is better for Iran if America is entangled in Afghanistan with the Taliban," wrote an analyst in Iran's largest-circulation daily.[204]

The dialogue over Iraq may have backfired—with reverberations felt in Afghanistan as well—but diplomats refused to admit defeat. In July 2008, Rice voided her own red line of May 31, 2006, by dispatching Under Secretary William Burns to meet Iran's nuclear negotiator even without an Iranian commitment to suspend uranium enrichment. The willingness to issue and then ignore frameworks and conditions hemorrhaged American credibility. Even with Burns present, Iran rejected any enrichment freeze.

Bush left the White House with Iran's nuclear program far more advanced than when he took office. By any metric, he failed to resolve the challenge posed by Iran to American national interests. While proponents of engagement attribute Bush's failures to a neglect of diplomacy, the opposite is true. Bush, like Clinton and Carter before him, would not acknowledge that rogue regimes engaged insincerely.

The Outstretched Hand

For those who insisted that the failure to bring Iran in from the cold resulted from insufficient diplomacy, Barack Obama's election offered a chance to test their strategy. Before he took office, Obama had become diplomats' favorite candidate when he promised to meet the leaders of Iran "without preconditions."[205] Nicholas Burns, a former under secretary for policy at the State Department, explained the logic, saying, "An unconditional offer deprives Iran's leaders of the excuse not to negotiate."[206] For many of Obama's supporters, the key to success was easy: simply remove any bone of contention from the agenda. Thus Roger Cohen, a *New York Times* columnist, urged Obama not to "obsess" over the nuclear issue.[207]

Iranian officials recognized that the American press "was in favor of talks . . . without preconditions,"[208] and they were willing to encourage the idea. Ahmadinejad sent Obama a congratulatory letter upon his election.[209] Iran's ambassador to the IAEA, Ali Asghar Soltanieh, also welcomed a broad dialogue with Obama.[210]

Obama was a man of his word regarding outreach to the Islamic Republic, which became his marquee foreign policy issue. The State Department sent a letter to Ahmadinejad to pave the way for face-to-face talks. Then, less than a week after taking office, Obama told Al Arabiya's satellite network, "If countries like Iran are willing to unclench their fist, they will find an extended hand from us."[211]

Soon there were signs that Iran's embrace of dialogue was merely tactical. The speaker of Iran's parliament, Ali Larijani, rebuffed a request from Howard Berman, a prominent Democrat chairing the House Committee on Foreign Affairs, to meet in Bahrain.[212] Then, Khamenei waved off Obama's outreach as "bogus gestures."[213]

Iranian culture is subtle, and its diplomacy is a reflection of its culture. The White House did not pick up on the hints. Instead, Obama called a news conference and again called for face-to-face talks.[214] William Perry, a former defense secretary and an influential figure for the Obama White House, met a high-level Iranian delegation led by a senior Ahmadinejad advisor, Mojtaba Samareh Hashemi, to emphasize the point. The Associated Press reported, "Not since before the 1979 Iranian revolution are U.S. officials believed to have conducted wide-ranging direct diplomacy with Iranian officials." If talking to a brick wall was diplomacy, then the press report was true.

As diplomats cycled through excuses for why diplomacy had yet to work, one theory became prominent: insufficiently respectful language. Just as Madeleine Albright tried to bypass the problem of rogue regimes by renaming them "states of concern," Obama tried to revamp American rhetoric in order to conjure up diplomacy. To Obama and his aides, Iran's inclusion in the Axis of Evil was original sin—never mind that Americans seemed to object to the phrase more than Iranians did.

The vocabulary makeover soon turned from the sublime to the ridiculous. For example, William Luers, Thomas Pickering, and Jim Walsh warned that Iranians "bristle at the use of the phrase 'carrots and sticks,'" because it depicted them as donkeys and because it implied a threat to beat Iran into submission if they could not be bought.[215] That Iranians would raise such manufactured grievances suggests that they saw elder statesmen like Pickering as useful idiots, willing to accept any reason short of Iranian insincerity to explain the failure of U.S.-Iranian engagement. After all, the phrase "carrots and sticks" had long been used in the Iranian press.[216]

Obama continued his efforts to set a new tone when he offered Iranians the traditional Persian New Year's greeting on March 20. Whereas Bush had taken care to differentiate between the Iranian people and the regime, Obama broke precedent and paid homage to the Islamic Republic rather than the Iranian nation. His attempt to ingratiate himself with the regime came to naught. Ali Akbar Javanfekr, an aide to Ahmadinejad, responded by calling on the United States to compensate Iran for previous American mistakes. If Americans believed that dialogue would lead to compromise, Iranians saw the process leading to American surrender. The Supreme Leader ridiculed the idea of diplomacy with the United States.[217]

Meanwhile, the Iranian nuclear program kept moving forward. Admiral Mike Mullen, chairman of the Joint Chiefs of Staff, warned that "the Iranians are on a path to building nuclear weapons."[218]

To jumpstart diplomacy, Obama offered a unilateral concession: recognizing the Islamic Republic's right to enrich uranium. With a single statement, he voided three Security Council resolutions forbidding further uranium enrichment by Iran. Rather than enable diplomacy, he poisoned it. Iranian strategists concluded that defiance pays.[219] It was around this time that a revolutionary court lodged espionage charges against Roxana Saberi, an Iranian American freelance journalist and former Miss North Dakota.

Persistent American outreach efforts, each coupled with new incentives, also eroded regional allies' faith in America's commitment to them. Arab allies worried that Obama might sacrifice their security for the sake of U.S.-Iran rapprochement. Israeli officials worried that the Iranian government aimed only to run out the clock.[220] Perhaps this is why Obama signaled that his patience was not infinite. "We do want to make sure that, by the end of this year, we've actually seen a serious process move forward," he declared.[221]

The American preconditions lifted, Ahmadinejad responded with his own.[222] The United States offered concessions to get Iran to the table, but from the Iranian perspective, the dance had long since begun. Iranian negotiating behavior represented a culturally different understanding of diplomacy: everything was about position. Formal dialogue was not the beginning of the process, but its middle. By playing hard to get, Tehran could win objectives even before the horse trading started. By offering concessions without demanding anything in return, Obama played into Iranian hands and encouraged Tehran to shift the goalposts and stake out more extreme positions.

The State Department operated as if it were in a vacuum, pursuing diplomacy with little regard to the Iranian response. Hence, American diplomats would pounce on the feeblest hints that Iran was willing to talk, even as Khamenei vetoed that possibility.[223] Embracing hot dog diplomacy, the State Department instructed American embassies to invite their Iranian counterparts to Fourth of July celebrations.[224] Reality intruded when Iranians took to the streets in outrage after blatant fraud in the June 2009 presidential elections. With Iranian security forces firing on crowds in the streets, Secretary Hillary Clinton reluctantly rescinded the July 4 invitations. Otherwise, the administration remained largely silent. "We respect Iran's sovereignty," Obama explained.[225] To speak publicly, the administration feared, would hinder efforts to engage. Shortly before the botched election, Obama had sent a second letter to the Supreme Leader seeking dialogue, but received no reply.[226]

In 1986, Ronald Reagan stood in solidarity with the people of the Philippines after the dictator Ferdinand Marcos had tried to throw an election. In 2000, Bill Clinton stood with Serbs who were troubled over

Slobodan Milosevic. By contrast, George H. W. Bush, in his infamous "Chicken Kiev" speech, elevated engagement with the Soviet Union above hastening its collapse. Obama likewise lost perspective, effectively favoring the preservation of the Islamic Republic out of a desire to engage the regime. Protestors' chants of *"Obama, ya una ya ba ma"* (Obama, you're either with us or against us) underscored the point. Silence born from the desire to talk had a cost.

As the protests over the Iranian election were about to enter their fourth week, Obama again proposed talks with the regime. Speaking at the conclusion of the Group of Eight summit in L'Aquila, Italy, he said the world's main powers would "take further steps" if Tehran failed to make good-faith efforts to resolve concern about its nuclear program by the time of the G20 summit two months later. He refused to elaborate on what steps he had in mind, and instead merely said, "Our planning is how to prevent us from getting too close to that point."[227] If Iran's leadership believed Obama had any remaining credibility, he soon disabused them of the notion as the deadline passed without immediate consequence.

That the Iranians would test Obama's ultimatum was a certainty. Iranian diplomats regularly allow deadlines to grow close if not pass before responding, in order to derail the Western response. Only a day before Security Council diplomats were to discuss new sanctions did Iranian officials signal their readiness to engage.[228] Any Iranian hint that they would negotiate in good faith was enough for diplomats to delay punitive action. With sanctions pushed back and pressure relieved, Ahmadinejad pivoted and again ruled out any Iranian compromise. "Iran's nuclear issue is over," he said. "We will never negotiate Iran's undeniable rights."[229]

The State Department did not regard Ahmadinejad's statement as sufficiently official, since it had not come through proper channels. This complaint was symptomatic of a mindset in which American diplomats judge rogue regimes by norms they do not accept. Accordingly, Secretary Clinton dispatched William Burns, the number-three State Department official, to meet his Iranian counterpart.[230]

Iranian authorities, meanwhile, quietly informed the IAEA of plans to build twenty nuclear reactors and ten new uranium enrichment plants.[231] As Condoleezza Rice had struggled to get the Iranians to the table, they were secretly breaking ground on a new enrichment facility at Fordo, near Qom. As Obama extended his hand, Iranian engineers were finishing their new underground facility. Iranian diplomacy was undertaken in bad faith, meant to buy time.[232] Nor was Tehran's acknowledgment of the Fordo facility made in good faith; it was only to preempt a Western announcement of its discovery.[233] Unbelievably, the White House rewarded Iran by allowing its foreign minister to visit Washington for the first time in a decade, a step that Iran remained unwilling to reciprocate.[234]

After months of angry posturing capped off with test-firing of new missiles, Iranian authorities hinted that they might return to the table only when new sanctions loomed.[235] This was completely typical Iranian behavior, yet Western officials breathed sighs of relief. "Iran has told us that it plans to cooperate fully and immediately with the International Atomic Energy Agency on the new enrichment facility near Qom," said Javier Solana at a press conference. In exchange, the Europeans and Americans "agreed to intensify dialogue."[236] Cheerleaders for Obama's outreach celebrated. "Barack Obama pwned Bush-Cheney in one day and got more concessions from Iran in 7½ hours than the former administration got in 8 years of saber-rattling," wrote Juan Cole, a fiercely partisan professor at the University of Michigan.[237]

Obama himself was more cautious. "We're not going to talk for the sake of talking," he said, adding, "we are prepared to move towards increased pressure." Over the next weeks, he gave his imprimatur to an IAEA proposal that would see Iran ship its enriched nuclear fuel to Russia, which would enrich it further and return it to Iran for use in medical research. An Iranian delegation in Geneva said they would accept the compromise, and Iran's foreign ministry called the deal "a national success." All the international community needed was Iran's formal acceptance. This never came. Rather, the Iranian regime tore up its agreement and demanded the right to enrich all uranium inside Iran.

Such a scenario would have replicated the North Korea fiasco: After the Bush administration had acquiesced to Pyongyang's demands to continue enrichment domestically, Kim Jong Il's regime expelled inspectors and enriched its uranium to weapons grade.[238] Even short of gaining consent to its demand, Tehran had already achieved its goal: derailing sanctions, while spinning its centrifuges without pause.

In the face of Iranian intransigence, Obama once again signaled weakness. He postponed punitive measures to give Iran time to reconsider.[239] Then, Clinton appointed John Limbert to be her point man on Iran policy. A former hostage, Limbert worked as an advisor to an anti-sanctions lobby group and was dismissive of concerns about a nuclear Iran.[240] The Iranian government had even celebrated his comments in its official press.[241] In effect, Limbert counseled surrender.

At a speech commemorating the thirtieth anniversary of the U.S. embassy seizure, Khamenei disparaged Obama's efforts at engagement. "The Iranian nation will not be deceived by the US government's apparently conciliatory words," he told university students in Tehran.[242] Obama ignored the Supreme Leader's remarks. To do otherwise would have required him to choose between accepting Iran's nuclear breakout and implementing a more forceful strategy. Obama's worldview did not allow him to admit that he had no Iranian partner, so instead he made excuses for the Iranians to explain why diplomacy floundered. "Part of the challenge that we face is that neither North Korea nor Iran seem to be settled enough politically to make quick decisions on these issues," the president explained.[243] This excuse assumed that the Great Leader in Pyongyang and the Supreme Leader in Tehran took public opinion into account when making decisions.

With the White House refusing to observe its own red lines, the head of Iran's atomic organization, Ali Akbar Salehi, announced plans for five more reactors.[244] The following week, the foreign ministry spokesman, Ramin Mehmanparast, acknowledged that Tehran had never had negotiations with Washington on its agenda.[245] The Iranian parliament disclosed a request by Senator John Kerry to visit Tehran, which it refused. Less than a month later, Iran's military launched a rocket capable of carrying a nuclear warhead.

The White House condemned the missile launch as "provocative,"[246] but Clinton still backtracked, saying, "We've avoided using the term 'deadline' ourselves . . . because we want to keep the door to dialogue open."[247] In effect, the Obama administration preferred to change its metrics rather than admit failure. Clinton's flexibility reinforced Iranian intransigence. "We share the same idea with her," said Mehmanparast. "Deadlines are meaningless."[248]

As the State Department and its European partners began discussing how to augment sanctions, Turkey and Brazil, both nonpermanent members of the UN Security Council, began negotiating their own nuclear deal with Iran. Turkey took the lead, motivated less by a desire to end the standoff—Turkey's prime minister had endorsed Iran's nuclear program, after all—than by a desire to raise its own prestige. Iranian officials embraced such efforts, consistent with a long pattern of deferring sanctions while seeking to exploit divisions in the international community. On May 17, the three countries agreed to a deal similar to the one Iran had walked away from the previous year in Geneva. The new agreement did not take account of enrichment done over the previous half year, and so it left Iran with sufficient uranium to build a bomb.[249] Nor did it bring Iran into compliance with UN resolutions.

What had begun as a confidence-building measure turned into the opposite. Not only the United States, but also the European Union, Russia, and China dismissed the deal. Turkey's diplomacy had transformed Iran from a culprit into a victim of supposed U.S. diplomatic persecution.[250] For the West and its partners, patience had run out. Almost nine months after the G8 leaders promised to punish Iranian defiance, the United Nations passed sanctions.[251] Even then, Iran could count on Russia and China to water down the results. The United States and Europe, along with Japan and Korea, augmented the multilateral sanctions with their own unilateral measures.

The Iranian response was bluster and defiance. "What have they achieved today after passing four resolutions?" Ahmadinejad asked. "They thought if they pass a harsh resolution, they can usurp the rights of the Iranian nation and now they say, 'We want to negotiate.'" Ahmadinejad made the Iranian position clear: "If you want to negotiate, you should abandon the behavior of those who rebel against God."[252] The Iranian foreign minister publicly rebuffed two attempts by Clinton to greet him at a security conference in Bahrain, and rejected her offer of diplomatic relations the following year.[253]

While Clinton renewed her outreach attempts, Iranian authorities intensified their crackdown on civil society.[254] They understood that they need not fear accountability when Washington wanted them at the table. A round of talks in Geneva in December 2010 went nowhere when Iran's chief nuclear negotiator, Saeed Jalali, refused to discuss any agreement that would have Iran forfeit its right to enrich uranium. In response, the West offered Iran more concessions.[255] Proponents of engagement worried that Ahmadinejad might fall, and then Washington would have to find a new partner for diplomacy. For all his "messianic fantasies" and Holocaust denial, Ahmadinejad was still the Islamic Republic's "most ardent advocate of direct nuclear negotiations with Washington," observed Ray Takeyh, a former advisor in Hillary Clinton's State Department, and his wife, Suzanne Maloney, a former Bush administration official.[256] Diplomacy advocates in Washington kept tilting at windmills in a quixotic quest to engage. The Supreme Leader's rejection of Obama's overtures, reiterated ad nauseam by underlings, fell on deaf ears.[257]

If Ahmadinejad was Iran's "most ardent advocate" of direct diplomacy, he would soon meet his match in Hassan Rouhani, Iran's former nuclear negotiator. Voters hoping for reform propelled Rouhani to a first-round victory in the elections of June 2013. Many American proponents of engagement saw Rouhani as a man with whom they could deal, and Rouhani did not disappoint. Shortly before his visit to the United Nations in September 2013, he published an op-ed in the *Washington*

Post urging world leaders "to make the most of the mandate for prudent engagement that my people have given me and to respond genuinely to my government's efforts to engage in constructive dialogue."[258]

When he arrived in New York, the press treated Rouhani like a rock star. The Iranian president demurred on a direct meeting, so Obama settled for a phone conversation, after which he reported triumphantly:

> *Just now, I spoke on the phone with President Rouhani of the Islamic Republic of Iran. The two of us discussed our ongoing efforts to reach an agreement over Iran's nuclear program. I reiterated to President Rouhani what I said in New York—while there will surely be important obstacles to moving forward, and success is by no means guaranteed, I believe we can reach a comprehensive solution. . . . The very fact that this was the first communication between an American and Iranian President since 1979 underscores the deep mistrust between our countries, but it also indicates the prospect of moving beyond that difficult history. I do believe that there is a basis for a resolution. Iran's Supreme Leader has issued a fatwa against the development of nuclear weapons. President Rouhani has indicated that Iran will never develop nuclear weapons.*[259]

Although the fatwa, or religious declaration, that Obama cited has been the subject of diplomatic banter, it does not appear to exist. It is not listed in the Supreme Leader's list of fatwas, and Iranian officials who mention it are not consistent on the text or even the date of issue. In his eagerness for a deal, Obama simply put trust before verify.

Some context for Rouhani's assurances could have been provided by a speech he gave in 2005 to clerics in Mashhad, titled "Iran's Measures Rob the Americans of Foresight." Here, Rouhani endorsed a strategy of unpredictability and misdirection. "An important factor in the defeat of the plots of the enemies of Islam and the victory of the Islamic revolution was the principle of surprise," he explained. "We always had another plan, which was both victorious and unpredictable for them as to exactly what direction we might take."[260] Obama assumed the best, never considering what, if anything, might have led Rouhani to a change of heart.

Obama used his press conference after the telephone call to celebrate a new opportunity, while Rouhani assured his domestic audience that he had not changed his position at all.[261] The Western press reported that Rouhani was prepared to shutter the underground nuclear facility at Fordo, but Rouhani's cabinet flatly ruled it out.[262] The same held true for the Supreme Leader. While Western officials interpreted Khamenei's talk of the need for "heroic flexibility" as a sign that he endorsed Rouhani's outreach, the Supreme Leader's advisors and aides explained that he had approved only a change in tactics, not in policy.[263] Because so many Western reporters cherry-picked the facts to accentuate the positive, Western officials began to base their policies on a false perception of Iranian flexibility.

That may have been Rouhani's goal all along. In his first television interview as president, Rouhani had announced that Iran's economy had shrunk 5.4 percent over the previous year.[264] Soon after he returned home from his appearance at the United Nations, the State Department dutifully requested that Congress delay new sanctions and roll back those already in place, in order to encourage diplomacy.[265] Loosening sanctions may have been Tehran's priority, but for the United States to fulfill the Iranian agenda before talks even begin does not make their success more likely.

* * *

"Cultivation of goodwill for goodwill's sake is a waste of effort,"[266] advised Bruce Laingen, the senior U.S. diplomat in Tehran, just weeks before the hostage crisis. More than three decades after Iran's revolution, diplomacy has failed to resolve disputes between the United States and the Islamic Republic, let alone restore trust. Quite the contrary, the American rush to talk has backfired, reinforcing Iranian radicalism and recalcitrance at the expense of American national interest. It is telling that the three U.S. administrations that pushed most persistently for diplomatic engagement—

those of Carter, George W. Bush, and Obama—suffered the greatest Iranian violence as a reward for their efforts.

Under Carter, an ill-conceived handshake and a willingness to take military action off the table transformed a hiccup at the embassy into a 444-day standoff. Persistent diplomacy empowered radicals. Under George W. Bush, the gap between rhetoric and policy reality was huge. Once Iranian leaders saw they would suffer no ill consequences for their defiance and, indeed, might even profit from it, Iran's nuclear program expanded rapidly and Iranian forces grew increasingly bold in their confrontations with American troops in neighboring Iraq and Afghanistan. Despite the track record of his predecessors and the statements of Iranian leaders, Obama pursued diplomacy with a vigor unseen since the Carter years. The Iranian leadership responded with disdain. For the first time in thirty years, the regime plotted an assassination in the heart of America. Human rights abuses multiplied in Iran.[267] The Iranian nuclear program progressed to the verge of weapons capability.

Debate remained fierce about why engagement with Iran failed. Many proponents of engagement said that Washington, at best, was equally at fault with Tehran; more often, they blamed America. After the exposure of Iran's bungled attack on Washington, D.C., a senior American official suggested that American aggressiveness explained Iran's inclination to lash out.[268] This, of course, is nonsense: whereas anti-American incitement is a staple of weekly Friday prayers in Iran, no American president, diplomat, or congressman has ever led crowds in anti-Iranian chants. George W. Bush's "Axis of Evil" speech may be an exception to the rule, though he drew a sharp distinction between the Iranian people and the Islamic Republic. The disproportionate American focus on that single utterance reflects the American tendency to self-flagellate rather than recognize the rogue's responsibility for diplomacy's failure.

Diplomats counseling engagement with Iran too often assume that they and the Iranians share a common objective. They are wrong. Western officials see diplomacy as a process of compromise and conflict resolution. Iranian leaders, on the other hand, view it from a Manichaean perspective. As *Kayhan* explained it, "The power struggle in the region has only two sides: Iran and America."[269]

Successive Iranian officials have bragged that America plays checkers while Iran plays chess. They have boasted about how Tehran deceives the West with diplomacy. For the ayatollahs, diplomacy is a tactic to divide the international community, pocket concessions, and hold off sanctions or military strikes. "Without violating any international laws or the nonproliferation treaty, we have managed to bypass the red lines the West created for us," bragged Hamidreza Taraghi, an advisor to the Supreme Leader.[270] The cycles of embracing and disengaging from talks have stymied the West for more than thirty years. That the State Department continues to grasp at Iran's proffered straws demonstrates a lack of strategic review within American diplomatic circles.

One reason for the failure of diplomatic outreach to Iran has been inattention to the circumstances under which it is initiated. Diplomacy toward Iran works only when the costs of intransigence have grown too great for the Islamic Republic to bear. In 1981, Khomeini released the hostages not because of Carter's persistence, but because Iraq's invasion had increased the cost to Iran of its own isolation and because Reagan's election signaled a resolve that Carter lacked. Likewise, Khomeini agreed to end the Iran-Iraq War only after the cost of continuing the stalemate grew too great. He likened his about-face, walking away from objectives he once swore he would never abandon, to drinking from a chalice of poison.

Channeling diplomacy through the United Nations can compound the problem. By embracing a UN framework, Obama diluted his threat to impose harsh sanctions.[271] Red lines matter. Wars in the Middle East are not caused by oil or water, but by overconfidence. When adversaries believe they can overstep red lines with impunity, they will. In 2006, Hezbollah leader Hassan Nasrallah acknowledged that had he understood Israeli red lines, he would not have conducted the terrorist attack that led to war.[272] The willingness of American administrations to disregard their own red lines signaled to Iranian leaders that they could accelerate their nuclear and missile programs and even kill American troops without consequence.

American outreach bolsters the Iranian leadership's perception of its own strength relative to the United States. Just as revolutionary authorities became more resolute with each Carter administration overture, so too did they grow defiant in the face of Obama's outreach. In September 2010, Ahmadinejad used his bully pulpit at the United Nations to suggest that 9/11 was an inside job,[273] the ultimate irony given that Joe Biden had justified American outreach by pointing to the spontaneous show of sympathy from Iranian citizens.

The Iranian leadership's bad faith condemns diplomacy to failure in the absence of crippling sanctions or even limited military strikes. Ultimately, force counts. In June 2010, the Iranian government announced that it would send a ship to supply Hamas despite the Israeli blockade of the Gaza Strip. Israeli officials publicly and repeatedly said they would intercept the Iranian ship. Iran blustered, but Israel stood firm and Iran blinked.[274] Never has an American administration implemented a comprehensive strategy to force Iran's Supreme Leader to blink, let alone drink from the chalice of poison and begin to negotiate sincerely.

Chapter Three

TEAM AMERICA AND THE HERMIT KINGDOM

Most Americans believe the Korean War ended more than six decades ago, when General William Harrison, representing the United Nations Command, and General Nam Il, representing the North Korean army and Chinese volunteers, signed an agreement to end fighting. The Korean War Armistice Agreement of 1953, however, was merely a ceasefire. Today, more than a million troops face each other across a demilitarized zone (DMZ) less than three miles wide. South Korea has transformed itself into an affluent democracy, while Kim Il Sung, his son Kim Jong Il, and his son Kim Jong Un have turned North Korea into a land of starvation, prison camps, and slave labor. Of all rogue regimes the United States faces, the Democratic People's Republic of Korea is the most isolated, most bizarre, and least understood. With its nuclear weapons and long-range missiles, and its refusal to abide by international norms, it is also the most dangerous. That it can now threaten Hawaii, and California may soon be within its strike range, is a testament to more than sixty years of failed American diplomacy.

The Korean armistice was the result of more than five hundred negotiating sessions spanning over two years.[1] The United States did not insist that North Korea recognize the South's legitimacy. To do so might have derailed sensitive talks.

With the armistice signed, Americans hoped to return home; but South Korea's president, Syngman Rhee, understood that the armistice was just the beginning of a new phase in the conflict. Three months after its signing, American, Korean, and Chinese officials met again at Panmunjom in the DMZ to discuss peace and withdrawal of foreign forces. These talks were even more hostile than the armistice negotiations. According to Arthur Dean, the American ambassador, "No individual ever spoke personally to anyone on the other side." North Korean representatives read every statement only after their Chinese allies approved it. "There was never an exchange of greetings or amenities on starting or ending a meeting," Dean recalled, describing the sessions as "negotiation without contact."[2] After four weeks, the Americans and the North Koreans could not even agree on an agenda. The Americans may have wanted to talk, but good intentions mean little in diplomacy. North Korea was a Chinese puppet and Mao Zedong preferred that Korea remain an open wound.[3] A follow-up conference in Geneva also ended without progress. Just because an adversary is willing to engage does not mean it is willing to agree.

The presence of American forces along the DMZ made it impossible not to talk. The armistice directed the two sides—American forces under the banner of the United Nations, and North Korea—to form a commission to communicate, settle violations, and handle repatriation of prisoners and displaced civilians. Today, American officers talk with their North Korean counterparts at Panmunjom if only over mundane matters such as the return of the bodies of North Korean villagers or farmers swept downstream during flash floods, or coordinating border crossings for international visitors. In practice, this requires a phone link between American and North Korean officials who occupy offices just a dozen meters away. If the North Koreans refuse to answer, American officers use a handheld bullhorn to shout messages across the divide.

When President Harry S. Truman excluded South Korea from his outline of America's defensive perimeter, Kim Il Sung assumed he had a pass to attack South Korea. By the end of the 1960s, it appeared that fighting could again erupt on the peninsula. Between 1966 and 1969, there were more than 280 North Korean attacks on Americans or South Koreans around the DMZ.[4] The North Koreans staged a brazen attack on the presidential mansion in Seoul, aiming to assassinate President Park Chung Hee. Two days later, North Korean forces seized the USS *Pueblo*, a U.S. Navy ship gathering intelligence in international waters off the North Korean coast, and took all the ship's personnel hostage.

Only after Lyndon Johnson dispatched the USS *Enterprise* battle group did the North Koreans even agree to discuss the *Pueblo*.[5] Johnson's approach to the *Pueblo* crisis presaged Carter's handling of the Iran hostage crisis years later, and with the same result: When Kim Il Sung concluded that American military force was off the table, talks went nowhere. It was almost a year before the North Koreans released the *Pueblo*'s crew, and then only after General Gilbert Woodward signed a humiliating "confession" on behalf of the U.S. government.[6]

In hindsight, the decision to negotiate a resolution of the *Pueblo* crisis was complicated. Engagement saved the lives of the ship's crew, but their rescue came at a high cost. Allowing North Korea to keep the *Pueblo* meant the exposure of secret American technology. The ship's capture remains a propaganda coup for the communist regime. Now a museum, the ship is a reminder to North Korea's starved population of America's supposed impotency. The symbolism went deeper, too: South Koreans juxtaposed the willingness of the White House to kowtow to North Korea after the *Pueblo*'s capture with its inaction after the assault on the South Korean presidential mansion, and said the contrast signaled that the life of the South Korean president was secondary to the return of the American crew. The fact that the North Korean commandos had passed through an area secured by American forces to reach the presidential mansion accentuated the point.[7]

American outreach to rogue regimes consistently erodes allies' confidence, and Seoul had reason to be nervous. It understood Pyongyang's tendency to couple diplomacy with provocation. On April 15, 1969—Kim Il Sung's birthday, one day after North Korean officials proposed a meeting in the DMZ—two North Korean MiG-21s shot down an unarmed U.S. surveillance aircraft over the Sea of Japan, dozens of miles from North Korean airspace, killing thirty-one American servicemen.

Nixon contemplated military action but embraced diplomacy instead. Still, he understood that *how* the Americans talked was consequential. With a greater appreciation for nuance than diplomats today, he considered a number of scenarios: attending the prearranged meeting at Panmunjom and then storming out when the North Korean delegation defended their actions; demanding a special meeting; or boycotting Panmunjom altogether. As Nixon considered the options, Henry Kissinger, his national security advisor, balanced the need to maintain Panmunjom as a channel with the need to avoid transforming it into a stage for North Korean propaganda.[8] In the end, American officials walked out of the meeting after the North Korean representative condemned the unarmed plane's flight as a "brigandish aggressive act."

Nixon's decision not to retaliate militarily had emboldened the North.[9] Over the next four months, a period in which there were no talks, North Korean soldiers attacked United Nations Command guard posts and personnel, and North Korean saboteurs attempted to infiltrate South Korea by sea four times. Then, four days after the two sides met so that the Americans could formally issue their litany of complaints, North Korean forces shot down an unarmed American helicopter that had strayed into North Korean airspace while on a training mission along the DMZ. Kim Il Sung calculated that with more than 150,000 American troops embroiled in Vietnam, the chance of American retaliation for his actions was slight.

North Korean authorities demanded that the United States acknowledge its criminality and apologize. For Kim Il Sung, it was irrelevant that helicopters patrolling the border often strayed across mountainous terrain in foggy conditions. He wanted a propaganda victory, not an explanation. Kim counted on the fact that the American public had little patience for Americans being held hostage.[10] Certainly, the West's lack of strategic patience is a lesson that other rogue leaders leveraged to their benefit, be it the Iranians through several hostage crises, or the Libyan leader Muammar Qadhafi, who threatened to execute five Bulgarian nurses on false charges that they had infected Libyan children with HIV.

Even as Kissinger moved to warm up relations with Beijing, America's relationship with North Korea remained frozen.[11] What little dialogue Kim Il Sung engaged in consisted of alternating bellicosity and outreach. For example, after telling the *New York Times* that he was preparing for war,[12] he sent the U.S. Congress an open letter requesting negotiation,[13] but then launched a military campaign to seize five South Korean islands off the North Korean coast. Between October and December 1973, North Korean military vessels crossed the maritime boundary around the islands almost every other day; then, in February 1974, they seized one South Korean fishing vessel and sank another.[14] True to form, once Kim Il Sung brought the peninsula to the brink of new conflict, he sent a proposal for talks to the U.S. Congress. No senators took the bait. The North's proposal to forbid foreign troops in South Korea would have left that country defenseless.[15]

That North Korea would make such an outlandish proposal should not be a surprise, given that Kim Il Sung thought he was engaging the United States from a position of strength. After all, the White House had agreed to withdraw from Vietnam, and North Korea's naval probing demonstrated that the United States was not serious about its commitment to defend South Korea. Kim Il Sung believed he could act without consequence. Over the following year, the North Korean navy grew increasingly aggressive. A conciliatory American approach had encouraged Pyongyang to push harder.

In August 1976, with the Ford administration in its final months, North Korea struck at Americans in the DMZ. A work crew supervised by Captain Arthur Bonifas was trimming a tree that obstructed an American observation post. When North Korean soldiers demanded that they stop, Bonifas refused. Some twenty North Korean soldiers then knocked him and Lieutenant Mark Barrett to the ground and hacked them to death with axes. The murders shocked Washington, but for North Korea they topped off a propaganda campaign that Pyongyang had initiated months before.

While the North Korean regime sought diplomatic advantage, blaming violence on the American presence, the brutality of the axe murders repulsed the international community. North Korea's traditional allies stayed quiet. If the murders were a gambit to damage America, the net effect was the opposite.

The United States did not offer a humiliating apology for Pyongyang to broadcast repeatedly, nor did it bomb North Korea as Kissinger proposed. Instead, the United States launched Operation Paul Bunyan to cut down the tree with the backing of U.S. Army engineers, combat troops, and South Korean special forces, along with squadrons of jet fighters, B-52 bombers, and the USS *Midway* strike group on full alert. Military bluster might not be American style, but Washington was playing by Pyongyang rules. It worked. Not only did North Korea stand down, but Kim Il Sung offered regrets.[16]

Carter's New Approach

Jimmy Carter rejected the lessons his predecessors had learned in blood. On January 16, 1975, shortly after declaring his candidacy for president, he announced his intent to withdraw American forces from Korea, although he later amended his pledge to include only ground forces and only on a timeline determined in consultation with Seoul.[17] A devout Christian, Carter was deeply committed to peace. If his proposals were initially ignored, it was because he was considered a longshot candidate. He would not remain so.

Carter clawed his way to the top and won his party's nomination. The Democratic National Convention adopted his platform calling for the gradual withdrawal of U.S. ground forces and nuclear weapons from South Korea, to be replaced with reliance on tactical air and naval forces.[18] Many diplomats shared Carter's ambivalence if not antipathy toward Park Chung Hee, South Korea's president, whose human rights record was appalling.

Carter's goodwill toward North Korea trumped strategic wisdom. American allies in Seoul, Tokyo, and Taipei saw his plan as dangerous.[19] They knew Kim Il Sung's mind. An aide to the Japanese prime minister saw Carter's announcement as a sign that America might abandon Asia, especially since it came so soon after the withdrawal from Vietnam.[20] Regional experts noted that Carter's logic fell flat when translated from theory to reality. "We should consider also the ripple effect of a round, shiny pebble from Washington suddenly tossed into a still Asian pond, causing undulations far beyond the point of impact," wrote Frank Gibney, an East Asia specialist, in *Foreign Affairs*.[21]

It was for this reason that Carter's more worldly advisors tried to rein him in. The secretary of defense, Harold Brown, who had served in senior Pentagon positions during the Johnson administration, advised the president against withdrawal, especially as the intelligence community noted the North's military buildup.[22]

Believing his opponent hopelessly naïve, Kim Il Sung wasted no time in offering diplomacy. Shortly after Carter's inauguration, Kim sent a letter to the president-elect proposing to replace the 1953 armistice agreement with a peace treaty. The North Korean foreign minister followed suit in a letter to Cyrus Vance, the secretary of state. Carter expressed interest, so long as South Korea might also participate. Kim Il Sung rejected that condition.[23] He was willing to embrace dialogue only if it did not require North Korean compromise.

Kim Il Sung sought to lull Carter into complacency. The DMZ enjoyed the longest pause in provocations since the armistice, and when North Korea downed an American helicopter that had strayed across the border, Kim released the bodies of those killed and the lone survivor within days. But while he wanted a quiet DMZ, Kim remained as belligerent as ever toward South Korea and Japan. Violence escalated in the Sea of Japan, the Yellow Sea, and the Joint Security Area.[24] Most abductions of Japanese citizens occurred between 1977 and 1983. These provocations followed Pyongyang's traditional pattern of matching conciliation toward one country with provocation toward its ally.

Kim's attempts to drive a wedge between the United States and its Asian allies did not work. When Carter shelved his withdrawal plan, Kim reacted bitterly, accusing the U.S. president of aiming to "deceive the world."[25]

Carter never gave up hope that he might broker peace on the Korean Peninsula. He had uncritical trust in his own power of persuasion. If past diplomacy had failed, it had to be the fault of his predecessors, not America's adversaries. Carter believed that if he was able to bring the two Korean leaders together in a Camp David–like setting, he could achieve peace. Fortunately, his aides and the U.S. ambassador in Seoul talked the president out of a "flaky" proposal to invite both leaders to the DMZ.[26]

Next, Carter proposed tripartite talks with American diplomats and their North and South Korean counterparts. This too went nowhere. The North Korean regime balked at including the South, and the South worried that Carter's aim was for the United States to abandon South Korea, much as it had South Vietnam four years earlier.

Diplomats and military leaders alike "were horrified by the peremptory and damaging way the issue was pursued by the Carter White House," noted Don Oberdorfer, who covered Asian affairs for the *Washington Post* for a quarter century.[27] Carter's intentions may have been noble, but his single-minded rush to diplomacy was costly. Ultimately, time ran out. An assassin's bullet felled the South Korean leader and ushered in years of political upheaval, while the Iran hostage crisis consumed Carter's attention through his last year in office.

Reagan and Korea

Ronald Reagan inherited a more dangerous Korea largely because Carter's desire for diplomacy had emboldened Kim Il Sung. Reagan turned Carter's approach on its head. Carter wanted to evacuate troops from the Korean Peninsula; Reagan increased their numbers. Diplomacy took a back seat. Halfway through Reagan's first term, a Soviet fighter jet downed a South Korean airliner that had strayed over Soviet territory, killing 269 people, almost a quarter of them Americans. Tension skyrocketed not only between the superpowers, but also between Seoul and Pyongyang.

It was against this backdrop that China again became central to the Korean conflict. A decade after Nixon visited China, Beijing was finding its stride. On October 8, 1983, Chinese diplomats passed the American embassy in Beijing a North Korean message expressing Pyongyang's willingness to participate in tripartite talks. In the face of Reagan's military buildup, the North Korean leadership had decided to cast aside its objection to South Korean participation, the basis for its rejection of Carter's offer.

Kim Il Sung's about-face might be seen as validation of the idea that engagement with rogues can work if it is conducted from a position of strength. Events the next day challenged that assumption, however. As South Korean cabinet members and presidential advisors awaited President Chun Doo-hwan's arrival at a wreath-laying ceremony in Rangoon, three North Korean army officers detonated a bomb they had hidden in the roof of the mausoleum, killing twenty-one, including the foreign minister and the deputy prime minister. It was no rogue operation. At the time, Pyongyang's foreign operations service was under the command of Kim Il Sung's eldest son and future successor, Kim Jong Il.[28]

If Western diplomats believe that transforming rogues into responsible regimes boils down to incentives, the Rangoon massacre should disabuse them of the notion. Rogues are proactive rather than reactive. They simply do not accept international norms. Limiting strategy to the tools of normal diplomacy will fail.

After the bombing, Reagan's attitude toward North Korea diplomacy cooled. In January 1984, the Chinese premier, Zhao Ziyang, passed a North Korean message to Reagan again endorsing three-way talks between the Koreas and the United States. The offer fit a pattern in which Pyongyang proposed engagement only to deflect consequences for its behavior. Many rogues understood that dangling the prospect of diplomacy can lead the West to put aside its disgust at earlier actions.[29] Diplomats look forward, and they are often willing to put atrocities behind in exchange for the promise of a better future. Seldom do olive branches offered by rogue regimes suggest a desire for peace, however.

There had been no softening of Kim Il Sung's complete refusal to accept South Korea's legitimacy. When the International Olympic Committee selected Seoul to host the 1988 Olympics, some South Korean officials hoped they might leverage the games for reconciliation.[30] The Dear Leader, for his part, saw any acceptance of Seoul as a blow to his claim to be Korea's only legitimate leader.[31] North Korean threats had forced the relocation of the 1970 Asian Games away from Seoul, but in the run-up to the 1986 games in Seoul, Kim Il Sung's complaints fell on deaf ears. Six days before the opening ceremony of the Asian Games, North Korean terrorists detonated a bomb at South Korea's main airport, killing five. The world might know that North Korea was guilty, but if other states hesitated to deal with the South, then Kim Il Sung could claim victory. For rogue regimes, terrorism is a fully legitimate tool in the diplomatic kitbag.

To drive home the point, North Korean agents placed a bomb on board a Korean Air flight from Baghdad to Seoul in November 1987, killing 115. One North Korean agent committed suicide, but police captured his accomplice, who confessed that Pyongyang had ordered the bombing to suggest that South Korea was unsuitable to host the Olympics.[32] The international community did not back down, and the games proceeded without a hitch. As for North Korea, it won a spot on the State Department's State Sponsors of Terrorism list.[33]

After the Olympics ended, South Korea's president, Roh Tae-woo, announced that the South would no longer seek to isolate the North. "The basic policy in the past was to try to change the North Korean position by isolating them," Roh explained. "We have changed this. We think that by encouraging them to be more open, we can have peace in this part of the world."[34] Later that week, Roh unveiled a program to promote trade, exchanges, and humanitarian contacts with the North.

North Korea initially brushed off the initiative, but the White House embraced it. The State Department effused, calling it "a major—indeed historic—reversal of traditional" South Korean policy.[35] Not everyone was happy with how diplomacy had become intertwined with incentives. Benjamin Gilman, a Republican and chairman of the House Committee on International Relations, observed, "We are paying for bad behavior by rewarding North Korean brinkmanship with benefits." He further noted, "North Korea is now the largest recipient of U.S. foreign aid in East Asia, and in response to recent North Korean provocations, the Administration proposes only to increase the level of our assistance."[36]

Skeptics abounded, but it was hard to argue when America's Korean allies wanted to talk. After Roh informed the Americans that he would seek a summit with Kim Il Sung, the State Department let Pyongyang know that Washington would also like to improve relations should North Korea cease its belligerence and terrorism.[37] The North Koreans agreed, and so began a series of nearly three dozen bilateral meetings spread over five years. Direct talks eased communication—no longer did the two sides have to use China as an intermediary—but the talks did little to address the chief U.S. concerns: North Korea's nuclear and missile programs.[38]

North Korea's Nuclear Program

In 1980, a spy satellite spotted construction of a nuclear reactor at Yongbyon, about sixty miles north of Pyongyang. Four years later, satellites detected craters suggesting that North Korea was experimenting with detonators used in nuclear bombs.[39] That North Korea had signed the Nuclear Non-Proliferation Treaty in 1985 should not have assuaged diplomats; the Soviet Union had promised North Korea four nuclear plants if it accepted the treaty.[40] Its signature allowed Pyongyang to import dual-use equipment. While the NPT requires states to sign a safeguards agreement with the IAEA within eighteen months, Pyongyang refused.[41]

The Pentagon monitored Yongbyon from afar as the complex grew. By February 1987, it was clear that North Korea intended to produce plutonium. The next year, satellites detected a new facility, two football fields long and six stories high, and more evidence that North Korea was experimenting with the explosions needed to set off a nuclear warhead.[42]

Whereas Reagan had kept concerns about Yongbyon secret in order to maintain the option of a surprise attack, George H. W. Bush put diplomacy front and center. Bush trusted that the world would see the North Korea threat just as he did. Secretary of State James Baker explained, "Our diplomatic strategy was designed to build international pressure against North Korea to force them to live up to their agreements."[43] In a national security review, the White House also embraced a carrots-and-sticks policy.[44] Bush's approach to Korea essentially paralleled Carter's strategy toward Iran. After cultivating international opinion, he sought to entangle Pyongyang in dialogue and nonproliferation obligations.[45] There was one big difference between Carter on Iran and Bush on North Korea: Bush understood the importance of deterrence.

Undermining Bush policy, however, was a lack of consensus about its goals. One camp, giving priority to arms control, viewed compliance with the NPT and IAEA inspections as the top goal. They argued that demands to end reprocessing violated rights recognized in the NPT and might lead North Korea to abandon the treaty altogether. Another camp, emphasizing security, argued that the threat North Korea would pose with weapons-grade material should override the universality of the treaty's privileges.[46]

Any pretense of secrecy ended when South Korean diplomats leaked word of North Korea's activities after being briefed by American diplomats.[47] International headlines soon broadcast predictions that North Korea might be nuclear-weapons capable by the mid-1990s.

North Korea responded with bluster. Pyongyang accused the West of hypocrisy, a card to which American diplomats are sensitive, as Iran and other rogues well understand. The North Koreans said they would not accede to inspections of Yongbyon so long as the American military maintained a nuclear arsenal in South Korea.[48] Whereas rogue regimes as a rule do not accept Western arguments, Bush yielded to the North Korean argument.[49] Those who elevated arms control over national security won the day.[50]

Bush hoped that removing nuclear missiles from South Korea would set the circumstances for successful negotiations. Rather than shape the move as a concession to Pyongyang, Bush's team depicted it as outreach to Moscow.[51]

Initially, it looked like Bush had found the magic formula. On December 18, 1991, Roh announced that American forces had completed the removal of the U.S. tactical nuclear arsenal. Just over a week later, North Korea agreed to sign the NPT safeguards agreement and permit inspections of Yongbyon. Over the next several weeks, North and South Korean officials signed a Joint Declaration on the Denuclearization of the Korean Peninsula, in which the two Koreas forswore plutonium reprocessing and uranium enrichment, and agreed not to test, manufacture, produce, possess, deploy, or use nuclear weapons. Both sides also agreed to inspections by a joint commission.[52]

Baker chalked up Pyongyang's compliance to patient diplomacy. "American diplomacy [was] directly responsible for an end to six years of intransigence by the North," he wrote in his memoirs.[53] But while Baker congratulated himself, the Dear Leader recognized that Baker was desperate and concluded he could outlast the Americans. In order to get the deal done, Baker accepted a clause that limited inspections to sites "agreed upon between the two sides," in effect giving North Korea a veto.[54] Baker offered this concession even though the CIA had warned that North Korea was hiding parts of its nuclear program.[55]

Other observers argued that the end—a North Korean agreement—justified the means. "The withdrawal of the American nuclear arsenal had a powerful effect in North Korea, contributing in important fashion to an era of compromise and conciliation," wrote Oberdorfer.[56]

Such a view is myopic. Just as Saddam Hussein's invasion of Iran did more than any Carter concession to force the ayatollahs to recognize the cost of holding Americans hostage, it was the end of the Cold War that forced Kim to reassess his position. Moreover, as Baker observed, "American diplomacy also had the benefit of a powerful new psychological weapon—our stunning victory in the Gulf War."[57] Engagement may change hearts, but military success can change minds.

Regardless of what brought about the agreement, the national security advisor, Brent Scowcroft, aimed to leverage the success with new high-level talks. The American team was led by Arnold Kanter, the number-three diplomat at the State Department, while Kim Yong Sun, one of the Dear Leader's most trusted aides, headed the North Korean delegation. Kanter offered the North Korean team good relations and perhaps even normalization should North Korea adhere to its commitments, including the denuclearization declaration it had signed only weeks before. That Kim Yong Sun refused should have raised red flags. But for diplomacy's cheerleaders, it is easier to blame America than to blame its enemies. Robert Gallucci, who would serve as the chief negotiator for North Korean issues during the Clinton administration, and his allies blamed North Korean reticence on Kanter's vagueness.[58] Even though the talks achieved nothing, some diplomats saw victory. According to Gallucci, "The New York meeting was significant for occurring at all."[59] Whenever meetings replace achievement as the metric of success, national security suffers.

In hindsight, the removal of U.S. nuclear arms from Korea and the subsequent agreement to cancel military exercises with South Korea in 1992 were mistakes. By the end of the year, all signs of progress had evaporated. Channels between the Koreas froze, and Pyongyang again blocked inspections. The chief thing that inspectors had learned was that North Korea was on pace to produce more plutonium than the Americans had earlier estimated.[60] Talks between North Korean and American diplomats petered out.[61] North Korea had never actually ceased work on Yongbyon. As Bush prepared to leave office, the depth of North Korean duplicity became clear.[62]

Kim Il Sung had played Baker and Scowcroft for fools. Chuck Downs, a Korea watcher and longtime Pentagon official, suggested that the North's actions were part of a distinct pattern: First, North Korean officials would reveal information to generate concern; then they would cut access and watch as Western desperation grew.[63] For American diplomats, engagement was a means to get that elusive signature on a piece of paper. For their North Korean counterparts, it was part of a broader strategy to alleviate pressure while they pursued a nuclear advantage over South Korea.

With its cheating exposed, Pyongyang backed out of its commitment to joint Korean inspections, while insisting that the concessions it had received should remain in place. The North Koreans did not accept that concessions should be tied to their behavior. When the Pentagon resumed its exercises with South Korea in 1993, Pyongyang in a fit of pique severed cooperation with both Seoul and the IAEA, and then, for the first time in a decade, declared itself "in a state of readiness for war."[64]

The Agreed Framework

Bill Clinton won the presidency as the crisis on the Korean Peninsula reached its peak. Hesitant to reward Kim Il Sung's defiance, Clinton initially shied away from diplomacy. The Dear Leader had no desire to make it easy for the neophyte president. Kim's last experience with a Democratic president was Carter. He hoped that, like Carter, Clinton might fold. Clinton had been president barely a month when Pyongyang refused to allow IAEA inspections, and just weeks later the regime announced that it would withdraw from the NPT in three months' time.[65] Over subsequent weeks, North Korean saber rattling grew louder. Rumors swirled that North Korea was expelling or quarantining foreign diplomats, recalling its own delegations from abroad, and cutting telephone lines.[66]

If Kim Il Sung expected Seoul and Washington to flinch, he was right. South Korea's president, Kim Young Sam, opposed any response that might isolate Pyongyang, while the State Department aimed to keep North Korea within the NPT at almost any price. Gallucci and his aides later explained, "If North Korea could walk away from the treaty's obligations with impunity at the very moment its nuclear program appeared poised for weapons production, it would have dealt a devastating blow from which the treaty might never recover."[67] Once again, diplomats elevated the preservation of the treaty over broader national security objectives. Their reaction was what Pyongyang wanted. The scramble to preserve the NPT distracted the United States from North Korea's greater interest: preventing inspectors from accessing sites that would demonstrate weaponization work.[68]

Clinton's team, unwilling to take any path that could lead to military action, sought to talk Pyongyang down from its nuclear defiance.[69] Talking, however, meant legitimizing brinkmanship. North Korean authorities believed crisis to be in Pyongyang's interest.[70]

Clinton replicated Bush's strategy of rallying world opinion.[71] The State Department tried to leverage China's influence on Pyongyang, but even Beijing's limited help came at a price. While coalitions augment pressure and legitimacy, policymakers seldom consider the sum cost of assembling them. China's IAEA representative, for example, refused to allow that body to refer North Korean filibustering to the UN Security Council. The Clinton administration did not press the matter. "Discretion seemed the better part of diplomatic valor," according to Gallucci and his aides; "it was more important to keep China on board than to send the issue immediately to the Security Council."[72] When, eventually, the IAEA acted over China's objections, the Chinese ambassador watered down the Security Council's condemnation to the point of irrelevance.[73] North Korea would subsequently claim Chinese endorsement for its positions.[74]

Clinton's willingness to negotiate North Korea's nuclear compliance was itself a concession, albeit one to which he was oblivious. The 1953 armistice agreement demanded that Pyongyang reveal all military facilities and, in case of dispute, enable the Military Armistice Commission to determine the purpose of suspect facilities.[75] By making weaker nonproliferation frameworks the new baseline, Clinton let North Korea off the hook before talks even began.

Just ten days before North Korea's deadline to leave the NPT, Gallucci met with Kang Sok Ju, the North Korean deputy foreign minister. The ticking clock advantaged Pyongyang since it added urgency. Because Gallucci's priority was preserving the NPT at any price, North Korea recognized that he would be desperate to reach agreement. Discussions were tense; for the first time, Kang claimed that North Korea had nuclear weapons capability.[76] North Korean bluster increased in the following sessions, but Gallucci's team saw progress simply because Kang never walked out. "The North Koreans no longer talked about withdrawing from the NPT, but rather about the circumstances under which Pyongyang could remain in the treaty," they recalled.[77] After ten trying days, the North Koreans agreed to "suspend" their withdrawal from the NPT in return for U.S. security assurances and further dialogue. The State Department saw "some success."[78]

Any optimism was misplaced. The negotiations had returned only to the *status quo ante*, before Pyongyang precipitated the crisis; the agreement addressed neither the refusal to allow inspections nor violations of past agreements. The North Koreans, however, had fulfilled their long-term goal for a direct relationship with the United States without sacrificing anything in return.[79] President Kim Young Sam of South Korea, clearly frustrated, complained to journalists that North Korea was leading America on and manipulating negotiators "to buy time."[80]

On July 14, 1993, Gallucci and Kang reconvened to discuss IAEA inspections. Kang refused to allow them outright, but two days later he suggested that North Korea would switch to light-water reactors, less susceptible to proliferation, if the international community would provide them.[81] Even before negotiators resolved the issue of suspect site inspections, James Laney, the U.S. ambassador in South Korea and close friend to Jimmy Carter, suggested that Washington might organize an international consortium to cover the billions of dollars necessary for the scheme.[82] After much haggling, Gallucci agreed to "support" the construction of the reactors. Once again, the American concession came without any North Korean movement to allow IAEA inspection of suspect sites.[83]

For diplomats to characterize the deal as a "step forward" was nonsensical.[84] American diplomats conceive the engagement process as a straight line: the start of dialogue marks the beginning, and a formal agreement marks its end. Projecting the same diagram onto adversaries is a mistake. North Korea conceived dialogue as the beginning, and a nuclear bomb the end. Talks along the way were intended to buy time rather than mark progress toward an agreement. Had the State Department understood the North Korean perspective, American diplomats would have realized that the agreement was less a step forward than a stumble.

North Korean officials claimed that their understandings with Gallucci overrode their commitments to the IAEA. They conceded that IAEA inspectors might change film and batteries in remote cameras, but refused to allow rigorous inspections to include sampling soil and nuclear fuel. The suspicious nuclear waste dump would be off-limits.

The IAEA held firmer to the demand that North Korea submit to inspections than did Washington. The issue came to a head in September 1993 after the State Department had pressured the IAEA to compromise on limited inspections. While the IAEA director, Hans Blix, wanted to ensure the integrity of inspections and continuity of safeguards, the Clinton administration worried that an IAEA finding of noncompliance might lead North Korea to leave the table. Engagement had become the Clinton administration's end goal. Clinton's team trapped themselves in a North Korean dance that left them no room to maneuver. For the

State Department, the diplomatic process had come to outweigh the results it was meant to achieve. It was in this context that the Clinton administration again agreed to suspend its annual U.S.–South Korea military exercises.[85]

In October 1993, Rep. Gary Ackerman of New York visited North Korea, carrying a White House letter seeking new talks. He met with Kim Il Sung and other senior officials, but was lukewarm in his assessment afterward, saying the talks were, in the words of the *New York Times*, "long on symbolism but short on substance."[86] North Korea continued to seek trade-offs and concessions before fulfilling its IAEA commitments. Gallucci was more positive. He spoke about a grand bargain floated by North Korean leaders in which the communist regime would remain inside the NPT and allow inspections in exchange for light-water reactors, diminished U.S. ties to South Korea, and a formal peace.[87] Gallucci ignored the North Korean claim of nuclear weapons capability in order to advance the possibility of a deal.

Clinton, however, was not yet ready to forget the cause of dispute. On November 7, he declared that "North Korea cannot be allowed to develop a nuclear bomb."[88] The discrepancy in interpretations between Gallucci and Clinton illustrates the tendency of diplomats to spend so much time among the trees that they miss the forest. Gallucci had forgotten the big picture: the imperative of preventing the totalitarian and destabilizing regime from getting weaponry that could kill millions.

In the face of Pyongyang's defiance, Clinton was also wary that coercion could be a slippery slope to war.[89] No president takes war lightly. At the same time, telegraphing a fear of using force leads rogues to regard the United States as spineless, which makes diplomacy more challenging. So too does the tendency of the State Department to isolate diplomacy from tougher strategies. Military academies teach that a coherent strategy should have diplomatic, informational, military, and economic components, all implemented in conjunction. Coercive measures cannot be imposed with a flick of a switch, though, and so rogues embrace brinkmanship. They bluster through months of sanctions preparation, and then derail the sanctions by offering to talk hours before their implementation. Kim Il Sung was confident, as Chuck Downs noted, that some voices in a democracy would always seek peace rather than the uncertainties of war.[90]

So it was in Washington. When Clinton's top national security officials met to discuss North Korea for the first time in half a year, they concluded that diplomacy was the only real choice.[91] Clinton began to mollify Pyongyang almost immediately. He canceled the joint U.S.–South Korea military exercise for 1994, so that North Korea would allow regular IAEA inspections. When North Korean officials balked at intrusive inspections, or indeed any effective verification of their activities, the Clinton team agreed to discuss the issue—in effect, turning Pyongyang's earlier commitment into a negotiable point. Adding insult to injury, the Clinton administration criticized the South Korean government for being unwilling to compromise.[92]

As soon as talks commenced, North Korea abandoned any pretense of flexibility on inspections. The State Department response was to double down on conciliation. Gallucci's team empathized with North Korean complaints about the supposed provocation of the Pentagon's Patriot missile deployment to South Korea, even though the Patriot was purely defensive and North Korea had aimed thousands of missiles at the southern capital.[93]

Ambassador Laney told the White House that South Korea was worried more about U.S. brinkmanship than about the North Korean threat. This was a lie; Laney free-lanced. He projected his own opinion onto South Korean interlocutors and urged the White House not to press North Korea hard on inspections.[94] For too many diplomats, engagement is the top priority, and defense concerns are dispensable. When the United States shows any chinks in its defense commitments, rogues are emboldened, as Koreans well know.

American and North Korean officials agreed on a choreographed diplomatic dance: As the IAEA began inspections, North and South Korean diplomats would prepare a meeting of special envoys. Seoul would announce the cancellation of the military exercises, after which

Washington and Pyongyang would set a date for Gallucci and Kang's next meeting.[95] The North Koreans then reneged on the understanding and refused to talk to their southern counterparts.

The State Department sought to finesse the situation: the Pentagon would announce cancellation of the exercises based on the "premise" that the North and the South would exchange envoys. The Clinton team justified this flexibility by arguing that it would end the seven-month pause on inspections.[96] North Korea, however, learned that it could violate deals with impunity. Pyongyang had tested American resolve and found it lacking. Gallucci's team defined a relationship with North Korea based on concession to bluster rather than the sanctity of agreements. This made escalation of tensions inevitable.

When North Korea refused inspectors access, the IAEA referred the matter to the Security Council, and the Pentagon scrambled to reschedule its canceled exercise. As the North Korean negotiating team broke contact, they threatened to turn Seoul into a "sea of fire." American officials had no choice but to take the threats seriously. North Korean defectors believed that if war broke out, North Korean authorities would use any weapons in their possession, even nuclear arms.[97] U.S. military officers—many with long Korea experience—describe these events as the tensest days in post-armistice Korea. At one point, North Korea launched more than half its air force simultaneously in what it described as an exercise.[98]

It was not only North Korea's saber rattling that worried the West, but also its opacity. Because the United States and North Korea had always been adversaries, few Americans had experience dealing with the hermit kingdom, let alone living in it. North Korea used its opacity to full advantage to manipulate the perception of risk.[99]

With talks breaking down, North Korea announced that it would remove irradiated fuel rods from Yongbyon, a process which would both eliminate evidence of Pyongyang's intentions and enable North Korea to separate plutonium.[100] There was little the West could do. The IAEA canceled its $500,000 annual technical assistance, but Security Council sanctions were dead on arrival due to China's opposition. The fuel removal marked a watershed in the North Korean nuclear crisis: for the first time, North Korea's current nuclear activity, rather than its past behavior, became the focus for diplomats.[101]

As the Pentagon refined its war plans and Clinton's cabinet debated what to do, Jimmy Carter, in Pyongyang for an ostensibly personal visit, announced that Kim Il Sung would freeze North Korea's nuclear program and leave IAEA inspectors in the country in exchange for American support for North Korean acquisition of light-water reactors.[102] Despite briefings from Clinton's national security team about American concerns and positions, Carter conceded to Pyongyang the right to reprocess nuclear fuel rods, in effect giving Pyongyang enough plutonium to construct five nuclear bombs.[103] Carter also told the Dear Leader that the White House would abandon its drive for UN sanctions, a concession that Clinton had not authorized.[104] Even though he had essentially accepted an old—and unsatisfactory—North Korean offer, Carter believed he had achieved a breakthrough and announced as much on CNN, effectively trapping Clinton.[105]

Kim Il Sung's sudden re-embrace of diplomacy was merely a replay of his strategy of pushing to the brink of war in order to win concessions. It was a risky scenario for all parties. Rogues risk war, but the United States risks credibility. Ted Koppel, the *Nightline* host, picked up on this idea when he said "this administration is becoming notorious . . . for making threats and then backing down."[106]

Diplomacy began again, albeit with a new partner. On July 8, 1994, a heart attack felled the Dear Leader. Kim Jong Il, his eldest son and mastermind of past terrorist attacks, assumed command. To the surprise of the State Department, the new negotiations progressed quickly.[107] North Korea wanted compensation for shuttering its reactors and energy assistance until the light-water reactors would come on line.

Gallucci and his team agreed that the United States would supply 500,000 tons of heavy fuel oil annually. The North Korean team agreed to submit to inspections of the suspect plutonium sites, the trigger for the initial crisis, but only after most of the light-water reactor components had been shipped. Only when confronted by the press did Clinton acknowledge that this might mean North Korea would be inspection-free for five years.[108] While some Clinton officials recognized the agreement's weakness, they assumed that the collapse of the Soviet bloc meant North Korea would fall before the Americans would have to make good on it. They did not realize that Kim Jong Il retained tighter control over society than his communist counterparts elsewhere, or that the incentives included in the agreement might actually help preserve his regime.

What had begun as an illicit North Korean filibuster had netted the rogue communist regime billions of dollars in aid. The conservative columnist William Safire traced the steps of concession. "Mr. Clinton's opening position was that untrustworthy North Korea must not be allowed to become a nuclear power," Safire observed, but the president "soon trimmed that to say it must not possess nuclear bombs, and stoutly threatened sanctions if North Korea did not permit inspections of nuclear facilities at Yongbyon, where the CIA and KGB agree nuclear devices have been developed. But as a result of Clinton's Very Good Deal Indeed, IAEA inspectors are denied entry to those plants for five years."[109] Many senators also questioned the deal. John McCain lamented that Clinton "has extended carrot after carrot, concession after concession, and pursued a policy of appeasement based . . . on the ill-founded belief that North Koreans really just wanted to be part of the community of nations." Frank Murkowski complained that the deal carried "the scent of appeasement."[110]

Clinton's high-stakes engagement had a cost beyond the price tag. On October 7, 1994, President Kim Young Sam of South Korea blasted Clinton's deal with the North, saying, "If the United States wants to settle with a half-baked compromise and the media wants to describe it as a good agreement, they can. But I think it would bring more danger and peril." There was nothing wrong with trying to resolve the problem through dialogue, he acknowledged, but the South Koreans knew very well how the North operated. "We have spoken with North Korea more than 400 times. It didn't get us anywhere. They are not sincere," Kim said, urging the United States not to "be led on by the manipulations of North Korea."[111] The fact that the agreement required South Korea to make concessions years before the North was particularly troublesome.

While Kim Young Sam was right to doubt Pyongyang's sincerity, his outburst drew Clinton's ire. The administration did not want any complications to derail a deal, and Clinton was willing to ignore evidence that might spoil the initiative. Two weeks later, Gallucci and Kang signed the Agreed Framework.

Gallucci and his team were "exhilarated." They later recalled how they "had overcome numerous obstacles in the negotiations with the North; survived the intense, sometimes strained collaboration with Seoul and the International Atomic Energy Agency; and marshaled and sustained an often unwieldy international coalition in opposition to the nuclear challenge, all under close and often critical scrutiny at home." Getting the agreement, however, "seemed to make it all worthwhile."[112]

That Gallucci's team believed they had salvaged North Korea's membership in the Non-Proliferation Treaty was self-delusion. Pyongyang has never been sincere in its membership. North Korean diplomats confided that they had joined only to receive a Soviet reactor, but the Soviet Union collapsed before the Kremlin made good on the deal.[113] Gallucci had been had. He rewarded defiance. Carl Ford, a Pentagon official during the elder Bush's administration with long service in the Central Intelligence Agency, attacked the logic predicating the Agreed Framework on a delicate house of cards and the assumption that Pyongyang would abandon its nuclear program.[114] He was right.

South Korea's president had opposed the Agreed Framework for another reason: North Korea was imploding economically. "Time is on our side," he remarked.[115] The Soviet Union's collapse ended its subsidies to Pyongyang. From 1990 to 1991, Soviet exports to North Korea fell by 75 percent.[116] Kim Il Sung refused to acknowledge the trouble into which his kingdom had descended. While the country starved, the authorities extolled the virtue of eating only two meals a day. They tried to hide the disaster. When Rep. Gary Ackerman was in North Korea, his interlocutors bragged of their bumper harvest.[117] That the famine was three years old before word leaked of its extent was a testament to North Korea's totalitarian controls.

On May 3, 1994, a family who had escaped from the North held a news conference to describe a famine so severe that children could no longer hold their heads up and elderly people died in the fields.[118] Defectors do sometimes exaggerate, so policymakers were skeptical. The next year's flooding gave the regime an excuse for the starvation.[119] The famine was manmade, though. As 5 or 10 percent of the country's population—perhaps more than a million people—perished, Pyongyang spent its money on military hardware and the nuclear program.[120]

Clinton's priority was his deal. Even though Pyongyang had threatened a new holocaust, he believed that American interests lay in ensuring regime survival. Andrew Natsios, an international aid specialist (soon to lead the U.S. Agency for International Development), argued, "The collapse of the regime may be superficially attractive, but it is a dangerous risk." Providing food aid was worthwhile, he said, even if suspending it could end the regime.[121]

Clinton tried to spin food aid to North Korea as a necessary price for diplomacy, but analysts were dubious. "While it was not an unconditional surrender, it was a negotiated surrender," said James Schlesinger, who was Carter's energy secretary.[122] Clinton, Gallucci, and other cheerleaders for the deal bristled at such descriptions.[123]

Between 1992 and 1994, as North Korea's crops failed, U.S. companies exported $120 million worth of corn and wheat in addition to medicine and other humanitarian supplies to the hermit kingdom. Pyongyang, meanwhile, ignored its commitment to prove that the aid shipments had reached their intended recipients. A North Korean doctor claimed, "Ten percent [of donated medicine goes] for war preparations, 10 percent for the people, and 80 percent for officials."[124] Kim Jong Il made no secret of his belief that food should go to the military first.[125]

On March 9, 1995, the U.S., South Korean and Japanese governments stood up the Korean Peninsula Energy Development Organization

(KEDO) to coordinate provision of the light-water reactors and heavy fuel oil.[126] Subsequent negotiations about KEDO's operation, however, showed the prematurity of singing the Agreed Framework's success, for Pyongyang almost immediately began to renege on its commitments.

Shortly after oil shipments to North Korea began, Pyongyang started to divert oil to its steel industry in violation of the Agreed Framework.[127] Diplomats began tough negotiations to monitor the shipments, but chose to see virtue in the regime's cheating. Although Gallucci and his team acknowledged that North Korea "was willing to look for ways to stretch the limits of or evade the terms of agreements," they rationalized that the regime's oil diversion "also demonstrated the North's ability to turn on a dime and to take surprising steps to resolve potential problems that might undercut its broader interests."[128] Gallucci had become so invested in the Agreed Framework's success that he and his team, behind the scenes, blamed the Pentagon for insisting that the Framework restrict the permissible use of fuel.[129]

Provision of the light-water reactors was the next hurdle. The Agreed Framework called for Washington's "best efforts" to finalize the contract for the reactors within six months. That was too optimistic under any circumstances, even before Kim Jong Il's holdups got in the way. He refused to credit Seoul, which was to provide the reactors, because his henchmen said it would affront their national dignity.[130] The Clinton administration, fearing that Pyongyang itself was looking for an excuse to scrap the deal, sought to renegotiate it. The result was another victory for the North. Washington agreed not to credit South Korea publicly, slighting a key U.S. ally for the sake of its adversary's propaganda.[131] Not only would Pyongyang receive a multibillion-dollar reward for its nuclear defiance, but Clinton signaled that it could also now micromanage the reactors' provision and design. Gallucci declared the Agreed Framework "back on track,"[132] but it was another year and a half before North Korea signed agreements with KEDO to enable it to begin building the two nuclear reactors.[133]

The Four-Party Talks

In the course of negotiations related to the Agreed Framework, there was not a single Pyongyang-instigated crisis in which North Korea did not win tangible benefit. Nevertheless, the Clinton administration aimed to catapult its "success" into new talks to address North Korea's missile program and move to a permanent peace treaty.[134] On April 16, 1996, Clinton and Kim Young Sam proposed that the United States, China, and the two Koreas participate in talks without preconditions. That North Korea immediately demanded additional incentives to participate should have raised red flags, but nothing could derail Clinton's enthusiasm for engagement.

At the height of the famine, the United States had answered UN humanitarian appeals for North Korea to the tune of almost $20 million.[135] American generosity did not alter North Korea's behavior, though. In September 1996, several well-fed North Korean commandos infiltrated South Korea by submarine, a clear-cut act of war. Rather than make good-faith efforts at rapprochement, well-fed nuclear scientists accelerated both missile development and proliferation.

While the Clinton administration was not blind to North Korea's bad faith, it still offered concessions and repositioned red lines to keep the North Koreans at the table. It bent to North Korean demands that food aid be not only a matter of humanitarian need, but also a reward for talking. The State Department first balked at the idea of making food a precondition for talks. After all, the North Korean government often provided food not to its needy population, but rather to its army. Secretary Albright relented, however, again signaling to North Korea that in the battle of resolve, America was weak.[136]

The United States and its diplomatic partners began a series of meetings in preparation for more formal, four-party talks in Geneva, scheduled for December 1997. As the North Koreans argued over agenda and protocol, these preliminary talks produced little agreement; yet for diplomats, the mere fact that the North Koreans were sitting down at all was progress. "It is significant to have a chance to have a meeting of this length and at this level to review the overall U.S.-DPRK relationship," one American participant remarked. "That is important to diplomats."[137] The State Department's description of a session in March 1997 as "a modest success," even though it had not achieved anything, indicated the emptiness of American diplomatic metrics.[138]

As the preliminary talks continued, the North Koreans would not commit to the idea that the formal talks in Geneva should lead to peace on the peninsula, yet the State Department rewarded them with bilateral talks, a key North Korean demand because it validated Pyongyang's claim to speak on behalf of all Korea.[139] Officials praised the "exceptionally broad" scope, level, and length of the talks, despite the lack of substantive results. Proliferation was one subject discussed bilaterally. Robert Einhorn, the deputy assistant secretary for nonproliferation, had struggled for more than a year to get North Korea to commit to nonproliferation agreements. The State Department claimed success when Pyongyang called off a missile test, which suggested that American diplomats now accepted a cancellation of provocation, rather than a cessation of proliferation, as success.[140] The signal sent to Kim Jong Il and to other rogue leaders was that they could gain much by creating provocations in order to reap incentives.

It was when incentives stopped flowing or when Kim Jong Il wanted to increase his price that he stopped cooperating. In June 1997, North Korean negotiators shrugged off American demands that they not deploy the Nodong missile and cease selling Scud missiles and parts. Then, in August, Pyongyang called off a new round of talks.[141] The official Korean Central News Agency later acknowledged Pyongyang's cynicism, saying, "Our missile export is aimed at obtaining foreign money we need at present. If the United States really wants to prevent our missile export, it should lift the economic embargo as early as possible and make a compensation for the losses to be caused by discontinued missile export."[142]

The next substantive session did not occur until March 1998. Much had changed in the interim. South Korea elected Kim Dae-jung, an enthusiastic proponent of dialogue, as president. Kim launched the Sunshine Policy, a comprehensive policy of incentives and engagement designed to bring North Korea in from the cold. The day after Kim's election, he announced a desire for direct dialogue with North Korea and for a presidential summit. North Korea, meanwhile, experienced an apparent insurrection, a possible coup attempt, and a series of high-profile defections. Albright's decision to admit the defectors to the United States exacerbated tension, but to Clinton's credit he did not bow to North Korean pressure on the issue. His actions stood in sharp contrast to the Carter administration's willingness to force the ailing shah from American soil in order to assuage Khomeini.[143]

The North Korean delegation bogged down meetings with procedural talks and the demand that the United States immediately withdraw its forces from South Korea. While Clinton hoped to advance peace on the peninsula, Pyongyang had a more financial goal in mind. Downs speculated that the International Monetary Fund bailout of South Korea during its currency crisis in 1997 had convinced the North Koreans that they had settled for too little in the Agreed Framework.[144]

The situation would soon go from bad to worse. On March 31, 1998, the Korean Central News Agency charged the United States with delaying both fuel oil delivery and construction of the light-water reactors. Over subsequent days, the verbal assault escalated—on the United States, the U.S.–South Korean alliance, and the Agreed Framework. Authorities in Pyongyang complained bitterly of American military activity in South Korea even though the White House had again canceled the annual Team Spirit exercise in 1998. North Korea had redrawn the baseline and voided its previous understandings. The crisis culminated on May 8, 1998, when the North Korean foreign ministry announced it would no longer abide by the Agreed Framework.[145]

Defiance once again worked, as the Clinton administration augmented its offer. In 1998, U.S. taxpayers provided almost $73 million in food aid to North Korea and another $50 million to KEDO. The State Department spokesman James Rubin defended U.S. policy even as the General Accounting Office highlighted North Korean cheating, including the hiding of weapons-grade plutonium. Rubin claimed that North Korean accounting discrepancies did not constitute a violation and said that the United States would therefore continue to support KEDO and provide heavy fuel oil.[146] The State Department had become so dedicated to engagement that it ignored the problems that dialogue was meant to solve.

In the year following the North Korean abandonment of the Agreed Framework, food aid almost tripled and American assistance to KEDO continued.[147] It was in this context that North Korean authorities demanded $300 million simply to permit inspection of an underground suspected nuclear site near Kumchang-ni and $1 billion to stop missile exports.[148] Pyongyang justified the bribe in grievance, claiming that the United States was "seriously insulting the DPRK's honor and dignity" by demanding the inspection, even though the suspect facility had not been mentioned in the Agreed Framework.[149] That it had walked away from the agreement was an irony lost on the North Korean regime.

Once again, Clinton succumbed to the extortion, first sending a State Department team to Pyongyang, expanding political and economic ties, and then upping agricultural assistance. Albright justified compensation in order to get the Agreed Framework back on track. "In the negotiations, we did not agree to North Korean demands for 'compensation' in return for access," she said. Instead, she explained, resolving questions over suspect sites would "enable us to resume progress in our relationship as outlined in the Agreed Framework."[150] Pyongyang gloated: "We came down hard on the United States without giving it a moment of respite and thus compelled it to partially lift the economic sanctions against us."[151] The regime then increased its price for ceasing missile exports to $3 billion.[152]

Any doubt about Pyongyang's sincerity should have ended on August 31, 1998, when North Korea launched a new missile over Japan while talks were ongoing in New York. The launch symbolized both the advancement of North Korea's military under the Agreed Framework and Pyongyang's continued defiance regardless of diplomacy and incentives. Like a gambler sacrificing everything for one more pull of the slot machine, the Clinton administration used the missile test not to reassess its process, but to justify more diplomacy.[153] Pyongyang concluded that it would suffer no serious consequences for its provocations. Just as important, it also divided its enemies: while Washington embraced further investment in the North, Japan had had enough and suspended its KEDO funding.[154]

The Clinton administration did not allow the North's defiance or its breaking of commitments to sidetrack diplomacy, even as a congressionally mandated group of nonpartisan experts found that the North Korean WMD threat had advanced in the period since the Agreed Framework was signed.[155] Bowing to reality might undermine the Sunshine Policy.[156] The October 1999 missile talks went nowhere, and North Korea resumed construction of launch pads and storage bunkers the following month. Pyongyang certainly did not feel chastised. The North Korean army boasted, "There is no limit to the strike of our People's Army and . . . on this planet there is no room for escaping the strike."[157] North Korea underscored its bluster with a steady violation of South Korean waters in the West Sea, an escalation that ended with the sinking of a North Korean torpedo ship.[158]

When the four-party talks restarted, the North Koreans could already claim victory. They were the center of attention and the recipients of billions of dollars in aid, all without any reciprocal cost. In August 1999, North Korean officials hinted that they would consider negotiations over the missile program, an opening that American officials seized upon.[159] The irony, of course, was that Pyongyang was seeking to leverage advances it made in contravention of the 1992 Joint Declaration and the 1994 Agreed Framework. Kim Jong Il's strategy was not without its merits: his dovish South Korean counterpart argued that the international community should provide Pyongyang with more incentives in exchange for a North Korean agreement to abandon further missile tests.[160]

As the Clinton administration wound down, William J. Perry, a former secretary of defense who headed a presidentially mandated task force to review U.S. policy toward North Korea, ruled out not only the status quo, but also efforts to reform or undermine North Korea. Instead, he proposed a two-track approach combining amelioration of pressure with verifiable assurances from Pyongyang on a cessation of testing, production, deployment, and export of missiles. He recommended a fallback position of containment should Pyongyang fail to engage.[161]

In May 1999, Perry visited Pyongyang to present the administration's plan to scale back sanctions in exchange for North Korea's commitment to halt the deployment and export of its ballistic missiles. The North Korean regime's extensive smuggling networks heightened concern about its proliferation activities.[162] Because Kim Jong Il refused to meet him, Perry settled for a promise by a lower-ranking official to stop missile tests. That was enough for Clinton. The United States again eased sanctions.[163]

For North Korea, Perry's visit was a success. Upon his return, Perry speculated that North Korea was really aiming for deterrence.[164] This was a dangerous misreading for two reasons: first, it ignored the possibility that North Korea sought the annihilation of South Korea; and second, it opened the debate again to the Carter-era proposal of American withdrawal from the peninsula.[165] Regardless, it took Pyongyang only a week to renege on its commitment while belittling Clinton's "appeasement policy."[166]

Talks still continued, but when the breakthrough came, it was on another track. Between June 13 and 15, 2000, South Korea's president, Kim Dae-jung, made a historic visit to Pyongyang, which culminated in the signing of a North-South Joint Declaration that was long on symbolism but short on specifics. The Clinton administration lauded the summit as a paragon of engagement. "President Kim Dae Jung's vision of engagement has been instrumental in breaking new ground at the Summit," said the State Department spokesman. "His support for the US–North Korea dialogue, for Japan–North Korea dialogue, and dialogue between Pyongyang and other nations has also opened the door for this historic step."[167]

Both Korean leaders agreed to strive for unity and enhance exchanges, although they did not mention peace. Because North Korea did not recognize South Korea, North Korean leaders argued that there was no other entity with which to make peace.

The photos from the event became the defining symbol of the Sunshine Policy, though not necessarily as a triumph of diplomacy. While the Sunshiners trumpeted the summit as the fruit of engagement, in reality it came about only after a huge payoff. Shortly before the summit, Kim Jong Il demanded $200 million from Kim Dae-jung, who was desperate to depict his policy as a success, and therefore he obliged. The secret payment, revealed only in a subsequent investigation, rocked the South. Kim Dae-jung defended it as necessary "for inter-Korean economic projects and sustained development of inter-Korean friendship."[168]

Engagement did not change behavior; money did, and then only fleetingly. While many Koreans had come to embrace engagement—Kim Dae-jung's attitudes reflected the desires of a younger generation—he bungled the process. As Sung-Yoon Lee, a research associate at Harvard University's Korea Institute, explained, "Kim Dae Jung had an opportunity to engage the ever-more isolated Pyongyang in a manner that would reflect and even define the great will of his time. Instead, despite the tremendous economic and political levers at his disposal, once he became president, he courted Pyongyang . . . in a manner that can be described only as fantastic."[169] Even though South Korea had unprecedented economic strength and international legitimacy, Kim Dae-jung still engaged as if he were the supplicant. His fanciful vision won him a Nobel Peace Prize, but aside from that it succeeded only in whetting Kim Jong Il's already insatiable appetite for concession.

Perhaps this is why, in August 2000, Kim Jong Il invited Clinton to visit him in Pyongyang. He dangled the prospect of a resolution of all outstanding security concerns. Clinton sent Albright to Pyongyang to assess the proposal's merits, and liked what he heard. Albright's visit, however, should have been a wake-up call. A mass performance she attended with the Dear Leader featured a depiction of a Taepodong missile launch. Albright laughed it off. "He immediately turned to me and quipped that this was the first satellite launch and it would be the last," she related, and praised Kim Jong Il for his "exceptional hospitality."[170] Talks continued at the White House when Clinton hosted Cho Myong Nok, the third highest ranking official in North Korea.[171] Joe Biden, then the ranking Democrat on the Senate Committee on Foreign Relations, was ecstatic, saying, "The results of this comprehensive and integrated engagement strategy have stunned even the most optimistic observers."[172]

Meanwhile, North Korean cheating reached new levels. Although North Korea suspended missile tests, it proceeded with missile development and continued its exports.[173] As Kim Jong Il courted Clinton, North Korean authorities also apparently decided to pursue a full-scale, covert uranium enrichment capability.[174]

Bush Reconsiders

When President George W. Bush took office, most of his senior advisors were skeptical of North Korean intentions and diplomacy's legacy.[175] The new administration was still eager to engage, but it was not willing to grant the North Korean leadership the legitimacy that Kim Jong Il demanded. Colin Powell, the secretary of state, was the notable exception. "We do plan to engage with North Korea to pick up where President Clinton and his administration left off," Powell told the press at the State Department.[176] When reproached by Bush, he apologized, saying that he had leaned "too forward in my skis."[177]

The North Koreans were nervous and wanted the new administration to commit to picking up talks where Clinton's team had left off. "It was hard for Pyongyang to realize that it had waited too long before seriously engaging," said Charles Pritchard, the Bush team's special envoy.[178] Kim would gain no presidential visit. Instead, the Bush team sought working-level meetings to discuss the Agreed Framework, North Korea's missile programs, and proliferation. Further, Bush made clear that he would tie the lifting of sanctions and provision of nonhumanitarian aid to progress on reconciliation between the two Koreas.[179]

Bush said he would not allow optimism to cloud analysis. "I've got a message to Kim Jong Il: fulfill your end of the bargain," Bush told Asian newspaper editors, adding, "No one in the United States is stopping him from [reciprocating Kim Dae-jung's visit]. He can blame it on who he wants, but he ought to fulfill his end of the agreement . . . ."[180]

North Korean authorities reverted to their traditional mix of bluster and aggrievement. The foreign ministry declared that North Korea was "prepared for both dialogue and war."[181] They told a visiting European delegation that they had been on the verge of entering into bilateral talks with the United States, but if they did so after Bush's chastisement, they would lose face.[182] No evidence supported this assertion, but Pyongyang understood that grievances and accusations of cultural insensitivity put Western diplomats on the defensive.[183]

North Korean claims of aggrievement reached fever pitch after Bush placed North Korea in the Axis of Evil. Albright called Bush's remarks "a big mistake."[184] Others whose legacies were tied to engagement also lashed out, and the North Koreans seized upon that criticism to justify their own position.[185] The Clinton alumni who condemned Bush for his moral clarity had remained silent when North Korean officials used far cruder language to describe the United States.[186] Verbal fusillades are a staple of North Korean rhetoric, so to believe Pyongyang's claims of aggrievement suggests a lack of perspective.

North Korea did not appear so aggrieved three months later when its UN ambassador signaled a willingness to renew direct dialogue. The State Department proposed to send Assistant Secretary James Kelly to Pyongyang for talks, but while they awaited North Korea's response, a North Korean ship sank a South Korean patrol boat in the West Sea. Continuing the pattern expressed in the 1983 and 1987 bombings, the regime coupled diplomatic outreach with atrocity.

Powell nevertheless pushed forward with efforts to engage, even after information surfaced with regard to the extent of North Korean uranium enrichment. On July 31, 2002, he met his North Korean counterpart, Paek Nam Sun, on the sidelines of an ASEAN conference.[187] Then, without White House clearance, Powell approved the attendance of Charles Pritchard, the special envoy, at a ceremony celebrating Agreed Framework progress, despite U.S. suspicion that the North was violating the accord by illegal uranium enrichment.[188]

The Pentagon was angry about Pritchard's trip, given the magnitude of North Korean cheating. The issue was not simply the Bush administration's reinterpretation of intelligence. Clinton had been unable during his last two years in office to certify that North Korea had stopped seeking uranium enrichment capability.[189] The evidence was damning: even as North Korea signed the Agreed Framework, the rogue Pakistani nuclear scientist A. Q. Khan had shared centrifuge blueprints and prototypes with North Korea. Indeed, Pritchard's visit came as Donald Rumsfeld, the secretary of defense, was proposing that the White House suspend the Agreed Framework and cut off shipments of heavy fuel oil to North Korea.

On October 3, 2002, during a meeting in Pyongyang, Kelly told North Korea's deputy foreign minister, Kang Sok Ju, that Washington knew that North Korea had produced highly enriched uranium in violation of the Agreed Framework.[190] The next day, Kang acknowledged that North Korea had maintained a covert uranium enrichment program in violation of both the 1992 Joint Declaration and the Agreed Framework.[191] KEDO responded by cutting off fuel oil shipments.

By this juncture, the United States had already provided North Korea with more than $600 million in food, with another $400 million channeled through KEDO. While many diplomats celebrated these subsidies as the stuff of successful diplomacy, North Korean actions belied the logic that incentives and diplomatic entanglements flip rogues.

Pyongyang responded to the termination of oil shipments by announcing withdrawal from the NPT, expulsion of IAEA monitors, and a restart of the Yongbyon reactor. "It is clear to everyone that the U.S. is wholly to blame for this," a North Korean commentary read.[192] The regime demanded direct talks with Washington to resolve the impasse. The Bush team agreed to talk, but only multilaterally. No longer would the United States be bound by the bilateral Agreed Framework if North Korea was not. "My predecessor, in a good-faith effort, entered into a framework agreement," Bush explained. "The United States honored its side of the agreement. North Korea didn't. While we felt the agreement was in force, North Korea was enriching uranium."[193]

Diplomacy is the State Department's raison d'être regardless of its wisdom at any moment in time. To jumpstart diplomacy, Deputy Secretary Richard Armitage downplayed allegations of North Korean cheating. He dismissed reports that North Korea was test-firing engines, saying that "there is nothing in itself wrong with that."[194] Armitage's ham-handed exculpation backfired: North Korea seized upon his report to affirm its own behavior, while those invested in North Korea engagement took it as a green light for Bush-bashing.[195]

"Instead of picking up the ball where Bill Clinton dropped it, George W. Bush moved the goalposts when he assumed the presidency in 2001," remarked Leon Sigal, a former *New York Times* editorial writer.[196] This was dishonest on two counts: it was North Korea that unilaterally sought to move the goalposts; and the cessation of fuel oil shipments—which set off the cascade of North Korean defiance—was a decision made multilaterally at KEDO.[197] Joel S. Wit, a former State Department official, opined, "the fact that [Pyongyang] had confessed to a secret nuclear program is a sign that North Korea may be looking for a way out of a potential crisis."[198] This logic was as ridiculous as praising North Korea for reducing its arsenal if it launched its artillery at South Korea.

Just as during the elder Bush's administration, analysts who aimed to protect the NPT argued that Bush erred by suggesting that North Korea's nuclear breakthroughs were a result of cheating. Perhaps, they argued, North Korean scientists had found new ways to meet their goals not covered by their agreements.[199] This was also disingenuous;

evidence pointed firmly to subterfuge. An even more ridiculous example of engagers' wishful thinking was the argument that North Korean bluster was simply a prelude to its offer of a grand bargain, one which Bush ignored.[200]

The blame game highlights two truisms about diplomacy with rogue regimes. First, American partisans are more likely to blame their political competition than to blame the rogue regime. Second, when high-profile talks make careers, those invested in the talks are loath to admit failure, and so they remain in a state of denial about their opponents' insincerity.

Kim Jong Il's regime, for its part, justified its violations on the basis of delays in the construction of the promised light-water reactors. The two sides disagreed over schedule, but that did not excuse North Korea's wholesale violation of its agreements.

Despite renewed discussion of sanctions, the Bush administration never stopped trying to lure Pyongyang back into compliance with more food aid.[201] Bush also floated the possibility of increasing energy and agricultural development aid if North Korea verifiably dismantled its nuclear program and addressed U.S. proliferation concerns. Instead, North Korean authorities stepped up their nuclear program. On February 12, 2003, the CIA director, George Tenet, reported that North Korea might already possess missiles capable of reaching the continental United States.[202]

Too often, the desperation for successful diplomacy leads diplomats to ignore evidence that the other side has no real interest in the process. North Korean rhetoric, in fact, clearly telegraphed the regime's priorities. "National sovereignty lies on the military-first road," the regime asserted, adding that North Korea "can live without candy but not without bullets."[203] The irony here was that Pyongyang complained bitterly whenever the United States would couple diplomacy with military posturing. "Dialogue and pressure cannot go together," according to a North Korean commentary.[204]

Then, on April 12, 2003, two days after North Korea's withdrawal from the NPT, French, German, and Egyptian authorities intercepted a twenty-two-ton shipment, destined for Pyongyang, of aluminum tubing that matched specifications needed for vacuum casings for a Urenco centrifuge.[205] The regime had been caught red-handed.

Bush sought to resolve the crisis in six-party talks, to include both Koreas, China, Japan, and Russia. Pyongyang balked. When, in the course of a trilateral meeting in Beijing, the U.S. delegation refused to consent to a bilateral meeting with North Korea's diplomats, the head of Pyongyang's delegation, Li Gun, threatened James Kelly, saying, "You have always thought we had nuclear weapons; well, I am here to tell you that we do. And what we do with them is up to you."[206]

After an unsuccessful six-party session in August 2003, Bush offered new security guarantees to entice the North back to the table.[207] As subsequent rounds of talks went nowhere, conflict raged within the Bush administration. The State Department opposed Vice President Dick Cheney's insistence that the United States aim for an "irreversible" dismantling of North Korea's nuclear program because they felt it might undermine the ability to engage productively with the North.[208] One official even went so far as publicly dismissing the legitimacy of American intelligence in order to bolster diplomacy.[209] Once again, the act of engagement rather than national security had become the diplomats' end goal. Even though the talks produced no agreement, the State Department described them as "largely successful."[210] To say otherwise might invite questions about the billions of dollars invested in engagement and inducements.

In June 2004, the U.S. team proposed to North Korea a process not unlike that applied to Libya: If North Korea froze and then dismantled its nuclear program, it would receive incentives and regime rehabilitation. North Korea refused, instead gambling that a John F. Kerry defeat of Bush would lead to a more generous package. It was a gamble that would suspend talks for more than a year.

Even though Kerry lost, Kim Jong Il's gamble paid off. The new secretary of state, Condoleezza Rice, aimed to jumpstart diplomacy at almost any price. She appointed Christopher Hill, assistant secretary for East Asian and Pacific affairs, to lead new talks. Together, Rice and Hill tried to infuse Bush's black-and-white approach with shades of gray. Diplomats saw Hill as a professional negotiator with a knack for finding new ways around problems.[211] To his detractors, however, Hill was a freelancer, willing to push ahead rather than seek guidance from a superior who might be less compromising. Hill kept his cards close to his chest. He negotiated alone, often without keeping a written record of the dialogue. While he adhered to instructions received from the State Department, at critical moments he would not report back to give the team at home an opportunity to issue new instructions. He would often rewrite cables to make himself appear more biting. When North Koreans outplayed him, Hill would rush into the next round, hoping to redeem himself.

Bush may have wanted a multilateral solution, but rather than stick by the six-party framework, Hill consented to North Korea's demands for bilateral talks. With sleight of hand, he planned a pro forma half-hour session before breaking out into direct bilateral talks with the North Koreans.

Meanwhile, Rice ordered concessions on other counts. No longer would the United States demand that North Korea cease its nuclear program. The State Department also ended its focus on highly enriched uranium. Renewed flexibility was "a far better tactic to keep the momentum of the talks moving in the right direction," Pritchard argued.[212] Should North Korea rejoin the NPT and accept IAEA safeguards, the United States would accept North Korea's right to a peaceful, civilian nuclear program.

While KEDO in 2006 formally terminated its project to build two light-water reactors in North Korea, Hill resurrected discussion of the reactors, a fantastic concession given Pyongyang's previous deception.[213] When North Korea reaffirmed the 1992 Joint Declaration and the 1994 Agreed Framework, Hill celebrated it as a diplomatic victory. "We had a great day," he said. "We finally have an agreement. This is a win-win situation. We got agreement on denuclearization of the Korean peninsula."[214] Hill was simply projecting sincerity onto his North Korean partners.[215]

No sooner had North Korean negotiators accepted a joint statement, however, than the regime issued another statement distancing itself from the joint statement and insisting it would not rejoin the NPT or accept IAEA safeguards until it received the light-water reactors.[216] That Hill dismissed the North Korean interpretation as merely "spouting off to internal audiences"[217] suggests a basic misunderstanding of Kim Jong Il's accountability to his public. Pyongyang's decision to launch seven ballistic missiles on July 4 and 5, 2006, and then conduct an underground nuclear test three months later underscored its defiance in the face of American outreach. So did its production of weapons-grade plutonium.

Engagement's cheerleaders redoubled their calls for more talks. Carter argued that the North Koreans "don't respond well to threats, intimidation and punishment." James Laney asserted that talking "is not appeasement or being a wimp. It is sensible."[218]

The Bush administration's response to the nuclear test was weak. Rice urged calm. "The United States has no desire to escalate this crisis. We would like to see it de-escalate," she said.[219] First-term Bush administration officials could not believe the about-face. John Bolton, former ambassador to the United Nations, called Bush's redoubling of engagement efforts a "complete U-turn."[220] Aaron Friedberg, former deputy national security advisor under Cheney, called the engagement "fanciful" and argued that "it is precisely the *absence* of sufficient pressure that has gotten us where we are today."[221]

Rifts within the administration further weakened the credibility of an accompanying push for UN sanctions. Tom Lantos, the ranking Democrat on the House International Relations Committee, noted how "profoundly divided" the administration was, and said "there are very senior people in the administration who agree with me that dialogue is needed."[222] When sanctions did finally come, they lacked an enforcement mechanism.[223]

With the war in Iraq growing deeply unpopular, Rice tried to cement a positive legacy for Bush by doubling down on efforts to win a breakthrough on North Korea. When American diplomats met with North Koreans in Beijing, they offered even more concessions. In November 2006, Rice and Hill offered to remove North Korea from the State Sponsors of Terrorism list and the Trading with the Enemy Act, scrapping the Clinton team's demand that North Korea provide a written guarantee that it had ceased terrorism, would acquiesce to international agreements for combating terrorism, and would address its past terrorism.[224]

Beyond the bombings in the 1980s, North Korea's refusal to come clean about its kidnappings of Japanese citizens had been a major factor in its listing on the terror sponsorship list. In 2004, the regime returned five surviving abductees of the ten it eventually admitted seizing, but the Japanese government maintains that Korean agents actually kidnapped eighty Japanese citizens. Rice pressured Tokyo to tone down its objections and told Prime Minister Shinzo Abe that the White House was under no obligation to classify the kidnappings as terrorism.[225] Appeasing the enemy had trumped honoring the ally.

In January 2007, Hill met with Kim Kye Gwan, a top North Korean diplomat.[226] Their discussions and agreements culminated the next month in a two-phase six-party agreement, which the White House celebrated as a "very important first step." In the first sixty-day phase, North Korea would freeze its nuclear program. A second phase—for which no time frame was set—would have North Korea disable its nuclear facilities and disclose all nuclear activities.

Hill's triumph was, in reality, a major step down: the agreement allowed North Korea to keep its nuclear weapons. For Kim Jong Il, it was a complete victory, capped off by the repatriation of laundered money frozen in a Macau bank. Bolton was blunt in his condemnation of the deal, saying, "It sends exactly the wrong signal to would-be proliferators around the world: 'If we hold out long enough, wear down the State Department negotiators, eventually you get rewarded.'"[227]

The *New York Times*, on the other hand, praised the agreement without equivocation, famously suggesting that the State Department's rule of thumb on any initiative should be to ask, "What would Chris Hill do?"[228] Kelly also applauded Hill's approach. "Diplomacy is not the same as accommodation," he said. "The very process assures that acceptance of North Korea as a nuclear-weapons state is not a *fait accompli*, nor is it seen as such."[229]

The Bush administration defended its strategy. "It's about actions for actions," the National Security Council spokesman explained.[230] He suggested that the chance for success was greater than with the deals struck in the 1990s because Beijing had dropped its obstructionism. But China's compliance had come at a huge price. In the waning weeks of his administration, Clinton had waived missile-proliferation sanctions on China in exchange for a promise not to proliferate technology. Chinese companies then proceeded to sell sensitive technology to Iran.[231]

To listen to the North Koreans, moreover, would be to understand that the deal had not changed their position. Despite the advantage Pyongyang had won, the North Korean press described the deal as a "wicked plot" meant to "benumb" the North's "anti-imperialist spirit."[232]

Between September 2007 and April 2008, the United States negotiated an agreement with North Korea that obligated the regime to disable its plutonium facilities at Yongbyon and provide a "complete and correct" description of its nuclear programs. In exchange, the United States would lift economic sanctions and finalize North Korea's removal from the terrorism list. In effect, the United States would no longer demand an end to and reversal of North Korea's illegal actions. All Bush's team demanded was that Pyongyang acknowledge American concerns.[233] It was the diplomatic equivalent of letting a serial killer go free if he only promised to say sorry.

The agreement raised eyebrows among veteran diplomats. Winston Lord, an assistant secretary for East Asia and the Pacific under Clinton, and Les Gelb, assistant secretary for politico-military affairs under Carter, warned, "If the administration accepts North Korea's hedging and reneging once again, it will increase, not decrease, the likelihood of confrontation down the line." To answer those who say that deals must be struck with the enemy, they added, "Sometimes Washington must hold its nose, make concessions and tolerate ambiguity. But not now. Not when it waters down compliance with a painfully reached prior agreement. If President Bush allows Pyongyang to brush away its pledges, he will reinforce its instinct for bluster and blackmail."[234]

Rice was so desperate for a deal, though, that she ignored North Korea's failure to uphold its end of the bargain. When Pyongyang failed to declare its nuclear activities by the deadline, Hill voided the deadline.[235] Diplomats hoped that the regime's acknowledgment of concerns would segue into a process to address them. But when they forfeited their leverage just to get to the table, they made it more unlikely that North Korea would fulfill such dreams.

When the North Koreans blew up the cooling tower at Yongbyon, the State Department congratulated itself. But the demolition was less than met the eye. It did not set back North Korea's plutonium program appreciably. North Korea's declaration of its plutonium reserves was far less than American estimates, but the agreement left no way to settle the discrepancy.[236] Because Hill had declared victory before committing North Korea in writing to accept sampling, Bush could do little once Pyongyang began backtracking on verification, which itself was limited to Yongbyon and declared complexes, not the myriad covert sites in which intelligence officials believed North Korea conducted nuclear work.

Bush entered office critical of Clinton's North Korea strategy and its legacy of inducement and compromise. By any reasonable standard, Bush did far worse. On his watch, North Korea built perhaps a dozen nuclear bombs and extended the range of its missiles. It would be wrong, however, to suggest that Bush's failure validated Clinton's engagement. After all, beyond his harsher rhetoric, by his second term Bush had simply adopted Clinton's approach with equal vigor.

Obama's Turn

Bush's legacy on North Korea may have been diplomatic surrender, but Pyongyang was optimistic that it might expand its advantage with a Democrat in the White House.[237] Indeed, Obama made engagement the cornerstone of his strategy, promising rogue regimes that he would "extend a hand if you are willing to unclench your fist," and stating his willingness to engage in "tough and direct talks" with the North Korean regime.[238]

Pyongyang used the change of administration to float new proposals that would, in effect, nullify previous agreements. A North Korean diplomat, for example, suggested that diplomatic relations with the United States should precede North Korean forfeiture of its nuclear weapons.[239] North Korean officials also seized upon Obama's announcement of his "road to zero" nuclear weapons to argue that North Korea will forfeit its weapons only if the United States gives up its own.

Rather than engage in the rhetorical bluster for which diplomats condemned Bush, Obama's team took a soft approach. As North Korea planned its first missile launch of the Obama era, Defense Secretary Robert Gates, a Bush administration holdover, said the administration was "not prepared to do anything about it."[240] Stephen Bosworth, the administration's special representative for North Korea policy, described "substantial progress" in his talks, even as North Korea set about to fuel its missiles.[241]

Obama's conciliatory rhetoric fell on deaf ears. On March 17, 2009, North Korean authorities detained two journalists working for Al Gore's Current TV who had crossed illegally into their country. A kangaroo court sentenced both young women to twelve years in prison with hard labor. It was traditional hostage diplomacy. Bill Clinton traveled to Pyongyang to appeal for their release. His visit rewarded Kim Jong Il for sparking an artificial crisis, and the North Korean dictator took full advantage of it to solidify the position of his third son and designated successor, Kim Jong Un. According to South Korea's Yonhap News Agency, North Korea's police force put out word that "General Kim Jong-Un's artifice let former US President Clinton cross the Pacific to apologize to the Great Leader. It was all made possible thanks to General Kim Jong-Un's extraordinary prophecy and outstanding tactics."[242] The deputy foreign minister, Kim Yong Il, confided to his Mongolian counterparts that the groundwork for the Clinton visit had been long prepared; the North Koreans hoped to use the crisis to jumpstart talks from a position of strength.[243]

True to the pattern of coupling atrocity with diplomacy, North Korea fired hundreds of artillery shells into the Yellow Sea near the international border on January 27 and 28, 2010, and then, on May 20, the North Koreans torpedoed a South Korean naval vessel without warning, killing forty-six. The American response was weak. The State Department tweeted, "North Korea must be made aware that unprovoked and provocative events are not the actions of a responsible nation."[244] Clinton described the U.S. inaction as "strategic patience."[245] A month later, North Korea added insult to injury by demanding $65 trillion in Korean War restitution from the United States.[246] As the Obama administration sought to censure North Korea in the Security Council, Pyongyang reverted to hostage diplomacy, threatening to punish an American serving an eight-year sentence for illegal border crossing. "If the US persists in its hostile approach toward the [North], the latter will naturally be compelled to consider the issue of what harsher punishment will be meted out to him," the official Korean Central News Agency reported.[247]

Against this backdrop, the engagement lobby played into the Great Leader's hands. "The answer is re-engagement. There aren't any other tools in the toolbox," Joel Wit wrote.[248] On cue, Carter traveled to Pyongyang, where he met with Kim Jong Il and promptly called for new talks. In a *New York Times* essay, he criticized Bush for the collapse of previous agreements, failed to mention North Korea's unprovoked torpedo attack, and accepted North Korean sincerity despite its two nuclear tests and development of a long-range missile.[249]

Two months later, North Korea launched an unprovoked artillery barrage against the South Korean island of Yeonpyeong, killing two marines and setting numerous structures ablaze. Again, the American response was weak. The White House condemned the attack and asked North Korea to "halt its belligerent action." Carter, true to form, blamed the United States and gave the benefit of the doubt to North Korea, writing that "it is entirely possible that their recent revelation of their uranium enrichment centrifuges and Pyongyang's shelling of a South Korean island Tuesday are designed to remind the world that they deserve respect in negotiations that will shape their future. Ultimately, the choice for the United States may be between diplomatic niceties and avoiding a catastrophic confrontation."[250] Carter argued that engagement was more important than ever, and the North Koreans encouraged him. "The U.S. would be well advised to reexamine its hostile policy toward the DPRK and make a U-turn towards dialogue and fence mending," the North Korean news agency warned.[251]

Like many engagers, Carter did not consider that Washington's failure to stand up to North Korean provocations might encourage belliger-ence and lead the regime to believe it was negotiating from a position of strength. The South Koreans had other ideas, and they defied the North's threats. "Fear of war is never helpful in preventing war," President Lee Myung-bak remarked.[252]

Kim Jong Il died on December 17, 2011, and Kim Jong Un suc-ceeded him as planned. After any rogue regime goes through a change of leadership, Washington hopes for a change of policy, and Kim Jong Un knew how to play on that hope. He promised to freeze missile tests, uranium enrichment, and missile launches, and he invited back the nuclear inspectors who had been expelled three years earlier. The Obama administration dutifully responded by providing 240,000 tons of food. The assistance may have been meant to encourage diplomacy, but in reality it simply bought time for Kim to entrench himself. Still, Obama kept trying. In August 2012, he secretly dispatched two aides to Pyongyang for discussions.[253] If the goal of these talks was to calm tensions, the White House failed.

Over subsequent months, the North Koreans successfully launched a new long-range missile, advancing toward their goal of putting the West

Coast of the United States within missile range. The regime also reverted to hostage diplomacy, seizing Kenneth Bae, an American citizen who led tourist groups into North Korea's special economic zones, and sentencing him to fifteen years of hard labor on spurious charges. The Kim Jong Un regime sought to auction Bae in exchange for concessions. Obama dispatched a State Department envoy, Clifford Hart, to meet secretly with Han Song Ryol, the North Korean deputy UN ambassador. No progress was made, and North Korea launched a new round of provocations soon afterward.[254] Then, on October 8, the South Korean press reported that North Korea had restarted the Yongbyon reactor, which had been mothballed since 2007.[255] Dialogue had cost the United States and its allies billions of dollars, but ultimately it achieved nothing. Meanwhile, North Korea's nuclear program continued apace in the nearly two decades since the Agreed Framework was signed.

* * *

North Korea has been a target of American diplomacy for longer than any other rogue regime. The strategy has failed by any objective standard. Successive American administrations have sought security if not peace for South Korea and the region, and an end to the North Korean regime's nuclear proliferation and missile development. The United States and its allies have also given Pyongyang more than a billion dollars in food and fuel aid, an investment which has bolstered the regime's military but has done little for the health and livelihood of ordinary North Korean citizens.

Not only did diplomacy fail to fulfill American goals, but it actually sabotaged them. Pyongyang never engaged sincerely; rather, successive North Korean leaders used diplomacy to distract the West while pursuing their nuclear aims unimpeded. Because money is fungible, the aid and incentives offered by the United States to catalyze diplomacy made it easier for the North Korean regime to achieve its goals.

While U.S. administrations conducted occasional reviews of North Korea policy, none acknowledged the pattern surrounding North Korean diplomacy. Pyongyang's playbook never changed: First they provoke, then they consent to accept an agreement in exchange for concessions, and finally they violate that agreement, before starting the cycle again. Never will the State Department's hope be fulfilled that the next round will be different. Both Albright and Gallucci acknowledged North Korean cheating, but such is the blind belief and addiction that, even in hindsight, Gallucci could name few circumstances in which he would walk away from the table.[256]

If the West uses diplomacy as a tool to resolve conflict, North Korea does not. The North Korean regime makes no secret of its antipathy to the very concept of engagement. Kim Yong Nam, president of North Korea's Supreme People's Assembly and the regime's second most powerful figure—citing the legacy and philosophy of regime founder Kim Il Sung—declared, "The reckless knife-wielding of imperialists and reactionaries should be countered with the gun barrel to the end."[257] Whether its target was American helicopters, its rival government in South Korea, or Japanese and Koreans abroad, North Korea employed violence to claim the upper hand against its enemies, real or imagined. Pyongyang employed a strategy of brinkmanship. More often than not, the White House assuaged the regime. In 1992, for example, the George H. W. Bush administration withdrew nuclear weapons from South Korea, but received nothing in return. Today, the only nuclear weapons in Korea belong to the North. Only when North Korean leaders believed that the United States was on the verge of acting militarily would the communist regime back down, but that seldom happened. First Kim Il Sung, then Kim Jong Il, and finally Kim Jong Un assumed that when the going gets tough, there will always be a useful idiot around to relieve pressure and enable the North Korean regime to avoid concession.

The cost of engaging North Korea extended beyond the concessions offered to North Korea itself. Successive American administrations have used Beijing to mediate with Pyongyang, and China is not an altruistic player. South Korean intellectuals warned the State Department that China's obsession with North Korean stability—to use the state as a buffer—conflicted with both U.S. and South Korean interests.[258] The Chinese government was the layover point for illicit technologies going into or out of North Korea.[259] Because the State Department sought Chinese assistance when crisis arose in North Korea, Beijing could encourage the occasional crisis so as to reap its own rewards. China also used the North Korea issue to drive a wedge between Washington and its chief regional allies, South Korea and Tokyo.[260] While the State Department repeatedly allowed China to influence U.S. policy and diluted policy to win Chinese approval, such efforts were for naught, since China's communist rulers did not share U.S. concerns nor did they seek to advance American interests. U.S. strategy empowered Beijing, while American incentives strengthened the North Korean regime.

Chapter Four

LYING DOWN WITH LIBYANS

On December 19, 2003, Libya came in from the cold. After almost thirty-five years of defying the world, the Libyan government announced that it would cease its efforts to develop and acquire chemical and nuclear weapons, would eliminate its existing stocks, and would open its facilities to inspection.[1] The turnabout was quick. Inspectors arrived in January 2004 and within two months had certified Libya's compliance with its agreement. While Iraq became symbolic of the chaos resulting from war, Libya became Exhibit A to prove the efficacy of American engagement with rogue regimes.

From Ally to Enemy and Back Again

Libya was a close American ally until September 1, 1969. Early that morning, while the moderate King Idris was abroad, a group of junior officers seized power. The twenty-seven-year-old Muammar Qadhafi soon emerged as the prime power within the Revolutionary Command Council, and then became the unquestioned dictator.

As they would with Iran a decade later, the State Department's regional experts welcomed the Libyan revolution. Some may even have betrayed the names of counterrevolutionaries who had Qadhafi in their sights.[2] Adopting a mix of Arab nationalism and anti-Western rhetoric, Qadhafi demanded the expulsion of Westerners, and even went so far as to exhume European and Jewish graves.[3] He evicted U.S. forces from Wheelus Air Base, the largest American base in Africa. "The United States has made itself an adversary to the legitimate objectives of the Arab nation," Qadhafi said. "We are faced with a hostile policy and we resist it."[4] Nevertheless, the Libyan regime announced its willingness to talk, if only the United States would change its foreign policy. Qadhafi advised Nixon to rid Washington of Zionist influence, and Qadhafi's press minister blamed the failure of dialogue on a lack of White House interest.[5] There was no change during Ford's administration, so Qadhafi celebrated Jimmy Carter's election and hoped that the new president might send an ambassador.[6]

It was not an ambassador who would eventually come, however, but Carter's younger brother Billy. The president distanced himself from his brother's antics, while behind the scenes he defended Billy and denied any impropriety.[7] The U.S. embassy in Tripoli, for its part, viewed the visit positively. "There has been no negative fallout from Billy Carter's visit," the senior American diplomat in Tripoli reported. "In fact, on the local scene we would rate it a very positive event which has opened some doors for this embassy."[8]

The doors would not be open for long. In December 1979, a Libyan mob attacked the embassy, inspired by the Iranian revolutionaries who had seized the embassy in Tehran a month earlier. Carter was not about to make the same mistake twice. He ordered U.S. diplomats withdrawn and shuttered the mission, although he let the Libyan embassy continue to operate in Washington, an inconsistency which the Reagan administration rectified in May 1981. Today, diplomats urge the United States to send ambassadors to engage rogues the world over, but during Carter's presidency there was a bipartisan understanding that dialogue might continue at a lower level, though the dispatching of an ambassador was a reward for adversaries to earn.

Over subsequent years, relations between the United States and Libya reached their nadir. U.S. Navy jets downed two Libyan fighters that fired on them over the Gulf of Sidra, international waters claimed by Libya, in August 1981. Libyan support for terrorism increased throughout the decade. Investigators found Libyan fingerprints on the 1985 terrorist attacks at the Rome and Vienna airports, which killed nineteen and wounded 138. The following year, the U.S. Air Force bombed several targets in Libya after Qadhafi sponsored the bombing of Berlin's La Belle disco, popular with U.S. servicemen.[9] Finally, on December 21, 1988, Libyan intelligence officers bombed Pan Am 103 over Lockerbie, Scotland, killing all 259 on board and eleven on the ground.

Under Reagan, there was little direct diplomacy between Libya and the United States. What dialogue occurred was by bullhorn, as Reagan and Qadhafi publicly lambasted each other. Reagan, for example, called Qadhafi "the madman of the Middle East" and described him as part of "a new, international version of Murder Incorporated."[10] To Qadhafi, Reagan was "the vile actor" and, after a retaliatory bombing allegedly killed Qadhafi's young daughter, a "child murderer" as well.[11]

Rather than seek dialogue, Reagan favored sanctions to penalize U.S. companies investing in Libya, a move that many American detractors called a "nuisance" more than a "heavy blow to either."[12] By 1988, the White House had concluded it could not get rid of Qadhafi, and decided instead to isolate him.[13] To that end, U.S. officials began to show their European counterparts satellite and aerial photos of a huge Libyan chemical facility under construction at Rabta, forty miles south of Tripoli.[14] A mysterious fire destroyed the plant the following year. Twenty years later, after Qadhafi acquiesced to inspections, the Libyan regime was still converting Rabta from a chemical weapons facility to a legitimate pharmaceuticals plant.[15]

It was the bombing of Pan Am 103, however, that dominated Libyan relations with the United States. The investigation was painstaking. Other countries had motive and means. Before settling on Libya, investigators theorized that Palestinian terrorists working for Iran may have targeted the flight in retaliation for the accidental downing of an Iranian passenger jet by the USS *Vincennes* the previous summer. But investigators had a gold mine of evidence because the Pan Am flight left Frankfurt late, so the time bomb detonated while the plane was over land rather than ocean; and that evidence pointed to Libya.

Reagan had considered the disco bombing in Berlin an act of war, and he responded in kind. The Pan Am bombing, however, occurred during the twilight of his presidency. Vice President George H. W. Bush, the president-elect, took the lead and chose to treat the Pan Am bombing as a crime. This may have been partly a policy decision and partly inevitable, since the weeks between the bombing and the investigation's conclusion created a barrier to anything other than diplomacy. Both Washington and London demanded that Tripoli surrender the suspects to a Scottish court. They backed this demand with a cascade of UN Security Council sanctions and resolutions calling for Libya to surrender the suspects, cooperate with investigators, and pay compensation. The United Nations also imposed an arms embargo, restricted air travel to and from Libya, banned export of oil equipment to Libya, and froze some Libyan assets.

Qadhafi initially refused to accept UN jurisdiction because both the United States and the United Kingdom sat on the Security Council. Instead, Libya tried to shift jurisdiction to the International Court of Justice, which did not have the power to impose national sanctions.[16]

The process for hammering out jurisdiction was itself engagement. Ronald Bruce St. John, a Libya scholar, argued that Qadhafi hoped to reconcile with Bush. In October 1989, Libya's foreign minister, Jadallah 'Azzuz al-Talhi, expressed a desire to normalize relations with Washington without preconditions.[17] This would have meant turning back the clock and welcoming diplomatic ties as if the Lockerbie bombing had never happened. Diplomacy's advocates might seize upon such an olive branch, but doing so would have meant rehabilitating Libya without requiring it to pay any consequences for Lockerbie. The White House concluded that the cost of engagement under such terms was too high.

Over the next years, U.S.-Libya relations remained moribund. Diplomatic exchanges were sporadic, usually conducted through third parties, and limited to discussions over Lockerbie and Libya's weapons programs. The erratic Qadhafi, however, craved direct contact. "The Bush administration must sit face to face with Libya so that we can agree on the issues in dispute," he told reporters in 1989.[18] Neither the elder Bush nor Bill Clinton after him would submit to Qadhafi's demand. Both understood that if they were to allow direct diplomacy, Qadhafi would be the winner. Qadhafi need never give a concession nor engage sincerely, for the moment he met an American diplomat, he would have all he craved. Not only would the White House have legitimized his rule, but he could then humiliate U.S. leaders through words and actions, enhancing his own stature in the process.

U.S. rejection of engagement did not stop Qadhafi from trying. In February 1992, a man claiming to be a naval attaché at the Libyan embassy in Athens approached Gary Hart, the former senator, who was then traveling in Greece on business. When Hart reported the contact to the State Department, he learned that the Libyans had already made several approaches to different intermediaries but the White House refused to pursue relations until Qadhafi turned over the Lockerbie bombers.[19]

Senators have tremendous egos, so they make useful idiots for dictators. Hart was no exception, and he decided to continue his dialogue with the Libyans. In March 1992, he met with Yusuf Dibri, head of the Libyan Intelligence Service, and two other Libyan officials in Geneva. Dibri told Hart that Qadhafi would turn over the Lockerbie suspects in exchange for an agreement to begin talks on normalization and lifting sanctions. Hart later complained that the Bush administration was dismissive of this offer, almost unreasonably so. "We might have brought the Pan Am bombers to justice, and quite possibly have moved Libya out of its renegade status, much sooner than we have," he wrote.[20] In giving the benefit of the doubt to Qadhafi, Hart followed a common pattern in U.S. engagement with rogue leaders: ambitious intermediaries place greater faith in their adversary's goodwill than in their own president.

At its core, the Libya debate was nonpartisan. Clinton also kept U.S. relations with Libya on ice, largely due to concern about Libya's WMD ambitions. In 1995, the IAEA found that Libya had made a "strategic decision to reinvigorate its nuclear activities, including gas centrifuge uranium enrichment."[21] The following year, Congress passed the Iran-Libya Sanctions Act, which authorized the president to impose sanctions on any company investing more than $40 million annually in Libya's oil industry.

Diplomats often describe the United States and the United Kingdom as sharing a "special relationship," yet the two states seldom approach rogue regimes in a coordinated manner. While Washington was isolating Libya, London was reaching out to Qadhafi to get him to end his assistance for the Irish Republican Army.

For Qadhafi, however, it was the United States and not Britain that was the big prize. When the Hart channel did not produce, he turned to Milton Viorst, a former *Washington Post* and *New Yorker* writer sympathetic to Arab autocrats. Dibri invited Viorst to visit. Viorst dutifully fulfilled his role, meeting Qadhafi in the desert south of Sirte. The Libyan leader complained to him, "we want a reconciliation with America, but America doesn't want a reconciliation with us."[22] A Libyan diplomat, Abdulati Alobeidi, reported that he had tried reaching out to Washington, not only directly but also through Egypt, Morocco, Italy, and South Africa. No matter where he turned, Clinton rebuffed him.

Qadhafi wanted sanctions lifted as soon as the Lockerbie trial began. This would, however, have removed any leverage for collecting reparations. The stalemate continued until April 5, 1999, when Libya handed the two Lockerbie suspects over to Dutch authorities for trial under Scottish law in The Hague.

The State Department, meanwhile, concluded that Libya had "not been implicated in any international terrorist act for several years."[23] In 1999, and in response to demands passed to him through private channels, Qadhafi expelled the Abu Nidal Organization from its Libyan safe haven, from which it had targeted Jews and Westerners in Europe and the Middle East for almost twenty years.

Qadhafi's about-face was the result of accumulated sanctions and low oil prices, which weakened his ability to resist isolation. His acquiescence to the Lockerbie trial began the process of reconciliation. Even though the British had intercepted an illegal shipment of missile parts bound for Libya in May 1999, two months later London and Tripoli resumed diplomatic relations, which had been suspended fifteen years earlier.[24]

On January 31, 2001, the Scottish court convicted Abdelbaset Ali Mohamed al-Megrahi of downing Pan Am 103, but declared motive and Qadhafi's culpability beyond the scope of the case.[25] It was a convenient dodge, for it enabled the State Department to pretend the Libyan regime did not directly have American blood on its hands. Soon afterward, Assistant Secretary William Burns began secret talks with Qadhafi's regime.

In the wake of the 9/11 attacks, Qadhafi condemned al-Qaeda and positioned himself as an ally in the Bush administration's war against terrorism. "Despite political differences with America, it is a humanitarian obligation to offer condolences to the American people on this serious and horrible incident, which has aroused the conscience of humanity," he said.[26] Given his past support for a host of terrorist groups—ranging from the Irish Republican Army to myriad Palestinian factions to Abu Sayyaf in the Philippines—his about-face was rich, but American and British diplomats were willing to embrace the fiction.

While British and Libyan diplomats and parliamentarians traded trips, it was intelligence agents like Stephen Kappes, the CIA's deputy chief of covert operations, who carried out the substantive dialogue. The British press noted the irony that MI6 was not only negotiating with Musa Kusa, head of Libya's external security service, expelled from Britain two decades earlier for endorsing the murder of Libyan dissidents overseas, but also providing him with sensitive intelligence to use against members of an anti-Qadhafi Libyan terrorist group.[27] The State Department also dismissed outrage about Musa Kusa, whom Lockerbie victims believed was complicit in the attack. Publicly, spokesman Richard Boucher explained that neither the Libyans nor the Americans had vetted each other's delegations.[28] Privately, diplomats argued that most of Musa Kusa's intelligence benefited the United States. Dialogue means talking with enemies; rogues are not antiseptic partners.

Simultaneously, lawyers representing Lockerbie victim families began negotiating with the Libyan government for compensation. Only in August 2002 did Qadhafi agree "in principle" to pay compensation.[29] For U.S. and British officials, the families' suit was both helpful and problematic. The State Department traditionally opposes lawsuits against foreign governments for fear that, in an age of moral equivalence, foreigners will bring lawsuits against the United States too. Burns resented the actions of the victims' families, but they forced the State Department to take a firm line and hold Tripoli to account. This became apparent with the announcement of a deal that tied family compensation to the lifting of sanctions. The State Department had never expected linkage between the private settlement and government action. Only when it became evident that most families accepted the settlement did the State Department agree not to oppose the deal.[30]

Dialogue continued through the winter and into spring. Just because his aides were talking, however, did not mean that Qadhafi's intentions were clear. After all, both Iranian and Palestinian officials had engaged in dialogue that their political leadership later disavowed. There was a breakthrough in March 2003 when Qadhafi's son Saif al-Islam met three MI6 officers in a London hotel to discuss WMD. The next day, he flew to Burkina Faso to get his father's blessing to continue. Diplomatic footsie was over; Libya had decided to put its cards on the table. There followed a meeting between Musa Kusa and top MI6 and CIA officers to hash out issues that had festered since the Reagan administration.

Lockerbie remained the major obstacle in Libya's quest to end its isolation. By August 2003, Qadhafi decided he had had enough. He formally accepted responsibility for the bombing and agreed to compensate victims' families to the tune of $10 million for each passenger on Pan Am 103, a total of $2.7 billion to be placed in escrow. The agreement stipulated that money would be paid to each victim's family in installments: $4 million when the United Nations lifted sanctions, $4 million when the United States lifted economic sanctions not related to its terrorism list, and the final $2 million upon the State Department's removal of Libya from the list. When the Security Council voted to lift sanctions less than a month later, Libya made the first payments.

The restitution agreement was not officially approved by the United States, but it reflected Libya's agenda and laid out benchmarks for negotiations. The non-terrorism-related sanctions mostly concerned Libya's WMD program. The talks over WMD were already at their five-month mark, but American and British policymakers were still not certain that Qadhafi was sincere.

With Bush's blessing, Prime Minister Tony Blair sent a letter to Qadhafi on September 6, 2003, agreeing to end sanctions and begin military cooperation should he come clean on WMD.[31] Qadhafi, it turned out, was not acting on good faith. Unbeknownst to diplomats, intelligence analysts were tracking a shipment of nuclear equipment heading to Libya from a Malaysian factory affiliated with A. Q. Khan, the rogue Pakistani nuclear scientist. On October 3, 2003, German and Italian authorities acting on behalf of the Proliferation Security Initiative, a U.S.-backed multinational antiproliferation effort, intercepted the suspect ship and forced it to dock in Italy. On board, inspectors found parts bound for Libya's covert nuclear program. The discovery was a game changer. "The capture of the *BBC China* helped make clear to Libya that we had a lot of information about what it was doing," said John S. Wolf, the assistant secretary for nonproliferation at the time.[32]

While the incident showed that Qadhafi had engaged in bad faith, hindsight suggests that the interdiction convinced him that his deception was not worth it. Successful diplomacy requires not merely agreeing to sit with an adversary, but possessing superior intelligence. Engagement with a rogue should be a high-stakes poker game in which the United States can see its opponent's cards. The invasion of Iraq also shifted Qadhafi's cost-benefit analysis. Whereas Qadhafi may initially have tried to achieve a détente at a limited cost, perhaps by sacrificing only his chemical weapons programs, he came to realize the extent of U.S. intelligence, to understand that he could not hide weapons without consequence, and to acknowledge that on some subjects Bush did not bluff.[33]

On December 19, 2003, Qadhafi announced that Libya would come clean. At first he had resisted a full public declaration, but the American negotiating team insisted. As Robert Joseph explained, "The U.S. and U.K. participants believed that, without such a public acknowledgment and commitment, the strategic decision was absent or would be easily reversible."[34]

On January 18, 2004, Donald Mahley, deputy assistant secretary for arms control, led a team of experts to Libya to inventory its nuclear program components. Nine days later, the U.S. airlifted twenty-seven tons of documents and components relating to Libya's nuclear and ballistic missile programs. The team worked quickly, knowing that the mercurial Qadhafi might reverse course at any time. On March 6, 2004, a U.S. tanker sailed from Tripoli, removing additional equipment and Scud missiles that North Korea had sold to Libya. Two days later, U.S., British, and IAEA officials arranged to fly thirteen kilograms of highly enriched uranium to Russia.[35]

It did not take long for Washington to begin Qadhafi's rehabilitation. Even before Mahley had departed, Tom Lantos, the ranking minority member on the House International Relations Committee and a fierce advocate of engagement, became the first U.S. congressman in decades to visit Libya. On February 26, 2004, the Bush administration lifted the ban on American citizen travel to Libya, invited the Libyan government to open an interests section in Washington, and publicly urged more people-to-people exchanges. Finally, on March 23, 2004, Burns met Qadhafi, becoming the highest-ranking U.S. official to visit Libya in thirty-five years. The *Washington Post* described the atmosphere at the State Department as "almost giddy."[36] Not all was well, however. Qadhafi was still dragging his feet on compensating terror victims. He knew that once the Western floodgates were opened, it would be difficult for the White House to close them again.

In the face of the diplomatic progress to that point, it was easy for American diplomats to believe Qadhafi was a changed man. But while the Libyan strongman had agreed to pay compensation for those he murdered over Lockerbie, among other attacks, he refused to accept that the penalty was due to terrorism. A day after Libyan negotiators agreed to compensate the disco bombing victims, Saleh Abd Ussalam, the head of Libya's quasi-governmental Qadhafi Foundation, demanded that Washington pay it compensation for the 1986 airstrikes on Libya.[37] "The families of the victims stress the need to prosecute those who caused their losses, and also the need for them to obtain their civil rights in terms of compensation," according to Libyan television.[38]

Qadhafi was correct in concluding that he could backslide with impunity. On April 23, 2004, Bush terminated the Libya component of the Iran-Libya Sanctions Act, lifted a ban on U.S. commercial investment in the Libyan oil industry, and dropped Washington's longstanding objection to Libyan membership in the World Trade Organization. Qadhafi responded by demanding that Bush stand trial for the Abu Ghraib prison abuse scandal in Iraq.[39] Nevertheless, on June 28, 2004, the United States resumed diplomatic relations with Libya. Qadhafi responded by starting a legal defense fund for Saddam Hussein, the deposed Iraqi dictator.[40] Still, on September 20, after the Qadhafi Foundation agreed to pay compensation to the Lockerbie victims, Bush canceled executive orders imposed by Reagan and Clinton that had frozen Libyan assets in the United States, barred overflights and air links, and placed sanctions on Libya and prohibited importation into the United States of petroleum products refined in Libya. A year later, Bush issued waivers to allow export of military equipment to Libya. And, on May 15, 2006, Rice announced Washington's intention to send an ambassador to Tripoli at the end of the month. Libya remained as autocratic as ever, denying freedom of movement to American diplomats.[41] No matter—few Bush administration officials sought to talk to anyone beyond Qadhafi's immediate family.[42]

As the State Department removed Libya from its State Sponsors of Terrorism list, it lauded Libya's about-face. "Libya has responded in good faith not only in the area of international terrorism but also in the related field of weapons of mass destruction," the department announced, adding, "Libya is an important model to point to as we press for changes in policy by other countries (such as Iran, North Korea, and others), changes that are vital to U.S. national security interests and to international peace and security."[43]

If Washington moved fast to rehabilitate Qadhafi, London moved even faster. On March 25, 2004, Tony Blair became the first British leader to visit Libya since Winston Churchill went there during World War II. Blair, perhaps too eager, allowed Qadhafi to stage-manage the encounter. Libyan television broadcast the meeting as Qadhafi pointed the sole of his shoe, a traditional sign of disdain, toward his partner in peace.[44] Nevertheless, Blair was followed to Libya by a half dozen other ministers.

After every major meeting, Qadhafi instigated a crisis. On May 6, 2004, a Libyan court sentenced five Bulgarian nurses and a Palestinian doctor to death on charges of infecting several hundred Libyan children with HIV, even though the French doctor who first identified the HIV outbreak concluded that it started a year before the Bulgarians' arrival. The Libyan government nevertheless used the scandal to demand $5.5 billion in compensation for the families. Despite the State Department's wishful thinking, Qadhafi had not reformed.

The Libyans claimed that delays in removing Libya from the terrorism list meant they need not make the final payment to Lockerbie victims. The reason for the delay, however, was Qadhafi's complicity in a plot to kill Crown Prince Abdullah bin Abdulaziz of Saudi Arabia. In August 2003, as Qadhafi was pledging his intent to change, British authorities questioned an American Muslim activist who had been stopped with $340,000 in a suitcase, and who admitted his involvement in the assassination plot. The Libyan foreign minister, Abdel Rahman Shalqam, called the allegation "completely unfounded," but Saudi authorities said a Libyan intelligence official in Saudi custody had corroborated the account and fingered Abdullah al-Sanusi, Qadhafi's brother-in-law and director of military intelligence, along with Musa Kusa, the chief interlocutor for American and British authorities.[45]

Even so, the State Department soon removed Libya from the terrorism list, albeit without an announcement.[46] Wishing to take the spotlight off its terror support, Libya made its final $1.5 billion payment on October 31, 2008. The White House was willing to turn a blind eye to terrorism for the sake of preserving the deal.

The deal, moreover, netted a profit for Qadhafi. Not only did Libya receive a flood of investment upon the lifting of sanctions, but the State Department actually provided Libya with aid for nonproliferation and antiterrorism programs, a curious use of taxpayer dollars given Libya's oil wealth.[47] Further, on August 14, 2008, Tripoli and Washington signed a comprehensive Claims Settlement Agreement, which allowed Libyan claimants to seek compensation for U.S. military strikes, in effect rewarding Qadhafi's past terror. Soon afterward, Rice visited Libya, the first secretary of state to do so since 1953.

Relations improved further under Obama, at least initially. While Qadhafi complained that normalization was not quick enough nor relations warm enough, Obama bestowed honors on the mercurial dictator that no predecessor ever had. On July 9, 2009, for example, Obama became the first U.S. president to meet Qadhafi as both attended the G8 summit dinner in L'Aquila, Italy. Less than a year later, the United States and Libya signed a trade and investment pact. Almost $60 billion in Libyan infrastructure projects was at stake.[48] Within two years, however, Obama would build a coalition against the rehabilitated rogue, supporting rebel forces who would capture and summarily kill the Libyan strongman.

Did Engagement Work?

Was it engagement alone that brought Libya in from the cold? Willingness to talk does not necessarily mean sincere engagement. Yasir Arafat, chairman of the Palestine Liberation Organization, won a Nobel Peace Prize for sitting with Israelis, yet he refused to abandon terrorism, and even after eight years of talks he simply walked away from the agreement his aides had accepted. Had U.S. diplomats rushed into negotiations with Qadhafi during the Clinton administration, Libya might have avoided accountability for the Lockerbie bombing.

Theories swirl as to why Qadhafi acted when he did. Years of sanctions played a role. One European diplomat told the *New York Times*, "He realized that Libya was on a path of international isolation and internal stagnation after 30 years of concentrated economic wrecking."[49] Qadhafi was also scared. In the wake of the 9/11 terrorist attacks, he reportedly began to "call every Arab leader on his Rolodex," worried that Bush would target him for retaliation much as Reagan had fifteen years earlier.[50]

The looming Iraq War also added to Qadhafi's anxiety. On February 11, 2003, the CIA director, George Tenet, reported that "Libya clearly intends to re-establish its offensive chemical weapons capability."[51] The Libyan press, reflecting the regime's mindset, warned that Bush might consider using nuclear weapons against Libya.[52] As U.S. troops advanced on Baghdad, John Bolton, under secretary for arms control and international security, suggested that the invasion of Iraq "sends a message that when the President of the United States says that all options are open in his determination to rid countries of weapons of mass destruction, that he is serious about it." Bolton singled out Libya, Iran, and Syria as countries that should learn a lesson from Iraq.[53]

The conservative commentator Charles Krauthammer argued that it would be counterfactual to ignore Iraq's importance. "After 18 years of American sanctions, Gaddafi randomly picks Dec. 19, 2003, as the day for his surrender. By amazing coincidence, Gaddafi's first message to Britain—principal U.S. war ally and conduit to White House war councils—occurs just days before the invasion of Iraq. And his final capitulation to U.S.-British terms occurs just five days after Saddam is fished out of a rat hole."[54] The conclusion was clear to Robert Joseph, senior director for nonproliferation in the National Security Council at the time: "Without the use of force in Iraq and the successful interdiction of the *BBC China*, the outcome almost certainly would have been different."[55]

Bush voiced similar logic in his 2004 State of the Union address when he said, "Nine months of intense negotiations involving the United States and Great Britain succeeded with Libya, while 12 years of diplomacy with Iraq did not. And one reason is clear: For diplomacy to be effective, words must be credible and no one can now doubt the word of America." For his part, Qadhafi himself had already hinted at the importance of Iraq in his own calculations, saying, "When Bush has finished with Iraq, we'll quickly have a clear idea of where he's going. It won't take long to find out if Iran, Saudi Arabia or Libya will be targets as well."[56] Libyan officials have subsequently confirmed the importance of Bush's mobilization against Iraq in Qadhafi's nuclear turnaround.[57]

The Iraq War was a polarizing moment, however. Many analysts, infected with "Bush Derangement Syndrome," refused to find any merit in Bush's policy. Ronald Bruce St. John, a historian of Libya, argued that Bush deserved no credit for the change in Qadhafi's behavior. "The bellicose policies of the Bush administration, as opposed to accelerating the long-anticipated change in Libyan policy, actually delayed it," he wrote, offering no evidence for his charge.[58] Still, some Bush critics grudgingly acknowledged that force played a part.[59]

Martin Indyk, a Clinton National Security Council official, spoke of how Qadhafi had actually offered to forfeit his WMD programs in May 1999 during secret negotiations. It is true that Qadhafi approached the administration, but had the White House agreed to engage at that time, it would have undercut the resolution of Lockerbie. It is a common malady among American diplomats to regard all engagement as beneficial. Too often, they believe that if they can entrap rogues in process—even insincere rogues—they can compel them to reach a resolution.

Libyan authorities approached Bush and Blair again in the spring of 2003, nine months before the eventual agreement.[60] Even then, Qadhafi was insincere, as the *BBC China* incident shows. Rather than abandon

WMD, he wanted to keep all options on the table. Through years of negotiation, he sought tactical diplomatic advantage, not sincere resolution.[61]

The Cost of Dialogue

While diplomats debate where credit should go for the dialogue that led Qadhafi to forfeit his WMD and reach a resolution of Lockerbie, there has been far less conversation about the cost of engagement. Certainly, it was a diplomatic coup to force Qadhafi to give up his nuclear program without a shot being fired. The CIA received a rare opportunity to calibrate its analysis to reality and found that it had underestimated the speed and sophistication of Qadhafi's missile program, the reach of A. Q. Khan's nuclear network, and the extent to which al-Qaeda welcomed Libyan members.[62]

If Qadhafi believed that Bush had an itchy trigger finger, and if sanctions had left him economically vulnerable, might the State Department have driven a harder bargain and demanded more concessions from Libya on terrorism and human rights? Seeking to avoid complications, U.S. officials refrained from criticizing Libya's human rights record too harshly. When Colin Powell said the United States had "no illusions about Colonel Qadhafi or the nature of his regime,"[63] Libya's foreign minister, Abdel Rahman Shalqam, threatened him with a lawsuit "because his statement implies insult and libel against all Libyans."[64] The following day, the Libyan daily *Az-Zahf al-Akhdar* printed a racist tirade against Powell.

The State Department traditionally avoids soapbox diplomacy and remains silent in the face of crude rhetoric; diplomats are conflict-averse. Following Libya's tirade, the State Department refrained from any serious criticism of human rights in Libya so as not to sour dialogue. The Bush administration did not speak out forcefully when Libya assumed the chairmanship of the UN Human Rights Commission in January 2003 beyond calling it "a rather odd choice."[65] Qadhafi concluded he had a free pass and proceeded to publish missives rebutting criticism of the human rights situation in Libya.[66] He grew so bold that he even called publicly for his supporters to "kill enemies" who sought political reform.[67]

In a 2003 study group report, the Atlantic Council argued that political reform need not be the focus of engagement, because it would naturally follow when Libya's isolation ended. Qadhafi's "arbitrary, authoritarian style is increasingly out of step with the rest of the world," argued Chester Crocker, a retired diplomat, and C. Richard Nelson, international security director at the Atlantic Council. "This suggests that more active engagement could influence changes in Libya more effectively than continued isolation."[68]

Major news outlets accepted Qadhafi's son Saif, the regime's chief interlocutor with the West, at face value. The *Washington Post* described Saif Qadhafi as defying hardliners to display a "commitment to political freedoms and free-market reforms," while the *New York Times* said he was aiming "to dismantle a legacy of Socialism and authoritarianism."[69]

Events proved them wrong. The decision to remain silent on human rights enabled rapprochement to continue apace, but dissidents like Fathi El-Jahmi paid the price. Libya's most prominent democracy advocate, El-Jahmi was imprisoned in 2002 for advocating free speech and democracy at a public meeting hosted by Qadhafi. When the Libyan government released El-Jahmi on March 12, 2004, it won White House praise. President Bush called his release "an encouraging step toward reform in Libya."[70] Two weeks later, however, Libyan security forces rearrested El-Jahmi after he spoke with Alhurra, a U.S.-funded satellite station, about his desire for democracy. Fearing that human rights advocacy could derail rapprochement, the White House declined to demand El-Jahmi's release. The Libyan government "have cautioned that they view discussion of individual cases as improper interference in their internal affairs," the American embassy in Libya warned Rice.[71] El-Jahmi languished in prison while the regime harassed his family. When he fell ill from chronic conditions, Qadhafi's regime refused him basic medical care. Through it all, the Bush administration remained largely silent. On May 21, 2009,

El-Jahmi died. State Department officials viewed his case as unfortunate, but saw in his death the possibility for better relations.

Libyan repression of El-Jahmi represented the rule rather than the exception. Bush's silence had a price. The Libyan government sponsored a pogrom against a large Berber town, and American diplomats avoided the issue so as not to antagonize the regime.[72] Regional dictators saw that they need not fear White House wrath, that Bush's rhetoric about democracy and dissent had become empty. Many realists argue that the human rights practices of other countries should not be an overriding U.S. policy concern, or that, at the very least, they should be subordinate to counterterrorism and counterproliferation. The human rights issue, however, has a direct impact on international credibility. Dispensing with it while possessing a strong hand means an opportunity lost.

Within the State Department, other motives may also have been at play. David Welch, assistant secretary for Near Eastern affairs and point man on Libya, retired from the Foreign Service in December 2008 and almost immediately began to work for Bechtel, helping the firm win lucrative contracts in Libya.[73] As Qadhafi gunned down dissidents three years later, Welch met with the Libyan strongman to help him avoid culpability. The revolving door with wealthy dictatorships creates a conflict of interest. Diplomats know that only those who cultivate good relations with autocratic rulers can expect a golden parachute. Had Welch antagonized Qadhafi too much with entreaties to free El-Jahmi, for example, he might have put his retirement at risk.

It is also unclear whether the State Department's engagement with Libya substantively altered Qadhafi's embrace of terrorism. The Libyan regime had already modified its behavior before it began direct engagement with U.S. diplomats.[74] And while it is true that Qadhafi cooperated with the United States with regard to the Libyan Islamic Fighting Group and al-Qaeda in the Islamic Maghreb, both of which targeted Qadhafi's regime, it was an exaggeration to call Libya "a top partner in combating transnational terrorism," as the American ambassador to Libya did.[75] Qadhafi continued to support other terror groups either materially or morally, from Abu Sayyaf in the Philippines to Palestinian groups fighting Israel. Qadhafi continued to welcome Ahmed Jibril's Popular Front for the Liberation of Palestine–General Command (PFLP-GC) at a time when the group still sponsored suicide bombings in Israel.[76] The British government reported that Libya sought to purchase 130,000 Kalashnikov semi-automatic rifles for questionable end users.[77] That the State Department did not require Qadhafi to accept a precise definition of terrorism allowed the regime a way to sidestep its commitments.

Qadhafi's subsequent actions underline the danger of believing that engagement alone changes behavior. As Qadhafi traveled through Europe on his first trip to the continent in fifteen years, he threatened to return to violence should he not get his way diplomatically. "We do hope that we shall not be obliged or forced one day to go back to those days where we bomb our cars or put explosive belts around our beds and around our women," he told a Brussels news conference.[78] The plot to assassinate Crown Prince Abdullah bin Abdulaziz of Saudi Arabia underscored his threats, and in January 2008, Iraqi officials accused Saif Qadhafi of sponsoring a group of foreign fighters who crossed into Iraq from Syria in order to conduct terrorism.[79]

Nor did it appear that Qadhafi had changed his stripes when it came to proliferation. While announcing, to diplomatic applause, that it would end its military trade with countries "of concern for the proliferation of weapons of mass destruction," Libya cheated, selling weaponry to Syria as that country was constructing a covert nuclear facility.[80] The list of equipment the Syrians wished to purchase from Libya left little doubt about their intentions.

The Syria episode was not Qadhafi's only bout of insincerity. On June 14, 2007, Libya canceled its contract with the United States to destroy its chemical weapons. Libyan officials blamed their reversal on the cost of clearing the chemical stockpiles, and laid blame on a grassroots environmental campaign.[81] The State Department, never letting discernment interfere with its public posture, continued to describe Libya as "a model of nonproliferation."[82]

If diplomats expected engagement to change Libyan behavior or usher in a period of Libyan responsibility, they were wrong. Questions over continued Libyan support for terrorism delayed the return of a U.S. ambassador to Tripoli until December 2008.[83] When the Libyan leader rose to the podium to address the United Nations General Assembly for the first time in September 2009, it was not the reformed Qadhafi but the old one, demanding $7.77 trillion in compensation from the West for its imperial crimes, and suggesting that swine flu was manufactured in a military laboratory.[84] American diplomats privately reported how tenuous Qadhafi's adherence to his agreements was, describing how the Libyan government sought to sell uranium yellowcake and also to keep highly enriched uranium, which it had agreed to dispose of in order to extract new concessions, including the provision of U.S. weaponry.[85] Indeed, as soon as Western leaders and the United Nations unfroze Libyan assets, Qadhafi began hoarding money to help him weather future rounds of sanctions.[86] His wholesale slaughter of Libyan civilians and wanton launching of Scud missiles at civilian population centers were the exclamation point to his insincerity.

* * *

The 2003 deal to bring Libya in from the cold became the marquee case to justify diplomacy with rogue regimes. The engagement clearly achieved its immediate goals: Qadhafi forfeited his nuclear program and agreed to compensate victims of Libyan terrorism. To credit engagement alone, however, would be naïve. Qadhafi treated U.S. diplomacy as credible only when he believed it his best option to avoid military force. Once America waivered in Iraq and he recognized second-term Bush administration rhetoric to be empty, his compliance with agreements fell short. While Bush was willing to deal with Qadhafi, he did so by sacrificing Libyan human rights. That might be a worthwhile price for U.S. national security, but it is irresponsible to pretend that the sacrifice of human rights is a price that does not need to be paid. Nor did diplomacy change Qadhafi's behavior. Even if talks did convince Qadhafi to strike a deal and stick by it, to believe that rogue leaders will ever change their personalities or behavior is fantasy. It was the Libyan people who demonstrated what Western diplomats never understood: the only way to end a rogue regime is to oust the rogue.

Chapter Five

TEA WITH THE TALIBAN

In spring 1994, Afghans from a small village outside Kandahar approached a local mullah to report that a nearby warlord's posse had kidnapped two girls, taken them back to their camp, and gang-raped them. The mullah, Mohammed Omar, gathered his students—*taliban* in Pashto—to rescue the girls and kill the perpetrators. The vigilante justice was extremely popular. Gathering new recruits and support from among a public long victimized by warlords, the Taliban steamrolled through a country exhausted by decades of war. In 1996 they seized Kabul, and by 1998 they controlled 90 percent of Afghanistan.

Almost from the time the movement emerged, American diplomats hoped to engage the Taliban. This desire outweighed concerns about legitimizing a group that was imposing a reign of terror against women and minorities, banning girls from school, and waging war on television and music. While only Pakistan, Saudi Arabia, and the United Arab Emirates recognized the Taliban formally, representatives of the Taliban argued that they were in Afghanistan to stay, that they brought stability, and that the Islamic Emirate of Afghanistan—the formal name of their regime—wished to have diplomatic relations with every state.

Within the Clinton administration, the Taliban's arguments had resonance. Afghanistan had been without a functioning U.S. embassy for almost two decades. The Taliban had restored stability, something neither the Soviet Union nor the mujahideen had done. True, the Taliban might execute women in soccer stadiums, but couldn't such issues be addressed through diplomacy? There was also the double-standard argument: The Taliban's social policies might be noxious, but they were little different from those of Saudi Arabia, a country with which the United States had tight relations.

First Impressions

American talks with the Taliban began just three months after the group emerged. Because the Taliban had caught everyone by surprise, diplomats and spies scrambled to figure out who they were, what they wanted, and the source of their support. In February 1995, American diplomats stationed in Pakistan met with seven high-ranking Taliban officials in Kandahar. The Taliban were willing to engage, but not to say much. The American diplomats observed that they "appeared well-disposed toward the United States," but the face-to-face meeting provided little clarity on their intentions.[1]

The meeting was just the first in a long series of discussions in which the Taliban played the State Department like a fiddle. That same week, for example, another diplomat met "a Taliban insider" who told him that the Taliban liked the United States, distrusted Saudi Arabia and Pakistan, and had no problem with holding elections in Afghanistan.[2] It was exactly what American officials wanted to hear. Diplomats say that learning about adversaries outweighs the negatives attached to sitting down with rogues, but seldom do they consider how the credulity of diplomats can spoil the gains. Their engagement may end up bolstering an adversary's public relations; or worse, it might skew intelligence. When taking tea with the Taliban, the State Department's hapless diplomats did both. After a year of meetings, it was clear that the Taliban were less concerned with counterterrorism than with improving their image. Indeed, they asked that an American diplomat "tell President Clinton and the West that we are not bad people."[3]

On September 27, 1996, the Taliban seized Kabul after promising international mediators that they would not. They immediately exacted bloody vengeance—seizing, emasculating, and hanging Najibullah, the former communist president, who had taken refuge in the UN compound. Despite the bad faith demonstrated by the Taliban's march on Kabul, the State Department instructed American diplomats that "We wish to engage the new Taliban 'interim government' at an early stage" and asked embassy officials to tell the Taliban, "We would like to make frequent trips to Kabul to stay in contact with your government."[4]

The talk went nowhere, as the Taliban simply lied. The American ambassador to Pakistan, Thomas W. Simons Jr., met with Mullah Ghaus, the Taliban's acting foreign minister, just six weeks after the group seized Kabul. Ghaus denied that Osama bin Laden was present in Afghanistan, and he suggested that the Taliban could be more helpful if they received U.S. funding.[5] What the Clinton administration saw as dialogue, the Taliban saw as an opportunity for extortion.

Nor was much of the American dialogue guided by any grand strategy. The American embassy in Pakistan sent other diplomats to meetings with the Taliban, even when the State Department had already passed the same messages to Taliban through liaisons such as Hamid Karzai, the future president, who at the time was a Taliban supporter at the United Nations.[6] By meeting repeatedly with Taliban representatives, the State Department broadcast symbolic recognition of the group to Afghans who might not be sophisticated enough to understand what formal recognition entailed. For all the discussion about engagement, there was little if any introspection within the Clinton administration on the frequency with which American diplomats should talk to the Taliban and the metrics by which they should judge progress.

The dialogue with the Taliban exposed another problem. The Taliban may have begun as a grassroots movement, but by the time they were on the outskirts of Kabul, Pakistan's Inter-Services Intelligence (ISI) had co-opted them and transformed them into its proxy. The Taliban admitted that they received Pakistani money, supplies, and advisors. The Pakistani foreign ministry even drafted some of the letters that the Taliban sent to foreign diplomats.[7] American diplomats, however, engaged Taliban representatives as if they represented only the Taliban regime and not Pakistani interests. In effect, American officials were like a cat batting a string, happy to ignore the hand dangling it.

Because the American dialogue with the Taliban had yielded no results on the terrorism front—the Taliban continued to protect Bin Laden—the State Department redoubled its efforts to talk. While in theory the State Department reserves meetings with senior officials for equals or as incentive for progress, Secretary Madeleine Albright dispatched an assistant secretary, Robin Raphel, even though there had been no progress. After capturing Kabul, the Taliban were determined to win recognition. Even if the United States was not willing to bestow it formally, showing the world that the Americans were coming to them was the next best thing. While Raphel chatted, the Taliban barred girls from school, banned women from the street, and implemented barbaric justice.

Nor did American diplomats make progress in stopping Taliban support of terrorism. The Taliban knew how to string Americans along. Wakil Ahmed Muttawakil, advisor to Mullah Omar, readily agreed to an American request to visit alleged terror camps. Diplomats reported success, but over subsequent weeks, the Taliban kept making excuses to delay the visit. First, it was Ramadan. Then, winter snows hampered travel. Finally, in the spring, the Taliban canceled the offer.[8] The whole episode took four months—during which al-Qaeda planned the East African embassy bombings. The delay for diplomacy was not only deadly but also completely unnecessary. After all, satellite imagery provided a more accurate picture than a Taliban-guided tour of sanitized camps would offer.

Even as the Taliban stonewalled diplomats over the terror training camps, an American delegation visited Kabul and Kandahar to ask senior Taliban leaders to expel Bin Laden. The Taliban simply denied any responsibility for the issue. Mullah Ehsanullah Ehsan, an influential member of the Taliban's governing council, categorically refused to expel Bin Laden. Quite the contrary, Mullah Omar said the Taliban "have to help Bin Laden because he is a good Islamic person, who is fighting the kaffirs (unbelievers)."[9]

American diplomats appeared to be living in a parallel universe. In the course of negotiations, more than a year into State Department engagement, Ambassador Simons wrote, "There is little evidence to suggest that Mullah Omar is an Islamic radical with an anti-Western agenda."[10] Donald Camp, the head of the American delegation, concluded that the Taliban's refusal to expel Bin Laden was actually a desire to engage.[11] Such is the culture of the State Department. Clinton and Albright rewarded Camp for his actions promoting dialogue with the Taliban, first with an appointment to the National Security Council and then with a promotion in the State Department.

Throughout its dialogue with the Taliban, American diplomats maintained an Afghan Coordination Group to discuss Afghanistan and American strategy. Even though the diplomats recognized that the Taliban negotiated in bad faith, they concluded that the best policy was more dialogue. "Not to engage the Taliban would be a mistake because such a policy will most likely leave them only more isolated, possibly more dangerous, and certainly more susceptible to those wishing to direct Taliban energies beyond Afghanistan," argued John Holzman, the number-two diplomat at the U.S. embassy in Pakistan.[12]

Such reasoning may be a staple of diplomacy, but no evidence supports it. Ending isolation does not moderate rogue regimes; it legitimizes them. Holzman's engagement did not diminish the Taliban's inclination to shelter terrorists and allow them to use Afghanistan as a safe haven from which to plan terrorist attacks.

Holzman was not so naïve as to embrace the Taliban without a test. He suggested that the State Department should fund projects in Taliban territory to test the group's goodwill. For example, he wrote, the United States might fund crop substitution programs to test Taliban willingness to crack down on opium, or finance girls' schools to test commitment to female education, something Taliban representatives said they would tolerate but not fund. Willingness to accept aid, however, does not demonstrate sincerity. Any assistance given to the Taliban regime increased its capacity to sponsor terror.

The State Department's inability to understand the Taliban and radical Islamism was encapsulated by Holzman's recommendation to promote engagement between the Taliban and "moderate Islamic states such as Saudi Arabia, Egypt, and perhaps Indonesia." This suggestion to encourage dialogue between the Taliban and Saudi Arabia, both prime enablers of al-Qaeda, demonstrates the danger of treating engagement as a cure-all.

Sharing the Spotlight with the Taliban

In the television age, ambitious politicians and diplomats make headlines by sitting down with rogues. Engagement with terrorist groups and their state sponsors brought fame and fortune to diplomats like Dennis Ross, Chris Hill, and William Burns; others wanted their shot, regardless of the strategic cost. On April 17, 1998, Bill Richardson, U.S. ambassador to the United Nations and a member of Clinton's cabinet, traveled to Afghanistan to meet the Taliban. He was the highest-ranking American to visit Afghanistan in twenty years.[13] Richardson aimed to get the Taliban to participate in peace talks to end Afghanistan's civil war. He played the press expertly. According to CNN, "Taliban, masters of a suffering people, took Bill Richardson's visit seriously."[14] After his meeting with the Taliban, Richardson said he succeeded where others had failed: the Taliban agreed to a ceasefire and to negotiations with rival Afghans. Agreeing to negotiate and doing so in good faith are two separate things, however. In the days after Richardson's "breakthrough," the Taliban and its rival, the Northern Alliance, engaged in some of the bloodiest fighting of the civil war—a war which, despite Richardson's triumphalism, continued up until the Twin Towers came crashing down.

Discussions with the Taliban did not occur only in Afghanistan and neighboring Pakistan, but also in the United States. Zalmay Khalilzad, a Reagan-era veteran of the State Department, tried to cultivate the Taliban in the hope of enabling a trans-Afghanistan oil pipeline. In 1997, the California-based oil company Unocal (which merged into Chevron in 2005) brought Taliban to the United States, where they were met not by junior diplomats, but by an assistant secretary of state, Karl Inderfurth.[15] Discussions broke no new ground: the Taliban dismissed criticism of their abuse of women by blaming Afghan culture. They understood that American diplomats embrace cultural relativism, so they could cite culture to blunt diplomatic censure.

In hindsight, the Inderfurth meeting shows just how rudderless was the Clinton administration's engagement and how unseriously it approached counterterrorism. Clinton argued after 9/11 that his administration had assigned a high priority to the fight against terrorism, but Inderfurth had actually delegated the discussion of terrorism to a subordinate, in effect signaling to the Taliban that they need not worry about American entreaties. When Inderfurth's deputy raised the issue, Amir Khan Mottaqi, the Taliban's acting minister of Islam and culture, lied outright, assuring the diplomat that they would not "allow terrorists to use Afghanistan as a base for terrorism."[16]

Truth was no obstacle for the Taliban. As evidence of goodwill, the Taliban's acting minister of mines and industry, Ahmad Jan, told the State Department that the Taliban had stopped Bin Laden from giving public interviews. The American diplomats were not agile enough to challenge the Talib's veracity. After all, CNN had aired a Bin Laden interview the previous spring, and the Taliban clearly did not muzzle him after that. In May 1998, just two months before the East African embassy bombings, ABC News aired an interview conducted with Bin Laden in Afghanistan, during which he said, "We have seen in the last decade the decline of the American government and the weakness of the American soldier who is ready to wage Cold Wars and unprepared to fight long wars."

When the Taliban lied, the State Department had a prescription: more talk. Thirteen days after the East African bombings, Clinton ordered a cruise missile strike on a factory in Sudan and a terrorist training camp in Afghanistan. Mullah Omar was outraged. The next day, a Taliban sympathizer—one who worked at Voice of America—approached Michael Malinkowski, the director of the Pakistan-Afghanistan-Bangladesh bureau, and asked whether he would speak to a top Taliban leader. Malinkowski agreed, and early the next morning he received a phone call from Mullah Omar. The Taliban leader, frightened by the cruise missile attacks, denied that Bin Laden had planned any terrorism while on Afghan soil and said he was "open to dialogue." Malinkowski's conclusion? The Taliban might finally talk seriously about Bin Laden. Malinkowski was realistic enough, however, to warn that Mullah Omar's willingness to talk did not equal a willingness to do the right thing.[17]

The Taliban shifted their strategy over the following months. No longer would they stonewall on Bin Laden; rather, they told American diplomats what they wanted to hear. Mullah Omar took the lead. "There is no terrorist in our country, nor will we offer shelter to any terrorist," he declared, and repeated the canard that they had confiscated Bin Laden's communications gear.[18]

In a subsequent meeting, Abdul Hakim Mujahid, the Taliban's unofficial representative at the United Nations, adopted the same strategy: he outright lied. He assured Americans that few Afghans wanted Bin Laden in their country, and that 80 percent of the Taliban leadership also opposed his presence.[19] The icing on the cake was his pledge that the Taliban would protect the Buddhas of Bamiyan, a World Heritage site that the group infamously destroyed three years later.

As the Taliban's fear of reprisal receded, their rhetorical flexibility also declined. Mullah Omar accused the United States of opposing Bin Laden because Washington feared the rise of Islam. It may have been an outrageous statement, but Omar's offer of further dialogue was enough to mollify the State Department, which responded that it was willing "to engage in a serious and confidential dialogue with the Taliban."[20]

And so it was. Less than two months after the U.S. missile strike on the terrorist training camp, William Milam, the U.S. ambassador to Pakistan, met with Wakil Ahmed Muttawakil, the Taliban spokesman and chief aide to Mullah Omar. Little came of the meeting. Muttawakil repeated the canard that Afghan popular opinion would not allow the Taliban to expel Bin Laden, as if the Taliban were a democracy. Even though the Taliban's insincerity had led to the deaths of a dozen Americans—and hundreds of bystanders—the State Department continued the dialogue without demanding any Taliban concession. By doing so, it embraced the Taliban as a government rather than an umbrella group for terrorism. Despite the lack of progress, Milam counseled further diplomacy. "Now is the time to notch up the diplomatic—repeat—diplomatic pressure. . . . A political/diplomatic solution to Bin Laden's expulsion from Afghanistan may be a mite more possible now."[21] For the State Department, whether talks succeeded or failed was irrelevant because their prescription would be the same: more talk.

Meanwhile, the Taliban put American diplomats on the defensive, saying that if the Americans wanted Bin Laden expelled, they should prove the al-Qaeda leader's complicity in terrorism. With little discussion about whether it was wise to humor the Taliban, the State Department bent over backward to provide proof.[22] Nothing was good enough for the Taliban; they wanted the State Department to bless a Taliban trial for Bin Laden. When diplomats refused, the Taliban again invoked cultural relativism—kryptonite for diplomats—and accused Americans of implying that Islamic courts could not be trusted.[23] Diplomats would not walk away from stalemate, however. Inderfurth recommended that Washington leverage the Taliban's desire to break their isolation. "It may not be fruitful, but it is a low-cost strategy," he explained.[24] He was wrong. The cost of his strategy was to lay the groundwork for 9/11.

On November 20, 1998, a Taliban court dismissed the American evidence and acquitted Bin Laden. Taliban officials insisted that he was under control and could not plot terrorism from Afghanistan.[25] The State Department's reaction was predictable: more diplomacy. The following week, the American chargé d'affaires in Islamabad went to the house of the Taliban's ambassador in that city to meet Wakil Ahmed Muttawakil. While the State Department still preferred to advance diplomacy with carrots rather than sticks, Alan Eastham, the deputy chief of mission at the U.S. embassy in Islamabad, acknowledged the importance of coercion. "Since Wakil mentioned the possibility of further airstrikes a number of times, the Taliban may well fear that, once we decide the diplomatic track has run its course, we will once again pursue the military option," he wrote. Still, despite the Taliban's decision exculpating Bin Laden, Eastham found hope. "While it is possible that the Taliban are simply playing for time in seeking to reinvigorate the diplomatic track. . . . It is at least possible that they—some of them—are serious about finding a peaceful way out," he concluded, setting the stage for more engagement.[26]

There is no evidence, however, that the Taliban ever sought a peaceful way out. In subsequent months, they dug in their heels on Bin Laden.[27] As the United States renewed diplomacy and Mullah Omar understood that the threat of further retaliation was behind him, the Taliban broke other promises. They allowed both ABC News and Al Jazeera to interview Bin Laden. A State Department cable called Taliban promises "basically worthless," but still held out hope that dialogue could succeed.[28]

At no time did diplomats gauge progress against predetermined metrics. They were so committed to dialogue, they refused to believe it might fail. The CIA embraced the same conventional wisdom. Milt Bearden, the former CIA station chief in Pakistan, twice wrote op-eds urging American authorities to undertake "serious dialogue with the Taliban." He vouched for their sincerity. If diplomacy did not provide a breakthrough, it was because the United States had not tried hard enough.

By late 1999, U.S. patience was wearing thin. The Clinton administration threw its weight behind UN sanctions, first freezing Taliban assets and banning Afghanistan's airline from flying internationally, and then banning arms sales and military advisors, and calling for a reduction of Taliban diplomatic representation abroad. These measures were directed largely at Pakistan, the Taliban's lifeline.[29] The Clinton administration claimed success, but without Pakistani cooperation the sanctions were little more than cosmetic.

If the Taliban thought the United States was taking a more forceful tack, such a perception would have evaporated in the aftermath of the December 1999 hijacking of an Indian Airlines flight. When the Islamist terrorists diverted the plane to Kandahar, Mullah Omar personally helped the hijackers and replenished their weaponry.[30] The American reaction demonstrated a bankruptcy of ideas: Inderfurth met with senior Taliban officials to emphasize "the importance of continued dialogue."[31] There had been no shortage of talk, however. Abdul Salam Zaeef, the Taliban's ambassador in Pakistan, was well acquainted with his American counterpart.[32] If the Taliban were to expel Bin Laden, the American ambassador assured Zaeef, American recognition of the Taliban's Islamic Emirate would be quick.[33]

The Taliban had little interest in an immediate resolution. Like Iran, North Korea, and the Palestinians, they decided to gamble on the American elections. They understood that the American administration changes every four or eight years. New administrations are more apt to blame predecessors than adversaries for diplomacy's failure.

The gamble did not work this time. Soon after George W. Bush took office, Wakil Ahmed Muttawakil, then the Taliban foreign minister, sent a letter to Secretary Colin Powell seeking a new start.[34] The State Department instead ordered the Taliban to close its office in the United States. When Christina Rocca, assistant secretary for South Asia, met with the Taliban in August 2001, they were shocked by her tone. "During the conversation she flouted every diplomatic principle, and every single word she uttered was a threat, hidden or open," Zaeef complained.[35]

The Clinton administration had pursued the Taliban with fervor, sending diplomats and trusted advisors to meet Taliban representatives on almost three dozen occasions. Over the course of this five-year courtship, the State Department not only failed to win the Taliban over, but actually harmed American security. Diplomacy delayed alternative strategies. The Taliban refused to isolate, let alone expel, Bin Laden, and al-Qaeda metastasized. The regime lied unashamedly to American diplomats. In the run-up to 9/11, Taliban representatives assured America's diplomats, "Afghanistan has no intention to harm the United States of America now or in the future. We do not condone attacks of any kind against America and will prevent anyone from using Afghan soil to train for such an attack."[36] Clinton's diplomatic game would cost nearly three thousand lives.

Engagement Post-9/11

George W. Bush had no interest in engaging the Taliban, but he continued humanitarian aid.[37] Policymakers may draw a sharp line between humanitarian and other assistance, but money is fungible, so any aid helps rogues strengthen their grip. Meanwhile, the State Department counseled further accommodation with the Taliban. As the Pentagon began planning military operations to oust the movement from Afghanistan, Secretary Powell spoke of reaching out to "moderate Taliban leaders."[38]

Talking to the Taliban may have been subject to ridicule in the wake of 9/11, but with time, the idea has caught on among proponents of engagement. The talk show host Fareed Zakaria, for example, argued that while the United States differs with the Taliban on issues including democracy and women's rights, such differences never stopped the United States from talking with other Islamist groups or even Saudi Arabia.[39] This argument ignores how intertwined the Taliban and al-Qaeda have become.

Many advocates for dialogue also disregard the question of how the enemy interprets a willingness to talk. Ayman al-Zawahiri, who would assume command of al-Qaeda upon Bin Laden's death, called Afghan efforts to engage the Taliban "a sign of the government's weakness."[40] It is no secret that the American desire to engage the Taliban is proportional to the military difficulties facing U.S. forces.[41] In the waning weeks of Bush's presidency, the secretary of defense, Robert Gates, triggered speculation that the administration might approve talks with the Taliban when he commented, "There has to be ultimately—and I'll underscore ultimately—a reconciliation as part of a political outcome" to end the conflict in Afghanistan.[42]

The fact that Americans negotiate under fire does not pass unnoticed in the region. Tariq al-Humayid, the editor of *Asharq al-Awsat*, the Arab world's most important newspaper, wrote that the Obama administration "forgets that excessive leniency is a grave mistake, no less dangerous than extremism. . . . Openness for the sake of openness makes the situation more complicated and sends the wrong message."[43] A columnist for the paper's chief competitor, *Al-Hayat*, concluded that "The message that others can infer from the 'diplomacy of dialogue' pursued by the Obama administration is that extremism is the most effective way to attract the United States' attention."[44] The website of Gulbuddin Hekmatyar, a fierce Afghan warlord allied with the Taliban and al-Qaeda, described Obama's offer to negotiate with moderate Taliban as a sign of U.S. defeat.[45]

Hasan Rahmani, a close aide to Mullah Omar, remarked, "Today the Taliban are successful and the Americans and the NATO forces are in a state of defeat. The enemy wants to engage the Taliban and deviate their minds. Sometimes they offer talks, sometimes they offer other fake issues. The Taliban never ever tried for such talks, neither do we want these talks to be held."[46] The Taliban had a field day after NATO confirmed it had paid tens of thousands of dollars to an imposter claiming to be a Taliban leader.[47] The Taliban called it a "stigma on the forehead of the Americans and her allies," and explained, "Just as all the enemies' military technology, their soldiers, their dollars, and their various attempts failed and suffered bitter defeat, so did their intelligence plots and their base intrigues, which have become useless and vain."[48]

Despite the evidence that militants interpreted negotiation as weakness and an indication that terrorism works, American officials encouraged Afghan authorities to talk to the Taliban.[49] Mullah Omar derided Hamid Karzai, Afghanistan's president, for his attempts to engage the Taliban. At first he called Karzai "Shah Shuja," a figure known to all Afghans as a British puppet whose ouster in 1841 led to his own death and the worst defeat in Britain's history. As American forces prepared to withdraw from Afghanistan, he referred to Karzai as "Najibullah," the last communist leader of Afghanistan, who fell from power three years after the Soviet withdrawal and subsequently died a horrible death at Taliban hands. Still, as American officials pushed and prodded Karzai to reconcile with the Taliban, insurgency exploded. The perception of weakness creates its own reality. Afghans never lose wars; they simply defect to the winning side.[50]

Davood Moradian, a former advisor to Karzai, criticized engagement efforts for losing sight of objectives. Speaking in London, he argued that reconciliation "must address the needs and imperatives of Afghanistan. It should not become a means for speedy disengagement of international troops from Afghanistan." The aim of reconciliation, he said, "must be making the Taliban an irrelevant movement and dangerous totalitarian ideology, rather than further empowering and legitimizing them as a group."[51] Moradian also pointed to a misunderstanding of the Taliban among those counseling talk. "It is a Eurocentric and simplistic view to see the Taliban in its entirety as an indigenous and authentic Afghan or Pashtun movement and phenomenon," he said.[52] Ideology matters. The Taliban embrace a narrow and backward interpretation of Islam, and care little for the niceties of Western diplomacy. Engagement might work with adversaries who place similar faith in diplomacy, but the Taliban's ideology ruled out such a view.

Nevertheless, it has become a truism among Western diplomats that victory comes through negotiation rather than the battlefield. Des Browne, as the British defense secretary, argued, "There is no successful peace-building process in the world that has not been a continued engagement. People need to stay with these discussions . . . through their difficulties." According to Browne, "In Afghanistan, at some stage, the Taliban will need to be involved in the peace process because they are not going away any more than I suspect Hamas are going away in Palestine."[53] David Miliband, who served as foreign secretary, concurred and insisted that

"Dialogue is not appeasement."[54] British officials have taken the lead in engaging the Taliban, often justifying their approach by pointing to their experience negotiating with the Irish Republican Army.

This comparison is nonsense. Unlike the Taliban, the IRA had little state support, and Ireland is not Pakistan. Moreover, when the British government faced communist rebels in Malaya, it did not rely on negotiations; nor did it defend the Falkland Islands against the Argentine military with words.

Western officials who promote negotiation are too inclined to believe that terrorists are motivated by grievance. Graeme Lamb, the former head of Britain's elite SAS, for example, argued that U.S. and British forces might be better off if they addressed Afghanistan's grievances, which he implied were material rather than ideological.[55] Before a major reconciliation conference in January 2010, Rahimullah Yusufzai, a prominent Pakistani expert on the Taliban, ridiculed the Western belief that money rather than religious sentiment motivated the Taliban rank and file.[56] Moradian similarly chided the West for "ignoring the totalitarian ideology that the Taliban openly and proudly subscribes to." Moradian drew a parallel not to the IRA, but to more culturally relevant models, such as the Khawarajites, an extreme religious faction that wrought havoc in Muslim lands 1,300 years ago.[57]

During his campaign, Barack Obama suggested that dialogue with the Taliban "should be explored." Upon his election, Obama's Afghanistan "Dream Team" made rapprochement with the Taliban a priority.[58] "We will support efforts by the Afghan government to open the door to those Taliban who abandon violence and respect the human rights of their fellow citizens," he declared in a speech at West Point on December 1, 2009. Obama announced a small troop surge to help rid Afghanistan of al-Qaeda, but also a timeline for their withdrawal, explaining that "these additional American and international troops will allow us . . . to begin the transfer of our forces out of Afghanistan in July of 2011."[59] Although he subsequently bumped the withdrawal date to 2014, the political timeline to end America's Afghanistan adventure added impetus to the administration's efforts to engage the Taliban.

Secretary Hillary Clinton compared U.S. efforts to sit with the Taliban to Reagan's willingness to sit with the Soviet Union.[60] "You don't make peace with your friends," she explained. "You have to be willing to engage with your enemies if you expect to create a situation that ends an insurgency."[61] Even General David Petraeus argued that reconciliation was possible at least among some Taliban groups.[62] Whereas pundits had once criticized Colin Powell for suggesting talks with "moderate Taliban leaders," the Obama administration made that proposal seem mild. Pakistan's *Express Tribune* reported that the United States had made direct contact with Mullah Omar through a former Taliban spokesman whom U.S. forces had arrested in 2007. Personal ambition led the State Department to intensify outreach. Richard Holbrooke, having failed in his quest to become secretary of state, sought to lead talks with the Taliban in order to keep himself in the spotlight.[63] After Holbrooke's death, talks continued. Vice President Joe Biden went so far as to assert that "the Taliban per se is not our enemy."

The cost of America's Taliban diplomacy was exorbitant. The State Department aimed to set the right circumstances for success with unilateral concessions. It scrapped preconditions that the Taliban lay down their arms, accept the new Afghan constitution, and break from al-Qaeda, and it began to describe these instead as "necessary outcomes."[64] Obama's chief of staff said the U.S. goal in Afghanistan was simply "to leave."[65] The United States tried to split Taliban sanctions from al-Qaeda sanctions at the United Nations, a move that would pave the way for lifting sanctions entirely from the Taliban. The Obama administration also agreed to release Mullah Mohammed Fazl, a Taliban master terrorist responsible for a massacre of over one thousand Afghan Shi'ites, from Guantanamo Bay detention, even before negotiations began.

Pakistan's ISI sought to use the American outreach to the Taliban to catapult that group back into power. "If the United States wants to hold a political dialogue in Afghanistan, it should directly contact Mullah

Omar," commented Sultan Amir Tarar, a retired ISI brigadier general, adding, "Any effort to divide the Taliban will be unsuccessful."[66] The Taliban underlined their disdain for negotiations when they assassinated Burhanuddin Rabbani, the former president, who was Karzai's point man for reconciliation. In the wake of the killing, Clinton traveled to Afghanistan to urge Karzai to continue a dialogue that both he and the Taliban agreed was pointless. "We were actually talking to nobody," Karzai remarked.[67] He was right.

Moradian described the American agreement to enable the Taliban to open an office in Qatar as counterproductive. "We have given them political space, we have provided them with another source of funding and undermined the anti-Taliban forces," he said.[68] The Doha office did not lead to a breakthrough in diplomacy. One official who took part in talks with Maulvi Shahabuddin Dilawar, the Taliban's chief negotiator, concluded that diplomacy was a sideshow for the group. "You could tell Dilawar was surprised that everyone else was talking about coalitions and elections," said the official. "They still think they can win on the battlefield."[69] In order to jumpstart talks, Pakistan—with U.S. acquiescence—released Mullah Abdul Ghani Baradar, the Taliban's former number-two figure, whom a joint U.S.-Pakistani operation had captured in 2010.[70] Prior to his capture, Baradar had effectively led the Taliban insurgency. Rather than empower diplomacy, however, his release gave the insurgency a shot in the arm.

Desperation undercuts success. That Obama's timeline for withdrawal bolstered Taliban morale was one of the few things on which senior U.S. military leaders and their ISI counterparts could agree[71] U.S. Marine Commander James Conway observed that Obama's deadline "is probably giving our enemy sustenance. . . . In fact, we've intercepted communications that say, 'Hey, you know, we only need to hold out for so long.'"[72] Diplomats might believe that dialogue never hurts, but unless efforts are made to set the right circumstances, its costs are enormous and can be measured in lives. The Taliban themselves underlined this fact in October 2011 when they attacked both the U.S. embassy and a hotel frequented by foreigners. Clinton acknowledged that diplomats had sat down and talked with the very groups who subsequently targeted American civilians.[73]

* * *

Albert Einstein defined insanity as doing the same thing repeatedly while expecting different results. That definition also describes the American approach to the Taliban. Since 1995, shortly after the group erupted onto the scene, American diplomats have repeatedly reached out, hoping to resolve concerns about terrorism. The Taliban negotiating strategy has been consistent: string America along, demand concessions, but make no compromise. Rather than see diplomacy as laying out a path toward resolving conflict, the Taliban interpret American outreach as evidence that the United States is weak and irresolute. While it has become the mantra of diplomats that wars end with talks, the reality of the Taliban is that talks lead to war. The Clinton administration's Taliban outreach enabled al-Qaeda to maintain its safe haven long enough to plan and carry out a strike against the United States in September 2001. That the Obama administration now repeats Clinton's strategy does not bode well.

Even if the most recent outreach is successful from the State Department's standpoint, the price of that success will be huge. The Taliban seek not only partnership but dominance in Afghanistan. Peace may come in our time, but achieving it will require sacrificing basic human rights and empowering a radical, terror-embracing Islamist regime. For the United States to gamble its national security on getting Mullah Omar's signature on a piece of paper would be risky indeed.

Chapter Six

DOUBLE DEALING IN THE LAND OF THE PURE

Pakistan is not a rogue regime in the traditional sense. Shortly after its creation in 1947, it became an American ally. As India drifted closer to the Soviet Union, Pakistan gained an ever more important position in U.S. strategic calculations. Between 1954 and 1965, Pakistan received more than $1 billion in arms sales and defense assistance, a huge amount for the time.[1] Military exchanges between the United States and Pakistan were common. Cooperation only increased after the Soviet invasion of Afghanistan. It was not long until Pakistan became the third largest U.S. aid recipient, after Israel and Egypt.[2]

What makes the decades-long U.S.-Pakistani engagement noteworthy is that despite the close alliance and high-level cooperation, the two countries seldom share the same perception of strategic threats, national interest, or goals. Washington's relationship with Islamabad is marked by a distrust more often reserved for rogue regimes than for partners, and the population's attitude toward Americans is little better. Decades of war in Afghanistan have brought the relationship to the breaking point.

Cold War Embrace

Upon the 1947 partition of India, U.S. policymakers wanted to engage both India and Pakistan in order to create a bulwark against communism. The Cold War may have been the paramount U.S. concern, but for Pakistan, unresolved issues with India loomed larger. India successfully pushed Pakistani "volunteers" out of much of Kashmir, a majority Muslim province claimed by Pakistan but ruled by a Hindu who elected to remain part of India.

President Harry S. Truman officially sought to maintain neutrality between the two countries, although Pakistan—not without reason—believed he tilted to India. On October 30, 1947, the State Department rejected Pakistan's request for $2 billion in financial and military aid, which the Pakistani government said was necessary to guard against Soviet designs.[3] Pakistani leaders also felt slighted when, in October 1949, Truman invited Prime Minister Jawaharlal Nehru to visit Washington without offering a similar invitation to Pakistan's leader.

From Washington's perspective, the Pakistani desire for equal treatment was not realistic. India was four times Pakistan's size in both area and population. It enjoyed stable democratic institutions. Its victory over Pakistan in the 1947–1948 war reinforced its importance in the Cold War context. Americans hailed Mohandas Gandhi and Nehru as pioneers of freedom. Pakistan, in contrast, struggled with domestic strife. On September 11, 1948, its leader Muhammad Ali Jinnah died suddenly, leaving a leadership vacuum. Not only did India challenge its security, but so too did Afghanistan, which disputed Pakistani sovereignty over the North-West Frontier Province. U.S. officials were not blind to the anti-Americanism that many Pakistani intellectuals embraced.[4] In September 1947, one junior Pakistani official commented, "Now we have cleaned out the Hindus, we are going to clean out you Americans."[5] Truman's support for Israel's independence exacerbated animosity toward the United States. Moulvi Tamizuddin Khan, the deputy president of the Pakistani parliament, blustered, "Well-trained, fully-equipped Pakistani crusaders will soon be sent to the Palestine front to fight the Zionist aggressors."[6]

The upper reaches of the Pakistani government, however, sought alliance with the United States. They understood that Pakistan was between a rock and a hard place. Pakistan had essentially three foreign policy choices upon independence: It could follow a nonaligned policy like India, align itself with the Soviet bloc, or seek partnership with the West.[7] Because Pakistan had border disputes with India and Afghanistan, Pakistani officials concluded that an alliance was necessary to protect Pakistan from external aggression and to help it economically.[8] The old adage about an enemy's enemy being a friend also came into play. As Soviet authorities cultivated India, Pakistan drifted away from the socialist camp.

After Truman failed to win India's support in his anticommunist efforts, Washington pivoted toward Pakistan. Prime Minister Liaquat Ali Khan became the first Pakistani leader to visit Washington on May 3, 1950.[9]

Relations between the United States and Pakistan warmed considerably during Dwight D. Eisenhower's presidency.[10] John Foster Dulles, the secretary of state, denounced India's "neutralism" as "immoral."[11] On February 25, 1954, Eisenhower announced a large-scale military aid program to Pakistan.[12] Three months later, the United States and Pakistan signed a Mutual Defense Assistance Agreement over protests from both the Soviet Union and India.[13] The United States also provided Pakistan with its first nuclear reactor under Eisenhower's "Atoms for Peace" program. In 1954, Pakistan joined the U.S.-led Southeast Asia Treaty Organization, and the following year it joined the Baghdad Pact, soon to be renamed the Central Treaty Organization.[14] Finally, on March 6, 1959, the Pakistani government defied Soviet threats and signed an Agreement of Cooperation with the United States in which Washington committed to the "preservation of the independence and integrity of Pakistan" and agreed to take "appropriate action, including the use of armed forces . . . in order to assist the Government of Pakistan at its request."

This agreement was to become symbolic of the misunderstandings that would plague U.S.-Pakistani relations. The Pakistani government assumed that it had a solid U.S. guarantee to support Pakistan against future Indian aggression. Mohammad Ayub Khan, Pakistan's first native commander in chief and its second president, quipped that Pakistan had become "America's most allied ally in Asia."[15] The U.S. government, however, looked at the agreement only through its Cold War lens. When war between Pakistan and India erupted in 1965, the U.S. government not only refused to side with Pakistan, but also imposed an arms embargo on both sides.[16] Washington may have seen its actions as neutral, but the Pakistani view was quite otherwise. After all, India was larger and already had greater resources.[17] Therefore, penalizing Pakistan the same as India amounted to betrayal.

Pakistan appealed the U.S. decision, but Washington hunkered down. On April 12, 1967, the Pentagon announced that it would end both the U.S. Military Assistance Advisory Group in Pakistan and the U.S. Military Supply Mission in India. In retaliation, President Ayub Khan rejected President Lyndon Johnson's request for a lease extension on an airbase in Peshawar. "I concede that this facility is valuable to your country but by its very nature, it lays us open to the hostility and retaliation of powerful neighbours," Ayub wrote Johnson.[18] Evicting Americans from Peshawar, however, only diminished Pakistan's importance. In 1977, two years before he would be killed in Afghanistan, Adolph Dubs, deputy assistant secretary of state, said, "Direct U.S. security interests in South Asia are limited. We have no military bases on the subcontinent and we seek no bases."[19]

Richard Nixon entered office sympathetic to Pakistan. He had toured the globe after his 1960 and 1962 election defeats, and India treated him poorly. "The Nehrus treated him not only like a defeated governor of California, but also like one who had lost an election for dog catcher," recounted Senator Charles Percy. Pakistan, on the other hand, laid out the red carpet.[20]

Bilateral tension increased, however, after the United States tightened sanctions on both Pakistan and India after the 1971 war over East Pakistan, a conflict which culminated in Bangladesh's independence.[21]

While some historians speak of Nixon's tenure as representing the nadir of U.S.-India relations, Pakistanis, with aggrievement so engrained, sometimes suspect that Nixon was actually sympathetic to New Delhi.[22] Indeed, India's military procurement between 1965 and 1971 was four times that of Pakistan. The United States also delivered $4.2 billion in economic assistance to India over the course of those six years, whereas Pakistan received less than a third of that.

It was during this period that Pakistani leaders made a decision that still reverberates, and from which they cannot turn back: they redoubled their efforts to Islamize the society. Pakistan was founded upon Islamic identity, although what that meant in practice was never clear. Initially, Pakistanis were hardly radical. The new country's leaders had grown up in a diverse India, knew non-Muslims intimately, and were aware of the difficulty of any attempt to impose homogeneity upon society. The Pakistani people, for their part, were just as likely to embrace ethnic identity as religion. But the birth of Bangladesh was a humiliating defeat, and Pakistan's leaders concluded that ethnic identity could tear their country apart. They resolved to intensify the political and ideological embrace of Islam in order to unite the state. The number of madrasas teaching a radical brand of Islam exploded.[23] If in Turkey the military traditionally served as a bulwark against political Islam, in Pakistan the military became its catalyst.

In 1975, a Cold War calculus led the United States to reconsider its embargo. Secretary of State Henry Kissinger called the embargo "morally, politically, and symbolically improper" because the Soviet Union continued to arm India, causing Pakistan to fall further behind.[24] The damage was done, however; Pakistani resentment toward the United States now ran deep. While Washington saw everything through a Cold War lens, Pakistan judged its relations with the United States through a comparison with how the White House treated India. Prime Minister Zulfiqar Ali Bhutto complained that the U.S. Congress was hampering Pakistan's right of self-defense.[25]

From a Pakistani standpoint, U.S. policy was cynical and inconsistent. The United States "showed no hesitation in promoting her own self-interest at critical moments even when such actions went to the gross disadvantage of Pakistan," recalled General Khalid Mahmud Arif, a key aide to President Zia ul-Haq.[26] Washington was interested in engagement only when it needed something from Pakistan; when it did not, it would simply dismiss Pakistani concerns. Despite the Cold War equation, the State Department saw Pakistan as a strategic backwater until the Soviet invasion of Afghanistan.

Just a month before that invasion, relations between Washington and Islamabad had reached their nadir when a Pakistani mob burned the U.S. embassy in Islamabad and set fire to U.S. cultural centers in Lahore and Rawalpindi. The violence came after Ayatollah Khomeini, Iran's revolutionary leader, accused the United States and Israel of involvement in the seizure of the Grand Mosque in Mecca on November 20, 1979.[27] The embassy attack should have been a wake-up call to the growing attitude gap between the Pakistani government and its people.

The White House was willing to forget everything when Soviet tanks rolled into Afghanistan. Zbigniew Brzezinski, the national security advisor, and Warren Christopher, deputy secretary of state, offered $400 million in immediate assistance. The Pakistanis held out for more. Meanwhile, two presidential envoys flew to New Delhi on the same day to make the case for India to take a stand against the Soviet invasion, but they were rebuffed.[28] India's decision made the Americans dependent on Pakistan, a reality which Pakistan would exploit. Because Afghanistan was landlocked, Pakistan was in the catbird's seat. With Iran in revolutionary turmoil, Pakistan was the only route through which aid could flow to Afghanistan. Islamabad was not shy about setting its conditions: Pakistan would accept as much aid and weaponry as the United States, Saudi Arabia, and other countries could provide, but insisted on monopolizing the distribution. The result was that money flowed to the so-called Peshawar Seven, a loose coalition of mujahideen groups for whom Islamism trumped or at least colored Afghan nationalism. Starved of supplies, more moderate and liberal Afghan nationalist groups faded away, and Afghanistan's political culture changed permanently.

Only with hindsight was the Pakistani strategy's impact on Pakistan's own political culture apparent.

Atoms and Afghanistan

Prior to the U.S. occupation of Afghanistan in 2001, much of the tension in the U.S.-Pakistani relationship revolved around Pakistan's nuclear program. Pakistan saw Cold War interests as largely irrelevant to its program. Containing Soviet expansion may have been the consistent U.S. goal, but for Pakistan the chief nemesis lay to the east, where Pakistani forces stared down their Indian counterparts. Pakistani distrust of America did not compare to its suspicion of India.[29]

Pakistan initiated its nuclear program in 1955.[30] A decade later, Pakistan inaugurated its first nuclear reactor with U.S. assistance. Pakistani leaders were already determined to acquire a nuclear weapon. In 1965, Zulfiqar Ali Bhutto declared, "If India builds the bomb, we will eat grass and live, can even go hungry. But we will get one for our own. We have no alternative."[31] Pakistan's defeat in the Indo-Pakistani War of 1971 strengthened Bhutto's resolve. On January 20, 1972, he launched Project 706 to develop an atom bomb, even as Pakistani leaders assured U.S. officials that they did not seek such a capacity.[32] Denials continued even after India's nuclear test in 1974. While the Pakistani foreign minister, Aziz Ahmed, called India's test a "new threat to our security," he also said, "We will not use those facilities for what India has done."[33]

Pakistan's chief concern was strategic parity with India, but it was willing to engage America in order to seek advantage. Ahmed called for a U.S. "protective guarantee" against any Indian attack. No such guarantee was forthcoming; India and Pakistan had already fought three wars, and the United States was just extracting itself from Vietnam. Pakistani leaders then asked for weapons. Bhutto said that the resumption of American arms shipments would "blunt his nation's yearning to develop a nuclear device." A poor nation such as Pakistan, he said, did not "want to squander away limited resources" to develop a nuclear bomb. "If we are satisfied with our security requirements in conventional armaments, we would not hazard our economic future and promote an economic and social upheaval by diverting vast resources for a nuclear program," Bhutto claimed.[34]

Meanwhile, Pakistani officials pursued their nuclear aims without intermission. In March 1976, Pakistan signed an agreement with France for supply of a nuclear reprocessing plant.[35] The United States raised objections, but failed initially to persuade France to annul the deal. Thus Kissinger traveled to Pakistan in August 1976 with a tough message to Pakistani leaders to cancel the reprocessing plant deal. But neither Kissinger's warning nor his offer of A-7 aircraft convinced Bhutto to stop the reprocessing plant.[36]

Pakistani ambitions increased diplomatic tension. After Fred Iklé, director of the U.S. Arms Control and Disarmament Agency, told the Senate's Subcommittee on Arms Control that Pakistan's nuclear program aimed for building a nuclear weapon against India,[37] Bhutto angrily responded that "No individual or State had a right to dictate [to] another sovereign and independent state like Pakistan."[38]

President Jimmy Carter's emphasis on nonproliferation caused the diplomatic quarrel to go public. Carter saw nuclear proliferation as one of the greatest dangers to global security. Pakistan's assessment was the opposite. It viewed the acquisition of a nuclear weapon as essential for its security. Pakistani leaders also believed that acquiring a nuclear weapon would deter any Indian aggression. Congress, however, moved to ban economic and military assistance to Pakistan.[39] It was U.S. self-interest rather than principle that changed matters. Two days after the Red Army entered Afghanistan, Zbigniew Brzezinski, the national security advisor, wrote to Carter arguing that the Soviet action would necessitate a "review of our policy toward Pakistan, more guarantees to it, more arms aid, and, alas a decision that our security policy toward Pakistan cannot be dictated by our nonproliferation policy."[40] Carter agreed.

It was a view that Ronald Reagan took to heart. "I just don't think it's any of our business," he said when asked about Pakistan's nuclear ambitions.[41] He wanted nothing to interfere with the overriding objective to defeat the Soviets in Afghanistan. In December 1981, Congress waived antiproliferation sanctions in order to pave the way for a multibillion-dollar assistance package to Pakistan, including four hundred advanced F-16 fighter jets, which could be used against India, but would not have much use in Afghanistan.[42]

With the United States turning a blind eye to its behavior, Pakistan pushed ahead in its nuclear program. "We were allying with the United States in the Afghan war. The aid was coming," the rogue nuclear scientist A. Q. Khan recounted. "We asked General Zia and his team to go ahead with the test. . . . They argued that, since the United States had to overlook our nuclear program due to our support in the Afghan war, it was an opportunity for us to further develop the program. They said the tests could be conducted any time later."[43]

The Pakistani government was willing to tell American officials what they wanted to hear. "Pakistan will neither acquire nor produce a nuclear bomb," Zia ul-Haq asserted. But then he added, "Pakistan will never give up its right to acquire nuclear technology."[44] Indeed, the formula he enunciated—technology but no bomb—became the standard mantra for North Korea, Iran, and other regimes developing covert programs. In reality, however, Pakistan's quest for a nuclear bomb was proceeding apace. By 1984, Pakistan was nuclear-weapons capable.[45]

The United States toughened its stance on Pakistan only when the Red Army withdrew from Afghanistan in 1989. In October 1990, George H. W. Bush concluded that he could not certify to the Congress, as required by the 1985 Pressler Amendment, that "Pakistan does not possess a nuclear explosive device, is not developing a nuclear device, and is not acquiring goods to make such a device."[46] On October 1, 1990, Washington cut off its economic and military assistance to Pakistan over the nuclear issue.

Pakistan expressed dismay at the U.S. decision, but remained defiant. The chairman of the Pakistan Atomic Energy Commission, Munir Ahmed Khan, told a news conference that Pakistan "would never compromise its nuclear program for the sake of American aid." He vowed, "Aid or no aid, there will be no change in our nuclear program," and continued with the fiction that Pakistan was not at work on a bomb. Then he voiced publicly what nearly all Pakistani officials say privately: in the absence of a threat in Afghanistan, Washington considered Pakistan expendable.[47]

U.S. sanctions remained in place through the 1990s, as efforts to encourage Islamabad to sign the Non-Proliferation Treaty fell on deaf ears. On October 2, 1996, Prime Minister Benazir Bhutto told the UN General Assembly that Pakistan was "prepared to sign any and all nuclear treaties if India simultaneously signs with us," but warned that Pakistan would escalate its program in step with India's.[48]

Whereas American officials in the past were blunt in their warnings to Pakistan about its nuclear program, Clinton's team took a more conciliatory approach. After Bill Richardson traveled to Islamabad, the Pakistani media noted that "The team did not exhibit the same 'sound and fury' that has commonly remained a part and parcel of every US official or delegation visiting this part of the world."[49] Richardson emphasized commonalities rather than differences. The gentle approach may have avoided confrontation, but it also led to confusion, as Pakistanis concluded that the nuclear issue was no longer a top U.S. priority.[50]

Nothing was further from the truth. Between May 11 and 13, 1998, India tested five nuclear devices. Madeleine Albright pleaded for Pakistani restraint.[51] On May 28, Islamabad announced that it too had successfully tested five nuclear devices. Two days later, Pakistan conducted an additional test, and the United States slapped on new sanctions.[52] The nuclear blasts sent U.S.-Pakistani relations to a new nadir.[53] "The U.S. decision . . . is regrettable and without any justification," Pakistan's foreign minister said.[54] Ahmad Kamal, Pakistan's ambassador to the United Nations, blasted the sanctions as "discriminatory."[55] A commentary in *Jang*, Pakistan's largest-circulation Urdu-language daily, subsequently accused the United States of "double standard and hypocrisy" because Washington had not taken action against India's import of missile technology from Russia, a sentiment echoed by A. Q. Khan, who added Israel to the double standard.[56]

International condemnation infuriated Pakistanis, who contrasted it with the muted reaction to India's 1974 test. "While asking us to exercise restraint, powerful voices urged acceptance of the Indian weaponization as a *fait accompli*," Prime Minister Nawaz Sharif said indignantly.[57] Pervez Musharraf, president from 2001 to 2008, speculated that the fierce condemnation of Pakistan's nuclear program might be rooted in anti-Islam bias.[58] "The much stronger condemnation by the world in 1998 was surely because Pakistan was the first Muslim state to go nuclear," he asserted. "This is perceived in Pakistan as very unfair. Surely any state whose chief rival has the bomb would want to do what we did. After all, we knew we could not count on American protection alone."[59] Many Western diplomats see their Pakistani counterparts as relatively secular; after all, Pakistani diplomats have traditionally been effete, and they also stock the best whiskey. Religion shapes culture, however, all the more so in a country founded solely on religious identity.

"What matters is that we are now a nuclear weapons state and we have lived to tell the tale," a senior Pakistani diplomat said defiantly.[60] The consensus within the U.S. government, regardless of administration, was that Pakistan's nuclear weapons undermined regional security. This was not simply because Pakistan is a Muslim country; American policymakers feared that Kashmir could become a flashpoint to nuclear war. Pakistani proliferation of nuclear technology also worried Washington. The Pakistani government not surprisingly came to a different conclusion about the value of a nuclear deterrent. Musharraf would credit Pakistan's nuclear capability for bringing quiet, if not peace. "We have mobilized significant forces twice, in 1999 and 2002," he later wrote, and suggested, "it may be that our mutual deterrent has stopped us from plunging into full-scale war."[61] But when discussions turned to conventional weaponry, at no time did Islamabad recognize that India, facing a threat from China, needed a larger arsenal.[62]

With the United States and Pakistan on such radically different pages, relations were strained through the remainder of Clinton's administration. The two countries were allies in name only. In April 2000, the head of the ISI, Lieutenant General Mahmud Ahmed, visited Washington. The number-three diplomat at the State Department, Thomas Pickering, told him bluntly, "The Taliban were harboring terrorists who killed Americans. People who do that are our enemies, and people who support those people will be treated as our enemies."[63] To Americans, such an observation might be a statement of fact. To Pakistanis, it was a humiliating chastisement.[64]

The Post-9/11 Embrace

After the 9/11 attacks, the White House needed Pakistan, and desperately. On September 22, 2001, Bush waived the 1998 sanctions and declared Pakistan to be "America's closest non-NATO ally" in the war on terror. This waiver was not without consequence. It sent a damaging message to other nations aspiring to nuclear power: the West will reconcile itself to your nuclear ambitions when they need you. Pakistani officials, meanwhile, saw through the cynicism of it. Shamshad Ahmad, Pakistan's ambassador to the United Nations at the time, later wrote, "It has been our experience that as soon as the US achieves its objectives vis-à-vis Pakistan it loses interest in cooperating with us. . . . This sequence of 'highs and lows' turned into a love-hate relationship between the two countries. Every US 'engagement' with Pakistan was issue-specific and not based on any shared perspectives."[65]

Musharraf pledged to extend "unstinted cooperation" to the United States in the fight against terrorism.[66] Colin Powell remarked that Musharraf "abruptly turned our stalled relationship around."[67] Wendy Chamberlain, the American ambassador in Islamabad, also underscored Pakistan's about-face. "This is a spectacular transformation in Pakistan's diplomatic position. Just two months ago, Pakistan was internationally isolated and burdened with sanctions. Relations with the United States were often strained," she told two visiting senators. "That changed almost overnight with President Musharraf's decision to support wholeheartedly the war on terrorism, despite considerable domestic costs."[68]

The public posture may have changed, but the shift was not whole-hearted. Musharraf's government maintained its close ties to the Taliban.[69] There was no convergence of interests in the new partnership with the United States.[70] An editorial in the *Nation*, Pakistan's largest English-language daily, highlighted the belief among many Pakistanis that U.S. and Pakistani interests were diametrically opposed, and called any cooperation with the United States "a virtual surrender."[71] The ISI, for its part, sought to avert regime change in Afghanistan and instead force the Taliban to extradite Bin Laden and his top associates, and to close terror training camps—the same demands that the Taliban had consistently defied in their five-year engagement with the State Department.[72] U.S. patience had run out, though. "Our willingness to continue discussions ended September 11," the State Department said, while General Mahmud Ahmed, the ISI head, pleaded for negotiations—anything to preserve the Taliban regime.[73]

Eliminating the Taliban was not a Pakistani objective, and Islamabad was agnostic at best on al-Qaeda. Musharraf partnered with the United States for four reasons: security, economic revival, safety of nuclear and missile assets, and the Kashmir cause.[74] When Bush addressed a joint session of Congress, however, he was unequivocal. "Deliver to United States authorities all of the leaders of Al Qaeda who hide in your land," Bush warned the Taliban, or "share in their fate."[75] While Bush did not mention Pakistan directly, it was clearly on notice as the Taliban's chief foreign patron. Years later, Musharraf complained that Richard Armitage, the number two in the State Department, had told the ISI director that if Pakistan did not cooperate, it should "Be prepared to be bombed. Be prepared to go back to the Stone Age."[76] While the famously bombastic Armitage denied making any such statement, the accusation alone suggests just how far the gap between the two countries had grown.

As Pakistani leaders realized that it was impossible to save the Taliban's regime in the face of the U.S. onslaught, they aimed to influence a post-Taliban government. Islamabad's worst fear was that the Northern Alliance, a coalition consisting largely of non-Pashtun ethnic Afghans hostile to Pakistan and friendly to India, would consolidate control.[77] The irony, of course, was that American diplomats spent so much time talking to the Taliban directly and to Pakistan about the Taliban that many other countries assumed the United States was party to the Pakistan-Taliban shell game.[78]

Pakistani leaders hoped that, just as during the 1980s, the United States might defer formation of the new government to them. General Mahmud Ahmed, who was in Washington on 9/11, pleaded with George Tenet not to depend on the Northern Alliance.[79] The CIA director ignored his request. When the Pentagon launched the air assault against the Taliban on October 7, the Northern Alliance conducted operations on the ground, sparking an outcry in Pakistan.[80]

Addressing Pakistan a day after the U.S. began military operations in Afghanistan, Musharraf acknowledged his government's failure to broker negotiations between the United States and the Taliban. He promised that the U.S. military campaign would be "short," "targeted," and without collateral damage, and he warned both Bush and Blair against allowing the Northern Alliance to take control of Kabul after the Taliban's defeat.[81]

But as U.S. forces and the Northern Alliance advanced, even those who backed Musharraf's decision to join the United States in the war on terrorism reconsidered their decisions. General Hamid Gul, a former ISI chief and the Taliban's chief patron, had, for practical reasons, initially endorsed Musharraf's support for the United States in the war against terror, but as the Northern Alliance swept into Kabul, he changed his tune and endorsed "jihad against U.S. aggression." He began to spin wild conspiracy theories about U.S. motivations and argued that Israel, not al-Qaeda, had struck the Twin Towers.[82]

Powell traveled to Islamabad on October 15 to ease Pakistan's concern about post-Taliban governance. He promised Musharraf that "the U.S.

supports the formation of a broadbased government in Afghanistan, friendly to its neighbors."[83] To the Pakistanis, this required the Taliban's inclusion. Indeed, the ISI welcomed the Taliban's foreign minister to Islamabad the same day as Powell visited.[84] Powell's acquiescence to Pakistan's suggestion that "moderate Taliban" be included in Afghanistan's government, however, sparked outrage in the United States.[85] Albright criticized the idea, saying, "I would be very wary of what kind of Taliban I would include in a coalition government."[86] Others called "moderate Taliban" an "oxymoron."[87]

Appeasing Pakistan antagonized America's Afghan allies as well. "There is no place for the Taliban in the future Afghan government," said Abdul Vadud Kudus, a Northern Alliance official based in Tajikistan.[88] Abdullah Abdullah, the Northern Alliance foreign minister, echoed this view.[89] According to Gul Agha Shirzai, a Pashtun leader and the last pre-Taliban governor of Kandahar, "Powell is a good military person, but he doesn't understand politics."[90]

Rogues will read into diplomacy what they want. Pakistan took Powell's comments as a green light to help "moderate" Taliban assume power. General Ehsanul Haq met the Taliban's foreign minister, Wakil Ahmed Muttawakil, to urge him to seek a settlement with the United States.[91] The White House rejected his request for a ceasefire, saying, "There will be no negotiations. The president . . . does not think it would be constructive."[92] The 9/11 attacks convinced policymakers, at least temporarily, that diplomacy was no panacea.

As the Northern Alliance advanced on Kabul, Pakistani leaders scrambled to create a new Pashtun alliance as a counterbalance.[93] When Musharraf met Bush after the UN General Assembly in November 2001, the Pakistani leader called the Northern Alliance "a bunch of tribal thugs." Bush said he understood Pakistan's concern and said he would urge Northern Alliance leaders to remain outside Kabul. The meeting, however, accentuated the divergence between U.S. and Pakistani strategic outlooks. Musharraf's concern was Afghan and ethnic nationalism; he pushed for guarantees that Bush would prevent Northern Alliance consolidation across Afghanistan.[94] For Washington, on the other hand, the fight against radical Islam was priority number one.

When the Northern Alliance captured Kabul on November 13, Musharraf was frustrated and called for a multinational force led by Muslim countries to intervene. A Bush administration official called the proposal a nonstarter.[95] A Pakistani newspaper called the capture of Kabul "a strategic debacle" and quoted ISI officials as saying that "Pakistan's worst nightmare has come true."[96] According to Ahmed Rashid, a well-connected Pakistani journalist, the ISI told Pakistani media contacts that Bush had double-crossed them, that Mohammad Qasim Fahim and other Northern Alliance leaders were actually Indian agents, and that, in effect, India controlled Kabul.[97] Rawan Farhadi, the Northern Alliance's envoy to the United Nations, told a Pakistani newspaper on November 18 that the alliance had entered Kabul with U.S. support and advice—adding to the Pakistanis' anger at the Bush administration's "double-dealing."[98]

The Pakistanis did not have a monopoly on aggrievement at perceived double-dealing. When Prime Minister Benazir Bhutto visited Pyongyang in December 1993, Pakistani officials denied that her trip included any nuclear deal. In July 2002, however, U.S. spy satellites tracked a Pakistani military aircraft landing at a North Korean airport carrying a payload of ballistic missile parts. The incident caused fear in Washington about Pakistan's proliferation to North Korea. The plane used for transport, ironically, was American-built and had been provided to Pakistan to help it hunt down al-Qaeda members—indicating a diversion of resources intended for the fight against terrorism.[99] The American reaction was muted because Washington needed Islamabad's cooperation, but the incident shook U.S. confidence in Pakistan at senior levels. When word leaked of Pakistan supplying nuclear technology to Pyongyang, there was an extensive debate in Washington on how to act. "There was a lot of pressure not to embarrass Musharraf," one senior administration official recalled.[100] Powell made clear his displeasure to Musharraf, saying that Pakistan's dealings with North Korea were "improper, inappropriate and would have consequences."[101] Musharraf responded with a "400 percent assurance that Pakistan has not supplied any nuclear know-how to North Korea."[102]

Musharraf's assurance was worth considerably less than 400 percent, however. The United States imposed sanctions on Pakistan's Khan Research Laboratories, highlighting Pakistan's culpability in North Korea's nuclear program. Musharraf, oddly, acted aggrieved at Washington's failure to alert him to Pakistani cheating. "If they knew it earlier, they should have told us," he said. "Maybe a lot of things would not have happened."[103] Rogue regimes deny responsibility for their actions, and Musharraf's complaint fit the pattern. U.S. diplomacy, with its emphasis on cultural sensitivity and appeasing rogues, indirectly encourages the strategy of denial.

U.S. pressure catalyzed a backlash in Pakistan, where anti-Americanism increased sharply after 9/11. In 1999, 23 percent of Pakistanis had a favorable view of the United States; by 2003, only 13 percent did.[104] Shamshad Ahmad, a former Pakistani foreign minister, theorized that one reason for the decline was the fact that, in the wake of 9/11, the Pentagon and the CIA had supplanted the State Department as the face of American diplomacy in Pakistan.[105]

On March 14, 2003, Bush waived sanctions that had been in place since Musharraf's 1999 military coup, in order to shore up support for Musharraf and to win Pakistan's backing in the Security Council for the war in Iraq. Waiving sanctions allowed almost $250 million in U.S. aid money to flow to Pakistan. Islamabad welcomed the move. If diplomatic pronouncements are to be believed, it set everything right. "We welcome this decision, and it shows the warm relations between Pakistan and America," said the information minister, Sheikh Rashid Ahmad.[106] But reaction was different among the Pakistani opposition. On March 16, thirty religious parties called on the government to reject the U.S. aid. They reminded Musharraf that Zia ul-Haq had called $500 million in aid "mere peanuts," and they urged the government to reject the offer and instead to mimic North Korea's defiant stance.[107]

Pakistani promises were often meaningless. A. Q. Khan reportedly admitted that Musharraf knew about the technology transfers as they were occurring.[108] In February 2004, Iranian officials admitted that they too had received Pakistani assistance in uranium enrichment.[109]

Bush and Musharraf again conferred on the sidelines of the UN General Assembly. The meeting lasted an hour and was followed by another meeting in which George Tenet, the CIA director, gave Musharraf irrefutable evidence that Khan was selling nuclear technology to other states. Musharraf later described discovering Khan's role as the "most embarrassing" moment of his life and perhaps his "biggest challenge." Almost two weeks later, Armitage met Musharraf in Islamabad and requested both independent verification of Khan's subterfuge and punishment for the guilty scientists.[110] To emphasize the issue's importance, the CENTCOM commander John Abizaid traveled to Pakistan to repeat the demand. The decision to have parallel civilian and military delegations underlines the military's increasingly important diplomatic role.

It took another four months for the Pakistani authorities to arrest Khan, a period during which Pakistan's proliferation activities continued full steam. In November 2003, Musharraf traveled to China in an unsuccessful attempt to finalize a deal for building a new nuclear power plant in Pakistan. "The past belongs to Europe, the present belongs to the United States and the future belongs to Asia," Musharraf declared.[111] Only when the deal fell through did Islamabad begin to take action. If Pakistan was America's ally of last resort, the opposite was also true.

On December 10, Pakistani security forces arrested several nuclear scientists for transferring nuclear technology to Tehran. Politicians and the press attacked Musharraf for "obeying" the United States at the expense of Pakistan's national interest. Khurshid Ahmad Khan, a senator from a religious coalition, told reporters, "The rulers are pleasing Vajpayee [the Indian prime minister] and acting upon American dictates."[112] Islamabad and Washington might be talking directly, but they were hearing radically different things. For the Americans, the chief concern was nonproliferation, while for many Pakistani politicians, national pride and the rivalry with India stood paramount.

Toward the end of January 2004, Powell called Musharraf and said, "We are now going to talk general to general." Powell explained that Bush was going to make a speech about Libya and that the U.S. government could no longer hide A. Q. Khan's involvement in the transfer of nuclear technology. "You may want to—and I strongly recommend that you do—act," Powell told Pakistan's leader.[113] Musharraf complied. "We are carrying out a thorough investigation of any proliferation that may have been done by any individual for their personal financial gain," he announced at the World Economic Forum in Davos. "We will deal with them as anti-state elements."[114]

Just over a week later, Musharraf placed Khan, a popular hero, under house arrest. The rogue scientist confessed in a private meeting with Musharraf, but warned that he would "expose everyone and everything if he was made a scapegoat."[115] Khan reportedly said he had the approval of Mirza Aslan Beg, chief of the army, to assist Iran and claimed he had the support of two other former army chiefs in his North Korean deals.[116]

Musharraf struck a deal with Khan. In exchange for a public confession and acceptance of sole responsibility, Musharraf would grant a presidential pardon. Khan took the deal. In Pakistan's conspiratorial society, however, the belief took root that the entire episode was a U.S. plot to weaken Pakistan and threaten its nuclear capability. Senior government officials accepted the conspiracy as fact. "I fear Americans will demand joint custody of Pakistan's nuclear assets. Or they may say Pakistan will have to roll back," Hamid Gul said.[117] Thousands took to the streets to voice support for Khan. Qazi Hussain Ahmad, the leader of the Islamist Jamaat-e-Islami party, demanded that Musharraf step down for humiliating Khan. The rogue scientist's supporters began an effective domestic campaign to prevent any extradition.

The conspiracies metastasized. When Powell stopped in India on his way to Pakistan in March 2004, Pakistani politicians and press speculated that India had delivered dictates to Powell to implement upon arrival in Pakistan. A commentary in the nationalist Urdu daily *Nawa-i-Waqt* read, "It has been proved during the last few years that the United States, Israel and India together form a troika, whose targets, besides China, are Pakistan in particular and the Islamic world in general. It is for this very reason that Powell is visiting India first. There he will decide the agenda and then come to Pakistan for its implementation."[118]

Yousaf Raza Gilani, an important politician in the Pakistan Peoples Party, suggested that the United States was using proliferation concerns to justify attacking Iran and other countries, and argued that Islamabad should not tolerate any crackdown on Pakistani scientists. "The present government policies are absolutely against the Muslim world, Pakistan's security and dignity. . . . In Pakistan, the heroes of nuclear program are being humiliated."[119] Gilani's views were mainstream. In 2008, he became the prime minister. Within a year, his government had not only released A. Q. Khan, but also enabled him to hold a triumphant news conference.[120]

Loose Nukes

Through the Cold War, Pakistan was America's default ally. Pakistan's support for the Taliban and its nuclear subterfuge led American policymakers to reconsider. On July 18, 2005, Bush and the Indian prime minister, Manmohan Singh, released a joint statement declaring the end of the three-decade U.S. moratorium on nuclear trade with India, and announcing U.S. assistance to India's civilian nuclear program and the expansion of U.S.-Indian cooperation in energy and satellite technology. Congress quickly approved the deal. Pakistanis reacted angrily, especially as Washington offered no such deal to Islamabad.[121]

When the U.S. Congress approved the India deal less than three months later, Gilani sought a similar agreement.[122] The United States refused to extend Pakistan any nuclear cooperation not linked to greater security for Pakistan's nuclear arsenal. Amidst assassination attempts, coups, and Pakistan's radicalization, fear permeated the United States that

Pakistan might become the world's first nuclear state to fail, and that loose nuclear weapons could find their way into the hands of Islamist terrorists.

Between 2001 and 2007, the Bush administration provided Pakistan almost $100 million to secure its nuclear weapons.[123] Pakistan responded not by heightening security, but by building a new reactor capable of producing enough plutonium for forty to fifty nuclear weapons a year, representing a twenty-fold increase in capability, and by augmenting its arsenal's quality as well.[124] Pakistan refused to document its spending, to reveal weapon locations, or to detail its weapons and enrichment program. "This is an extremely sensitive matter in Pakistan," Musharraf explained. "We don't allow any foreign intrusion in our facilities."[125] Pakistanis believed the United States was aiming to dismantle their nuclear arsenal.[126] Pakistani officials, meanwhile, complained about American reports casting doubts on Pakistan's stewardship of its nuclear weapons.[127]

The Bush administration responded from the traditional American playbook. On one hand, it aimed to build a multilateral coalition to convince the Pakistanis of the error of their ways. On the other hand, it tried to offer money as an incentive. Strategies of this kind might have influenced Americans, but when applied to Pakistan they backfired. Gul scorned the idea of bringing international opinion to bear. "What is the international community?" he asked. "The one that I can see is a mafia in the service of the United States."[128]

Jamaat-e-Islami urged Gilani to refuse American aid if it came with strings attached to Pakistan's nuclear program.[129] He needed no such encouragement. Pakistan bluntly rebuffed an American request to return highly enriched uranium from a reactor that the Eisenhower administration had provided to Pakistan.[130] The Islamic parties lashed out at the U.S. offer of aid, arguing that it was a pretext to get hold of Pakistan's nuclear weapons. Maulana Fazlur Rahman, chief of Jamiat Ulema-e-Islam, accused the United States of using a "strategy of politics of fear" when it questioned the safety of Pakistan's nuclear assets.[131]

The Pakistanis responded with defiance and aggrievement. The foreign ministry suggested that the West was targeting Pakistan because it was a Muslim state with nuclear weapons.[132] Fazlur Rahman charged that Pakistan had become an "American colony" and that its "sovereignty and independence was sold cheaply."[133] The lesson should have been clear to Washington: throwing money at proliferators seldom constrains their arsenal or changes their anti-American attitudes.

The Relationship Unravels

Pakistanis resent their colonial era. Decades of British control instilled a complex that leads Pakistanis to interpret anything short of equality as an affront to their sovereignty. It was a political third rail that American policy often touched.

In the first eight years of war in Afghanistan, the United States paid Pakistan almost $9 billion for its military and logistical support, on top of $3 billion to support development, education, and health.[134] Rather than assuage Pakistani feelings, the money antagonized them. By the end of the Bush years, resentment was boiling over. "From the way the armed U.S. personnel have been wandering freely on our streets and towns, it appears as if Pakistan has become a U.S. colony," a columnist in a Lahore paper lamented.[135]

President Obama entered office convinced he would turn a new page. His aides assumed diplomatic problems to be more the fault of Bush than Pakistan. In October 2009, for example, Secretary Hillary Clinton assured a group of Pakistani students that there was "a huge difference" between Obama and Bush. "I spent my entire eight years in the Senate opposing him," she bragged. "So to me, it's like daylight and dark."[136] Alas, while the Pakistani students applauded her indictment of Bush, they were not partisan so much as anti-American.

On October 15, 2009, Obama signed the Kerry-Lugar Act into law as the cornerstone for a new Pakistan strategy, emphasizing civilian aid and development. The bill was generous. It would provide $7.5 billion to Pakistan for development but only on the condition that Pakistan would allow U.S. investigators direct access to Pakistani nationals involved in proliferation and ensure civilian authority over military promotions. Each year, the secretary of state would need to certify Pakistani counterterror cooperation.

Rather than welcome the cash, Pakistani politicians and the public reacted with fury. Less than one-sixth of Pakistanis supported accepting the aid because the strings attached would infringe on Pakistani sovereignty.[137] When Clinton called the Pakistani reaction "insulting" and "shocking," one Pakistani newspaper editor explained the "cultural gap": "When you're dealing with countries like Pakistan which are very sensitive about their own identity, which take a lot of pride in their so-called sovereignty, there needs to be some cultural sensitivity involved when you word your legislation, when you word your statements, when you word your interactions with our people, with our government."[138] Clinton, however, may have made matters worse when she appointed Richard Holbrooke, whom Pakistanis said often acted like a viceroy, to be her special representative to Pakistan and Afghanistan.[139]

Juxtaposing the cases of Aafia Siddiqui and Raymond Davis exacerbated both distrust and resentment. In July 2008, U.S. forces in Afghanistan arrested Siddiqui—a Pakistani national who was a U.S.-educated neuroscientist and wife of Khalid Sheikh Muhammad's nephew—on charges of terrorism. She was wounded during her interrogation after she allegedly grabbed an unattended rifle, and was subsequently extradited to New York, where she was sentenced to eighty-six years in prison.

In Pakistan, Siddiqui became a cause célèbre.[140] Pakistan's president, prime minister, and foreign minister all brought up her case with their American counterparts, and the Pakistani senate called on the United States to release her.[141] While the news of Siddiqui's arrest passed with little notice in the United States, her conviction led to widespread anti-American demonstrations, and to demands that Pakistani authorities suspend the delivery of supplies for the war effort in Afghanistan.[142] Her incarceration occupied headlines in Pakistan for months.

Pakistani umbrage increased after Raymond Davis, a CIA contractor, gunned down two Pakistanis he alleged were trying to rob him in January

2011. When Pakistani police arrested Davis—who did not have a diplomatic passport—the Americans demanded his release. According to a Pakistani monthly, "The tone adopted in the first statements from the US Embassy, and later on even the State Department, was not just insensitive. It had the touch of imperial Rome about it. The regret was muffled; the arrogance shone through: release our man or there will be consequences."[143]

The Davis case symbolized Pakistan's sensitivity to the inequality of its relationship with the United States. Newspapers contrasted the treatment Davis was receiving in prison with that of Pakistanis incarcerated in the same facility.[144] The leaders of Jamiat Ulema-e-Islam Punjab described Davis's punishment as "a question of the honor of the nation,"[145] while their clerics demanded his execution.[146] Other Pakistanis congratulated the ISI on so masterfully exploiting the Davis arrest in order to put the United States on the defensive and to renegotiate the terms of the U.S.-Pakistani relationship.[147]

When a Pakistani court freed Davis, and American officials whisked him out of the country, Pakistan erupted in demonstrations.[148] One Pakistan senator wrote, "The true face of the rulers has been unmasked before the entire world. Finally, the United States secured the release of its citizen, who is a criminal, while the Pakistani rulers fear even talking about their innocent national Dr. Aafia Siddiqui."[149] Mufti Muhammad Saifuddin, chairman of the Pakistan Shari'at Council in Islamabad, said that "Davis' release had slurred Pakistan's prestige and lowered heads of Muslims across the world."[150] Pakistani officials questioned why Pakistan had not traded Davis for Siddiqui.[151]

It was not only Pakistanis who resented the relationship, no matter how lucrative it might be. As the Taliban insurgency grew in Afghanistan, Washington's focus turned once again to Pakistan's support for the militants. Musharraf acknowledged that Islamabad did not share Washington's assessment of the Taliban. He drew a sharp distinction between al-Qaeda and the Taliban, which he alleged had popular support and recruitment driven by occupation.[152] Even relatively pro-American figures like Ashfaq

Parvez Kayani, the army chief of staff, suggested that the Taliban were a reality that needed to be accommodated.[153]

When the Pakistanis arrested senior Taliban leaders, they frustrated their American partners by breaking their promise to extradite them.[154] Nor did the arrests themselves show true Pakistani cooperation. When Pakistani security forces detained Taliban shadow governors, they exclusively went after those who were primarily Afghan nationalists and the least reliable in following Pakistani orders. Without exception, the ISI then installed Taliban replacements more loyal to Pakistani paymasters.

Behind the scenes, the Pakistani government reacted with umbrage to questions about its activity. When a congressional delegation questioned Musharraf on the ISI's role in Afghanistan, he rejoined, "We are not a banana republic and the ISI is not a rogue agency," adding that the ISI follows his orders.[155] If the ISI did subordinate itself to the presidency, that raised troubling questions about its involvement in terrorism, such as the July 2008 bombing of the Indian embassy in Kabul.[156] Likewise, the Haqqani network, a client of the ISI, was complicit in killing American troops.[157] And, as became apparent after the raid that killed Osama bin Laden on May 2, 2011, the ISI had been protecting the al-Qaeda fugitive in Abbottabad, the Pakistani equivalent of West Point.

Given the widespread suspicion that the Pakistani government subverted American goals in Afghanistan, the natural inclination of the U.S. embassy in Pakistan was to compromise. "We should ask what kind of government Islamabad can accept in Kabul," Ambassador Anne Patterson wrote in 2009, as the United States undertook its strategic review.[158]

* * *

Is Pakistan an ally? More than sixty years after Pakistan gained independence, there remains little institutionalized basis for the relationship, and decades of diplomacy have failed to repair it. There is a pervading awareness across the Pakistani political spectrum that Pakistan is an ally of last resort. "It is a fact that the more the United States engages with our government the angrier people get," the columnist Cyril Almeida observed after Clinton's visit to Islamabad.[159] Neither side trusts its partnership or the alliance. Each sees the other as guilty of betrayal. Part of the reason for this is that the United States traditionally views the relationship from a global perspective, while Pakistan's focus is regional. When engagement occurs, it is tentative and for limited duration.

The power differential defines the relationship. "The Americans are well aware of our weakness and they are taking advantage of the situation. This is what international diplomacy is all about," explained Abdul Sattar, a former Pakistani foreign minister.[160] According to Asaf Durrani, a former ISI chief, Musharraf's pledge to assist Bush in the wake of 9/11 was a tactical blunder. "We lost the bargaining power to defend Pakistani interests," he said. "Pakistan should have negotiated tougher. That's realism." It was perhaps following this logic that Pakistan decided in September 2010 to halt U.S. supply convoys to Afghanistan amidst a dispute over drone attacks in Pakistani territory.[161]

By any objective standard, Pakistan is a rogue regime. It sponsors terrorism, it maintains a secret nuclear program, and it promotes radical ideology antithetical to American interests. Even during periods of rapprochement, the United States and Pakistan act at cross-purposes. When the Pakistani government cooperates with U.S. objectives, it is more often due to pressure than to mutual objectives.[162]

American diplomacy with Pakistan ignites a volatile mix of insecurity and pride.[163] Pakistani figures resent American questions about Pakistan's terror sponsorship. While still ambassador to the United States, the liberal-minded Husain Haqqani sought to address U.S. suspicions about Pakistan. "Since the return of democracy in 2008, Pakistan has paid a terrible price for its commitment to fight terrorism. More Pakistanis have been killed by terrorism in the last two years than the number of civilians who died in New York's Twin Towers," he argued, adding, "Over the past nine years more Pakistanis than NATO troops have lost their lives fighting the Taliban."[164] This, of course, is like a bomb maker seeking sympathy for losing a finger in an explosion. Hamid Gul was blunter.

"The Pakistani Army is engaged today in fighting against its own people on behalf of US interests," he lamented.[165] Haqqani dismissed accusations about Gul's complicity in terrorism, arguing, "This is a man who hasn't held any position within Pakistani intelligence or the military for more than 20 years."[166]

It is in the nature of rogue regimes that often the most powerful figures hold no position in government, enabling the state to maintain plausible deniability for its actions. If diplomats look at Pakistan as it appears on paper, it might seem to be an ordinary country with an ordinary government. But behind the window dressing, the ISI is in charge, pursuing policies at odds with Pakistani diplomatic pronouncements and with international norms. As the ISI has consolidated power, it has lodged Pakistan firmly in the camp of rogues.

Chapter Seven

SITTING WITH SADDAM

In its first decades of independence, Iraq had a love-hate relationship with the United States. It joined President Dwight D. Eisenhower's Cold War alliance against the Soviet Union, but withdrew from the Baghdad Pact in 1959, a year after Abdul Karim Qasim overthrew the monarchy. In 1961, Qasim threatened to sever relations with Washington after the United States recognized Kuwait's independence. Six years later, after the Arab defeat in the Six-Day War, Baghdad followed through on its threat.

Saddam Hussein intrigued the State Department, however. "Hussein is a rather remarkable person," said Alfred Atherson, assistant secretary for Near Eastern affairs, in a meeting with Secretary Kissinger in April 1975. " . . . He's the Vice President of the Command Council, but he is running the show; and he's a very ruthless and—very recently, obviously—pragmatic, intelligent power."[1] When Kissinger met the Iraqi foreign minister, Sadoun Hamadi, in Paris later that year, he tried to lay the groundwork for reconciliation. "We do not think there is a basic clash of national interests between Iraq and the United States," Kissinger explained, adding, "we see no overwhelming obstacles on our side." From the Iraqi perspective, on the other hand, U.S. support for Israel was a deal breaker.[2] Kissinger, seeing Iraq as a Cold War prize and Saddam Hussein as the hope, abruptly withdrew American support for the Kurdish uprising in order to court Saddam.[3]

Jimmy Carter spoke of human rights, but when he entered office, his policy differed little from that of his predecessors. Seeking to restore relations around the world, Carter pursued ties with Baghdad. The secretary of state, Cyrus Vance, approached Hamadi to raise again the possibility of resuming relations; the Iraqis said no.[4] Next, Carter sent Philip C. Habib, a seasoned diplomat, to Baghdad. Again, Saddam Hussein rebuffed the overture.[5]

Grievances went both ways. Because of its support for Palestinian and European terrorist groups, the CIA included Iraq in its inaugural *Patterns of International Terrorism* report, which in turn led to the imposition of sanctions.[6] Ironically, it was the Iran-Iraq War that provided opportunity for reconciliation. On September 30, 1980, Secretary Edmund Muskie held a surprise meeting with Hamadi. Carter sought assurance that Saddam's war aims were limited, while Saddam worried—not without reason—that the White House might consider trading arms to Iran in exchange for the American hostages.[7]

Ronald Reagan initially continued Carter's efforts to engage Saddam. In April 1981, Secretary Alexander Haig sent a message to his counterpart asking for regular dialogue.[8] He dispatched Morris Draper, a midlevel diplomat, to Baghdad reiterating the desire to engage.[9] Saddam rejected proposals to re-establish relations, but the State Department was not dissuaded; engagement had become the end rather than the means. While Draper acknowledged that Iraq had no interest in formal relations, he insisted that he was "frankly pleased" with his trip because "the stage is set for a free dialogue."[10] There soon followed a meeting between Bill Eagleton, the U.S. chargé d'affaires in Baghdad, and Tariq Aziz, the Iraqi government's foreign policy spokesman—the highest-level meeting the U.S. interests section had held since the break in relations.[11]

Two months later, the State Department again tried to transform crisis into opportunity. On June 7, 1981, an Israeli airstrike destroyed the Iraqi nuclear reactor at Osirak, just eleven miles southeast of Baghdad. Rather than support Israel at the United Nations, Jeane J. Kirkpatrick, the U.S. ambassador to the UN, consulted with Hamadi on a resolution to condemn the Jewish state.[12] Punishing allies to ingratiate adversaries is historically a bipartisan strategy.

Wooing Iraq by condemning Israel failed. Saddam continued to rebuff America's embrace and refused to modify his behavior. In order to entice Baghdad, the State Department dropped Iraq from its list of terror sponsors.[13] The move had far less to do with any cessation of terror sponsorship than with enabling Iraq to receive export credits and U.S. arms.[14] Saddam responded by allowing the Palestinian terrorist Abu Nidal to re-establish his headquarters in Baghdad, four years after his expulsion.[15]

None of this stopped Reagan's outreach. Even after concluding in July 1982 that Iraq had used chemical weaponry against Iran, the administration remained silent, and the next year it extended almost a half billion dollars in credits to Iraq so Saddam Hussein's government could purchase agricultural goods.[16] Lawrence Eagleburger, under secretary for political affairs, welcomed his Iraqi counterpart, Ismat Kittani, in Washington to discuss both the war and the State Department's desire to exchange ambassadors.[17] Meanwhile, intelligence continued to flow in showing that Iraq had used chemical weapons.[18]

Saddam, however, had finally begun to respond positively to the American outreach, although the main reason was likely to have been the shifting fortunes of war. By 1983, Iran had expelled the Iraqi army from almost all Iranian territory and was threatening to go on the offensive. Just as Iranian setbacks during Iraq's initial invasion had led Khomeini to release his hostages, the possibility of military disaster brought Saddam around. In December 1983, Reagan dispatched Donald Rumsfeld, then working in the private sector, as a special envoy to meet with Saddam in Baghdad. The State Department reported that Saddam was pleased with Rumsfeld's visit and the letter he carried from the president: "His remarks removed whatever obstacles remained in the way of resuming diplomatic relations, but did not take the decision to do so."[19] Rumsfeld himself recalled, "I began to think [during the meeting] that through increased contacts we might be able to persuade the Iraqis to lean toward the United States and eventually modify their behavior."[20]

Dialogue continued throughout 1984, greased by the Reagan administration's decision to share military intelligence about Iran with Iraq.[21] The State Department did not want Iraq's use of chemical weapons to interfere with rapprochement.[22] When Kittani visited Washington, Eagleburger told him that Washington's condemnation of Iraqi chemical weapons use was routine and should not be taken too seriously.[23] In view of that condemnation, the State Department saw the second Rumsfeld mission in March 1984 as a barometer, telling him, "If Saddam or Tariq Aziz [the foreign minister] receives you against this background, it will be a noteworthy gesture of the [Iraqi government's] interest in keeping our relations on track."[24] The State Department made clear that Iraq's use of chemical weapons would not affect relations and even worked to minimize any UN action.[25]

The willingness to bend over backward for Saddam paid off. In October 1984, Saddam said he would resume diplomatic relations after the U.S. presidential elections.[26] Tariq Aziz flew to Washington, where he visited Reagan and George Shultz, the secretary of state, in the White House, and the two countries restored full diplomatic relations on November 26.[27] The Reagan administration began issuing export licenses for high-technology and dual-use goods. When some officials— most notably Richard Perle—raised alarms about the combination of lax export controls and Iraqi nuclear ambitions, they were overruled by Shultz and Caspar Weinberger, the secretary of defense, even though the Defense Intelligence Agency had concluded that Iraq would "probably pursue nuclear weapons."[28]

Playing Footsie with Saddam

Elite Washington society often treats engagement with rogues as chic and sophisticated. The Iraq experience was no different. In December 1985, the *Washington Post Magazine* gave a swooning account of a dinner party hosted by the new Iraqi ambassador, Nizar Hamdoon.[29] It was the first of many.[30]

Engagement had not changed the regime's behavior, though; it had only changed American tolerance for evil. When reports surfaced about the use of chemical weapons against Iraq's own Kurdish population, one American diplomat explained, "The approach we want to take is that, 'We want to have a good relationship with you, but that this sort of thing makes it very difficult.'"[31] It was a weak response, especially as Shultz moved to crush the Prevention of Genocide Act, a Senate bill to ban dual-use goods, stop Export-Import Bank credits, mandate U.S. opposition to IMF loans, and sanction Iraqi oil in order to punish the regime for using chemical weapons.[32] Hussein Kamil, Saddam's son-in-law, "vented his spleen for one and a half hours" because of the proposed sanctions, the U.S. embassy in Baghdad reported.[33]

Saddam's use of chemical weapons occurred after Iraqi engagement with the United States had begun. Once he understood that he could get away with murder, his chemical weapons use became more frequent. Far from moderating the Iraqi regime, engagement emboldened Saddam to believe himself immune from consequence.

It was not only Saddam's campaign against the Kurds that diplomats were willing to ignore. On May 17, 1987, an Iraqi warplane fired two missiles at the USS *Stark*, an American frigate in the Persian Gulf, killing thirty-seven sailors. Saddam apologized immediately. "I hope this unintentional incident will not affect our relations and the common desire to establish peace and stability in the region," he said.[34] Diplomats initially wanted to use the incident to strengthen ties between Washington and Baghdad. For example, Richard Murphy, an assistant secretary of state, proposed creating a joint inquiry with Iraq, and saved most of his criticism for China's supplying of anti-ship missiles to Iran. In effect, the State Department was giving Iraq a free pass.

As the Iran-Iraq stalemate was drawing to a close, Saddam realized he did not need the United States anymore. Washington may have sought rapprochement, but Baghdad's goals were situational. Soon the Iraqi government began dragging its feet on compensation to the *Stark* victims and the U.S. Navy.[35] The Pentagon accused the Iraqi government of stonewalling, but diplomacy clouded the U.S. response. Abraham Sofaer, the State Department's negotiator on the issue, swore that "the Iraqis now seem ready to engage in serious discussions."[36]

Tension also increased over Saddam's demands that American diplomats only meet with Iraqis approved by him. Tariq Aziz canceled a meeting with Shultz after mid-ranking U.S. diplomats met the Iraqi Kurdish leader Jalal Talabani.[37] Shortly afterward, Iraq expelled a U.S. diplomat whom it accused of meeting with Kurds.[38]

Diplomatic relations continued, and Iraqi embassy dinner parties remained A-list events for Washington society. On October 2, 1989, President George H. W. Bush signed a national security directive declaring, "Normal relations between the United States and Iraq would serve our longer-term interests," and calling for the U.S. government to provide economic and political incentives to increase influence and encourage Iraq to reform its behavior.[39] The directive did warn Iraq that further chemical weapons use or nuclear weapons development would endanger rapprochement. Not surprisingly, this "logic of accommodation," as the political scientist Bruce Jentleson labeled it, fell flat: Iraq did not temper its behavior in response to incentive offers, but grew more defiant.[40]

The Bush administration tried to temper Saddam in other ways. On February 15, 1990, after the Voice of America broadcast an editorial into several Arab countries celebrating the collapse of dictatorship in Eastern Europe and castigating Iraq as a member of a club whose leaders maintained power "by force and fear, not by the consent of the governed,"

Saddam was furious. The Bush administration, instead of defending the premise and maintaining moral clarity, apologized and decided that the secretary of state, James Baker, would personally clear future editorials.[41]

Any pretense that Saddam was moderating his regime evaporated with the execution of Farhad Bazoft, a journalist for London's *Observer*, on March 15, 1990, on espionage allegations. Saddam refused to speak with the British foreign secretary prior to carrying out his sentence. Adding insult to injury, the Iraqi government shipped Bazoft's body back to Heathrow Airport with a terse statement: "Mrs. Thatcher wanted him. We've sent him in a box."[42] U.S. diplomacy fared little better. In April 1990, the United States expelled an Iraqi diplomat involved in a plot to kill dissidents in the United States.[43] In light of this and Iraq's burgeoning weapons program, *U.S. News and World Report* branded Saddam "The World's Most Dangerous Man."

Still, proponents of engagement refused to give up. Senator Arlen Specter traveled twice to Baghdad to meet Saddam. So impressed was Specter with Saddam's air of sincerity that he helped block military sanctions on Iraq.[44] "There is an opportunity, or may be an opportunity, to pursue discussions with Iraq," he said two months later. "And I think that it is not the right time to impose sanctions."[45] Less than two months after that, in August 1990, Iraq invaded Kuwait. Only after several years had passed did Specter acknowledge that Saddam had exploited him and his Senate colleagues as useful idiots. Specter recalled,

> *I went to Baghdad twice, in 1989 and 1990. Senator Shelby and I met with Saddam Hussein and had a very productive meeting, I thought. When I got back to Washington, I urged Bob Dole to go to Iraq; he happened to be going to the Mideast in April 1990, so he arranged an ad hoc meeting in Baghdad. The Iraqis broadcast the transcript of that meeting. They got Howard Metzenbaum calling Saddam Hussein a man of peace, Alan Simpson saying he understood Saddam Hussein's problems with the press because he had similar problems.[46]*

The Kuwait Crisis

It was not only the senators who had egg on their faces after Iraq invaded Kuwait. The invasion was unexpected, but there had been warning signs. When Saddam had threatened force against Kuwait the previous month, the official U.S. response came not via the White House, but in the person of David Mack, a midlevel diplomat—leaving Saddam with the impression that the United States was not serious.[47] The following week, Ambassador April Glaspie told Saddam, "We have no opinion on the Arab-Arab conflicts, like your border disagreement with Kuwait."[48] Glaspie later insisted that she gave Saddam stern warnings, but the transcript of the meeting released by the Iraqi leader suggested the opposite.[49]

While Glaspie is rightly pilloried, it is unfair to make her the sole scapegoat. The State Department had instructed Glaspie to deliver a message of friendship from Bush to Saddam at her meeting. "I also welcome your statement that Iraq desires friendship, rather than confrontation with the United States," the message said. "My Administration continues to desire better relations with Iraq."[50] The Pentagon worried that Bush's request to the Iraqis to step back from their threats against Kuwait might lead Saddam to conclude that the United States would not confront Iraqi aggression. "We were already seeing troops moving," recalled Henry S. Rowen, the assistant secretary of defense. "We were getting worried and we were putting up this piece of pap. It was just very weak. We should have been much more threatening."[51] Diplomats, however, had dismissed the dissent.

The Kuwait debacle is instructive for another reason. Diplomats justify engagement with rogue regimes because they say it enables them to gauge personalities and thus enhances intelligence and provides a sense of intentions. Glaspie's meeting with Saddam defies this theory. She had concluded that "His emphasis that he wants peaceful settlement is surely sincere."[52]

Saddam favored engagement only because he believed he could play American diplomats for fools. He almost succeeded. Ten days after capturing the sheikhdom, he proposed talks to resolve the conflict. Top

U.S. advisors, including Richard Haass of the National Security Council, argued for diplomacy. Prime Minister Margaret Thatcher famously told Bush "don't go wobbly on me now" when he appeared to favor diplomacy in the wake of Iraq's invasion.

Bush did not shut the door on diplomacy, but he refused to reward violence with compromise. He first won a UN Security Council resolution demanding Iraqi withdrawal from Kuwait by January 15, 1991.[53] Then he invited Tariq Aziz to the White House and offered to send Baker to Baghdad. Any engagement, however, would be from a position of U.S. strength. The president deployed 250,000 U.S. troops in the region, along with 55 warships and 500 aircraft. "I don't think there will ever be a perception that the United States is going to blink in this situation," Bush asserted.[54] Saddam's Revolutionary Command Council complained, "The enemy of God, the arrogant President of the United States, George Bush, always rejected dialogue," but they understood the message. "Despite the fact that Bush's call for the meeting came after he had mobilized all the criminal forces on the holy places of the Arabs and Muslims . . . we accept the idea of the invitation and the meeting."[55]

Having agreed to engage, Saddam then repeatedly delayed Baker's visit in order to miss the January 15 deadline.[56] After his capture in December 2003, Saddam explained that Iraq's goal had been, in the words of his interrogator, "to exploit any chance for peace regarding the situation with Kuwait."[57] He understood that as soon as one ultimatum collapsed, other demands could crumble as well. Baker met Aziz in Geneva days before the deadline, but it was too little, too late. The war began on January 16, 1991, and the Iraqi army surrendered six weeks later. Bush left Saddam in power, believing that a weak Saddam was better than a leadership vacuum.

Prominent Democrats slammed Bush for his prewar attempts to woo Saddam. Al Gore opined, "If George Bush's prosecution of the war is part of his record, so too is his involvement in the diplomacy which led to it."[58] According to Joe Biden, "in his prewar diplomacy, President Bush was guilty of a sustained act of appeasement constituting a colossal foreign policy blunder."[59] The appeasement was made worse by subsequent discoveries of how much more advanced Iraq's nuclear program had been than the CIA realized.[60] Documents showed that the Iraqi government had deceived the IAEA about its nuclear program for more than a decade.[61]

If Bush thought defeat would humble Saddam, he was wrong. No sooner had the U.S. military released Republican Guard prisoners than Saddam ordered them into action against Iraq's own Shi'ite and Kurdish populations. Rolf Ekeus, the director of the United Nations Special Commission on Iraq (UNSCOM), complained that the Iraqi government was refusing to abide by a UN-mandated disarmament. Years later, Saddam said he refused to comply fully because "a country that accepts being violated will bring dishonor to its people." While the Security Council resolutions were cut-and-dried, Saddam believed he had a green light to quibble since negotiation is the "way of the UN."[62]

Courting Clinton

Bush's election defeat in 1992 diminished Saddam's willingness to make further concessions, since he considered Democrats to be weaker. In one of his first interviews as president, in fact, Bill Clinton signaled flexibility, saying, "If [Saddam] wants a different relationship with the United States and the United Nations, all he has to do is change his behavior."[63] Clinton quickly backtracked amidst a congressional uproar. "There is no difference in policy," he clarified. "I have no intention of normalizing relations with [Saddam]."[64]

To woo the new president, Saddam turned to Ramsey Clark, who had been Carter's intermediary to Khomeini and was a champion of radical causes. "I simply believe that we can pave the way for building new relations based on mutual respect and the exchange of legitimate interests regardless to what has happened," Saddam said.[65] It appeared to work. On March 27, 1993, Secretary of State Warren Christopher announced that the United States would "depersonalize" the conflict and would drop the demand that Saddam step down before lifting sanctions.[66] Rather than meet concession with concession, Baghdad doubled down on its defiance.

In April 1993, George H. W. Bush traveled to Kuwait to commemorate its liberation. Kuwaiti authorities rounded up a cell that was plotting to kill him with a car bomb. Two months later, Clinton responded with a cruise missile strike on the Iraqi Intelligence Service headquarters.

Iraq, meanwhile, not only refused to meet its postwar Security Council obligations, but again sent its forces to the Kuwaiti border, on October 7, 1994, apparently testing U.S. mettle. Christopher publicly noted that the United States had "adequate authority" in existing Security Council resolutions to attack Iraq again. "Next time we'll probably not wait. We will take action, strong action, against him," Christopher declared.[67] Facing a credible military threat, Iraq backed down and did not threaten its southern neighbor anymore.

Hostage diplomacy again brought Iraqi and U.S. officials face to face. In March 1995, Iraqi security forces seized two American defense contractors who strayed into Iraqi territory from Kuwait. Sentenced by an Iraqi court to eight years, they served 114 days before Bill Richardson, a congressman from New Mexico, flew to Baghdad to retrieve them. While American media lauded Richardson, his trip was not without cost: Saddam used it to depict Iraq as strong and America as weak. "President Saddam Hussein told Richardson that he accepts the pleas by Bill Clinton, the Congress and American people," the Iraqi News Agency reported.[68]

Clinton's Iraq policy was dominated by sanctions and inspections. Iraq resisted both. Speaking in the Senate, Biden implied that diplomacy must have a timeline and that the White House must gauge an adversary's sincerity. "Vigorous diplomacy has been pursued over the past three months, but, thus far, Saddam Hussein has shown that he has no interest in a peaceful solution on anything other than his own terms," he said. "We cannot allow this tyrant to prevail over the will of the international community."[69] Congressional doubts about the Clinton administration's backbone led to the passage of the Iraq Liberation Act, which called for the United States to support regime change.

Iraqi diplomats argued that American hostility toward Saddam was a problem. On October 19, 1998, for example, the Iraqi government delivered a letter to the Security Council chronicling American hostility. According to Iraq's foreign minister, American aircraft had violated Iraqi airspace almost 42,000 times, while American officials spoke about the desire to see Saddam's government fall.[70]

Iraq's refusal to comply with its international commitments culminated in Operation Desert Fox, a four-day bombing campaign to force Iraqi cooperation with international inspections. In the aftermath of the bombing, grievance became Saddam's major diplomatic theme. It is a strategy that serves rogues well. Iraq's trade minister claimed that the United States had prevented Iraq from purchasing "even one pill."[71] Any American officials who might be Jewish, such as Defense Secretary William Cohen, received special animus.[72] Anti-sanctions activists—some financed by the Iraqi regime—jumped on the remark made by Secretary of State Madeleine Albright, "we think the price is worth it," when she was confronted with the false claim that sanctions had killed 500,000 Iraqi children.

On February 11, 2000, Baghdad announced its refusal to allow United Nations weapons inspectors to return to Iraq. Across the American political spectrum, there was little patience for Iraqi defiance. Lee Hamilton, Brent Scowcroft, and James Schlesinger argued that the State Department should label Iraq rather than Iran the leading state sponsor of terrorism.[73] Senators criticized the Clinton administration for repeatedly scaling back demands in order to win fleeting Iraqi cooperation.[74] As Clinton's term wound down, there was no appetite for serious dialogue with Saddam either in the White House or in the Republican-controlled Senate.

September 11, 2001, was a paradigm shift. Saddam cheered the attacks on the United States, and his regime created a mural of Saddam, chomping a cigar, with the World Trade Center collapsing in the background. After his capture two years later, the Iraqi leader was not so haughty. He claimed that Tariq Aziz had written letters to American interlocutors like Ramsey Clark to denounce the attacks informally, and said he had wanted to have a relationship with Washington but the United States would not listen to anything he had to say.[75] This was nonsense, of course. When he believed himself to be strong or his adversaries uncertain or weak, his diplomatic strategy was to stall.[76] Aziz often preconditioned talks on easing U.S. pressure.[77] There was one exception: on December 8, 2002, in the face of U.S. military preparations, the Iraqi government released a 12,000-page document detailing the decommissioning of its WMD programs. Colin Powell, the secretary of state, dismissed the report out of hand. In the weeks before war began, Saddam again offered talks, saying, "I am ready to dialogue with Mr. Bush and to appear together before the television."[78] He would not get the opportunity. On March 21, 2003, American forces invaded Iraq.

* * *

It is an irony of America's relations with Saddam Hussein's Iraq that peace was inversely proportional to dialogue. Washington and Baghdad may not have been friendly during the period in which the two lacked diplomatic relations, but they respected well-established red lines. Problems began along with dialogue: as successive U.S. administrations courted Saddam, they empowered him, at least in his own mind.

The more that U.S. diplomats talked to them, the less the Iraqi authorities listened. What they did hear, they misinterpreted. Throughout the twelve-year period between Kuwait's liberation and the invasion of Iraq, Saddam consistently misread U.S. policy and determination. Tariq Aziz said Saddam was "very confident" that the United States would not attack Iraq, but if it did, he believed, the assault would be curtailed under international pressure. Part of the problem was that Iraq's totalitarian system reflected Saddam's rhetoric back at him. Even after U.S. troops invaded, Saddam believed his own propaganda.[79]

The Iraqis may have gone through the motions of dialogue periodically, but they were seldom sincere. Saddam may have disarmed in the months before the U.S. invasion, but years of deception made trust impossible. What disarmament did occur was the result of military coercion and sanctions. Iraqi documents seized after the 2003 invasion show that Saddam intended to reconstitute his WMD arsenal as soon as the United Nations lifted sanctions. Sometimes, a regime's character is so engrained in its leadership that only regime change can enable a new order.

Chapter Eight

HIJACKERS INTO PEACEMAKERS

The Palestine Liberation Organization (PLO) is the prototypical rogue. From its founding in May 1964 through the establishment of the Palestinian Authority three decades later, the PLO was synonymous with terrorism.

Soon after Yasir Arafat took the helm, the PLO began to commit spectacular acts of terror. On February 21, 1970, a PLO bomb destroyed a Swissair passenger jet in flight, killing forty-seven. The following September, the PLO hijacked three planes to the Jordanian desert. Terrorists answering to Arafat massacred the Israeli team during the 1972 Munich Olympics, in footage beamed around the globe. The following year, Arafat himself gave the order to execute Cleo A. Noel Jr., the U.S. ambassador to Sudan, whom Palestinian terrorists had earlier taken hostage.[1]

Through all this, the Palestinian issue remained outside respectable diplomatic parlors. As Henry Kissinger explained, "Before 1973, the PLO rarely intruded into international negotiations. In the 1972 communiqué ending Nixon's Moscow summit, there was no reference to Palestinians, much less to the PLO. . . . The idea of a Palestinian state run by the PLO was not a subject for serious discourse."[2]

It soon became one, however. Not long after Noel's murder, the PLO approached an aide to Richard Helms, the U.S. ambassador to Iran, who had been the director of the Central Intelligence Agency until shortly before. The PLO, Helms reported, sought dialogue. Arafat, it seemed, was willing to accept Israel's existence, but wished to bargain over Jordan's. After Kissinger demurred, Arafat persisted, approaching intermediaries in Morocco and Lebanon.

The Yom Kippur War was a watershed. The Arab invasion surprised Israel, which beat back the onslaught but at a tremendous cost in blood and treasure. More than 2,500 Israelis were killed, compared with fewer than 1,000 Israelis in the Six-Day War. Questions about its initial complacency brought down the Israeli government. Arab states may have failed in their aim to eradicate the Jewish state, but they inflicted enough damage to worry statesmen.

It was in this context that Kissinger authorized Vernon Walters, the CIA's deputy director, to meet with a PLO representative in Rabat. The meeting was not a success. With Israel's victory in the 1973 war, the PLO turned again on Jordan, which it considered weaker. Walters simply informed the PLO that the United States would stick by its friends. Washington saw the Palestinian question as an intra-Arab issue, not an international one. In his memoirs, Kissinger rationalized the dialogue, noting that negotiations took time and led the PLO to curtail attacks on Americans, at least briefly. He described the engagement as limited in extent: "As it turned out, the beginning of our dialogue with the PLO was also its end. There was only one more meeting, in March 1974, but it did not advance matters beyond the point of the first one."[3]

This was not quite true. The PLO and American intelligence maintained low-level ties in Beirut, where they engaged periodically on security issues.[4] Americans may have talked, but the PLO's notion of diplomacy was not identical to theirs. Addressing the United Nations, Arafat described diplomacy only as a supplement to armed struggle. "We are also expressing our faith in political and diplomatic struggle as complements, as enhancements of armed struggle," he said.[5] Kissinger's willingness to engage the PLO, even briefly, had opened Pandora's box. Once engagement with a rogue occurs, it is almost impossible to retract. Even when talks are suspended, the precedent leads inevitability to new talks. Hence, it was in the wake of the 1973 war that the "peace process" was born.[6]

After the 1974 Arab League summit recognized the PLO as the "sole legitimate representative of the Palestinian people," realists began to argue that the United States had no choice but to engage. No longer could the PLO be dismissed as just one among many groups. In September 1975, Kissinger pledged that the United States would not engage the PLO until it accepted UN Security Council Resolutions 242 and 338, which laid out the principles upon which the parties could negotiate a peace agreement. Congress later wrote this pledge into law.[7] Nevertheless, the CIA kept up its contacts, although it took pains to keep its channels covert.[8] This did not stop the PLO from trying to open an information office in Washington. In October 1976, two PLO members obtained visas under false pretenses to open the office. When the State Department learned of the subterfuge, it urged consulates to be on the lookout for PLO operatives.[9]

The PLO again made diplomatic headlines in the summer of 1979. On July 26, as the Security Council considered amending Resolution 242, Andrew Young, a civil rights hero whom Carter had appointed to be the U.S. ambassador to the United Nations, met secretly with Zehdi Terzi, the PLO's representative at the UN, ostensibly to determine whether there was any formula by which the PLO would accept 242.[10] Young had not cleared his meeting with the State Department or the White House. A day after Carter reprimanded him, Young resigned. He remained defiant, however, and sparked an international debate about the wisdom of the U.S. refusal to talk to the PLO. Carter, for his part, privately blamed the Israelis for the matter coming to a head.[11]

Carter had a soft spot for the PLO. It was the PLO to which he turned after Iranian revolutionaries seized the U.S. embassy in Tehran. While the State Department credited the PLO with winning the release of black and female hostages, a gesture the Iranians likely would have made regardless, it ignored the cost.[12] Not only did fifty-two diplomats remain hostage for another fourteen months, but diplomats also granted the PLO legitimacy at a time when it refused to abandon terrorism. Congress stepped in to constrain Carter's outreach, opposing both the UN Special Committee on Palestinian Rights and American participation in the International Monetary Fund if the PLO joined.[13]

When Reagan took office, it looked as if the PLO might be in decline. During his campaign, Reagan swore he would not negotiate with terrorists. The State Department had come to a different conclusion.[14] Even though Israel's 1982 Lebanon invasion dealt the PLO a defeat and forced its leadership into exile, the group remained committed to terrorism, most famously when a faction hijacked the cruise ship *Achille Lauro* in 1985. The execution, reportedly on Arafat's orders, of an elderly, wheelchair-bound American Jew reinforced the PLO's status as a pariah not only in Washington but to many previous sympathizers.[15]

That the PLO was a pariah, however, did not mean that Washington ignored it. Rather than gear policy to undermine the weakened PLO further, the State Department again engaged the group. At one point in 1985, U.S. diplomats were willing to accept the fiction of a joint Jordanian-PLO delegation so long as Arafat accepted Resolution 242, renounced terror, and acknowledged Israel's right to exist. At the last minute, Arafat refused even this, so talks were canceled.[16]

In the aftermath of the *Achille Lauro* hijacking, Congress passed the Anti-Terrorism Act of 1987, which formally declared the PLO to be a terrorist organization for purposes of U.S. law, and reinforced the prohibition on U.S. dialogue with the group. This act forced the State Department to close the PLO's offices in Washington, although the United Nations treaty protected the PLO offices in New York.

With the outbreak of the first intifada in December 1987, the PLO got a new lease on life. The next February, in the midst of almost daily violence, Mohamed Rabie, a Palestinian academic close to the PLO leadership, approached William Quandt, a Carter-era National Security

Council aide at the Brookings Institution. Rabie sought Quandt's help with an introduction to NSC officials to explore U.S. interest for dialogue with the PLO. This dialogue began on February 16, when Rabie met with Robert Oakley, the NSC's director for Near East affairs, and Dennis Ross, his deputy. While the meeting was polite—and, according to Rabie, Oakley agreed that Israel's occupation of the West Bank and Gaza Strip was untenable—Oakley listed two obstacles to dialogue. The first was the PLO's inability to speak with a unified voice, and the second was U.S. law that prohibited engagement with the PLO until it accepted UN Resolutions 242 and 338, renounced terrorism, and accepted Israel's right to exist.[17]

This did not mean that U.S. officials called a halt to indirect communication with the PLO. Diplomats maneuvered around the congressional prohibition on engagement by using intermediaries to pass oral messages. Every Arab capital the State Department used had its own competing objectives. As Rabie noted, "The PLO received as many different signals as the number of channels used. As a result of this Tower of Babel communications arrangement, the United States could not get straight answers to the questions it posed to the PLO. And the PLO could not understand the U.S. objective behind sending apparently contradictory messages."[18]

When, on July 31, 1988, King Hussein renounced Jordanian claims to the West Bank, he removed any pretense that Jordan could negotiate the fate of West Bank Palestinians. Proponents of engagement could claim that the Arab League's designation of the PLO as "the sole legitimate representative of the Palestinian people" was now true.

In the wake of Hussein's declaration, Rabie and Quandt sought to craft State Department and PLO statements that would fulfill the prerequisites to allow direct negotiation. Over subsequent weeks, Quandt served as middleman for the State Department, and Rabie served as Arafat's proxy. As these unofficial negotiations progressed, George Shultz briefed Reagan on the initiative, and on September 16, 1988, he told the Washington Institute for Near East Policy that "Palestinian political rights must also be recognized and addressed." He then defined the Reagan administration's position: "Our approach . . . calls for direct negotiations, launched—if required—through an international conference. It requires acceptance of 242 and 338 and renunciation of violence and terrorism."[19]

There was little discussion of the Palestinian issue in the run-up to the U.S. presidential elections of 1988. Less than two weeks after those elections, the Palestine National Council met in Algiers and issued a Palestinian Declaration of Independence, along with a political program. While it implicitly accepted Israel's existence and limited objectives to statehood in the West Bank, the Gaza Strip, and East Jerusalem, the declaration was vaguely worded and backtracked from the agreements that Rabie and Quandt had reached. The PLO seldom honored its own diplomatic deals. Still, the declaration pushed the Palestinian issue to the forefront of U.S. diplomatic debate. Shultz resisted those who sought an explicit U.S. call for Palestinian self-determination.[20] Arafat sensed momentum, however, and announced his intention to take his case to the UN General Assembly against U.S. wishes. When Shultz rejected his visa, the General Assembly moved its session to Geneva. For its efforts to break new ground, the Reagan administration ended up with egg on its face.

Engagement continued nevertheless. Arafat traveled to Sweden, ostensibly to meet with American Jews, but that was a sideshow. In Stockholm, Swedish diplomats presented Arafat with the State Department's revisions to a proposed PLO statement that would meet American demands. To reach agreement, Shultz consented to the PLO's demand to excise language requiring a moratorium on "all forms of violence."[21] This provided Arafat with the wiggle room he needed. Shultz also agreed not to object either to the Palestinian desire to put statehood on the agenda or to an international conference, so long as it did not bypass direct PLO-Israel engagement.[22]

On December 14, 1988, just five weeks before Reagan left office, Arafat appeared to fulfill American preconditions. He avowed, "our desire for peace is a strategy and not an interim tactic. . . . Statehood provides salvation to the Palestinians and peace to both Palestinians and

Israelis."[23] He reiterated acceptance of Resolutions 242 and 338 as the basis for negotiations at an international conference, and repeated his condemnation of terrorism, although he used an Arabic term suggesting temporary rejection rather than permanent renunciation.[24] That evening, Shultz responded as promised. Based on Arafat's statement, he said, "The United States is prepared for a substantive dialogue with PLO representatives."[25] Reagan also affirmed that the PLO met U.S. conditions. Two days later, Robert H. Pelletreau Jr., the U.S. ambassador in Tunisia, met with a PLO team.

Dialogue proceeded slowly. The PLO resisted U.S. pressure to end violence and embrace dialogue, but what truly angered them was the State Department's acceptance of an Israeli proposal that Palestinians hold elections.[26] The PLO leaders—who had spent most if not all of their lives in exile—feared they would lose an election to grassroots activists. The PLO activists based in Tunisia or elsewhere were radical and detached from reality. Those who remained quietly in Gaza or the West Bank were more disposed to compromise and they had a better understanding of Israelis, with whom they had been forced to live. The U.S. consideration of the Israeli proposal was, according to Rabie, "a wound from which the dialogue could never recover."[27] American diplomats backed down. The dispute highlighted diplomacy's cost: When Reagan agreed to dialogue, the PLO was down and out. U.S. engagement resurrected the group, which was more radical than grassroots Palestinian activists. Israel's justice minister, Dan Meridor, explained to Dennis Ross, "We can deal with the internal PLO; indeed, we must be able to live with them. But we cannot deal with the external PLO because their aim is to eradicate Israel. . . . If you legitimize the external PLO in your dialogue or you give them a role in this process, you will legitimize their agenda."[28] Alas, this is exactly what Ross did.

Too many American officials conflated Palestinian nationalism with the PLO, but Congress was not so certain. In 1989, noting that the PLO continued its terrorism with Arafat's cognizance, Congress passed the PLO Commitments Compliance Act (PLOCCA), which required the State

Department to affirm every 120 days that the PLO was abiding by its commitment to abandon terrorism and recognize Israel's right to exist.[29] If the PLO did not meet its commitments, then dialogue should cease.

Dialogue had not changed the PLO. On May 30, 1990, seaborne Palestinian commandos attacked a Tel Aviv beach. When Arafat refused to discipline Abu Abbas, the PLO executive committee member who planned the attack, the State Department suspended dialogue. The PLO continued to show its true colors when it, alone, cheered Iraq's invasion of Kuwait, and then cheered again when Iraq launched missiles at Israel during the coalition campaign to liberate Kuwait.

Ross argued that the time was ripe for new talks. "Radicals would be discredited, Arafat would be weak, regional moderates would be ascendant, our standing and authority in the region would be unprecedented, and the Soviets would be on our side," he explained.[30] Rather than use the momentum to end Arafat's claim to leadership permanently, the State Department threw him a lifeline.

Being a proponent of diplomacy means never having to say you're sorry. When outreach to Arafat again failed, Ross blamed Yitzhak Shamir, the Israeli prime minister, for not offering enough concessions at the 1991 Madrid Conference. "Had he permitted the Palestinians in negotiations to demonstrate that they were producing increasing Palestinian independence," Ross argued, ". . . he might have truly empowered the Palestinians from the territories and made it possible for the 'internal PLO' to become an alternative to Yasir Arafat's PLO in Tunis."[31]

The Oslo Accords

In the end, it was not American diplomacy that enabled a breakthrough. In August 1993, an Israel-PLO back-channel talk, hosted by Norway in a secluded location near Oslo, culminated in a "Declaration of Principles on Interim Self-Government Arrangements." A Palestinian Authority would take control over portions of the West Bank and the Gaza Strip. While Israeli settlements would remain, Israeli forces would redeploy into military zones. The two sides would begin talks to resolve their conflict within two years, and conclude them within five.

Warren Christopher and Dennis Ross insisted that the two sides recognize each other, and also that the PLO renounce terrorism, an item which, in theory, the Reagan administration had already won as a precondition for U.S.-PLO talks. Arafat and Yitzhak Rabin consented to mutual recognition, and Arafat agreed to take responsibility for the PLO's constituent parts. At the White House signing ceremony four days later, Arafat said, "My people are hoping that this agreement which we are signing today will usher in an age of peace, coexistence and equal rights."[32]

The Oslo Accords forever changed U.S. engagement with the Palestinians. Arafat now headed a pseudo government, not just a terror group. In October 1993, Congress passed the Middle East Peace Facilitation Act, which waived prohibitions on contacts with the PLO, and allowed the organization to open its de facto embassy in Washington so long as the PLO continued to abide by its commitments to cease terrorism and recognize Israel.[33] Congress also enabled the president to waive legislation that prohibited U.S. government employees from negotiating with the PLO and prevented the United Nations from channeling U.S. donations to the PLO.[34]

In theory, the creation of the Palestinian Authority sounded good: responsibility for governance would moderate former terrorists. Unfortunately, the State Department's assumption was wrong. Arafat wanted the trappings of state without its constraints. He cared little for good governance, and instead sought only to consolidate power. He demanded that all aid flow through his coffers to bolster his patronage and strengthen his grip.[35]

As implementation of the Declaration of Principles floundered, the State Department's instinct was to preserve the peace rather than the agreement. Thus, when Arafat adopted a radically divergent interpretation of his commitments, diplomats scrambled to appease him. As December 13 approached—the day on which the Palestinian Authority was to become established—Arafat engaged in brinkmanship. Ross observed, "He'd decided that he could frighten Christopher into pushing the Israelis to accommodate him." Ross argued that this tactic backfired because "Arafat convinced Christopher that he, Arafat, was irrational and that dealing with him might be necessary but unpleasant."[36]

Prior to Christopher's next meeting with Arafat, Ross coached the Palestinian leader. "I told him that his meeting in Amman had been a disaster," Ross recalled, adding, "If the meeting later in the day was a repeat performance, I doubted Christopher would see him again. I told him, 'Be practical, don't shout, and don't just spend your time complaining.'"[37]

For Clinton's peace team, the Oslo Accords were too big to fail. It was not until May 4, 1994, that the Israelis and the PLO reached an agreement to allow Arafat to return to Gaza to establish the Palestinian Authority formally.

In Western diplomacy, agreements settle issues, enabling negotiators to move on to unresolved issues. Not so with rogues: Arafat did not feel himself constrained by the rules of diplomacy. Nine hours after reaching an agreement, he reneged. Ross recalled, "On live TV, in front of the world . . . Arafat would not sign the maps attached to the agreement."[38] Arafat cared little for the agreement, and instead aimed to shore up his support by simultaneously defying the United States, Russia, Egypt, and Israel. A decade later, Muammar Qadhafi did much the same thing when he pointed the soles of his feet at the British prime minister, Tony Blair, on live television. In their enthusiasm for peacemaking, Clinton's team ignored Arafat's insincerity. It would be a lethal mistake: terrorism skyrocketed as Israel handed over territory to the Palestinian Authority.

U.S. diplomats had little chance to rest. After Arafat returned to Gaza, he was dismissive of his commitments to ensure security and revoke portions of the PLO's charter that called for Israel's destruction. Adding insult to injury, Arafat would fantastically blame Israeli agents for Palestinian terrorist attacks.[39]

Because the State Department pressed forward with talks regardless of Arafat's backpedaling, the Senate tried to rein in engagement. On July 15, 1994, the Senate prohibited release of taxpayer funds to the PLO unless the PLO complied with its commitments to renounce and control terrorism.[40] If the PLO failed to change its covenant, the Palestinian Authority risked losing U.S. funding.[41] Congress also cut off funding for the Palestine Broadcasting Corporation, as Arafat transformed that body into a partisan pulpit.[42] Congressional action did not necessarily filter down to diplomats on the ground, though. "I took every opportunity I could to see Arafat," recounted Edward Abington Jr., the U.S. consul general in Jerusalem. "I just felt it was important to be seen as very active, as understanding Palestinian positions, showing sympathy and empathy."[43] That Albright reprimanded Abington did not matter; on his retirement, Arafat rewarded him with a golden parachute.[44]

The peace process continued, while Israelis complained about Palestinian terrorism, and Palestinians expressed frustration that the Israeli withdrawal had not ended Israeli involvement in their daily affairs. U.S. diplomats mostly cajoled the two sides as they sought an interim agreement to determine security and governance throughout the West Bank. This agreement was signed on September 28, 1995. Five weeks later, a lone gunman assassinated Rabin after a rally in Tel Aviv, and Shimon Peres became the acting prime minister.

Almost twice as many Israelis died at the hands of Palestinian terrorists in the eighteen months after the Arafat-Rabin handshake as during the same length of time before it.[45] Not surprisingly, Israeli public opinion started turning against the peace process, while Benjamin "Bibi" Netanyahu, the Likud leader, grew more popular. Clinton's team then began to interfere in the Israeli elections. "On the eve of the mandated thirty-day campaign period, Peres visited Washington and we all but endorsed him," Ross recalled.[46] On May 29, 1996, Israelis elected Netanyahu.

Ross tried to reassure Arafat. "I told him that we were not going to walk away from peace, and neither could any Israeli government," Ross recounted.[47] Arafat cracked down on terrorism—at least, the terrorism committed by Hamas and Palestinian Islamic Jihad. "As I had asked, he was not giving Bibi an excuse on security,"[48] Ross explained. While Clinton and Ross resented Netanyahu's tougher line, they failed to understand that it was Netanyahu's brinkmanship rather than their own conciliation that delivered results.

Ross's desire to engage, meanwhile, caused blindness to Arafat's complicity in terrorism. Documents subsequently captured from Arafat's Ramallah compound showed the depth of his personal involvement in financing and directing terror attacks. Clinton was unwilling to consider the possibility that pushing engagement was destabilizing the Middle East.

After the Netanyahu government opened the Hasmonean Tunnel alongside (but not under) the Western Wall, Arafat spread the fiction that the tunnel would undermine the Temple Mount.[49] Dozens died in the ensuing violence. To resolve the conflict, Clinton invited Arafat and Netanyahu to the White House. Ross was frustrated with Netanyahu, whom he later described as "not willing to concede anything" and "riveted on his political base rather than on the needs of the process." Clinton was furious with Netanyahu.[50] Arafat had incited violence, but Clinton wished to extract concessions from a democracy in order to preserve engagement with a rogue.

There followed months of U.S.-brokered negotiations between Palestinians and Israelis over Hebron, a flashpoint West Bank city. Complicating negotiations was Arafat's refusal to abide by his own agreements.[51] Ross explained the duplicity as a negotiating tactic, saying that "Arafat usually created a crisis before finally closing just to test whether he had gotten all he could."[52] American negotiators were loath to question Arafat's sincerity. Meanwhile, despite the evidence of his culpability in terror, the State Department refused to report his guilt in its mandated reports to Congress.[53]

Immediately after Palestinian and Israeli representatives, on January 15, 1997, signed a protocol for redeploying Israeli forces around Hebron, Ross began work to win further Israeli redeployments. Each interim agreement merely sowed greater distrust. The White House grew so frustrated with obstacles that it would condemn both Israeli and Palestinian govern-ments whenever either would undertake an activity that complicated talks. A perverse moral equivalence infected American diplomacy. To Clinton's peace team, there was little difference between Israeli construction in Jerusalem and Palestinian suicide bombers. At no time was this more apparent than after the suicide bombing of the Apropos Café in Tel Aviv on March 21, 1997. Netanyahu refused to negotiate until Arafat acted against terror, as he had long ago pledged to do.[54] The Clinton team, for their part, were so immersed in the details of daily mediation that they seemed unable to see Arafat's violation of his commitment.

The peace process had granted Arafat both land and power. Although he moderated his rhetoric at times, he had not changed the Palestinian position at all. After almost every terror attack, as Ross related, the major concern of diplomats was how to preserve the dialogue and prevent an Israeli response. Secretary Albright and Sandy Berger, the national security advisor, blamed Netanyahu for the impasse and even discussed cutting him off altogether.[55]

Seeking the Final Status

After their talks on Hebron, Clinton's team shifted from graduated talks to comprehensive negotiations meant to settle the Israeli-Palestinian conflict once and for all. Moral equivalence solidified. On January 22, 1998, Clinton met Arafat at the White House. For the first time, he treated Arafat in a manner equal to Netanyahu. Because the president had received Netanyahu in the residential East Wing of the White House, he would also meet Arafat there. "This was as much a statement of unhappiness with Bibi as it was an effort to use symbolism to try to move Arafat on the substance," Ross explained.[56]

In order to entice Arafat to dispense with further interim talks and instead look toward a final settlement, Clinton promised to support an independent Palestinian state. As far as Arafat was concerned, however, he had already won that by meeting with Clinton alone.[57] To reset diplomacy—especially after the Monica Lewinsky scandal in Washington—the Clinton peace team proposed a Middle East summit. As they prepared for it, Clinton again welcomed Arafat to the White House. "Seeing the President on his own—in effect, having the same standing as the Israeli Prime Minister—was a big deal for Arafat," Ross wrote. "It played to his hunger for stature and also to his own sense that he was producing a relationship with the United States."[58]

Ross traveled to the region to ready both sides for the summit to be held in October 1998 at Wye Mills, Maryland. In Gaza, he met with the Palestinian security chief, Muhammad Dahlan, who objected to any agreement in which Palestinian forces would forfeit illegal weaponry or have prisoners vetted prior to their release.[59] As Clinton bestowed the respectability of diplomatic partnership upon them, Palestinian officials placed the desire to be treated like statesmen above any willingness to reform. U.S. diplomats played along, blurring compliance on security issues to mollify Palestinian feelings.

The Wye River Summit began on October 15. Two weeks earlier, the international community had pledged $2.4 billion for the Palestinian Authority, of which the United States offered $500 million.[60] It was a mistake. Committing funds before talks were concluded only squandered incentive.

At the summit, Clinton pushed Netanyahu to strengthen Arafat, arguing that a strong Arafat could better deliver.[61] This reflected two common misassumptions among diplomats: first, that dictators deliver; and second, that rogues accept the concept of give-and-take, rather than participating in peace processes only to take. Facing stalemate, the White House blamed Israel and accused it of insufficient flexibility. After Netanyahu demanded that the Palestinian Authority arrest terrorists and formally amend the Palestinian National Covenant as they had agreed at Oslo, Clinton lost his temper. "That SOB doesn't want a deal. He is trying to humiliate Arafat and me in the process," the president reportedly grumbled.[62]

Clinton's team were so intent on getting a deal that they were willing to overlook Arafat's duplicity and instead fault Netanyahu for making an issue of it. Arlen Specter summed up the illogical approach when he argued that the Americans should both subsidize the PLO and simultaneously chide it for failing to take action on the covenant.[63]

After eight days of negotiations, Netanyahu and Arafat signed the Wye River Memorandum, which fleshed out further Israeli redeployments in the West Bank, security cooperation, a Palestinian crackdown on incitement, and an agreement that the PLO Executive Committee would reaffirm the nullification of covenant provisions delegitimizing the State of Israel. The White House then rewarded the Palestinians with $400 million in additional funding.[64]

Israelis were ambivalent about the Wye River Memorandum.[65] Shortly after its signing, suicide bombers attacked a market in Jerusalem, killing twenty. Arafat announced—falsely—that the 750 prisoners that Wye committed the Israelis to release would all be security prisoners.[66] When Israel released only 100 security prisoners, Palestinian anger boiled over. Fatah sought to channel Palestinian anger by leading demonstrations and clashing with Israeli soldiers. These demonstrations violated Wye, but the negotiators had invested so much personally in the process that they refused to question Arafat's sincerity. After a Palestinian mob attacked an Israeli vehicle outside of Ramallah, Netanyahu suspended the implementation of the Wye River Memorandum.

It was against this backdrop that Clinton traveled to Israel and Gaza. His visit to Gaza was a huge boon for Arafat.[67] After significant American strong-arming, the Palestinian Legislative Council excised language calling for Israel's eradication from the covenant. Arafat hoped Clinton would reward him by inaugurating the Gaza airport while surrounded by Palestinian flags, or by speaking from a lectern bearing the PLO insignia. Clinton's advance team ensured that there would be no such propaganda coup.[68]

While Palestinian action settled Israeli concerns over the covenant, other issues remained unresolved. Ross was frustrated, and claimed that

"Bibi did little to set things right. He acknowledged that action had now been taken on the charter. But he immediately read a laundry list of Palestinian failings, among them the alleged stockpiling of illegal weapons, including heavy weapons."[69] Almost half the weaponry in Palestinian hands was illegal under the Oslo Accords, smuggled into Gaza through tunnels from Egypt, or from Jordan across the Dead Sea by small boat.[70] But Ross refused to allow the reality to endanger diplomacy.

When Netanyahu lost the 1999 election to Ehud Barak, Western officials could barely conceal their glee.[71] Barak's premiership did not translate into immediate progress, however. He was more interested in the Syria track, which angered Arafat, who did not like to be ignored. In February 2000, amidst arguments about whether villages near Jerusalem would be included in a transfer of territory to the Palestinian Authority, Arafat suspended talks.[72] Ross pressured Barak to compromise in order to keep the engagement alive. Barak did so, in an agreement that he and Arafat both tried to keep secret.[73]

Arafat's ego complicated engagement. The Palestinian Authority was a dictatorship: the only voice that mattered was Arafat's, and Palestinian negotiators knew it. As the teams met to hash out comprehensive peace, Palestinian negotiators dragged their feet.[74] They realized that any concession might lead to Arafat accusing them of betrayal, as Ross noted. "Without Arafat's readiness to assume responsibility for any concessions that might be negotiated, Abu Ala [Ahmed Qurei, a chief Palestinian negotiator] would be under personal threat," he observed.[75] Even so, Ross never demanded that Arafat take the lead in negotiations. If Arafat liked the deal, he could take credit. If he did not, he could dismiss the deal while pocketing the concessions granted to reach it.

Arafat chose the latter. "In retrospect," Ross later explained, "I believe Arafat felt violence at this point served several useful purposes. It was a safety valve for releasing the anger that . . . was building up on the Palestinian street. It highlighted the consequences of not satisfying the Palestinians. And, in his eyes, it put pressure on the Israelis to be more forthcoming."[76] There had been no Israeli provocation.[77] While the Clinton administration barely hid its animus toward Netanyahu's democratically elected government, Arafat often got a free pass. Bashing friends to court adversaries is a constant theme of diplomacy with rogues. The PLO pretended to abide by diplomacy, but embraced violence to win what it could not get at the negotiating table. Ross saw in the violence a reason to accelerate engagement.[78] He would not acknowledge that the push for diplomacy was exacerbating the problem.

Like many second-term presidents, Clinton looked increasingly toward his legacy. He wanted to be the president who won Arab-Israeli peace. On June 15, 2000, Arafat met Clinton in the Oval Office, and then dined with Albright at her townhouse in Georgetown. Although Arafat would not commit to peace, secret talks went forward. Negotiators made progress, but Sandy Berger, the national security advisor, was cautious. After Ross reported that the two sides were on the verge of an agreement, Berger asked, "How do we know what you heard represents either Barak or Arafat?"[79] It was to become the key question. While Israeli negotiators certainly represented their leaders, the same was not true of the Palestinian side.

When Albright subsequently traveled to Israel to meet Barak and Arafat, she found both inflexible. Barak felt he had offered enough concessions and would not go further without an indication that Arafat would compromise. With Clinton desperate for a deal, Arafat was in the driver's seat.[80] Barak complained, "We will be negotiating with ourselves. We propose, they reject, and tell us to give more."[81] He had encapsulated the Palestinian strategy, one enabled by Clinton. Berger argued for more pressure on Barak.[82] To placate rogues, the path of least resistance is to force allies to make concessions.

On July 9, 2000, Arafat and Barak arrived at Camp David to continue talks. Clinton and his aides pushed the Palestinians and Israelis to work through their remaining differences on territory, Jerusalem, and refugees. By the fifth day, Clinton was livid.[83] Palestinian negotiators had rejected every offer, but had refused to put forward their own proposal. Clinton met with Arafat and offered the Palestinians 89.5 percent of disputed territory, sovereignty in outer areas of East Jerusalem, and control over their border with Jordan. Arafat belittled the offer and claimed that Rabin had offered more. This was an outright lie, and Clinton called him on it.[84] Arafat's fabrications had a purpose: they established a false conventional wisdom and a new baseline from which to negotiate.

Because rogue engagement develops its own momentum, it took Ross almost twelve years to consider Arafat's true character. "Arafat may simply not be up to making a deal," Ross wrote. "He is a revolutionary; he has made being a victim an art form; he can't redefine himself into someone who must end all claims and truly end the conflict."[85]

Clinton cloistered himself with Arafat to push him to a deal. Arafat, he yelled, had "been here fourteen days and said no to everything."[86] Clinton was desperate for a legacy, but he would leave office with a foreign policy failure rather than a crowning success. Gambling on a rogue had exacted a tremendous cost. Clinton blamed Arafat.[87]

The PLO chief was intent on perpetuating the gravy train that engagement with the United States had become. He believed, however, that concessions flowed most generously when he provoked violence. He found his excuse when, on September 28, 2000, the Likud leader Ariel Sharon visited the Temple Mount.[88] Commentators often mark this as the beginning of the second intifada, although the situation remained calm until the next day. Imad Falouji, the Palestinian communications minister, said that Arafat planned the intifada as soon as the Camp David talks collapsed, and Arafat's wife later acknowledged that the Palestinian uprising was premeditated.[89] Despite the violence, Clinton requested additional funding for the Palestinian Authority as well as Israel in the last weeks of his presidency. Congress, however, was not willing to reward bad behavior and adjourned without acting on his request.[90] On December 23, 2000, Clinton sketched out a new proposal in which Israel would cede 94 to 96 percent of the West Bank to a Palestinian state, with the remainder addressed by a land swap; a redivision of Jerusalem; and an international commission to adjudicate refugee issues. Israel accepted the proposal, but Arafat rejected it. In February 2001, Fahd al-Fanek, a columnist for the Jordanian paper *Al-Ra'y*, argued that the intifada should wind down because it had served its purpose of forcing Israeli concessions.[91]

Clinton's peace team had gotten so involved in engagement with Arafat that they never stopped to assess the impact of their diplomacy. Clinton had gone to bat for Arafat, a man responsible for the deaths of dozens of Americans, and had gotten stiffed. Violence in the West Bank and Gaza was worse than before the U.S. government had lifted its restrictions on talks with the PLO and helped create the Palestinian Authority. Nevertheless, the diplomats were more inclined to blame Netanyahu than Arafat when diplomacy bogged down.[92]

Arafat understood that winning the public relations war was as important as winning in negotiations, so the Palestinian Authority spent $2.25 million to hire Edward Abington to be his lobbyist.[93] Given how American aid had flowed to the Palestinians and how much of it Abington had lobbied for when he was the U.S. consul general in Jerusalem, this hire was problematic. Abington did not disappoint his paymaster. He unstintingly sang Arafat's praises and consistently blamed diplomacy's failure on Israel and the United States.[94]

A New Roadmap

When George W. Bush took office, Palestinians expected him to be more sympathetic to their cause than Clinton had been. For the State Department, it was business as usual.[95] Talks continued despite the ongoing terrorism, and Colin Powell, the new secretary of state, even pressured Israel to transfer $54 million in taxes to the Palestinian Authority.[96] The talks sometimes led to a ceasefire, which never lasted. The problem was always the same: Arafat would agree to talk, but would always try to enhance his hand with force. Finally, on December 14, 2001—after nearly a year of violence—Bush blamed Arafat squarely.[97] Congress also renewed its demand for reports on PLO compliance with its commitments, a requirement the State Department would too often let slide.[98]

Palestinian Authority involvement in terrorism soon became indisputable. On January 3, 2002, the Israeli navy intercepted the Gaza-bound freighter *Karine-A*. It carried fifty tons of Iranian weaponry purchased by the Palestinian Authority.[99] The *Karine-A*'s captain admitted to being an officer in the Palestinian navy and a salaried Palestinian Authority employee.[100] The Palestinian Authority had made the purchase during a ceasefire.[101]

After initial denials, Arafat acknowledged responsibility and promised not to purchase such weaponry again.[102] That was good enough for Bush. When the Israeli prime minister, Ariel Sharon, asked him in February 2002 to sever diplomatic relations with the Palestinian Authority, Bush refused. Bush was not Clinton, however, and he would not play along endlessly in Arafat's game.

In April 2002, after a wave of suicide bombings, Israeli forces besieged Arafat in his Ramallah compound and launched an operation to eradicate bomb-making factories. With bloody fighting in Jenin, and the Church of the Nativity in Bethlehem occupied by Palestinian terrorists, Bush called on Arafat to stop the violence. "The Chairman of the Palestinian Authority has not consistently opposed or confronted terrorists," the president said. "At Oslo and elsewhere, Chairman Arafat renounced terror as an instrument of his cause, and he agreed to control it. He's not done so. The situation in which he finds himself today is largely of his own making."[103] While Bush sought to force Arafat to be accountable, the strongest proponents of engagement were frustrated that he would place accountability before diplomacy.

At the height of the terror campaign, Arlen Specter counseled further engagement. "The risks for the United States of doing nothing are much greater than the risks if we try, even if there is not immediate success."[104] The State Department concurred. On April 22, William Burns met the besieged Arafat in his Ramallah compound. After six days of hard negotiations, Arafat accepted an American plan to imprison Palestinian gunmen who had seized the Church of the Nativity, and Israel agreed to lift its siege. Bush urged Arafat to use his freedom to push for peace with Israel.

When Arafat reverted to form and continued to encourage violence, Bush had had enough. "Peace requires a new and different Palestinian leadership, so that a Palestinian state can be born," he said in a White House speech on June 24. "I call on the Palestinian people to elect new leaders, leaders not compromised by terror."[105] Bush's decision to isolate Arafat stood in sharp contrast to the policy of Clinton, who had welcomed Arafat to the White House more than any other foreign leader.[106]

"The Arabists in the State Department were appalled" by Bush's speech, recalled Condoleezza Rice, the national security advisor.[107] The State Department resisted the new approach and refused to accept Arafat's foreknowledge or funding of terrorism as conclusive evidence of participation; even Arafat's signature on a $20,000 payment to the al-Aqsa Martyrs' Brigades, a terrorist group, was dismissed as inconsequential.

Under White House pressure, Arafat rediscovered flexibility. Bush, for his part, was reluctant to see him completely isolated or humiliated. When Israeli forces surrounded Arafat's compound after back-to-back suicide bombings in Israel, the Bush administration forced Sharon to lift the siege. Arafat claimed victory.[108]

Throughout Arafat's supposed isolation, the State Department continued to fund the Palestinian Authority over which Arafat still wielded control.[109] These millions, in theory, were to be spent on sewers, water, and infrastructure. In reality, the money enabled the Palestinian Authority to continue funding terrorism.

In short order, facing persistent pressure from the State Department to engage, Bush backpedaled on diplomatic isolation. On April 30, 2003, the United States and its Quartet partners—representatives of the European Union, Russia, and the United Nations—launched a "Roadmap" laying out phased steps to peace, first and foremost of which was an end to Palestinian terrorism, the original commitment to which Arafat had agreed a decade before. Still, Bush's team did not repeat the conciliation that marked Clinton's approach. When the Palestinian negotiator Sa'eb Erekat complained about Israeli actions in Gaza, for example, John S.

Wolf, the chief American monitor, responded by reminding the Palestinian Authority about Americans killed by Palestinian terrorists.[110]

It was Arafat's death that enabled diplomacy to move forward, albeit not at the same level to which Palestinian officials had grown accustomed under Clinton. Meetings with Bush and the secretary of state were hard to come by, but Palestinian officials met with more junior counterparts. Some Palestinian officials also reached out to their former interlocutors from the Clinton years.[111]

During his second term, Bush had a change of heart and re-engaged in peacemaking. From the time he made Arafat a pariah, the U.S. strategy had become strengthening Mahmoud Abbas.[112] On May 26, 2005, President Bush not only welcomed the new Palestinian Authority president to the White House—the first time a Palestinian leader had visited the Oval Office since Clinton's presidency—but also pledged $50 million in direct aid. Five months later, Bush renewed his call for Palestinian statehood during another White House meeting with Abbas.[113]

It was Israel, and not the United States, that finally shook loose the status quo. On September 12, 2005, Israel completed its unilateral disengagement from the Gaza Strip. U.S. negotiations with the Palestinian Authority focused on two issues: fine-tuning Palestinian rule in Gaza and preparing for elections. Israel's pullout caught Palestinian negotiators flatfooted. Sa'eb Erekat complained that the pullout was cosmetic and did not address larger issues relating to statehood, and he scoffed at the U.S. request that the Palestinian Authority put a positive spin on the Gaza disengagement.[114]

Democratization and transformative elections were the centerpiece of Bush's first-term Middle East policy. Arafat's death had removed the chief impediment to Palestinian elections. Condoleezza Rice—who had revived the Clinton-era approach of her predecessors and lent her prestige to the minutiae of border crossings, the Gaza airport, and greenhouse infrastructure—curiously took a hands-off approach to the crafting of the election law.[115] It was a fateful mistake. Hamas, an unrepentant terrorist group, won 44 percent of the vote in the Palestinian elections on January 25, 2006, edging out Fatah at 41 percent.

Hamas was clearly a rogue, but Arab states and Turkey argued that free and fair elections legitimized it. While the State Department asked the Palestinian Authority to return funding the United States had provided to regenerate Gaza's economy, Arab states opposed any cutoff of aid to the Palestinians.[116] Diplomats maintain that engagement entangles rogues in a process, yet after the Hamas victory it was the State Department that found itself entangled, as tensions persisted with both Hamas and Fatah.

The Palestinian Authority, facing certain Israeli retribution, had agreed to jail those who assassinated the Israeli tourism minister in October 2001, so long as American and British monitors kept the Israelis at bay. After the Palestinian Authority rebuffed demands to bolster security for the American and British monitors, Washington and London recalled the monitors, and Israel seized the prisoners. The Palestinian Authority was livid.[117] Never had Clinton's team held them to such account. It would prove to be the exception, not the rule.

By 2007, the Bush administration had reversed its June 2002 demand that cessation of terror support be a prerequisite for government legitimacy. Rice declared, "I have heard loud and clear the call for deeper American engagement in these processes."[118] Once again, process trumped substance. As Bush met Abbas, the State Department requested an additional $86 million in assistance to Palestinian security forces run by Abbas. Rice began a full-court press to restart Middle East peace talks.[119]

Any real difference between the Clinton and Bush policies had disappeared. The no-nonsense approach to terrorism was gone, and in its place was pressure on Israel to offer unilateral concessions, ostensibly to bolster Abbas against his militant opposition. Bush pressured Israel to release 255 Palestinian prisoners, including convicted terrorists. Abbas celebrated, but the move did not win Israel much gratitude. Prime Minister Salam Fayyad denigrated the gesture: "The conflict between us and you is not over prisoners. A prisoner release is better than doing nothing, but it is better to do something significant."[120] The Palestinians demanded ever-increasing sums from the United States. Erekat opened one 2007 negotiating session by complaining, "The money the US is thinking of giving is too little. In Wye River, Clinton coughed [up] $450 million."[121]

As the Bush administration geared up for a peace conference in Annapolis in November 2007, the State Department requested more than a quarter billion dollars to shore up the Palestinian government.[122] For that money, the White House achieved little more than a photo opportunity at Annapolis. In the months following the conference, Rice met Ahmed Qurei often, but struggled to agree even on the agenda. Granted, with the Bush administration coming to a close, the Palestinians had little incentive to reach an agreement. Whatever Rice offered was essentially free money. Qurei spent his time complaining about Israel but not moving forward on his own.[123]

Even if Annapolis had been a success, it would have done nothing to address the challenge posed by Hamas, which, like Hezbollah, used territory ceded by Israel to attack the Jewish state. In the year following the conference, Palestinian rocket launches from the Gaza Strip increased more than 60 percent—to over two thousand.[124] American and Fatah negotiating teams ended up commiserating over a common adversary in Hamas.[125]

State Department efforts to resolve the dispute with Egyptian mediation failed. Sitting directly with Hamas would not have brought better results; the problem was not who sat at the table, but rather their ideology. When faced with an armed threat, a military response is often more effective than a diplomatic one. On December 27, 2008, Israel launched Operation Cast Lead, an assault on Gaza to force a cessation of rocket attacks. The strategy worked. In the month before the assault, there were more than six hundred rocket and mortar strikes in Israel; in the month following it, there were fewer than sixty.

American efforts to bolster Fatah relative to Hamas were no more successful than the efforts to bolster Iranian reformists versus hardliners.[126] Many rogues engage in good cop / bad cop strategies, which are always lucrative for the rogue but do little to achieve peace. Thus, when the

State Department contributed nearly $200 million to the UN Relief and Works Agency for Palestine Refugees in the Near East (UNRWA) in 2008, much of the money was spent in Hamas-controlled Gaza.[127] The State Department also reinstated Fulbright grants for Palestinian students in Hamas-controlled universities after a brief suspension.[128]

The Obama Approach

Even before he won the presidency, Barack Obama signaled his intention to give priority to the Israeli-Palestinian conflict. In August 2008, he wrote to Abbas and subsequently met the Palestinian president in Ramallah. Abbas found a sympathetic ear in the Illinois senator, and began to send Obama reports on Israeli settlement activity.[129] On January 22, 2009, just two days into his presidency, Obama appointed the former senator George Mitchell to be special envoy for the peace process. Symbolism mattered. With wars going on in Afghanistan and Iraq, diplomats took note of Obama's quick action.[130]

Coached by Rashid Khalidi, a Palestinian historian and PLO veteran, Obama sought to recalibrate the American position. He accepted Abbas's entreaties to make Israeli settlements the top priority.[131] Over subsequent months, both Mitchell and Secretary of State Hillary Clinton met with Abbas. Both hinted at a tougher American stance toward Israel. On May 28, Obama met Abbas at the White House and, standing next to him, demanded a halt to Israeli settlement activity.[132] He did not distinguish between settlement outposts and construction on existing homes within Jerusalem's post-1967 neighborhoods. His demand for cessation of Israeli activity led the Palestinian Authority to suspend negotiations until Israel had fully halted construction. Obama did not acknowledge that this represented a step back from past practice, which had encouraged the Israelis and Palestinians to talk constantly.

Obama then made the Palestinian cause his own when he addressed the Islamic world during a visit to Cairo in June 2009. "Let there be no doubt: the situation for the Palestinian people is intolerable," he said.

"America will not turn our backs on the legitimate Palestinian aspiration for dignity, opportunity, and a state of their own."[133] In his zeal for outreach, Obama turned a blind eye to Palestinian incitement of violence. Just weeks after his Cairo speech, the U.S. government announced that it would finance the construction of a computer center in Hebron named after a terrorist who killed thirty-seven, including twelve children and an American citizen.[134]

Hewing closer to the Palestinian cause—accommodating the former rogue—did not jumpstart the peace process. Abbas continued his boycott of talks for the first nine months of Netanyahu's ten-month moratorium on settlement construction. The more Obama engaged the Palestinian Authority, the more Abbas felt he could extract greater Israeli concessions. It took twenty months for Israeli and Palestinian representatives to sit down together. Behind the scenes, Erekat hectored American diplomats, and Abbas hardened his stance further, declaring that the Palestinian Authority would never recognize Israel as a Jewish state.[135] Finally, in November 2012, Abbas went directly to the United Nations to request unilateral recognition of Palestinian statehood. The move, followed by the Authority's rebranding itself "The State of Palestine," was in violation of the Oslo Accords and all previous agreements. Once again, rather than hold the Palestinian leadership to account, the Obama administration waived U.S. law requiring Palestinian offices to be closed should they claim to recognize an independent state prior to a formal peace agreement. Obama and John Kerry, the secretary of state, invested too much hope in a new round of diplomacy, which unsurprisingly led nowhere.

* * *

Securing Israeli-Palestinian peace has been the dream of generations of American diplomats. Decades of diplomacy, first with the PLO and then with the Palestinian Authority, has not achieved its promise. Far from reducing conflict, diplomacy has increased it. Despite billions of dollars in U.S. aid, self-administration of their own territory, and the trappings of statehood if not universal recognition, the Palestinian street remains fiercely anti-American, just as committed to terrorism, and more likely to partner with Tehran than Tel Aviv. Palestinian attitudes toward diplomacy have not changed since Arafat described talking as a complement to armed struggle. Palestinians may complain about uneven Israeli fulfillment of the Jewish state's commitments, but Palestinian frustration cannot excuse terrorism.

What went wrong? From the Oslo Accords onward, diplomats embraced the idea that engagement with former terrorists could bring peace in the Middle East, an article of faith that Aaron David Miller, an advisor to six secretaries of state, calls "the false religion of Mideast peace." He explains:

> *Like all religions, the peace process has developed a dogmatic creed, with immutable first principles. . . . They were a catechism we all could recite by heart. First, pursuit of a comprehensive peace was a core, if not the core, U.S. interest in the region, and achieving it offered the only sure way to protect U.S. interests; second, peace could be achieved, but only through a serious negotiating process based on trading land for peace; and third, only America could help the Arabs and Israelis bring that peace to fruition.*[136]

When George W. Bush briefly challenged the idea that the peace process should continue regardless of Palestinian terrorism, diplomats and media roundly criticized him until he reversed course.

Rather than hold Palestinian leaders to account, the White House often blamed Israel. Neither the White House nor the State Department did much to hide its animosity toward Netanyahu, in particular. Once, a microphone caught Obama complaining about the Israeli prime minister to the French president, Nicolas Sarkozy: "You've had enough of him, but I have to deal with him every day!"[137]

The root of the tension was a divergence of goals: American officials put a premium on talk for its own sake, while their Israeli counterparts focused more on results. The State Department has never questioned its strategy or fundamental assumptions, but has merely shifted standards to accommodate Palestinian behavior. Consequently, a perverse pattern has developed: the harder Americans push for peace, the more rapid is the descent into violence.

Chapter Nine

IS IT TIME TO TALK TO TERRORISTS?

Not long ago, no senior official would publicly suggest working with an unrepentant terrorist group and expect to keep his job, but times have changed. In May 2010, John Brennan suggested that the United States work with "moderate elements" of Hezbollah.[1] Less than three years later, Brennan became the CIA director. The State Department now considers the Muslim Brotherhood a partner, and the group has received U.S. taxpayer largesse. The Palestine Liberation Organization still does. As a senator, Chuck Hagel proposed talking to Hamas, a position endorsed by senior statesmen like Jimmy Carter and Brent Scowcroft. Engaging terrorists is now vogue. After engaging rogue states like Libya and Iran, it is not a huge leap to sit down with rogue groups. Indeed, many intellectuals find talking to terrorists the epitome of sophisticated statecraft.

France and Britain long fought terrorist insurgencies in their colonies before granting them independence. "One man's terrorist is another man's freedom fighter" became a catchphrase that was often used to justify engagement with terrorist groups. Abdel Bari Atwan, editor of *Al-Quds al-Arabi*, expressed a common Arab view of how the United States distinguishes between terrorists and freedom fighters: "If you are with the Americans, you are a legitimate fighter, you are a hero, but if you are fighting against a country supported by America, then you are a terrorist."[2] Chris Patten, the European Union's chief foreign policy official between 1999 and 2004, saw terrorism as a launching pad for Third World political careers. "For years, terrorist groups have fetched up in government," he explained. "Their access to respectability, from Israel to Kenya to South Africa to Ireland, has been part of the political settlement of one dispute after another."[3] Bobby Sayyid, a research fellow at the University of Leeds, went further, calling the designation of terrorist groups a racist attempt by the West to keep formerly colonized peoples subjugated.[4] In American circles too, the idea of David versus Goliath imbues terrorism with a romantic aura. There is hardly a college campus where Che Guevara, Latin American revolutionary and mass murderer, does not adorn T-shirts or posters. Diplomats seeking talks can always massage the definition of terrorism to justify dialogue. Today, the West uses more than 250 definitions of terrorism.[5]

Many diplomats justify talking to terrorists by pointing to the militant Zionists who waged a violent campaign against British rule, leading to the birth of Israel. But insurgency is not always terror. If terrorism is the deliberate targeting of civilians for political gain, then Jewish militants were not terrorists: they telephoned warnings to evacuate targets before striking. By the same token, French World War II partisans were not the brethren of Hamas suicide bombers. Not every colonial struggle is legitimate, nor do all groups cloaking themselves in national liberation have popular support. Moral equivalence is a dangerous foundation for policy.

Even so, the idea that Western states do not negotiate with terrorists is nonsense. Spain talks to Basque separatists, Turkey talks to the Kurdistan Workers' Party (PKK), and Israel talked to the PLO in the years preceding the 1993 Oslo Accords.[6] The Clinton administration invited Gerry Adams, the head of an Irish Republican Army (IRA) front group, to the White House despite British complaints; Prime Minister John Major refused to take Clinton's phone calls for days.[7]

Talking to terrorists has costs beyond antagonizing allies. Sometimes reconciliation sparks backlash. In 1962, French soldiers upset with Charles de Gaulle's ending of hostilities in Algeria tried to assassinate him. Yitzhak Rabin was not so lucky: in 1995, an Israeli who was disgruntled over the talks with Arafat succeeded in gunning down the prime minister.

Spoilers can derail engagement on either side.[8] After the British began negotiations with the IRA, a group calling itself the "Real Irish Republican Army" launched attacks to disrupt the peace process, most famously with a massive bomb in the town of Omagh. Some academics see spoilers sowing mistrust between groups that honestly seek peace.[9] But there is another possibility: splinter groups can provide plausible deniability for terrorist organizations seeking to win more concessions through violence while they are pocketing diplomatic gains. Arafat became the most frequent foreign visitor to the Clinton White House even while paying supposed rogue factions to continue the terror campaign.[10]

For these and other reasons, few who advocate talking with terrorists do so blindly. Many realists question whether terrorism should be a black-and-white issue, at least when it comes to state sponsors. While still a Brookings scholar, Meghan O'Sullivan, whom George W. Bush appointed to a top national security position, argued that Washington should be more "nuanced" and "calibrate the penalties to relate to the different levels of state sponsorship."[11] This is dangerous, however, as it legitimizes a certain degree of terror.

Some suggest that the terrorists' ideology should be the litmus test. If terrorists see themselves as freedom fighters, then dialogue might work. But if they are absolutists dedicated to wiping out another country, or if they hold apocalyptic goals, little good can come from dialogue. Diplomats hold out more hope for groups who turn to terrorism as a result of specific grievances.[12] These diplomats would find it reasonable—if not advisable—for the United States to sit down with Hamas and Hezbollah.[13] Justifying terrorist ideologies, however, is subjective.

Legitimizing terrorism can also be costly. In 1979, the Carter administration reached out to the PLO, seeking that group's help in resolving the Iran hostage situation. After all, the PLO chairman, Yasir Arafat, had been Khomeini's first official foreign guest. When the channel failed, Carter aides felt they were no worse off for the effort, but in fact the United States paid a high price. Carter's outreach bestowed legitimacy upon a group that refused to renounce terrorism and had murdered a U.S. ambassador just seven years earlier. To avoid this problem, states sometimes farm out engagement to third parties like the International Red Cross. Intermediaries can be useful in hostage situations, or with repatriation of bodies, but their utility is limited.

Is There Ever a Time to Talk to Terrorists?

Robert Malley, an advisor to President Clinton on the peace process, proposed conditions for engaging terrorist groups: There should be no engagement with any organization on Washington's terrorist list—such as Hamas and Hezbollah—or those like the Muslim Brotherhood that are banned by allies.[14] Malley argued that Washington should not, however, stop local regimes from engaging Islamists. He urged the Bush administration, for example, not to oppose Mahmoud Abbas's outreach to Hamas, a strategy which would undermine the Arab-Israeli peace process while allowing rogues to play good cop / bad cop. Richard Haass, director of policy planning at the State Department and a consistent proponent of engagement, agreed that some groups are beyond the boundary of diplomacy. "There are some groups out there you can negotiate with. You have to decide whether there are terms you can live with," he explained. "But groups like Hamas . . . have political agendas that I would suggest are beyond negotiation. And for them . . . there's got to be an intelligence, a law enforcement, and a military answer."[15]

George W. Bush recognized that negotiation alone had failed to solve the Palestinian issue. In his first four months as president, Israel suffered more than twenty terrorist attacks, at a cost of more than three hundred dead or wounded. Israel responded with Operation Defensive Shield in April 2002, which led to spurious allegations of a massacre in

Jenin. Bush decided to alter course and take a zero-tolerance approach to terrorism. "There is simply no way to achieve peace until all parties fight terror," he said.[16]

Pundits and diplomats have promoted negotiation with Hamas by pointing to the relative success of the British deal making with the Irish Republican Army. Peter Beinart, for example, noted that the IRA had not renounced terrorism until seven years after signing the Good Friday Agreement.[17] George Mitchell also employed the IRA analogy to justify talks in the face of repeated failure. "In Northern Ireland, we had about 700 days of failure and one day of success," he quipped.[18] Mitchell referred to the Northern Ireland peace process in almost every press briefing he gave as Obama's special envoy for Middle East peace.[19]

The IRA analogy is tenuous. Beinart omits that the IRA never aimed to eradicate Great Britain. Northern Ireland's peace process was launched only after the IRA declared its war to be over. By contrast, Hamas seeks political legitimization without abandoning its military struggle.[20] Unlike the IRA, Hamas does not separate its military and political wings.[21] While religion was a factor in the Irish dispute, the IRA's political platform was Irish unification.[22] The Hamas Charter, by contrast, defines Palestine as "an Islamic Waqf" (a trust or inalienable endowment) and asserts that "Until the Day of Resurrection, no one can renounce it or part of it, or abandon it or part of it." Hamas also remains profoundly anti-Semitic. According to its charter, "The Prophet, Allah bless him and grant him salvation, has said: 'The Day of Judgment will not come about until Moslems fight the Jews (killing the Jews), when the Jew will hide behind stones and trees. The stones and trees will say O Moslems, O Abdullah, there is a Jew behind me, come and kill him.'"[23] Unlike Hamas, the IRA did not engage in suicide terrorism, and it was not a client of a state developing nuclear weapons or promoting genocide. Most importantly, the Good Friday Agreement aimed to undermine terrorism, not legitimize it.[24] These are but a few of the problems with the IRA-Hamas analogy; the same problems hold true with IRA-Hezbollah parallels.[25]

Terrorist groups have become adept at exploiting dialogue for propaganda purposes. In August 2004, Bobby Muller, an American peace activist, Beverley Milton-Edwards, an Irish academic, and Alastair Crooke, a former British official, met with senior Hamas and Hezbollah figures in Beirut in what they called "an exercise in mutual listening."[26] Retired American and European diplomats and intelligence officials followed suit. Hamas took advantage of Western naïveté. Mark Perry, a former intelligence operative and participant, reported back that Hamas "had rethought its goals of . . . destroying the Jewish state."[27] Alas, the statement was as fleeting as it was false. In the following year, Hamas fired more than 1,200 missiles into Israel proper, a fivefold increase over the previous year. As Israel withdrew from Gaza, the Hamas political leader Khaled Meshaal declared the "beginning of the end for the Zionist project in the region."[28]

Jimmy Carter and, subsequently, a delegation of British lawmakers fell into the same trap. Carter sought out Meshaal in Damascus, and came away convinced that Hamas had moderated and would accept Israel's existence.[29] Meshaal told the British delegation, in another highly stage-managed visit, that Hamas wanted "real peace" and would not demand Israel's destruction.[30] Upon his return, Carter acted more like a propagandist than a statesman. He claimed that Hamas had upheld its ceasefire with Israel—seemingly unaware that Hamas had fired over six hundred mortars and rockets into Israel over the previous month.[31] Hamas has learned that the most enthusiastic engagers will accept any peaceful statement at face value, however false. Three years after ruling out engagement with Hamas, Richard Haass suddenly began to advocate for it.[32] Meanwhile, Arab leaders with broader experience refused to grant recognition to a group they considered an Iranian puppet.[33]

Hamming It Up with Hamas

Enthusiasm for direct talks with Hamas increased after the group's victory in the January 2006 elections. Claude Salhani, editor of the *Middle East*

Times, predicted that its election would mature the group. "Democracy is not a choose by numbers game," he observed. "You take it all, plusses and negatives in one pill."[34] The Carnegie Endowment's Marina Ottaway argued that political power might moderate Hamas by forcing its accountability to a constituency.[35] This ignores the international subsidies that insulate Hamas from government accountability. Chris Patten counseled forgetting Hamas's past, saying, "We should judge the new government, including Hamas, by results."[36] Such hopeful scenarios fail to consider that Hamas makes no promise to abide by the rules of democracy. In the run-up to the elections, Hamas cofounder Mahmoud Zahar vowed, "We will join the Legislative Council with our weapons in our hands."[37]

The United States government and its Quartet partners agreed that diplomatic recognition of Hamas would be premature because of the group's refusal to recognize Israel, accept previous agreements, and forswear terror.[38]

It was not long, however, before first Turkey and then European foreign ministries began to shift their tune. When Hamas staged a violent putsch against its Palestinian rivals in July 2007 and consolidated control over Gaza, European diplomats argued that they had no choice but to engage Hamas since there was no longer any pretext of a Palestinian coalition. The French sent a retired diplomat to begin "unofficial" contacts with the group,[39] and the Italian foreign minister, Massimo D'Alema, urged the European Union to rethink its policy.[40] The European Union Institute for Security Studies called for "watering down" the Quartet preconditions.[41] Once again, talks for their own sake had become the end goal.

Too often, the mere passage of time legitimizes dialogue with rogues in Western eyes. It is a pattern that can discourage actual reform and compromise among pariahs, and it is a trap into which proponents of engagement often fall. Patten, Paddy Ashdown and ten other former statesmen and politicians signed a letter published in *The Times* of London saying, "We have learnt first-hand that there is no substitute for direct and sustained negotiations with all parties to a conflict, and rarely if ever a durable peace without them. Isolation only bolsters hardliners and their policies of intransigence. Engagement can strengthen pragmatic elements and their ability to strike the hard compromises needed for peace."[42] This view was echoed by Taghreed El-Khodary, a *New York Times* reporter; Joe Klein, a *Time* columnist; and Charles Grant, a *Guardian* writer.[43] Pundits may find it compelling, but in reality it falls flat. Engaging the most violent factions incentivizes terrorism and disadvantages groups that play by the rules.

When it comes to terrorist groups and other rogues, retired officials traditionally conduct the bulk of engagement. While this gives the White House plausible deniability, it can also sow confusion when self-appointed intermediaries lack influence or the means to impose sanctions. Ramsey Clark, the Kennedy-era attorney general, does not have the same credibility in Washington that he has had in Tehran, Tripoli, or Baghdad. The chief intermediaries under Obama, however, have both mainstream credibility and close ties to the White House. Malley and Thomas Pickering, a former senior diplomat, have taken the lead in engaging Hamas.[44] Both advised the Obama campaign. In July 2009, Pickering and Malley met with Mahmoud Zahar, Hamas's foreign minister, and Osama Hamdan, the movement's chief representative in Lebanon.[45]

Obama's election opened the floodgates to engagement. Ahmed Yousef, Hamas's chief political advisor in Gaza, claimed he had spoken with Obama's aides regularly, even before the election.[46] Prior to accepting a post as President Obama's chief economic advisor, Paul Volcker led a group that advocated engaging with Hamas regardless of any change in the group's strategy.[47] Less than a month into Obama's presidency, John Kerry, chairman of the Senate Committee on Foreign Relations, traveled to Gaza, the first trip there by an American congressman in nearly a decade. Hamas was thrilled. "This is a very good step reflecting the seriousness of this administration to follow up and get information about what is happening on the ground," Yousef said. Later he remarked, "This administration is different from the previous administration. We believe Hamas's message is reaching its destination. . . . Now we know the people coming to see us are so much more connected to the White

House."[48] Indeed, the U.S. diplomat Rachel Schneller publicly debated Hamdan in Qatar on February 23, 2010, and then privately chatted with him over tea. While technically on leave from the State Department on an academic fellowship, Schneller nonetheless cleared her meeting with Secretary Clinton. Khaled Meshaal subsequently claimed that Obama had sent a succession of envoys to engage Hamas.[49] Perhaps the White House differentiated between official and unofficial contact, though. Ismail Haniya, the Hamas leader in Gaza, complained that letters he sent to Obama went unanswered.[50]

Hamas may be willing to engage in order to further its goals, but this does not mean it is prepared to compromise on the issue of Israel's existence or to abandon the conflict. Some academics and diplomats cite Hamas's willingness to accept a *hudna*, a truce, as a sign that engagement can work, but they overlook the historical context.[51] Arabic has several other words for ceasefire (including *muhadana, muwada'a, muhla, musalaha, musalama, mutaraka,* and *sulh*). Islamists associate *hudna* specifically with the Prophet Muhammad's truce at al-Hudaybiyya, near Mecca. There, Muslim forces broke their nonaggression pact after two years when they had grown strong enough to defeat the local garrison.[52]

Engaging Hezbollah

Hezbollah, like Hamas, is a top target for those who embrace engagement even with terrorist groups. Like Hamas, it controls territory. Since 1988, six years after its founding, Hezbollah has administered much of southern Lebanon. Like Hamas, it also operates as a political party, holding seats in Lebanon's parliament and in its cabinet. Just as Hamas has killed Americans in various attacks, Hezbollah too has targeted Americans. Before 9/11, it was the most lethal terrorist group the United States faced. Perhaps for this reason, it has been America's European allies that have taken the lead in engaging the group.

Britain established relations with Hezbollah in 2001, but severed them in 2005 after the British government designated Hezbollah as a terrorist group. The suspension of ties did not last long. Between the Hezbollah-Israel war of 2006 and Hezbollah's formidable showing in Lebanon's 2009 elections, diplomats argued that there was too much to lose by treating Hezbollah as a pariah. "It's not helpful to couch this war in the language of international terrorism," said Mark Malloch-Brown, the UN's deputy secretary-general. "Hezbollah employs terrorist tactics, but it is an organization that draws on a strong political well of support in southern Lebanon."[53]

The argument that Hezbollah is a legitimate partner for diplomacy because it participates in Lebanese politics is dangerous. Augustus Richard Norton, a leading academic expert on Hezbollah, noted that the group rejected political participation in its first years, viewing politics as hopelessly corrupt, and then later changed course.[54] But that occurred only after Hezbollah had used military force to eliminate rivals and gain a near-monopoly over Lebanon's Shi'ites. Norton subsequently argued that moderate Islamists, especially compared with Osama bin Laden, "have goals that are in many ways pragmatic and even prosaic, and they are amenable to reasonable solutions and compromise."[55]

The British Foreign Office announced a formal dialogue with Hezbollah in March 2009. "Hezbollah is a political phenomenon and part and parcel of the national fabric in Lebanon," explained Barry Marston, a Foreign Office spokesman. "I believe such contacts will help push this movement to engage in the political process and achieve peace in the region."[56] When Frances Guy, the British ambassador to Lebanon, met the Hezbollah parliamentarian Muhammad Raid, the group bragged that the Foreign Office had requested the meeting. The State Department reacted with outrage, but British officials were unapologetic. Hezbollah, meanwhile, basked in its newfound legitimacy. "Western countries are rushing to speak with us and will so even more in the future," said Sheikh Naim Qassem, the group's deputy chief.[57] While the British Foreign Office said it would limit contacts to Hezbollah politicians but continue to shun the group's military arm, British parliamentarians were not so selective: three MPs met with senior Hezbollah and Hamas officials.[58]

Hezbollah, for its part, scoffed at British efforts to differentiate between political and military wings. Omar al-Mussawi, a Hezbollah Central Council member, reiterated that Hezbollah was "one entity."[59]

Upon the death of Mohammed Hussein Fadlallah, Hezbollah's spiritual mentor, Ambassador Guy eulogized him, saying:

> *People in Lebanon like to ask me which politician I admire the most. . . . Until yesterday my preferred answer was to refer to Sheikh Mohammed Hussein Fadlallah, head of the Shia clergy in Lebanon and much admired leader of many Shia Muslims throughout the world. When you visited him you could be sure of a real debate, a respectful argument and you know you would leave his presence feeling a better person. . . . The world needs more men like him willing to reach out across faiths, acknowledging the reality of the modern world and daring to confront old constraints.*[60]

The ambassador neglected to mention Fadlallah's role as the ayatollah who gave religious sanction to suicide bombings and embraced genocidal attitudes toward Jews.

Perhaps time heals all wounds. This was, at least, the argument of Steven Simon, an adjunct scholar at the Council on Foreign Relations, and Jonathan Stevenson, a professor of strategic studies at the Naval War College. "Except for its suspected logistical support for the bombing of the Khobar Towers in 1996 and its alleged training of the Mahdi Army in Iraq several years ago, Hezbollah hasn't targeted the United States in a generation," they wrote in 2010.[61] Of course, these exceptions meant the deaths of several hundred Americans, a reality whitewashed in the desperation to engage.

Ryan Crocker, a veteran ambassador, also recommended outreach. "We should talk to Hezbollah. One thing I learned in Iraq is engagement can be extremely valuable in ending an insurgency. Sometimes persuasion and negotiation change minds," he told the Senate Committee on Foreign Relations in June 2010. Crocker also insisted that negotiating with Hezbollah would bring an intelligence boon. "We would learn far more about the organization than we know now—personalities, differences, points of weakness," he said, adding, "We cannot mess with our adversary's mind if we are not talking to him."[62] This is nonsense on a number of levels. It is possible to mess with the minds of terrorist leaders without sitting down with them; that's what psychological operations are for. Moreover, it is an open question whether the advantage of learning personality quirks outweighs the drawback of legitimizing terrorist groups.

Embracing the Muslim Brotherhood

For decades, U.S. diplomats considered the Muslim Brotherhood off-limits. Since its founding in 1928, the Brotherhood has embraced violence, preached intolerance, and incubated terror groups. Its founder, the twenty-one-year-old Egyptian schoolteacher Hassan al-Banna, preached complete rejection of the West and taught that there was no aspect of life that fell outside Islam's bounds. The movement spread like wildfire. In 1935, the Muslim Brotherhood opened an office in Aleppo, Syria; and during World War II, al-Banna established branches in Palestine and Jordan.

The Brotherhood's rise disproves the conventional wisdom that the Israeli-Palestinian dispute is the cause of terrorism. In 1946, the military intelligence division of the U.S. War Department, the predecessor of today's Defense Intelligence Agency, examined over-the-horizon threats. Among them was speculation that the "Muslim world" would pose the next "threat to world security." Its evidence? The Muslim Brotherhood, an organization led by "demagogues and political opportunists," as the agency described it. "They issue clandestine pamphlets, attack the government, stir up hatred . . . and sow the seeds of violence."[63] Hassan al-Banna had become an unabashed admirer of Adolf Hitler and Italian fascism. In the waning weeks of World War II, the Brotherhood had unleashed a wave of terror that killed the Egyptian prime minister, Ahmad Maher, and wounded his predecessor, Mustafa al-Nahas. Shortly after Israel's creation, the Brotherhood chalked up the life of another prime minister, Mahmoud an-Nukrashi, in its tally of terror.

"It is the nature of Islam to dominate, not to be dominated, to impose its law on all nations and to extend its power to the entire planet," al-Banna declared.[64] His followers put his words into action, seeking to cleanse Egypt of Western influence by any means. As recently as 2005, the Muslim Brotherhood's webpage promoted the slogan, "Allah is our objective. The Prophet is our leader. The Quran is our law. Jihad is our way. Dying in the way of Allah is our highest hope." More liberal politicians might eschew the Brotherhood's violence but cannot disregard them. "Even the more enlightened Muslim leaders must cater to their fanaticism in order to retain their positions," the 1946 report observed.

When Gamal Abdel Nasser consolidated power in Egypt in the 1950s, he persecuted the Muslim Brotherhood mercilessly. So too did a succession of military rulers across the Arab world. Brotherhood activists had two choices: to go underground, or to flee. Most chose the latter. They may have condemned everything about the West as immoral and corrupt, but they did not hesitate to exploit Western freedoms to establish themselves in exile.

Diplomats preach that cultural interchange promotes understanding, but that was only half true of the Muslim Brotherhood exiles in the West. While they learned how to interact with Westerners, speak their language, and lobby governments, they didn't learn to appreciate Western culture. Their core ideology remained unaltered. Rather than liberalize them, the Western interlude aided Brotherhood groups in their propaganda.

Diplomats initially greeted the rhetoric of political Islamists with skepticism. After Algeria nullified elections won by an Islamist group in 1992, the diplomat Edward Djerejian remarked, "While we believe in the principle of 'one person, one vote,' we do not support 'one person, one vote, one time.'"[65] The latter principle was endorsed by Recep Tayyip Erdoğan, who would later become the Turkish prime minister and the toast of Washington, when he said, "Democracy is a streetcar. We only travel on it until we have reached where it is we want to go."[66]

Those who see the Brotherhood as a potential partner argue that the group has evolved over the decades and has shed its ideological rigidity. According to Robert S. Leiken and Steven Brooke, both Nixon Center scholars, "Jihadists loathe the Muslim Brotherhood . . . for rejecting global jihad and embracing democracy."[67] That other groups are more extreme, however, does not prove the Brotherhood's sincerity about democracy. Still, the success of Brotherhood-affiliated candidates, running as independents, in the 2005 Egyptian elections was enough reason for even the Bush administration to engage. "The Muslim Brotherhood was illegal in Egypt, but certain parliamentarians who were connected to the Muslim Brotherhood were, we felt, worth talking to," remarked Elliott Abrams, the deputy national security advisor.[68]

When Obama took office, Islamist advocacy groups and those seeking engagement with the Muslim Brotherhood finally found a receptive audience in the White House. The U.S. embassy in Cairo invited ten members of the Brotherhood's parliamentary bloc to attend Obama's address to the Muslim world from Cairo on June 4, 2009. In order to claim that the Muslim Brotherhood had moderated, diplomats focused on the group's assurances in English rather the messages it conveyed to its own membership. The previous year, the Brotherhood had posted a series of articles encouraging hatred of and violence toward Christians and Jews.[69] The discrepancy in tone and message from one audience to another is strategic. "I must speak in a way that is appropriate for the ear hearing me," said Hassan al-Banna's grandson Tariq Ramadan, a popular figure with American liberals, to an Islamist audience. "We must know how to speak to those who do not share our history."[70] This strategy has been effective in gaining acceptance by U.S. observers. In March 2009, scores of prominent intellectuals including Beinart and the conservative scholar Robert Kagan signed an open letter to Obama in which they maintained that "most mainstream Islamist groups in the region are nonviolent and respect the democratic process."[71] Two years later, while Egyptians were protesting against Hosni Mubarak's nearly thirty-year rule, Bruce Riedel, who had been a top Middle East hand in the Clinton administration, asserted, "If we really want democracy in Egypt, the Muslim Brotherhood is going to be a big part of the picture."[72]

The Arab Spring uprising caught the Muslim Brotherhood by surprise, but with a decades-old organization and ample funding from Turkey and Persian Gulf donors, it was the group best positioned to benefit from Mubarak's resignation. While diplomats, advisors, and pundits applauded Obama's direct outreach to the Brotherhood, the warning signs were dire. On February 18, 2011, hundreds of thousands of Egyptians greeted the exiled Brotherhood preacher Yusuf al-Qaradawi back to Cairo. Journalists and advocacy organizations regularly labeled Qaradawi a moderate even though, less than two months after al-Qaeda's 9/11 attacks, he had described suicide terrorism as religiously legitimate. "These are heroic commando and martyrdom attacks and should not be called suicide under any circumstances," he said.[73]

The rise of the Muslim Brotherhood acolyte Mohamed Morsi to the presidency seemed to cement the group's legitimacy in American policy circles, even if Morsi repeatedly violated pledges not to seek Brotherhood domination. On July 14, 2012, Secretary Hillary Clinton was meeting Morsi at the presidential palace in Cairo. Her meeting bestowed Washington's blessing on Egypt's new order, and she promised "the strong support of the United States for the Egyptian people and their democratic transition." Less than three weeks later, Defense Secretary Leon Panetta underlined the U.S. endorsement, using almost the exact same phrase.

Their outreach achieved little. After Egyptian Islamists tried to storm the U.S. embassy on the anniversary of 9/11, claiming outrage over an Egyptian American's polemical film ridiculing the Prophet Muhammad, Morsi was silent. The Muslim Brotherhood's English Twitter account professed relief that "none of @USembassycairo staff was hurt," but in Arabic the group urged that "Egyptians rise to defend the Prophet."[74] When Morsi seized dictatorial powers, his Western supporters were apologetic.

Professor Noah Feldman of Harvard, for example, suggested that Morsi had turned tyrant in order to save Egypt's nascent democracy.[75]

Despite revelations that Morsi, just a year prior to the Arab Spring, had unleashed an anti-American rant and called Jews "bloodsuckers . . . descendants of apes and pigs," the Obama administration pushed forward with plans to deliver billions of dollars in aid and debt forgiveness, topped off by sixteen F-16 fighters and two hundred Abrams tanks.

The irony of the Obama administration's embrace of the Muslim Brotherhood is that the United States ended up accepting what Egyptians would not. After promising a pragmatic and inclusive approach to governance, Morsi instead focused on imposing his narrow religious agenda. The economy plummeted as Egypt's tourism and manufacturing industries ground to a halt and security unraveled. With the first anniversary of Morsi's presidency approaching, Egyptians took to the streets to protest the Muslim Brotherhood, and soon, crowds of millions were demanding that Morsi step down. Rather than stay silent, Anne Patterson, the U.S. ambassador to Egypt and a career diplomat, criticized the protestors. "Some say that street action will produce better results than elections. To be honest, my government and I are deeply skeptical," she explained.[76] Her comments infuriated the Egyptian public, many of whom had supported the Muslim Brotherhood until Morsi turned his back on the democratic system and seized dictatorial power for himself. The Egyptian military offered Morsi a stark choice: compromise with the opposition, or suffer the consequences. When Morsi ignored the threat, the Egyptian military forced him from power.

The ensuing debate in Washington—about whether Morsi's ouster was a coup or not—was actually a sideshow to the main feature. In the course of a year, the Muslim Brotherhood had managed to antagonize tens of millions of Egyptians and force them back into the arms of a military against whose rule they had rebelled. Not only had the Egyptians rejected the Brotherhood, but many of the Gulf States that once supported the group cut off aid. The Brotherhood had become too radical even for Saudi Arabia, a bar that few groups exceed. There was little introspection in either the White House or the State Department about how the quest for engagement had led the United States into a position where it stood firmly against the people in whose behalf its outreach was supposedly conducted.

* * *

American statesmen once took pride in the fact that the United States did not negotiate with terrorists. Over the last quarter century, that principle has become more the exception than the rule. Terrorists no doubt realize that if they remain intransigent—and if they can acquire territory—the West will fold first, abandon preconditions, and water down its demands. Indeed, already there are murmurings in Western circles that perhaps even al-Qaeda could be a target for talks.[77]

Nevertheless, diplomats have little positive to show for the experience of negotiating with Hamas, Hezbollah, and the Muslim Brotherhood. Each group remains as radical and committed to terror as it was before dialogue began. Nor did the intelligence benefits of meeting one's enemies materialize. U.S. diplomats and informal intermediaries still find themselves blindsided by these groups.

The experiment of dialogue with terrorists has been costly. Treating terrorists as diplomatic partners has legitimized their rise to power, at the expense of more moderate groups that eschew violence. Perhaps the experiment would be worth the price if terrorists put down their weapons, but it was naïve to believe that terrorists—accustomed to achieving their aims through violence—would not revert to that strategy when the benefits of diplomacy had run their course. Sixty percent of Palestinians may endorse a two-state solution, but two-thirds of these believe that the two-state solution is merely a stepping stone on the path to Israel's eradication.[78]

Proponents of engagement may be loath to admit it, but sometimes refusal to talk has merits. Talking to terrorists can embolden their state sponsors, enabling them to reap concessions while maintaining the fiction of plausible deniability. Diplomacy can also entrench and preserve the most hardline elements, be they in Palestine, Egypt, Afghanistan, or Pakistan. Conversely, a firm refusal to legitimize terrorism diminishes the benefits of engaging in terrorism. No compromise was granted to the Baader-Meinhof Gang or the Japanese Red Army, and both groups faded from existence. In 2009, the Sri Lankan military did what the United Nations and scores of diplomats had failed to do: they eliminated the Tamil Tigers, ending their thirty-three-year reign of terror. Diplomats might criticize the Sri Lankan army for its brutality, but ordinary citizens can now get on with their lives, unafraid of kidnapping and suicide bombers. Talking to terrorists is not sophisticated; it is harmful. Perhaps U.S. policy should go back to the future and once again send the message that terrorism will not pay.

Chapter Ten

PLAYING POKER WITH PARIAHS

Diplomacy is never a panacea; often it has a heavy price. Whether talks fail or succeed depends on careful preparation to set the right circumstances. That can take years.

When diplomats criticize the refusal to talk to enemies, they often point to Ronald Reagan's willingness to sit with Mikhail Gorbachev, against the advice of Reagan's advisors. But Reagan met Gorbachev in Reykjavik only after years of preparation. During the 1980 election campaign, he spoke of the need to reassert U.S. nuclear "superiority" over the Soviet Union. He later quipped that he wanted "parity, with a margin to spare." As Reagan deployed intermediate-range and cruise missiles across Europe, antagonism toward the United States soared.[1] But Reagan's jokes about bombing Russia convinced Soviet officials that he might just be crazy enough to use those missiles. It appeared to be in Moscow's interest to negotiate.

If diplomacy is to work, both allies and adversaries must believe that the United States is willing to use force. On August 14, 1981, two Libyan fighter jets challenged two American F-14s operating over international waters claimed by Libya. In less than a minute, both Libyan aircraft were down. Looking back on the incident, Defense Secretary Caspar Weinberger commented, "We had demonstrated not only a greatly increased American resolve, but also a greatly increased American capability for dealing with the enemy quickly and decisively. That alone did more to reassure our allies than any budget amounts we were committed to spend, or any amount of rhetoric no matter how well delivered."[2]

The Importance of Credibility

None other than Joe Biden emphasized the importance of credible threat when he spoke on the floor of the Senate just before Operation Desert Fox, the 1998 bombing campaign in retaliation for Iraq's expulsion of international inspectors. "Doing nothing would encourage Iraqi defiance and lead to a complete collapse of the constraints that have been placed upon Iraqi behavior since the end of the Gulf War. It would be the surest way to rehabilitate Saddam Hussein," he said.[3] Two years earlier, Osama bin Laden had galvanized his al-Qaeda followers with the suggestion that Reagan's withdrawal from Beirut in 1983 following the Marine barracks bombing was evidence that America was a paper tiger. Likewise, when Obama unveiled his Afghan strategy at West Point and announced a timeline for withdrawal, the Afghan Taliban and their supporters received a huge morale boost.

Setting the circumstances for diplomacy is a complicated process. Diplomats may want to believe that soft statements create the right atmosphere for diplomacy to succeed, but the opposite is often true when it comes to dealing with rogues. For instance, on April 21, 2004, Jacques Chirac said that Franco-Iranian ties were "excellent." The state-controlled Iranian press turned the French president's comments into an endorsement of Iranian actions in Iraq as the insurgency swelled. "Expressing his concern over the critical situation in the war-torn Iraq, President Chirac said Tehran and Paris share identical views regarding the latest developments in Iraq. France believes that Iran's stands regarding

Iraq are in line with the interests of the world and regional states," the official news agency asserted.[4]

Another mistake that diplomats make in setting the circumstances is holding talks too frequently, particularly at the highest ranks. The president or secretary of state can lend great prestige to talks, but to dispatch either of them too often erodes the value of their involvement. Writing about the incoming secretary of state for the George H. W. Bush administration, Dennis Ross noted, "From the beginning, [James] Baker had one proviso for Middle East policy: he didn't want to be 'flying around the region the way Shultz did.' He would not go to the Middle East unless there was a chance of real progress—a point he made to every Middle Eastern leader who came to Washington in the spring of 1989."[5] In the end, Baker did not adhere to this principle: he traveled to Syria twelve times, twice the number of trips that Shultz had made. Baker's successor, Warren Christopher, made the trip twenty-nine times, resulting in a profound erosion of his prestige.[6]

Senators too often fail to recognize the downside of frequent diplomatic travel. In 2006, Arlen Specter bragged that he had made almost thirty trips to the Middle East, including fifteen to Syria; he would visit Syria more than twenty times before he retired from the Senate.[7] He refused to acknowledge the harm that resulted from the appearance of being a supplicant. "We can't expect someone to hit a home run every time they go to bat," he said.[8] True, but batters do not win respect when they strike out every time. Not only did Specter fail to achieve any meaningful diplomatic breakthroughs, but his visits instead often led to Syrian entrenchment.[9]

Projecting desperation to negotiate can only convey weakness. On the other hand, communicating a sense of indifference can help build a perception of strength and give force to deadlines in diplomacy. "If there was one reality about negotiating with Arafat, it was that he would never agree before he thought he had to," Ross recalled. "The greatest leverage we had was walking away, telling him we had done all we could, this was the best he was going to get, and that holding out for more would cost him dearly."[10] Ross's advice was sound, but Bill Clinton ignored it. George W. Bush understood the power of conveying nonchalance. In June 2002, he declared that he would no longer deal with Arafat so long as the Palestinian leader continued to sponsor terrorism. It was a sound strategy, but one which the State Department fiercely resisted.

When rogues doubt American power, deadlines backfire. Senators Carl Levin and Hillary Clinton pressed for deadlines on North Korea, saying, "It doesn't matter who is at the table as long as we and the North Koreans are there, and as long as both sides negotiate with seriousness and urgency." But they demanded that any penalties for failure to meet deadlines be applied through the United Nations, and so Pyongyang understood that there would be little consequence for ignoring the timeline.[11]

Diplomats often set deadlines and red lines, but then fail to enforce them. When the gap between rhetoric and action grows wide, rogues calculate that America is a paper tiger. In defending the Agreed Framework with North Korea, for example, Secretary Christopher laid down clear red lines: "The path to full implementation has defined checkpoints. If at any checkpoint North Korea fails to fulfill its obligations, it will lose the benefits of compliance that it so clearly desires."[12] Pyongyang almost immediately began violating its agreement, and the Clinton team simply looked the other way in order to avoid disrupting engagement. Kim Jong Il learned that there would be little consequence for violating agreements.

During the George W. Bush years, red lines were erased with abandon. Addressing a joint session of Congress after 9/11, Bush declared, "Either you are with us or you are with the terrorists." And yet, in the months and years that followed, only Iraq paid a price for its terror sponsorship. The Bush team offered lucrative incentives to Iran, turned a blind eye to the Palestinian Authority's complicity in terrorism, and offered diplomatic legitimacy to North Korea. In contrast, countries enjoyed no discernible benefits for aligning themselves with the United States. Georgia, for example, sent two thousand troops to Iraq, but when it faced a Russian invasion, the United States did little more than issue vague condemnation.

In his 2002 State of the Union address, Bush vowed that the United States "will not stand by" as Iran, Iraq, and North Korea develop weapons of mass destruction. The U.S.-led invasion of Iraq in 2003 certainly ended any plans that Saddam Hussein may have had to reconstitute his weapons programs. Yet the Bush administration did little of substance to block Tehran's continued pursuit of nuclear weapons, and by the end of 2002 it had also retreated from its declaration that a nuclear North Korea would not be tolerated.[13]

Iranian authorities gloated. In 2005, the Iranian nuclear negotiator Hossein Mousavian bragged, "Thanks to our dealings with Europe," which theoretically had taken the international lead on the Iran file and had sought to mitigate sanctions in order to test Iranian feelers, "even when we got a 50-day ultimatum, we managed to continue the work for two years." That was how they had been able to complete the uranium conversion facility in Isfahan, he noted, adding, "During these two years of negotiations, we managed to make far greater progress than North Korea."[14]

Still, North Korea would give Iran a run for its money in the contest to gather Western concessions among shredded red lines. In February 2007, the United States along with four other nations offered North Korea approximately $400 million in fuel oil and aid in exchange for North Korea's beginning to dismantle its nuclear facilities within sixty days.[15] The two-month period came and went without progress. Pyongyang negotiated as if it were the stronger party. Kim Kye Gwan, North Korea's top negotiator, reportedly told the American delegation that Pyongyang would not allow nuclear inspections until a Macau bank released $25 million in frozen North Korean profits from narcotics and counterfeiting. Even after the Bush administration blessed the account's release, Pyongyang still missed the deadline.[16]

During September 2007 negotiations in Switzerland, North Korea agreed to disclose its nuclear activities and disable its nuclear programs by year's end.[17] The New Year arrived without any consequence when Pyongyang failed to abide by its agreement. Only in June did Pyongyang submit its nuclear inventory. And while Washington rewarded the communist state by beginning the process to remove it from the State Sponsors of Terrorism list, North Korea continued its nuclear development, leading to new UN sanctions. Even though North Korea had not kept its part of the bargain, the White House did not retract the concessions it had granted.

Ultimatums against Syria were just as tenuous. In April 2003, the State Department announced that Colin Powell would travel to Syria to give Bashar al-Assad an ultimatum to cease supporting terror or face consequences. The threat was empty, though. When journalists asked Powell what those consequences would be, he replied, "That will be taken into account as we decide on our future strategy."[18] While Assad transformed Syria into an underground railroad for suicide bombers targeting Americans in Iraq, Bush slapped on some sanctions, but these were more symbolic than real, given the low volume of bilateral trade.

Transitions between administrations can erase red lines. In 2008, Bush declared, "Our message to the leaders of Iran is also clear. Verifiably suspend your nuclear enrichment so negotiations can begin." At the same time, however, Senator Obama was pledging to negotiate without preconditions. For the Islamic Republic, it was a simple calculation to stonewall until the U.S. elections, a decision for which Obama amply rewarded them.

Even if strategists establish the right circumstances, successful diplomacy requires partners who are both strong and sincere. "Big decisions require strong leaders" like Jordan's King Hussein or Israel's Menachem Begin, argued Aaron David Miller, a member of Ross's team, since peacemaking in the Middle East could be "politically risky and life-threatening."[19] When Anwar Sadat announced a willingness to go to Jerusalem, he captured the world's imagination. He had tried and failed to achieve his objectives for Egypt through war and had decided that diplomacy was a better way. Israeli officials concluded that Sadat was sincere. Moshe Dayan told *Newsweek*, "If you want to make peace, you don't talk to your friends. You talk to your enemies."[20] Alas, many proponents of engagement cite Dayan approvingly without understanding the strategic context of his remarks. Arlen Specter, for example, cited Dayan to justify outreach to Iran, although no Iranian leader had abandoned violence as the means to win objectives.[21]

American policymakers often rationalize insincerity. As Arafat encouraged terrorism, Ross noted that "Defiance, being so much a part of Arafat's appeal to Palestinians, always took precedence over accommodation, particularly if he judged the mood to be negative on his street."[22] Congressmen are notoriously bad at gauging sincerity. In 1982, Saddam Hussein told Stephen Solarz, an influential Democratic representative from New York, that he recognized Israel's legitimate defense needs.[23] At the same time, Saddam continued to feed his domestic audience a steady diet of rejectionism, and within a decade he was launching missiles at the Jewish state. In January 2003, Senator Specter participated in a U.S.-Syrian dialogue and afterword reported, "The Syrians left with a better understanding of our revulsion to suicide bombings targeting civilians after our own experience of 9/11." Yet within months, Syria would become the main conduit for suicide bombers targeting American forces in Iraq.[24]

The best-laid plans are for naught if the timing is off. The end of the Cold War made possible what had been impossible only a few years earlier. In 1991, for example, Gorbachev cut President Hafez al-Assad loose and Syria joined the U.S.-led coalition against Iraq.[25] As the Soviet Union curtailed support for rogues, sanctions against states like Libya and Iraq gained new efficacy.[26] When these regimes enjoyed outside patronage, diplomacy had little hope.

The American election cycle plays an outsized role in the timing of diplomacy, as rogue rulers consider whether they might get a better deal from the incumbent or his challenger. At the same time, second-term U.S. presidents often seek foreign policy breakthroughs to define their legacies. With the clock ticking down, they may rush the process and eschew normal political considerations. As Clinton prepared to leave office, he worried little about the domestic repercussions of forcing Israel to make unilateral concessions. The Palestinian Authority, however, did not seize the chance, for Arafat calculated that with Arab solidarity growing, he stood to gain more by delaying.[27] Three months before the end of Clinton's second term, Secretary Albright announced that she would visit North Korea to pave the way for a possible presidential visit.[28] Just days before leaving office, she gave approval for direct dialogue with Libya.

When timing is not right for effective diplomacy, should the State Department sit on the sidelines? Many diplomats argue that rather than merely wait for opportunities like Sadat's change of heart, they can "actively encourage, seek out, and create opportunities for peacemaking."[29] This was the philosophy that the Carter administration embraced during the Iran hostage crisis. Caspar Weinberger, Reagan's defense secretary, was dismissive of such an approach. "Occasionally, an article or paper would appear by one of the so-called strategic experts who gravitate from one conference to another arguing that we should try to develop 'openings' to the Iranian government; that there was hope that they may want a friendlier relationship with the United States; and similar nonsense, as it seemed to me," Weinberger wrote.[30]

Joel Wit, a Clinton administration diplomat, credited the persistence of dialogue for success in North Korea talks. "The Clinton administration succeeded in negotiating access to a suspected nuclear production site in 1999 because it had an ongoing dialogue," he claimed, as he criticized the Bush administration's failure to maintain that engagement in the face of North Korean violation of the Agreed Framework. While Wit understood the need to penalize Pyongyang, he argued that Washington should never cancel engagement. Any suspension of reactor construction or fuel shipments, he insisted, "must be coupled with a sustained, serious diplomatic dialogue with North Korea."[31]

For those who make peace negotiations their niche, any suspension of dialogue, however strategic, is anathema. But establishing a process in the hope that it might create opportunities can carry a high cost. Many diplomats were critical of the no-nonsense attitude toward terrorism that George W. Bush projected in his first term. According to a United States

Institute of Peace study group comprising many former diplomats, "Bush 43 appeared to be uninterested in testing whether possible openings could be exploited to create diplomatic opportunities."[32] Bush's team, however, viewed engagement in the face of terror as equivalent to letting the PLO perpetrate terrorism without consequence.

Alas, the counsel to ignore rogue behavior is common among the foreign policy elite. In an Atlantic Council study group, Lee Hamilton, James Schlesinger, and Brent Scowcroft lamented the congressional tendency to wield sticks rather than carrots against rogues. "The most important difference between members of Congress and the principal foreign policy decision makers in the executive branch is that the latter do not have the luxury of being able to focus narrowly on single issues," the group concluded. "Instead, they must act with a *global* perspective that includes a whole array of *cross-cutting* U.S. foreign policy interests."[33] The study group criticized legislation requiring the State Department to produce an annual *Patterns of Global Terrorism* report, since such reporting placed Iranian terror sponsorship front and center in the public debate. They also argued that an effective U.S. strategy for engagement with Iran would entail "unilateral steps to remove unnecessary irritants in the U.S.-Iranian relationship," such as lifting the fingerprint requirement for visiting Iranians and facilitating trade.[34] As is often the case, there was no reciprocal demand for the rogue to address U.S. grievances.

The question about when to offer concessions lies at the heart of the debate over how to engage rogue regimes such as Iran and North Korea. The retired diplomats Thomas Pickering and William Luers, writing with Jim Walsh, an academic, criticized George W. Bush for failing to set the stage for successful engagement. They advised Obama "to talk directly to all nations, without preconditions," and suggested a number of steps to build confidence, most of which involved granting unilateral concessions to Iran.[35] The fact that they suggested no confidence-building measures that Tehran might undertake played into Iranian hands and implied U.S. responsibility for a lack of progress. Ironically, the Bush administration had on its own proposed two of their suggestions—putting a U.S. interests section in Tehran and establishing a naval hotline in the Persian Gulf—only to be rebuffed. The United States Institute of Peace has likewise argued for unilateral concessions. "U.S. policymakers must envision a comprehensive set of incentives aimed at attracting as wide a constituency in Iran's ruling elite as possible," they recommended.[36] But unilateral concessions serve only to incentivize rogue behavior.

Is the Home Front an Achilles' Heel?

America will be hard-pressed to succeed diplomatically against rogue actors until the domestic debate about when to engage and when to walk away is settled. Foreign policy is not exclusively foreign. Success requires consensus at home. After Saddam Hussein had invaded and annexed Kuwait, Senator Specter argued that the situation could best be resolved if Congress lined up behind the president and showed that "we mean business and are prepared to fight."[37] Either America's demands are credible, or the United States becomes a paper tiger. Some rogues influence public opinion through nongovernmental institutions that are their ideological allies. During the Cold War, the Institute for Policy Studies abetted Soviet propaganda efforts in the United States.[38] The Alavi Foundation, which the FBI believes is a front for the Islamic Republic of Iran, has supported American academics.[39] But rogues do not need to sponsor academics and journalists if national security is politicized. When Senator Edward Kennedy compared Iraq to Vietnam, he gave succor to insurgents who understood how divided U.S. public opinion was on the war. The Taliban too have sought to capitalize on American public opinion. When Leon Panetta visited Kabul as secretary of defense in December 2011, the Taliban spokesman crowed, "New mujahedeen have been entering the ranks of Taliban every day. They conduct attacks with new tactics and higher morale on occupying troops in every corner of the country."[40] In an era of 24/7 news coverage, rogues know they can use the Western press to fray consensus.

Success in one arena can rally public support, boost credibility, and build momentum in diplomacy broadly. As Warren Christopher recognized, "Diplomacy cannot be compartmentalized, and credibility is not divisible. Our ability to manage one important challenge enhances our ability to handle others."[41] Thus, in describing the willingness of North Korea to come to the table, James Baker noted that "American diplomacy also had the benefit of a powerful new psychological weapon—our stunning victory in the Gulf War."[42] By contrast, Clinton's difficulties in Haiti and Somalia eroded confidence at home and made it more difficult to coerce rogues abroad. Success in Bosnia resurrected the credibility of U.S. diplomacy and bolstered U.S. influence internationally. Eight years later, the U.S. drive to Baghdad had a profound impact on Qadhafi.

In 1993, the State Department announced its hope that the Oslo Accords would be a springboard to broader success. "The secretary does intend to use the momentum created by this historic breakthrough to continue the hard work on some other tracks," the department spokesman said.[43] The following year, Christopher stressed the importance of maintaining "the momentum for peace."[44] Clinton recognized that momentum could go either way. Prior to the summit at Sharm el Sheikh in October 2000, he warned Ehud Barak, the Israeli prime minister, that failure there would "kill Oslo."[45]

The Obama administration made building momentum central to its strategy, at least in theory. "Everything in the process is interrelated," said P. J. Crowley, the State Department spokesman, referring to Israeli-Palestinian peace talks. ". . . That creates momentum and trust and confidence that the process can, in fact, yield results and yield progress toward an ultimate agreement."[46] The same view applied to Iran policy. Concerning a U.S. proposal to swap uranium for the Tehran research reactor, Crowley said, "We thought it was a confidence-building measure that could provide some momentum to enhance the discussions of our core concerns."[47] He also acknowledged the multiplier effect of maintaining momentum against all rogue states simultaneously, saying,

"I think we now have very significant momentum that this is the second major sanctions regime that the international community has passed against outlier states—North Korea last year, Iran this year."[48]

Failing to build momentum can exact a heavy price. Jeane Kirkpatrick, former U.S. ambassador to the United Nations, illustrated the "unintended consequences of inaction" when she spoke about UN passivity in the face of the Rwandan genocide in 1994. She noted that it was followed by mass murder in Srebrenica the next year, and later by genocide in Darfur.[49]

Strategists ignore the importance of momentum at their peril. In July 2010, after what had been NATO's worst month in Afghanistan, Robert Blackwill, who had been deputy national security advisor under Bush, advocated ceding southern Afghanistan to the Taliban. He dismissed worries that the Taliban would not respect the de facto partition, suggesting that the U.S. military would ensure that it did.[50] The Taliban seized upon Blackwill's recommendation as a sign that they were winning.

It can be useful to see momentum as a zero-sum game: when America falters, rogues build momentum. When rogues coordinate their efforts, the equation can become perilous. Ronald Reagan spoke of how rogues conspired against the United States in a 1985 speech:

During his state visit to North Korea, Nicaragua's Sandinista leader, Daniel Ortega, heard Kim Il-song say this about the mutual objectives of North Korea and Nicaragua: "If the peoples of the revolutionary countries of the world put pressure on and deal blows at United States imperialism in all places where it stretches its talons of aggression, they will make it powerless and impossible to behave as dominator any longer." And Colonel Qadhafi, who has a formal alliance with North Korea, echoed Kim Il-song's words when he laid out the agenda for the terrorist network: "We must force America to fight on a hundred fronts all over the Earth. We must force it to fight in Lebanon, to fight in Chad, to fight in Sudan, and to fight in El Salvador."[51]

Even during the Cold War, Pakistan and North Korea were trading arms. As their nuclear trade accelerated after the fall of the Soviet Union, Pakistan's prime minister, Benazir Bhutto, visited Pyongyang. Rather than remit cash for North Korean missiles, Pakistani authorities apparently provided highly enriched uranium, enabling Pyongyang to bypass restrictions on its own enrichment program under terms of the 1994 Agreed Framework.[52] A. Q. Khan, the rogue Pakistani nuclear scientist, acknowledged there was cooperation among rogues. "Since Iran was an important Muslim country, we wished Iran to acquire this [nuclear] technology," he said. "Western countries pressured us unfairly. If Iran succeeds in acquiring nuclear technology, we will be a strong bloc in the region to counter international pressure. Iran's nuclear capability will neutralize Israel's power. We had advised Iran to contact the suppliers and purchase equipment from them."[53]

The dangers posed by weapons of mass destruction push the stakes higher as rogue regimes use diplomatic pauses to proliferate. At the same time, the inability of American officials to factor cooperation and coordination among rogues into their calculations undercuts strategy. Many diplomats criticized Bush's "Axis of Evil" speech for its implication that rogues cooperated, but that debate should now be settled. Iran and North Korea work together to increase their military capacity, against the backdrop of American outreach. North Korean transfers of Scud missiles to Iran began in 1987, long before the Agreed Framework and the six-party talks. The relationship continued even as the Clinton administration made diplomacy with the hermit kingdom a priority. In 1993, both the head of the Islamic Revolutionary Guard Corps, Mohsen Rezai, and the Iranian defense minister, Mohammad Fourouzandeh, led delegations to North Korea to gain assistance for Iran's missile program. The North Koreans helped the Islamic Republic assemble missiles inside Iran.[54] The assistance intensified as the United States prepared for the invasion and occupation of Iraq.[55]

Traditional twentieth-century engagement is not well equipped to handle rogue alliances. At no point did U.S. diplomats working the

North Korea portfolio include North Korean programs overseas, even as Pyongyang's allies allowed it to continue work on prohibited programs. North Korea's assistance to rogue regimes increased under the Agreed Framework. North Korean scientists and engineers from the IRGC were behind the construction of Syria's nuclear reactor, destroyed by Israel on September 6, 2007, and numerous news reports put North Korean and Iranian scientists at each other's missile and nuclear tests.[56] As the George W. Bush administration reached out to both Pyongyang and Tehran in its waning days, North Korea transferred items "of proliferation concern" to Iran.[57] Such transfers only increased after Obama extended his hand.[58]

Measuring Success, Measuring Failure

The military can spend as much time studying past successes and failures as it does preparing for new challenges. Seldom do diplomats, however, conduct after-action reports to determine why diplomacy has failed or to highlight what they might have done differently to succeed. As secretary of state, Hillary Clinton launched high-profile engagement with many of the same Taliban leaders whom diplomats had engaged during her husband's administration, without ever asking why previous diplomatic efforts failed or explaining why she now expected a better result.

Self-assessment is difficult for diplomats because of their aversion to metrics. Often, when the going gets tough, the metrics get tossed; but embracing illusory success raises the price of talking to enemies. To understand the lack of precision with which diplomats consider their track record, one needs to go no further than the State Department's daily press briefing. Invariably, the spokesman talks of success; seldom will he acknowledge any failure.

The Arab-Israeli peace process is a case in point. While negotiating with Palestinians has been a staple of State Department strategy for more than two decades, at no point have diplomats established firm metrics to gauge success. In December 1992, Edward Djerejian, assistant secretary of state, defined "progress" as merely getting the two sides to talk. "Let's not forget the beginning where we couldn't get one of the delegations off the couch in the lobby of the State Department to go into the negotiating room," he said.[59] State Department spokesmen often talked of progress over the course of the next several years. Even as talks between the Israelis and the PLO bogged down over security issues, Michael McCurry spoke of "productive, interesting exchanges."[60] And when the Oslo Accords' Declaration of Principles remained unimplemented almost six months after the deadline, McCurry talked about "enormous progress."[61]

North Korean behavior is bizarre even at the best of times, yet the State Department often describes its talks with North Korea as "cooperative and constructive."[62] When the Clinton administration acquiesced to North Korean demands that the U.S. extend a humiliating apology after a U.S. helicopter strayed into North Korean territory, McCurry called it "good progress."[63] Nicholas Burns also equated talking with progress during the Clinton administration's attempts to engage North Korea. Discussing a March 1997 bilateral meeting between U.S. and North Korean officials, Burns defined "modest progress" as a meeting in which all that had occurred was the delivery of an American letter to the North Korean delegation.[64] After reaching agreement to hold a second day of meetings on a proposal for talks about a peace agreement on the Korean Peninsula, Charles Kartman, deputy assistant secretary of state, told the press, "We made some encouraging progress."[65] This was not quite true, since Pyongyang had demanded additional aid as a precondition of further talks. Extortion is not a good indicator of progress. Likewise, James Rubin described discussions as "useful and productive" simply because the North Koreans had behaved "in a businesslike and cordial manner."[66] Only once did the Clinton team suggest more precise metrics with regard to North Korea diplomacy. On September 1, 1993, Winston Lord, assistant secretary of state, outlined two conditions for continued dialogue with Pyongyang: "Meaningful engagement with the IAEA" and "a meaningful dialogue, including on the nuclear question, between South and North Korea."[67] When the going got tough, even these vague metrics were cast aside.

The American distaste for metrics is not shared by all partners. While the Israelis accepted some ambiguity to reach an agreement with the Palestinians, they also demanded an "unambiguous" mechanism to verify Palestinian compliance. This took the form of a checklist and a timeline.[68] When the metrics showed the agreement to be in trouble, Rubin dismissed the metrics. "There are some commitments that still have to be fulfilled," he admitted, "but in our view, overall, they are making progress here."[69]

The Clinton peace team's claims of "progress" were seldom based on anything other than a desire to justify talking.[70] Warren Christopher defended his twenty-nine trips to Syria in terms of "progress" made. Yet the State Department, when challenged, explained that the purpose of his travel was "to figure out what further substantive progress must be made in order for Israel and Syria to narrow their differences."[71] Progress, it seems, is a word the State Department throws around freely.

Seldom does the press challenge diplomats' claims of progress, but diplomats can get defensive when it does. "We've always called it as we see it," asserted Nicholas Burns in 1996. "I've often said up here that there hasn't been any progress made on this particular day. We haven't always claimed progress, but, when we've claimed progress—when we've said there's progress—we've done it because we think there is, and I would judge us by our record."[72] In reality, however, Burns had never acknowledged a lack of progress. Similarly, Dennis Ross's memoirs show a dissonance with the claims of progress that he and his team had made while they were engaged in diplomacy.[73]

In effect, rather than gauge diplomacy by any objective measure, the State Department would make it up along the way. It was a very rare occasion when the State Department spokesman acknowledged the lack of metrics. In 1998, when a Palestinian negotiator reported that 90 percent of the interim agreement was yet to be resolved, Rubin argued, "There's no easy way to put a percentage on this. If an issue is largely resolved but there is one outstanding part of it, one can either say that's 95 percent completed, or one can say that it's zero percent completed."[74]

The same is true with regard to Iran. In June 1998, Rubin pronounced Mohammad Khatami's declaration that "Terrorism should be condemned in all its form" to be "significant."[75] The State Department's finding of significance was based more on hope than on reality. If the Iranian funding, arming, and support for terror had been considered as a metric, then Iranian terror sponsorship had increased. In a 2000 briefing, Richard Boucher acknowledged that the State Department had no way of determining progress when he said, "I'm not sure I can give you sort of a barometer of ups and downs in the support of terrorism."[76] A decade later, the State Department still had not defined its Iran metrics. In 2010, when a Washington Institute study group set out to assess U.S.-Iran diplomacy, disagreements about diplomacy's achievements centered on one question: "what are the appropriate metrics by which to measure progress?"[77] If diplomats are willing to ignore U.S. strategic interests, then it is possible to remove impediments to good relations. Many diplomats prefer this method; it is the path of least resistance.

The Bush team was little better when it came to peace process metrics. Even if they pointed to the "Roadmap" as a means to measure success, the State Department acknowledged in a confidential 2003 memorandum that "The US Mission has not developed benchmarks by which to assess progress and monitor implementation of the Roadmap."[78] Likewise, in 2004, Boucher described talks aiming to win a "complete, verifiable and irreversible dismantlement" of North Korea's nuclear program as "largely successful" simply because they put the U.S. goal on the agenda. Those talks, however, failed completely.[79] As the war in Iraq dragged on, the constant declarations of progress unattached to any fixed measure led the U.S. Congress to impose eighteen benchmarks upon which the Bush administration would report—everything from the creating of a constitutional review committee, to a viable security plan for Baghdad, to agreement on how to divide oil resources among Iraq's ethnic and sectarian groups.[80]

The European approach to Iran, at least initially, was rooted in firm metrics. When launching its "critical engagement," the European Union tied its dialogue to improvement in human rights, resolution of the Rushdie issue, and reduction in terrorism. "Improvement in these areas will be important in determining the extent to which closer relations and confidence can be developed," the European Council concluded.[81]

Karl Inderfurth, an assistant secretary of state in the Clinton administration, came to understand the importance of metrics after the Taliban strung along American diplomats ahead of the 9/11 attacks. As the Obama administration sought to negotiate, Inderfurth argued that Secretary Clinton should ask several questions to determine whether talks could be successful, not the least of which would be, "Do the Taliban accept a political solution to the Afghanistan conflict, and what is their vision of it?"[82]

Although the State Department routinely speaks of "progress" in the absence of solid metrics, it is possible to identify a shift in language when there is actual progress. When a PLO-Israel deal on a Declaration of Principles to serve as a framework for negotiations in the Oslo process appeared imminent, McCurry mentioned "substantial progress" three times on the same day.[83] When Israel and the PLO finally reached agreement the following week, McCurry effused that it was "a very important historic agreement" and a "psychological sea change in the history of the Middle East."[84] After Libya agreed to forfeit its WMD programs, Paula DeSutter, assistant secretary for verification and compliance, declared that "the success of Libya is a ray of light in the otherwise dark world of the WMD black market" and labeled Libya cooperation "absolutely amazing."[85] Likewise, Boucher spoke of "the remarkable progress that we've made with Libya."[86] Perhaps the standard of success is found after the fact.

* * *

In many ways, diplomats diving into negotiations with rogues are like compulsive gamblers who, no matter how much they lose, believe that one more round might reverse their fortunes. But unlike a gambler leaving a casino, a diplomat cannot determine whether he has gained or lost by the cash in his pocket. The State Department's aversion to metrics enables diplomats to keep playing no matter how far in the hole they fall.

The idea that it never hurts to talk is wrong. Poorly planned dialogue can exact a high cost, and even the most skilled diplomats will fail when their governments do not demonstrate strength and leverage. Ronald Reagan entered into negotiation with the Soviet Union only after a substantial military buildup. Unilateral concessions may win Western hearts and minds, but few rogues are the products of Western culture. In dealings with Iran, North Korea, the Taliban, Hamas, and the Palestinian Authority, concessions eroded the façade of strength needed to effect a successful outcome.

Engagement represents just the tip of the diplomatic iceberg. Success usually comes only after robust military and economic efforts to set the right circumstances. Muammar Qadhafi flipped—at least temporarily— not only because of "commitment, dialogue, and co-operation," as the British Foreign Office claimed,[87] but even more because of superior American intelligence and a demonstrated U.S. willingness to use force. The international community's sweeping sanctions on Libya had imbued the diplomatic process with greater leverage. The real inducement was the lifting of sanctions, rather than giving incentives that would risk encouraging bad behavior. In the diplomatic poker game, the West had the aces, and Qadhafi's hand was a mess. Without leverage, years of preparation, and the willingness to walk away from the table, talk can exacerbate the very problems that diplomats hope to resolve.

Chapter Eleven

CORRUPTING INTELLIGENCE OR CORRUPTED INTELLIGENCE?

If diplomatic battles over rogue regimes are bad, the intelligence battles can be even worse. Any diplomatic engagement with rogue rulers is a high-risk undertaking. Because rogue regimes are also among America's most opaque adversaries, intelligence is a major tool. When intelligence gets in the way of political and diplomatic goals, something has to give. Often it is the intelligence: seldom do presidents want their diplomatic initiatives to be the sacrifice.

When the CIA created its Directorate of Intelligence, social scientists believed they could predict international affairs. In reality, social science proved far more social than scientific. It is likewise for intelligence analysis. The personal biases of analysts inevitably intrude into their assessments even if they see themselves as neutral. Often, analysts equate any questioning of their conclusions with political malfeasance.[1] Allegations of the politicizing of intelligence in the lead-up to the Iraq War have been the stuff of headlines, but the problem goes far deeper.

The value of intelligence to policymakers rests in large measure on its independence. When the stakes are especially high, analysts sometimes shape intelligence to support policy, or they may suppress information that politicians might use to build a case for war. This corruption may sometimes be deliberate, as career analysts with agendas might assume they know better than politicians who are new to the job. Many CIA analysts opposed George W. Bush's re-election and tried to undermine his chances. "Of course they were leaking," said W. Patrick Lang, a former Defense Intelligence Agency official. "They told me about it at the time. They thought it was funny. They'd say things like, 'This last thing that came out, surely people will pay attention to that. They won't re-elect this man.'"[2]

More often, analysts unconsciously follow their personal biases or project their own beliefs and logic onto an adversary. This "mirror imaging" can particularly affect the analysis of rogues, since the intelligence community's security clearance procedures favor those with limited overseas experience. Most analysts of Iran, for example, have never set foot in that country. Likewise, even Langley's best Arabists are unlikely to have had more than a fleeting visit to PLO-run refugee camps or Hezbollah strongholds. They may fill in the blanks without realizing it.[3] As the adage goes, if all you have is a hammer, everything looks like a nail.

The mirror imaging can go both ways. North Koreans who engage in informal, nongovernmental dialogue believe their American interlocutors act on government orders because North Koreans cannot act apart from the Dear Leader's instruction. Likewise, Middle Easterners embrace conspiracy theories about the United States and the American press because the opacity of their own society encourages conspiracy.

Analysts' gatekeeper role enables them to project their bias up to policymakers. A day's worth of intelligence could take more than a year to read, so the CIA sorts it. There is a direct relationship between the seniority of any official and the breadth of information he might read. A deputy assistant secretary, for example, might supervise policy relating to a dozen or more countries. The portfolio of an assistant secretary might include several dozen, and so on to the secretary and the president, whose portfolios encompass the world. Every day, the CIA produces the President's Daily Brief, a report encapsulating the top news and intelligence to be read only by the president, the vice president, and perhaps a few other officials.[4] News selection affects policy. For example, if the CIA omits evidence of direct Palestinian Authority complicity in terror or Iranian outreach to al-Qaeda, policymakers may believe that the Ramallah and Tehran regimes are more benign than the facts indicate.

Intelligence analysts accuse policymakers of cherry-picking when they ignore findings that do not support their policy. Too often, analysts believe their own conclusions to be gospel, but analysis is often open to interpretation. And while discussions in the intelligence community can be ongoing, policy debates are not. When a leader makes a decision, the debate ends.[5] Once politicians invest in a policy, they resent the intelligence community playing spoiler. President Lyndon Johnson used to describe his frustration with spoilers by telling a story about his cow Bessie: "One day, I'd worked hard and gotten a full pail of milk, but I wasn't paying attention, and old Bessie swung her shit-smeared tail through the bucket of milk. Now, you know that's what these intelligence guys do. You work hard and get a good program or policy going, and they swing a shit-smeared tail through it."[6]

Intelligence and Politics during the Cold War

Arms control was the focal point of U.S.-Soviet Cold War diplomacy. The stakes were huge, not only for national security, but also in politics. If disarmament talks succeeded, a president might reap political rewards. The worst-case scenario was not that talks would fail, but rather that the Soviet Union would be found to have violated its agreement and gained a competitive advantage. Hence, American administrations were often tempted to interpret data in the best possible light.

In 1961, the Kennedy administration founded the Arms Control and Disarmament Agency (ACDA) to create a firewall between arms control and politics. Housed within the State Department but reporting to the president, the agency was shrouded in suspicion. Diplomats feared that the ACDA would interfere with the State Department's mission to foster good relations with other countries, while conservatives feared that ACDA employees, anxious to prove their utility, would promote arms control even when it was detrimental to national security.[7] Robert Lovett, who had been secretary of defense under Truman, worried that the agency was "going to be a mecca for a wide variety of screwballs."[8]

Controversy swirled around the ACDA during its nearly four-decade existence. During the Johnson administration, the agency clashed repeatedly with the Joint Chiefs of Staff, who felt that its interference endangered American military preparedness.[9] The Nixon White House slashed the ACDA's budget after some senators used its findings to criticize Nixon's agreements in the Strategic Arms Limitation Talks (SALT I).[10] Nixon had reason to be sensitive about challenges to SALT I. The talks concluded with the Anti-Ballistic Missile Treaty of 1972, which did not usher in a new era of security. On the contrary, the Soviet Union immediately began to upgrade the size and lethality of its nuclear arsenal.[11]

During the 1980s, the ACDA clashed with the State Department. Dov Zakheim, a longtime Pentagon official, and Robin Ranger, a political scientist at St. Francis Xavier University, explained why in a 1990 article. "The Department of State finds life without enforcement of treaties politically easier," they wrote. "Ignoring compliance policy allows the many arms-control enthusiasts in and out of government freely to develop schemes without worrying about enforcement."[12]

The Arms Control and Disarmament Agency was not the only focus of Cold War intelligence battles. When the CIA reported to Congress that multi-warhead Soviet missiles would not threaten America's ability to retaliate against a first strike, Kissinger dismissed the CIA's conclusions as based on speculation more than hard evidence, and he ordered the director of central intelligence to revise the findings.[13]

In 1974, Professor Albert Wohlstetter from the University of Chicago accused the CIA of underestimating Soviet missile deployments and allowing the Soviet Union to gain an edge.[14] Wohlstetter's paper sparked an initiative to form the so-called Team B, an outside group of experts to assess the same intelligence. Arms control was a hot issue, not only between but also within parties. For example, in his first tenure as secretary of defense, Donald Rumsfeld distrusted Soviet compliance and worried that President Ford's desire for a legacy might color his judgment on SALT II.[15] The CIA initially resisted any outside appraisal, but on May 26, 1976, its director, George H. W. Bush, signed off on Team B. The group began operating the following autumn.

In December 1976, shortly after Carter won the presidency, Team B issued its report finding that the CIA had consistently underestimated the intensity, scope, and threat of Soviet strategic programs. The report suggested that Moscow embraced SALT to seek comparative advantage, not to reduce mutual threat and advance peace.[16] Critics, on the other hand, argue that hindsight shows Team B to have exaggerated Soviet capabilities, leading directly to Ronald Reagan's decision to embark on an expensive military buildup.[17]

Carter enthusiastically sought détente. Rumsfeld recalled how, when he was briefing Carter and his national security team, Carter excitedly said that he had an "unprecedented" communication from the Soviet Union expressing interest in new arms-control talks.[18] Whereas Ford blamed Pentagon intransigence for his failure to get SALT II passed, Carter's defense secretary, Harold Brown, was less hostile to the treaty than Rumsfeld had been. When Carter launched the SALT II talks, he wanted nothing to stand in the way of agreement. Against the wishes of his European allies, therefore, he omitted the Soviet Union's SS-20 intermediate-range nuclear missiles from the agenda; to include them might risk the agreement.[19] Carter sang SALT II's praises,[20] but the strategic community harbored doubts, and the Democrat-controlled Senate refused to ratify the agreement. "The Carter team had invested so much in believing that the Soviets were well-intentioned that they found it almost impossible to reverse course," Rumsfeld observed.[21] Reagan scuttled the agreement seven years later.

Throughout the late 1970s and early 1980s, reports persisted that the Soviet Union was using chemical and biological weaponry in Laos, Cambodia, and Afghanistan, in violation of the 1972 Biological and

Toxin Weapons Convention.[22] Tribesmen in Laos described clouds of colored gas or oily liquid emerging from bombs or rockets that exploded at tree-top level. Twice in 1980, Dutch journalists filmed a Soviet helicopter dropping canisters emitting a yellow cloud on a village outside of Jalalabad, in eastern Afghanistan.[23]

When the governments of Laos, Vietnam, and the Soviet Union ignored State Department inquiries, the Carter administration went public with its charges, and the United Nations decided to investigate. The American intelligence community was able to collect samples of plants with mysterious lesions, as well as tissue samples, blood, and urine from refugees exposed to the "yellow rain." In July 1981, a toxicologist at the Armed Forces Medical Intelligence Center suggested that the symptoms suffered by those exposed were consistent with thichothecene mycotoxins, a poison produced naturally by certain types of mold that grow on wheat, corn, and other grains.[24] In February 1982, a Special National Intelligence Estimate concluded that the Soviets were mass-producing thichothecene mycotoxins as chemical weapons. Diplomatic pressure and lack of access to Vietnam and Laos meant that the investigating UN Group of Experts was unable to determine if chemical weapons had been used on the refugees. Many American allies conducted their own studies affirming the American conclusion, but refused to release their results for fear that definitive proof of Soviet cheating would torpedo arms-control talks.[25] They were unwilling to let intelligence get in the way of diplomacy.

So too were many ideologues. Revisionists feared that Reagan might employ proof of Soviet chemical weapons use as justification to renew chemical weapons research and production.[26] Harvard and Yale scientists suggested that the yellow rain might have been natural in origin, a mixture of pollen and bee feces. The State and Defense departments reassessed Hmong refugee interviews and dismissed them.[27] The bee feces story ignored the geographically divergent occurrences of yellow rain, their correlation with battlefield operations, traces of the toxin on a gas mask, extensive Soviet literature on mycotoxins, and the failure of yellow rain episodes to recur after the conflict ended.[28] The skeptics cherry-picked data to reach the desired conclusion.

Reality would soon intervene. In early 1980, reports surfaced of an "outbreak of disease" in Sverdlovsk, today's Yekaterinburg, in the Ural Mountains.[29] Intelligence suggested that an anthrax outbreak originated at a biological weapons facility. The Soviets blamed tainted meat. American assessments, however, placed the casualty count above one thousand and pointed to inhalation anthrax rather than the gastric variety. Witnesses and émigrés reported quarantine and decontamination efforts. Satellite imagery showed that a building in the suspect military complex was abandoned after the incident.[30] Some intelligence officials questioned Soviet guilt, disputing both the difference in symptoms between gastric and inhalation anthrax, and the possibility of determining an accurate casualty count.[31]

Once Reagan left office and there was no need to worry about his aggressiveness, the intelligence community restored its initial conclusion that the Soviet Union had used chemical weapons.[32] More damning, in 1990, the press exposed the KGB cover-up at Sverdlovsk. Two years later, President Boris Yeltsin acknowledged that the Soviet Union had maintained an offensive biological weapons program.[33]

Debate surrounding both the yellow rain and Sverdlovsk incidents centered on burden of proof.[34] Shifting the proof is one way that intelligence analysts and policymakers will shape conclusions. During the Reagan administration, Congress mandated that the White House report regularly on Soviet noncompliance with arms-control agreements. These reports often sparked more debate than they resolved. Sometimes, the State Department would seek to dilute a report's findings.[35] Even when the reports concluded there was "a pattern of Soviet noncompliance," evidence supporting the conclusions remained a subject of heated debate. That the intelligence community qualified its findings with modifiers like "probable," "likely," and "potential" was enough to create reasonable doubt. Adding to the uncertainty was the fact that subsequent reports often used the same information to draw opposite conclusions. For example, the president's February 1985 report on Soviet noncompliance found no violation resulting from the Soviet use of dismantled SS-7 missile sites to support the SS-25. The next report, however, determined the Soviets to be in violation of SALT I for the same activity.[36]

Soviet behavior challenged even the most dovish Americans' determination to prove that treaties worked. In 1983, an American spy satellite detected a Soviet radar complex near Krasnoyarsk, in the middle of Siberia. Its configuration suggested a military purpose. The sheer size of the complex underlined the scale of Soviet subterfuge of the Anti-Ballistic Missile Treaty.[37] To confirm the cheating, however, would undermine future arms-control agreements with the Soviet Union, so the Kennedy and Johnson advisors McGeorge Bundy and Robert McNamara, along with Gerard Smith, a SALT I negotiator, pronounced the facility to be "of only marginal importance." The Arms Control Association also dismissed Krasnoyarsk as insignificant, and the Federation of American Scientists suggested that suspicion was "more a product of faulty deduction than of analysis of the facts."[38]

Reagan thought otherwise. "No violations of a treaty can be considered to be a minor matter, nor can there be confidence in agreements if a country can pick and choose which provisions of an agreement it will comply with," he explained.[39] While this might sound self-evident, it was a controversial statement to analysts and academics. "The Soviets can respond to U.S. concerns only if Washington establishes politically realistic standards of compliance," observed Gary Guertner, a professor at California State University.[40] William D. Jackson, a professor at Miami University in Ohio, actually recommended that the United States "avoid inordinately intrusive inspection and verification procedures which hinder progress in arms control."[41]

Even those willing to excuse Soviet cheating had difficulty finding a credible legitimate purpose for the Krasnoyarsk complex. Although its construction began while Carter was in the White House, some suggested that the threat posed by Reagan's policies motivated Soviet cheating.[42] Soviet attempts to link dismantlement of the Krasnoyarsk complex with that of a thirty-year-old American missile-tracking facility in Thule, Greenland, belied the Kremlin's initial claim that the complex was merely a space tracking system.[43] Only in 1989 did the Soviets, after years of angrily denying the accusations, finally admit that the radar violated the ABM Treaty.[44] The Soviet foreign minister, Eduard Shevardnadze, called it "a clear violation."[45]

The fall of the Soviet Union did not end the manipulation of intelligence. As Russia revived its capabilities, the CIA simply denied knowledge of new defenses that violated the ABM Treaty, despite having in its files new evidence on Russian antiballistic capabilities and command-and-control.[46]

Is Manipulation the Exception or the Rule?

Accusations of intelligence manipulation went beyond arms control and the Soviet Union. Any area subject to sharp policy debate became a battleground for conflicting analyses. Sometimes, the manipulation was by omission. In 1983, *Foreign Relations of the United States*, an annual declassification of documents, usually after a thirty-year embargo, omitted key documents discussing the 1954 CIA-backed coup against Jacobo Árbenz Guzmán in Guatemala. It took an act of Congress in 1991 to force declassification of documents that described events more accurately.[47] And, sometimes, intelligence became a high-stakes football because of its policy implications. Throughout the 1970s and 1980s, American diplomats often clashed with the White House regarding both the degree of communist influence in leftist movements and the culpability of right-wing juntas in human rights abuses. Robert White, U.S. ambassador to El Salvador in 1980, accused the Reagan administration of weaving "a consistent tissue of lies" about the region.[48] In 1993, ahead of the U.S. intervention in Haiti, Bill Clinton resisted intelligence assessments that Jean-Bertrand Aristide, the leader whom the White House sought to install, was neither mentally stable nor committed to democracy.[49]

The easiest way to manipulate intelligence is to change the terminology. If the Clinton administration initially embraced the concept of rogue regimes, diplomats in its waning years believed that the rogue label hindered diplomacy by stigmatizing partners. Speaking on National Public Radio, Madeleine Albright announced that no longer would the United States designate certain regimes as rogues. "We are now calling these states 'states of concern,'" she said. Richard Boucher, State Department spokesman, explained that the category of rogue regime "has outlived its usefulness."[50] Robert S. Litwak, a National Security Council staffer under Clinton, elaborated, "No longer thinking of this very disparate group of states as a specific category . . . will permit the necessary differentiation to deal with each country in its own terms."[51]

Such logic transcended parties. In the months before 9/11, the elder statesmen Lee Hamilton, James Schlesinger, and Brent Scowcroft complained that the State Department's definition of terrorism unfairly targeted only "one strand of the whole spectrum of politically motivated violence." It was not much different from asymmetrical warfare, they argued.[52] If terror sponsorship hampered diplomacy and trade, they suggested it would be both easier and better to redefine terror than to demand real change. Rather than condemn all terror sponsors, they recommended that the State Department distinguish "between different kinds of terrorism."[53] George W. Bush delinked religious ideology from al-Qaeda terrorism in order to avoid hurting Muslims' feelings, regardless of how Bin Laden and terrorists such as the 9/11 hijackers justified their actions.[54] The Obama administration took political correctness to an even greater extreme when Janet Napolitano, the secretary of Homeland Security, aimed to replace the word "terrorism" with "man-caused disasters."[55]

Perhaps the most egregious example of political manipulation of terror designations across administrations involves the Mujahedin al-Khalq (MKO). In 1997, the Clinton administration designated the MKO a terrorist group as a concession to Iran's newly elected president,

Mohammad Khatami, whom Clinton hoped to woo. In the years prior to the Islamic Revolution, the MKO had killed Americans, and subsequently it had aimed its terrorism at the Islamic Republic's leadership. To erase their terror designation, the MKO did not forswear terrorism but rather paid five- and six-figure speaker fees to a bipartisan array of former ambassadors, cabinet secretaries, and even General James Jones, Obama's first national security advisor. Their investment paid off. In 2012, after repeated endorsements from their own unofficial lobby, a U.S. court demanded that the State Department delist the MKO. Secretary Clinton complied. Diplomacy determined the timing of the group's listing, and bribery—for lack of a better word—determined its delisting. Intelligence played little role.

From Carter to the present, peace on the Korean Peninsula has been a major diplomatic goal. Carter had set his sights and staked his legacy on Korea years before Anwar Sadat and Menachem Begin made Arab-Israeli peace possible. Carter did not want intelligence assessments to get in the way. He refused to consider any intelligence that did not support his desire to withdraw troops from the Korean Peninsula. "I have always suspected that the facts were doctored by DIA and others, but it was beyond the capability even of a president to prove this," Carter explained.[56] When Secretary Cyrus Vance assigned Richard Holbrooke to oversee the Korea policy review, he was forbidden to offer the option of not withdrawing forces.[57]

North Korea's nuclear program kept advancing through the 1980s. By February 1987, analysts suspected that North Korea intended to produce plutonium. When satellites the following year detected a new structure at Yongbyon, two football fields long and six stories high, it looked as if they had found the smoking gun. But some intelligence analysts, intent on avoiding conflict, suggested the building might be a factory producing a nylon-like fabric.[58] This was nonsense, but it was enough to inject uncertainty into the debate and avoid offering politicians a cut-and-dried case to establish North Korean cheating.

The Clinton administration too would not allow conflicting assessments of North Korean sincerity to get in the way of making a deal. Shortly after Clinton took office, the White House pressured the International Atomic Energy Agency to downplay North Korean noncooperation. To describe events accurately might precipitate a crisis.[59] Later, when Kim Young Sam, the South Korean president, told the *New York Times* that the Dear Leader was simply buying time, the State Department was furious.[60] When he repeated his criticism the following year, Clinton blew his top.[61] Of course, in hindsight, the South Koreans were right.

Diplomats had become so invested in the process that they refused to recognize the obvious. After the Agreed Framework had been signed, the *Washington Post* columnist Jim Hoagland noted the difficulty of trusting North Korea, let alone celebrating the deal: "North Korea's government is isolated, Stalinist and economically crumbling. Only a few months ago it was listed as a 'backlash state,' an appellation the Clinton administration awards only to a half-dozen certified stinkers of the earth." Hoagland then demanded that Clinton's team answer three basic questions: "(1) Do they really believe that North Korea has ceased being a backlash state and should therefore be trusted? (2) Why did Kim Jong Il do the deal now? (3) Won't it serve as an incentive for other backlashers to pursue nuclear weapons programs, to get bought off by the United States if for no other reason?"[62]

Clinton not only refused to answer such questions, but also refused to budge on his assessments.[63] By 1997, there was little doubt that the Agreed Framework had failed. The State Department would not accept the intelligence community's findings. To do so would invalidate Clinton's approach. Nicholas Burns, the State Department spokesman, asserted, "We are absolutely confident . . . that the agreed framework put in place two and a half years ago is in place, it's working. We are absolutely clear that North Korea's nuclear program has been frozen and will remain frozen."[64] Stephen Bosworth, the U.S. ambassador to South Korea, also insisted that the Agreed Framework was on track. Nothing was further from the truth.[65]

In 1999, the General Accounting Office (GAO) reported that it could no longer verify how North Korea distributed or used its food aid.[66] The communist regime allowed World Food Program monitors to visit only 10 percent of institutions receiving food aid. The North Korean military would block access to inspectors. The State Department refused to accept the GAO findings because to accept them would be to admit North Korean cheating and to undermine the premise of engagement in which they had already invested too much.[67] Likewise, when the GAO reported that monitoring of heavy fuel oil had gone awry, the State Department informed Congress that they trusted that the regime's use of the heavy fuel oil was consistent with the Agreed Framework.[68] Congress did not buy it, but in an angry exchange of letters, Secretary Warren Christopher in effect covered up North Korean noncompliance.[69] The State Department continued to insist that the Agreed Framework was "a concrete success."[70]

It was not only in Washington that diplomats and politicians cast aside intelligence to preserve diplomacy. Kim Dae-jung had made the so-called Sunshine Policy his cornerstone policy. Sunshiners could point to the June 2000 summit between the South and North Korean presidents as a victory for their persistence. Only subsequently did Kim Dae-jung's secret $200 million payoff come to light. As South Koreans began to turn on the Sunshine Policy, the desperation to justify it grew. "What had begun as a means to an end had become an end itself—an end from which there could be no deviation and a dogma to which, as the Sunshine Policy approached its denouement, there could be no official denunciation," explained Sung-Yoon Lee, a professor at Tufts and researcher at Harvard.[71] Indeed, South Korean politicians and often their American partners bent over backward to avoid the conclusion that the policy was a failure. Hence, they found ways to blame everything but the Sunshine Policy or the North Korean regime for multiple North Korean missile tests and the 2006 nuclear test.

When George W. Bush entered the Oval Office, engagement with North Korea had failed. The intelligence community may have been suspicious of North Korean intentions, but it was wary of the policy track that Bush was taking. After he included North Korea in the Axis of Evil, the CIA consciously diluted its intelligence estimates on the regime's plutonium possession.[72] With the Iraq War looming, they did not wish to give Bush any fodder for another war. Diplomats also remained invested in Korea diplomacy. In 2007, Christopher Hill, the point man on North Korean nuclear issues, presented to Congress an artificially rosy picture of the diplomatic process with North Korea, so as not to undercut support for engagement.[73]

Condoleezza Rice's push to remove North Korea from the terrorism list was perhaps the most blatant example of intelligence suppression on the Korea file. When Rice's State Department attested, for purely political reasons, that the North Korean government had not sponsored terrorism since the 1987 airline bombing, information available to the U.S. government suggested the opposite. Sources in France, Japan, South Korea, and Israel allege robust North Korean involvement with both Hezbollah in Lebanon and the Tamil Tigers in Sri Lanka.[74] Ali Reza Nourizadeh, a London-based Iranian reporter close to Iran's reformist camp, described North Korean assistance in the design of underground Hezbollah military facilities, assertions supported by a diverse array of reporting.[75] These tunnels allowed Hezbollah to shield rockets from Israeli surveillance prior to the 2006 war and to evade during it. Chung-in Moon, a professor at South Korea's Yonsei University, has reported Mossad allegations that Hezbollah missiles included North Korean components.[76]

North Korean efforts to aid the Tamil Tigers were more blatant. The *Far Eastern Economic Review* reported in 2000 that North Korea had supplied the insurgents with weaponry, citing intelligence sources in Bangkok. The State Department's *Patterns of Global Terrorism* made similar claims in 2001, 2002, and 2003, rendering its subsequent claims that Pyongyang had abandoned the terrorism business curious. Three times between October 2006 and March 2007, the Sri Lankan navy intercepted cargo ships flying no flag or identifying marker and found to be carrying North Korean arms.[77] For Rice and Bush, though, diplomacy outweighed intelligence reality.

Cooperation between rogue regimes can compound the challenge. In advance of James Kelly's visit to North Korea in October 2002, some U.S. officials—presumably those who were skeptical of engagement with North Korea—leaked word that Pakistan was supplying nuclear technology to Pyongyang. An extensive debate arose in Washington over how to respond. "There was a lot of pressure not to embarrass Musharraf," one senior administration official told the *New York Times*.[78] Likewise, the White House was reluctant to castigate North Korea for its assistance to Syria's nuclear program, fearing that the revelation of such assistance would undermine diplomacy.[79]

A willingness to let diplomatic considerations override intelligence affects China policy too. Despite intelligence pointing to Chinese proliferation, the Clinton administration approved an export license for a Cray supercomputer to China, convincing itself that Beijing was being upfront in saying the computer was for weather forecasting and would save lives. In reality, China used supercomputers for its ballistic missile programs.[80]

In April 2010, the treasury secretary, Timothy Geithner, delayed the submission of a report to Congress in order to avoid accusing China of manipulating exchange rates. Senators criticized this move. "The past few years have proven that denying the problem doesn't solve anything," wrote Charles Grassley of Iowa, the top Republican on the Senate Finance Committee.[81]

Russian relations are likewise subject to intelligence manipulation. On June 27, 2010, three days after the Russian president visited the White House, the FBI arrested ten Russian spies. The bust raised questions not only about Russian behavior, but also about the Obama administration's emphasis on "resetting" U.S. relations with the Kremlin. Still, the White House was determined not to let Russian subterfuge disrupt diplomacy.[82] U.S. officials released the Russian agents in a hastily arranged spy swap, which raised eyebrows in the Senate and among former intelligence officials. "We have to do a damage assessment, and when you do a damage assessment, you want to have access to the individuals involved for an extended period of time so you can get new leads and ask questions," commented Michelle Van Cleave, a former head of U.S. counterintelligence. "We lost all that. We lost a clear window into Russian espionage, and my question is: What was the rush?" The obvious reason for the rush was to avoid a trial that might expose Russian malfeasance and further undermine Obama's outreach.[83]

The Middle East has long been an intelligence battlefield. Seeking rapprochement with Baghdad, the Reagan administration wanted to remove Iraq from the State Sponsors of Terrorism list, "both to recognize Iraq's improved record and to offer an incentive to continue this positive trend," according to the White House congressional liaison. The idea that Iraq had abandoned terror was fiction, however; its support for Palestinian groups was well known. Years later, Noel Koch, former assistant secretary of defense, acknowledged that removing Iraq from the list had nothing to do with terrorism and everything to do with Reagan's strategic goals.[84] Indeed, the administration was even willing to overlook Saddam Hussein's granting of refuge to Abu Abbas, mastermind of the *Achille Lauro* hijacking.

Rep. Howard Berman, a Democrat from California, was less willing to turn a blind eye to Iraqi terror and introduced a bill to return Iraq to the terrorism list, but Secretary George Shultz adamantly refused. "Iraq has effectively disassociated itself from international terrorism," Shultz wrote, warning that Berman's bill risked "severely disrupting our diplomatic dialogue on this and other sensitive issues." He promised that he would not hesitate to return Iraq to the list if he concluded that any Iraqi-sponsored groups conducted terror attacks.[85] Evidence of Iraqi complicity in terrorism continued to pour in, but the State Department refused to report it. Similarly, the White House shunted aside concerns about Iraqi nuclear ambitions in the interest of selling high technology to Iraq.[86] The Pentagon even dressed down its employees for obstructionism when they raised red flags. It was the same logic that led the administration to bury reports of Iraqi use of chemical weapons against Iran and, later, its own Kurdish minority.[87]

Things came to a head in 1990 when Iraq invaded Kuwait. After Saddam Hussein was pushed back, Senator Joe Biden criticized successive administrations for long ignoring evidence that the Iraqi dictator had not changed. The White House, he said, acknowledged reality

> *only after . . . disregarding a mountain of incriminating evidence that Saddam was using American aid to buy arms; only after ignoring Saddam Hussein's genocidal slaughter of his own Kurdish citizens; only after fostering high technology exports to Iraq even as Saddam Hussein provided safe haven for the world's most infamous terrorists; only after overlooking his manifest quest for nuclear and chemical weapons; only after supplying Saddam Hussein with military intelligence almost until the eve of the invasion.*[88]

A decade later, the opposite charge was made concerning the lead-up to the second Iraq War. Partisan critics claim that George W. Bush manipulated intelligence to concoct a justification for invading Iraq—a case often cited as the archetype for the politicization of intelligence. In fact, it was anything but. Certainly, the intelligence that influenced Bush's decisions was flawed. The 2002 National Intelligence Estimate overstated the conclusiveness of intelligence on Iraq's WMD programs, as did the President's Daily Brief.[89] But there is no evidence that intelligence agencies bowed to political pressure. Superiors did not change products to conform to political orders. Indeed, European countries, Arab allies, the United Nations, and even Saddam's own underlings believed that Iraq had a covert weapons program.[90]

The intelligence community's conclusions were wrong, but were they corrupted by politics? As one analyst puts it, "Politicization is like fog. Though you cannot hold it in your hands, or nail it to a wall, it does exist, it is real, and it does affect people."[91] Ego and politics often mingle to color intelligence analysis. Joseph Wilson, having been dispatched by the CIA to Niger to investigate charges that Iraqi officials had tried to purchase uranium there, jumpstarted a flagging career by accusing the Bush administration of politicizing intelligence on that subject.[92]

Not every error is the result of politicization, although some are. Just as the intelligence community overstated Saddam's weapons programs, so did the CIA exaggerate the shah's strength in the years leading up to the Islamic Revolution in Iran. When a young Farsi-speaking diplomat, Stanley Escudero, questioned the firmness of the shah's grip on power in the early 1970s, the State Department almost ended his career.[93] Likewise, when Carter finally received a cable describing how turbulent the situation actually was in Iran, he was incensed at the ambassador who authored it, for it contradicted much previous reporting.[94]

In the wake of the Islamic Revolution, reconciliation became diplomats' top goal. After terrorists bombed the Khobar Towers in Saudi Arabia, killing nineteen U.S. Air Force personnel, suspicion centered on Iran. The Senate Intelligence Committee concluded that the attack "was not the result of an intelligence failure"; the U.S. intelligence community was already following Iranian intelligence activities in Saudi Arabia's Eastern Province.[95] President Clinton refused to allow Iranian complicity to disrupt his diplomatic efforts. When the official investigation fingered Tehran, Clinton ordered the report withdrawn and destroyed. It was par for the course according to Caspar Weinberger, the former defense secretary, who in Senate testimony described how hope for diplomacy often led administrations to table retaliation.[96] The State Department's willingness to cherry-pick intelligence can be downright dangerous for American travelers. After Khatami called for a "dialogue of civilizations" in 1998, the State Department revised its travel warning to make the Islamic Republic seem like a safe destination. It was, of course, wishful thinking not grounded in intelligence. Soon afterward, Iranian hardliners attacked a bus carrying Americans.[97]

Diplomats lambasted Bush for including Iran in the Axis of Evil, but this inclusion rested on intelligence that Iran was seeking nuclear weapons and sponsoring terrorism. It is often the proponents of engagement who massage the intelligence. Deputy Secretary Richard Armitage even cast the Islamic Republic as a democracy.[98] Diplomats long tried to cover up Iranian complicity in Iraq's insurgency. "I think there's a dearth of hard facts to back these things up," said Adam Ereli, a State Department spokesman.[99] There was a growing body of evidence that suggested the opposite, however.[100] Hezbollah was not only active in Basra, but was so bold that it openly shared a building with the Badr Corps, an Iraqi militia created and trained by the Islamic Revolutionary Guard Corps.

Perhaps the most blatant case of political manipulation of intelligence involves the 2007 National Intelligence Estimate (NIE) regarding Iran's nuclear program and its government's intentions. The U.S. intelligence community had warned since the 1990s that the Islamic Republic was covertly pursuing uranium enrichment as part of a nuclear weapons program, and that Iranian scientists were experimenting with plutonium and uranium. In 2002, an opposition group revealed the existence of a secret enrichment facility at Natanz, a revelation that Tehran confirmed when confronted with it. In November 2007, the National Intelligence Council released a new estimate in which it declared, "We judge with high confidence that in fall 2003, Tehran halted its nuclear weapons program."[101]

The National Intelligence Council based its 2003 and 2007 findings on much the same evidence. What had changed was the political climate. The rise of Mahmoud Ahmadinejad to the presidency and the Iranian assistance to militias in Iraq brought a sharp downturn in U.S.-Iranian relations. Some in the intelligence community feared that evidence suggesting Iranian nuclear progress might lead Bush to launch military strikes against Iran. Rather than look impartially at the intelligence in hand, the estimate's authors gamed how policymakers might react to the information. Indeed, the three primary authors—Tom Fingar, a former analyst for the State Department's Bureau of Intelligence and Research; Vann H. Van Diepen, the national intelligence officer for WMD; and Kenneth Brill, former U.S. ambassador to the International Atomic

Energy Agency—all had reputations for hyperpartisanship and distrust of the Bush administration.[102]

Politicization occurred two ways: First, it changed definitions. A footnote attached to the NIE's finding "We judge with high confidence that in fall 2003, Tehran halted its nuclear weapons program" redefined "nuclear weapons program" to exclude uranium conversion and enrichment.[103] The underlying fiction was that military and civilian enrichment are distinct enterprises, even though it is impossible to differentiate between them, and the ability to produce highly enriched uranium is the biggest technological hurdle on the way to building a nuclear bomb. The redefinition also absolved Iran for the secrecy that surrounded the Natanz enrichment plant until its cover was blown. After all, if covert enrichment outside of inspectors' monitoring was no longer considered military in nature, then diplomats, with sleight of hand, could say that Tehran's secrecy was no cause for concern.

The NIE's authors also cherry-picked evidence. Discounted intelligence included Iran's experimentation with polonium 210, a key component for nuclear bomb triggers, and documents showing that Iran sought a warhead that would detonate at a level too high for anything but a nuclear warhead. The intelligence community's assertion that Tehran had abandoned its nuclear weapons drive because of "increasing international scrutiny and pressure" was tenuous. Even if Iranian authorities had abandoned their program—although evidence points more toward a tactical pause—there are alternative explanations. First, by ousting Saddam Hussein over WMD questions, the U.S. military achieved in three weeks what the Iranian army was unable to do in eight years. Second, the Iranians suspected that an Iranian defector had informed the CIA about facilities in which Iranian scientists and engineers conducted nuclear weapons design work.[104]

Further, by suggesting with false certainty that it was diplomacy rather than military coercion or intelligence prowess that had changed Iranian behavior, the intelligence community was trying to guide officials toward a specific policy. Desiring to avert military action might be noble, but corrupting the intelligence process is not. It was for these reasons and more that foreign intelligence services criticized the American report.[105]

The Obama administration, desperate to withdraw U.S. troops from Iraq in order to fulfill a campaign pledge, was just as willing to ignore Iranian malfeasance in Iraq. "Many people point . . . and talk about an Iranian influence," said Vice President Biden in a speech to the Veterans of Foreign Wars in 2010. "Let me tell you something, Iranian influence in Iraq is minimal. The Iranian government spent over $100 million trying to affect the outcome of this last election, to sway the Iraqi people, and they utterly failed."[106] The WikiLeaks document dump showed Biden to be lying, for they are replete with warnings about growing Iranian influence.

The decision to designate Iran's Revolutionary Guards as a terrorist organization in August 2007 should have raised questions about the politicization of intelligence, not because the designation was made, but rather because the Guards' behavior had been consistent for decades; diplomats had simply refused to draw the logical conclusions earlier. Too often, advocates of engagement indulge in wishful thinking. Whichever way the tea leaves fall, diplomats will read them as proving an Iranian desire for rapprochement.[107]

As diplomats sought to bring Libya in from the cold, they buried intelligence demonstrating that Muammar Qadhafi remained a rogue. Shortly before London restored ties with Tripoli, British authorities confiscated thirty-two crates of Scud missile parts—labeled automotive parts—from a British Airways flight bound for Malta en route to Libya. The British foreign secretary, Robin Cook, hushed up the incident so as not to derail his diplomatic efforts.[108] A decade later, the Scottish government released Abdelbaset Ali Mohamed al-Megrahi, the mastermind of the Lockerbie bombing, on compassionate grounds after determining that he had terminal cancer and less than six months to live. Leaked ministerial letters between British and Scottish officials, however, show that London hoped to trade Megrahi for oil contracts. The doctor who had publicized the dire diagnosis had lied.[109] Megrahi lived for three more years.

American diplomats were little better. When a Libyan plot to assassinate the Saudi crown prince came to light, the Bush administration promised consequences should the Libyan regime be found culpable. When such evidence did emerge, diplomats cast it aside. Instead, they had a stern conversation with the Libyans to remind them of their commitment "to cease all support for terrorism."[110] The State Department spokesman refused to detail the Libyan response and explained that the terror question would not affect the decision to set up a permanent U.S. office in Tripoli.[111] Just a year later, William Burns called Libya a true ally in the war on terror, effectively perjuring himself during a congressional hearing.

Nowhere has political filtering been more consistent than in the Arab-Israeli peace process. Leading peace processors like Dennis Ross are overt about it. Discussing efforts to empower the exiled PLO leadership at the expense of grassroots Palestinian activists, Ross related how the George H. W. Bush administration tried to "preserve the fiction that the PLO was not responsible for the dialogue."[112]

Clinton put Palestinian-Israeli peace at the forefront of his foreign policy. Politically, he was loath to admit failure, so the State Department painted failure as progress. Years of heightened expectations took a toll, though. When Bill Clinton went to the Camp David talks in 2000, he expected to leave as the triumphant broker of Middle East peace. Instead, he went away embarrassed and angry. Albright shamelessly described the summit as achieving "incredible progress."[113] Over subsequent weeks, the State Department repeatedly spoke of the summit's "success" to an increasingly skeptical press.[114]

George W. Bush was less willing to ignore Palestinian terror, a change that frustrated the State Department and jeopardized a career ladder built on negotiating with Palestinians. When the State Department issued its semiannual report on Palestinian behavior to Congress in April 2001, it refrained from assigning responsibility for violence to any senior PLO or

Palestinian Authority official, citing a lack of "conclusive evidence," even as the report acknowledged that Palestinian leaders did not discipline those involved in violence.[115] Arafat had provided money to Tanzim and the al-Aqsa Martyrs' Brigades to conduct attacks, though.[116] The State Department basically lied to Congress about intelligence in order to avoid complicating a diplomatic mission in which it believed, and continued to embrace the "no conclusive evidence" line even after the seizure of documents showing a direct link between Yasir Arafat and an illicit shipment of Iranian arms.[117] Likewise, the State Department chose to ignore the involvement of Maher Fares, head of military intelligence in Nablus, in a Tel Aviv bus bombing.[118]

Near the end of his second term, Bush tried to kick the moribund Palestinian-Israeli peace process into high gear. As the political stakes grew larger, the State Department again began to claim success even where none existed. "Well, the Israelis and Palestinians have both made quite a bit of progress on a lot of issues," said the spokesman in October 2008. "Now, they've kept that progress quiet in terms of the details, which, as you've heard from us, are a positive thing."[119] In effect, the State Department argued that secret details equaled success, and that a skeptical public should take diplomats' word for it. Officials simply ignored intelligence suggesting otherwise.

Sometimes American policymakers feel that diplomatic necessity leaves them no choice but to turn a blind eye. For example, so long as the Red Army remained in Afghanistan, the Reagan administration bypassed sanctions designed to kick in as a result of Pakistan's nuclear program. Either the State Department and the intelligence community did not pass information about Pakistan's nuclear program up to the White House or, more likely, Reagan cast aside such information for the sake of greater U.S. security interests, at least until the Soviet withdrawal from Afghanistan.

After 9/11, the White House again needed Pakistan. The Bush administration waived sanctions implemented because of Pakistan's nuclear program and transformed the country overnight into "America's closest non-NATO ally." Again, Pakistan got a free pass. The Bush administration even downplayed the danger posed by A. Q. Khan. In June 2004, Donald Rumsfeld professed confidence that Khan's "network has been dismantled," and four months later, Condoleezza Rice declared the network to be "out of business."[120] This was nonsense.

Obama aides also twisted intelligence to court Pakistan. While rumors of subterfuge by Inter-Services Intelligence were rife among regional specialists and intelligence analysts, both Pentagon and CIA briefings to Congress were "vague and inconclusive."[121] Aid continued to flow. In July 2010, Secretary Clinton announced an additional $500 million, calling the United States and Pakistan "partners joined in common cause."[122]

When terrorists attacked Indian targets in Afghanistan, Richard Holbrooke, Obama's special representative for Afghanistan and Pakistan, blatantly denied Pakistani complicity, although evidence suggested it.[123] After WikiLeaks exposed intelligence gathered regarding Pakistani involvement in terrorism, the *New York Times* observed, "The behind-the-scenes frustrations of soldiers on the ground and glimpses of what appear to be Pakistani skullduggery contrast sharply with the frequently rosy public pronouncements of Pakistan as an ally by American officials, looking to sustain a drone campaign over parts of Pakistani territory to strike at Qaeda havens."[124] Perhaps no person better exemplified the cavalier treatment of intelligence than Leon Panetta. As CIA director, he warned, "We really have not seen any firm intelligence that there's a real interest [in reconciliation] among the Taliban, the militant allies of al-Qaida, al-Qaida itself, the Haqqanis, [and] . . . other militant groups."[125] Yet when he became the defense secretary, he pushed reconciliation with the same groups. The State Department got in on the act. When it issued its list of terrorist organizations on August 6, 2010, it added the Pakistani Taliban but omitted any Afghan Taliban group.[126]

Osama bin Laden's death was Obama's counterterror triumph, but this victory against terrorism resulted in more twisting of intelligence to fit political aims. The controversy over *Zero Dark Thirty*, a cinematic recounting of the raid that took out Bin Laden, received criticism for its depiction of waterboarding as efficacious. In a partisan report, Democrats on the Senate Intelligence Committee approved findings denying the utility of torture. Whether or not waterboarding al-Qaeda detainees was responsible for locating Bin Laden, the sharp partisan divide among senators investigating the matter suggests the political filter by which intelligence is judged.

As the 2012 election neared, Obama's national security record looked strong: He had not only killed the world's most wanted terrorist, but had also effected regime change in Libya at a fraction of the cost of the Iraq War and with no U.S. casualties. That changed on September 11 when terrorists stormed the U.S. consulate in Benghazi and murdered the American ambassador. Because political operatives surrounding Obama feared that acknowledging the incident as a terrorist attack might undermine his election claims, they constructed the fiction that the riot was a spontaneous reaction to an amateur video mocking the Prophet Muhammad. In the aftermath, the administration even changed CIA talking points—the epitome of intelligence politicization.

* * *

The value of intelligence derives from its ability to serve as an independent check on policy. The firewall between intelligence and policy has never been as solid in reality as in theory, however. While journalists and academics denounced the George W. Bush administration for allegedly manipulating intelligence to justify war with Iraq, the problem is actually far greater when administrations wish to make peace with rogue regimes. Once a president launches a high-profile peace process, not only is his legacy at stake, but so is the prestige of entire departments. Fear of failure creates a tremendous temptation to ignore dire intelligence, for when peacemaking fails, then war looms. Intelligence officers are only human, and they can allow fear of the alternative to color their work.

The problem has grown along with the intelligence bureaucracy. Analysts may believe they are apolitical, but every individual is burdened with bias. All it takes is a few politicized analysts to taint the entire community, a threshold long since passed. Most may not cherry-pick or spout falsehood; simply manipulating definitions or shifting burdens of proof has been enough to alter conclusions. The failure of the intelligence community to stand up to diplomats with the same firmness they show in resisting politicians is to the benefit of no one, except perhaps the rogue regimes.

Chapter Twelve

BLESSED ARE THE PEACEMAKERS?

When diplomats cannot sit with rogues or terrorists, others lead the way. People-to-people dialogue has become the staple of peace studies programs and organizations devoted to conflict resolution. If official diplomacy is Track I, then Track II involves unofficial talks between retired but well-connected officials, academics, and activists. Between them is an intermediate track in which high-ranking politicians and decision makers back-channel. Such talks fulfill an important role. In polarized societies, the plausible deniability afforded by informal talks can be the difference between success and failure.[1] The PLO and American Jewish activists, for example, maintained a quiet but effective dialogue before formal U.S. recognition of the PLO enabled direct talks.[2]

Back channels are important, but they can be effective only outside the limelight. "We made enormous progress through the secret channel in Stockholm between Abu Ala and myself," wrote the Israeli negotiator Shlomo Ben-Ami. "But the exposure of the channel destroyed any possibility for further progress."[3] Both North and South Korean intelligence agents talked under the guise of the Red Cross.[4] At the same time, back-channeling has a cost, as theoretical concessions may undercut official negotiating positions. Both Ehud Barak and Yasir Arafat resisted understandings that their back-channeling proxies had reached.[5] Informal dialogue can result in wasted time, or worse. Poorly timed talks, self-serving intermediaries, and insincere adversaries can actually exacerbate conflict.

People-to-people dialogue became popular during the Cold War. With tensions rising after the downing of Francis Gary Powell's spy plane in 1960, President Dwight D. Eisenhower and Nikita Khrushchev, the Soviet premier, encouraged meetings of American and Soviet citizens. After the Soviet invasion of Afghanistan, diplomats grew frustrated at the lack of dialogue between Cold War adversaries. "A great many folks felt you could not simply cut off communications with an adversary who had so many nuclear weapons and missiles aimed at you," explained Joseph Montville, the veteran American diplomat who coined the "Track II" concept.[6]

What works with one adversary may not work with another, however. As Ronald Fisher, an expert in dialogue at American University, has noted, culture matters in diplomacy.[7] Westerners might embrace an escape from straitjacket diplomacy—and Russia is rooted in Western culture—but any North Korean who veered off script would end his life in a labor camp. Iranians too are constrained in options for talking. In late 2007, the foreign minister, Manouchehr Mottaki, informed American Track II participants that the Iranian government was suspending its dialogue. When some Iranians tried to continue, security forces confiscated their passports.[8]

Cultural differences affect interpretation in diplomatic talks. American officials would sometimes see the North Koreans as little more than cult drones, while North Koreans found the jocular Americans to be disrespectful.[9] North Koreans project formality onto any discussion, and thus treat theoretical options as true concessions. "Track II efforts could literally dissuade North Korea from recognizing reality," argued L. Gordon Flake, an Asia specialist.[10]

If there was one thing North Koreans liked, it was the money that came with Track II dialogue. Myriad organizations, from Stanford University to the Social Science Research Council, tried dialogue with

Pyongyang. Each brought hard currency to the regime at a time when it was scraping the barrel to fund its nuclear and missile programs.[11] Harvard University played into North Korean hands when it organized a twelve-day alumni trip to the hermit kingdom. Most of the more than $6,000 spent per person went to North Korean hotels and travel companies. For Harvard, totalitarianism had become little more than a Disney World attraction.[12] Nor was it much more than that for Google's execute chairman, Eric Schmidt, who handed Kim Jong Un a propaganda victory when he visited the hermit kingdom and North Korean television filmed him touring computer labs just a month after Pyongyang had launched a satellite—defiantly demonstrating much the same technology required to launch an intercontinental ballistic missile. Even though the Obama administration generally supported rapprochement with North Korea, the State Department spokeswoman, Victoria Nuland, said of Schmidt's visit, "We don't think the timing of this is particularly helpful."[13] Indeed, it was not.

Congressional trips had a different cost. "We were received with great courtesy and had the opportunity to engage in genuine dialogue," reported Senator Ted Stevens of Alaska after traveling to Pyongyang with four colleagues in April 1997. "We did not go there to negotiate; we went to listen and to learn."[14] North Korea achieved a propaganda coup for the price of a few visas. Rogue tourism is epidemic among limelight-seeking congressmen. Arlen Specter's many visits to Syria never changed the regime's behavior, but did undercut efforts to isolate Syria. Dana Rohrabacher, a Republican congressman from California, met with a Taliban representative in 2001—just months before 9/11—to pitch a peace plan. The Taliban couldn't have cared less about peace, but welcomed the legitimacy that Rohrabacher's visit brought.[15]

The Problem with Intermediaries

In times of crisis, clarity is crucial. Alas, intermediaries often sow confusion. William H. Sullivan, the U.S. ambassador to Iran in the late 1970s, recalled how his "communications from Washington grew increasingly confused" as the shah teetered. Sullivan described "the increasing number of visitors who came from Washington to Iran in official or quasi-official capacities, carrying various messages to the shah."[16] One of these visitors was a businessman, the second a cabinet official, the third a CIA agent, and the last a senator. Each emphasized different points.

The hostage crisis amplified the pattern. The UN secretary-general, Kurt Waldheim, and former attorney general Ramsey Clark both began negotiating with Iranian intermediaries against Carter's instructions.[17] "Throughout this period," recalled Harold Saunders, the assistant secretary of state, "there was a proliferation of private groups and individuals who felt that their going to Tehran in an unofficial capacity could prove an American sounding board for Iranian expression of grievances." Later, some intermediaries even went so far as to propose that a revolutionary tribunal try the hostages prior to their release.[18]

The wrong Iranian intermediary could be just as disastrous. The Reagan-era arms-for-hostages scheme went awry when Robert McFarlane, the national security advisor, chose a serial liar, Manucher Ghorbanifar, as his intermediary.

The situation becomes murkier when intermediaries self-appoint. In 1990, as diplomats scrambled to force an Iraqi withdrawal from Kuwait, Jimmy Carter wrote to UN Security Council members lobbying against efforts by Brent Scowcroft, the national security advisor, to win authorization to use force.[19] Self-appointed intermediaries continue to blight U.S.-Iran relations.[20] Professor Hooshang Amirahmadi of Rutgers University has made a career of pushing himself forward as a go-between for Washington and Tehran. Because Iranian leaders seldom tolerate intermediaries unsympathetic to their positions, access requires a willingness to parrot Iranian lines. Speaking in Iran, Amirahmadi asserted, "The problem of terrorism is a true myth. Iran has not been involved with any terrorist organization. Neither Hezbollah, nor Hamas are terrorist organizations."[21] Affirming American adversaries does not aid understanding, but sabotages it.

The temptation to try improving relations at the expense of core interests also afflicts senior officials. In 2001, an Atlantic Council study group chaired by Scowcroft and Lee Hamilton proposed loosening sanctions to encourage Iranian moderation.[22] The recommendation was naïve, since the Iranian regime invested any hard currency it could get in its covert nuclear weapons program.

Perhaps it is not surprising that the Iranian government treats American interlocutors as useful idiots. In 2003, proponents of dialogue seized upon a supposed grand bargain from Iran to resolve all outstanding differences. While Iranian officials privately acknowledged that the offer was fake, self-styled citizen diplomats embraced the fake offer as evidence of Iranian altruism and a reason to bash Bush.[23] Javad Zarif, Iran's ambassador to the United Nations who has since become the Islamic Republic's foreign minister, cultivated numerous American journalists, professors, and politicians. Those who met him considered him sincere and trustworthy, but as John Bolton, the U.S. ambassador at the United Nations, observed, "He's very used to Western habits, so he is the perfect face for an unreasonable regime."[24] Zarif's private emails show he played Americans for fools.

It is for this reason, rather than to resolve conflict, that Iranian authorities so often embrace Track II processes. During the George W. Bush administration, Americans were invited to Iran by the reformers, who may be the Islamic Republic's soft face but are nonetheless loyal to the regime. Their message was consistent: Stop funding civil society. Participants returned to the United States and parroted the Iranian line.[25]

When Track II proponents disagree with American policy, they often complain that policymakers fail to listen to the true specialists. In reality, Washington seldom lacks for experts; it just lacks consensus among them. If area experts feel ignored, it is sometimes because their perspective is too narrow. For example, some diplomats and Iran experts—like Ambassador Sullivan, Secretary Cyrus Vance, and Deputy Secretary Warren Christopher—strongly advised Carter to deny the shah entry into the United States for medical treatment, but such a refusal would have reverberated among other longstanding American allies. At other times, academics try to amplify narrow specialties into false claims of expertise. The case of Professor Rashid Khalidi is instructive: his academic work centers on Palestinian nationalism, yet he complained that the Bush administration failed to consult him prior to the Iraq War, a country he had neither visited nor studied. Hypocrisy is also a factor: Diplomats often dismiss warnings from more experienced parties who counsel against talks, as many Korea experts did when Clinton's team pushed forward with plans to engage the North.[26] Perhaps ignorance is bliss.

North Korea, like other rogues, seeks out sympathetic intermediaries. Kim Il Sung initially welcomed the Reverend Billy Graham, but then rejected him in order to choose someone more favorable.[27] In 1980, Kim expelled Rep. Stephen Solarz of New York, the first American public official to meet with him, after Solarz not only conveyed U.S. concerns but also challenged the Dear Leader's truthfulness.[28] Kim then looked for a statesman who would not have the temerity to challenge him.

Few senior statesmen are as sympathetic toward rogue rulers as Jimmy Carter, so Kim invited him to Pyongyang annually. The State Department waved off the former president each year, but as crisis loomed in 1994, Jim Laney, Carter's friend and the ambassador to South Korea, urged him to visit the North.[29] Carter made no secret of his free-lancing.[30] Clinton's team began to suspect that he was more sympathetic to communist North Korea than to the democratic South.[31]

Carter was not the North's only handpicked intermediary. Selig Harrison, a fellow of the Carnegie Endowment for International Peace, visited Pyongyang frequently. The more he projected the North Korean line, the more exclusive access he received.[32] Over the years, Harrison consistently blamed America in any dispute. Tony Namkung, a Korean American academic, also became a communist tool, whether by conviction or a desire for access. He went so far as to coach North Korean officials on their statements and strategy.[33] While his contemporaries saw Namkung's mediation as helpful, subsequent North Korean cheating suggests that Pyongyang had cultivated him as a means of disinformation.

A sincerity gap regularly undermines outreach. Too often, proponents of Track II diplomacy project their own sincerity onto adversaries. Joe Biden repeatedly applauded efforts at dialogue by the Open Society Institute, the Nixon Center, and the American Iranian Council; and in the wake of 9/11, he urged the Bush administration to permit American organizations to spend money in Iran.[34] But when Bush agreed to allow the American Iranian Council to open an office in Tehran, the Iranian government refused to allow it to proceed.[35]

Targeted Outreach

Tailoring outreach to specific sectors is an approach that many people consider promising. For example, the National Academies, describing themselves as "advisers to the nation," reported in 2007 that over the course of a decade they had enabled more than five hundred Iranian and American scientists from eighty institutions to meet and discuss scientific issues.[36] The Academies also sponsored a visit to Iran by four American Nobel laureates, and afterward effused that the Iranians gave the laureates a "truly astounding" reception.[37] The State Department encouraged these exchanges, with diplomats praising the "long-term payoff . . . of positive international relationships and mutual understanding."[38] But the Iranian scientists had admired their American counterparts even before the dialogue began. The exchanges did little to address the real problem: Iran's revolutionary ideology.

Meanwhile, the Islamic Republic—under fire because of Ahmadinejad's Holocaust denial and genocidal threats—got a public relations reprieve. Thomas Jordan, a participant who was a geology professor at the University of Southern California, acknowledged that the Iranian government might exploit the visit, but he did not object; indeed, he "was hoping it would be" used for public relations.[39] The Iranian press gladly used the visits for propaganda. For example, the state-controlled Fars News Agency interspersed its story about the visit of a physicist, Burton Richter, with commentary about the justness of Iran's nuclear program. The story printed statements by Richter out of context, such as his pronouncement that "Iran wants to join the group of countries that want to know about the biggest things, like space."[40] Ordinary Iranians would only see a Nobel laureate's endorsement of Iranian ambitions, even while the U.S. government was concerned that the Islamic Republic was using its satellite program as cover for its missile program.

Likewise, when the National Academies hosted Khatami in Washington, D.C., they handed a propaganda platform to an unabashed supporter of Iran's military buildup. Khatami used his meeting with scientists to lobby for passenger-plane spare parts, which the Iranian government then proceeded to pirate for military use. Rather than see exchanges as a means to convince the Iranian government to alter its behavior, the National Academies questioned the U.S. policy of sanctions on Iran. The sanctions may have complicated Track II dialogue, but this was a minor price to pay for retarding Iran's nuclear programs. The desire to continue dialogue resulted in a warped perspective on a national security issue.

One particularly trendy form of people-to-people engagement is sport diplomacy. The theory is simple: Athletics transcends politics and can break down walls. The record is spotty, however. Proponents of sport diplomacy say that American participation in the 1936 Berlin Olympics, in which the African American runner Jesse Owens won five gold medals, discredited Nazis on their home turf.[41] But Owens's triumph did not discredit Hitler in German eyes; on the contrary, hosting an international sporting event added legitimacy to his rule.

American officials revisited the same question as the 1980 Moscow Olympics approached, in the wake of the Soviet invasion of Afghanistan. The *New York Times* opined, "Any occasion that brings people from all over the globe together in peace and concord, to compete and cooperate in honest friendship, has to merit vigorous support." But George Ball, a senior diplomat during the Kennedy and Johnson administrations, argued for a boycott of the games in order to deny Brezhnev the legitimacy that Roosevelt had granted to Hitler.[42] Secretary of State Edmund Muskie likewise recognized, "Losing the Olympics would be a severe blow to the Soviet Union. It might give them a greater measure of respect for our own firmness and determination."[43]

The most famous example of sport diplomacy is the ping pong match credited with breaking the ice between the United States and communist China. As Kissinger notes, however, this iconic moment did not initiate relations but followed months of secret diplomacy.[44] To credit "ping pong diplomacy" with the China breakthrough puts the cart before the horse.

Although its record was overblown, both Clinton and George H. W. Bush turned to sport diplomacy to reach out to the Iranian people. In 1998, Iranians warmly welcomed five American wrestlers to Tehran. Two hundred reporters greeted them at the airport. "Our hope was, with Iran, that sports could once again provide an opening wedge in improving relations," said John Marks, head of the Search for Common Ground. The State Department was self-congratulatory about such events. After one tournament in Bandar Abbas, the department reported, "When the Americans arrived in the arena . . . they were greeted to a standing ovation."[45] Ordinary Iranians' admiration for Americans was never in question, however. The sporting events did little to change the hearts and minds of those directing Iranian policy. When Iran's soccer team defeated America in the 1998 World Cup, the Supreme Leader crowed, "Tonight, again, the strong and arrogant opponent felt the bitter taste of defeat at your hands."[46]

Still, diplomats' hopes may not have been without basis. Iranian hardliners recognized the risk that too much interaction could erode walls. After one U.S.-Iran soccer match, for example, a hardline paper asked whether the matches served any purpose "other than destroying the barriers toward negotiations with the United States and destroying the hatred toward the Great Satan in public opinion?"[47]

Athletic contests may not provide a magic solution, but there are other advantages to high-profile events. When Iran lost to Bahrain in a World Cup qualifying match in 2001, Iranians took to the streets, inflamed by rumors that the regime had ordered the team to throw the game in order to avoid mixed-gender celebrations afterward. If diplomatic talks can pass without notice, millions tune in to televised sporting events, be they wrestling in Iran, soccer in Libya, or baseball in Cuba. Defeat embarrasses dictators. Losing Iraqi teams faced torture when they lost matches. After North Korea lost 0–7 in the 2010 World Cup, Kim Jong Il sent the team's coach to a slave labor camp. The "Miracle on Ice" at the 1980 Winter Games, in which the U.S. hockey team defeated the heavily favored Soviets, humbled the Kremlin and reversed American malaise.

Educational exchanges have also become staples of people-to-people dipomacy. Nicholas Burns, as under secretary of state, sought to bring more Iranian students into the country. "We've all seen the huge, long-term impact of having someone study in our country and get to know the American people and what that means in 30, 40 years," he explained. Such logic may not be so airtight, however. Sayyid Qutb, a Muslim Brotherhood ideologue, studied in Colorado between 1949 and 1951. Rather than develop a love for Americans, he reacted against Western liberalism and doubled down on terrorism. Likewise, Khomeini did not embrace Western culture after his sojourn in France.

Ordinary citizens do not necessarily benefit from educational exchange either, since ideological fealty often outweighs academic quali-fication for Iranians seeking university admission and scholarships to American universities. Unless rogue regimes allow Americans to administer qualifying exams like the Scholastic Aptitude Test or the Test of English as a Foreign Language, and unless truly independent bodies handle the local scholarship process, only the regime's most trusted supporters will benefit. When the United States was intervening in Haiti twenty years ago, diplomats differentiated "ordinary Haitians" from "MREs," the morally repugnant elites, whose children would win places in American universities. The inability of U.S. officials to conduct background checks on students from rogue regimes can have serious repercussions, especially given the recent Iranian attempts to surveil American targets for potential terrorist attacks and the Syrian efforts to spy on opposition activists in the United States.[48]

The Iranian government has tried to hijack academic exchange in other ways. To achieve tenure, Iranian studies professors must conduct fresh research, often based on resources available only inside Iran. Tehran can control the fate of those traveling on U.S. passports simply by refusing visas. In 2000, during the height of the "dialogue of civilizations," the United States granted Iranian passport holders approximately 22,000 visas; the Iranians reciprocated by granting U.S. passport holders fewer than 1,000. The discrepancy has only grown with time. Those who criticize Iranian policy receive no visa, while those who wish to ensure access will parrot the Iranian line. Seyyed Hossein Nasr, a professor at George Washington University and father of the former Obama administration official Vali Nasr, went so far as to encourage Tehran to use its leverage to purge Iranian studies programs of Jews and Baha'is.[49]

Sometimes an opportunity to improve relations comes through tragedy. Disaster diplomacy, such as the provision of aid after the Ardabil earthquake in 1997 or the Bam earthquake in 2003, can win hearts and minds. In contrast, failure to intervene effectively, such as after the 2005 earthquake in Pakistan or the flooding five years later, can let extremists fill the gap. The shah's bungled relief effort for the victims of the 1978 Tabas earthquake was a death knell to his already shaky regime.

It would be a mistake, however, to believe that altruism in the midst of tragedy is always a formula for reconciliation. The United States provided North Korea with billions of dollars in food aid only to have Pyongyang divert the food to its million-man army, leaving ordinary citizens to starve. It is also in the nature of ideological regimes to let hatred override the need for assistance. Iranian acceptance of disaster aid is inconsistent. In 2005, as hardliners consolidated control, the regime refused American assistance for victims of the Zarand earthquake. Tehran has also refused to accept Israeli aid. So too has the Islamist government in Turkey, which chose to let residents of the earthquake-decimated town of Van die rather than receive aid from Israel in the initial days after the disaster.

* * *

An entire industry has grown up around the idea that Track II exchanges work. People-to-people dialogue, however, is a risky gamble. Participants seldom can leverage their relationships into conflict resolution. The cost, meanwhile, can be high. Rogue regimes have mastered the art of hijacking dialogue for propaganda gain, to buy time, and to maintain momentum. Even disaster diplomacy can fail, as rogues often place their antipathies above the well-being of their citizens.

Can talks be designed in a way to make success more likely? Often, those engaged in dialogue seek high-ranking participants on the assumption that they can better forge back channels to senior policymakers. But the fact remains that there is no correlation between rank of participants and outcome of dialogue when one side remains uninterested in resolving the impasse. The former defense secretary William Perry may have met Iranian officials under the auspices of the Pugwash Group, but with hardliners consolidating control in Iran, even he could not prevent a worsening of relations.

This is not to say that unofficial dialogue always fails. Back channels are useful when rogues seek to come in from the cold. The decision to flip, however, must come first. Seldom if ever do back channels lead rogue regimes to change their heart. Even when they do succeed in advancing talks outside the public eye, there comes a time when private dialogue outlives its usefulness. After all, if the goal of dialogue is to resolve conflict, eventually this requires rogues to demonstrate to publics shaped by years or decades of incitement that a new dawn is approaching. To continue back channels alongside maturing processes simply allows rogue leaders like Khamenei, Arafat, or perhaps even Kim Jong Un to game the process while dispensing with the peace.

Conclusion

IS TALKING THE SHORTEST PATH TO WAR?

On January 21, 2013, President Barack Obama outlined his vision for his second term and legacy, saying, "We will show the courage to try and resolve our differences with other nations peacefully—not because we are naïve about the dangers we face, but because engagement can more durably lift suspicion and fear." His desire to engage was both genuine and in alignment with long-held conventional wisdom among senior statesmen. A half century worth of experience, however, does not support the thesis that diplomacy with rogue regimes or terrorist groups brings peace. Rather, diplomacy misapplied can be the shortest path to war.

False assumptions undermine strategic interests. Rogues do not accept American standards of diplomacy or the sanctity of agreements. By Western standards, North Korea, Iran, and the PLO cheat, but if judged by their own goals, they triumph. The West may consider economic integration a benefit, but adversaries do not share motivations. Throughout the 1990s, diplomats spoke of the "China model" for Iran, in which trade might bring economic liberalization and, in turn, spark political reform. The result was a cash infusion into Tehran that ended up fueling its nuclear and missile programs.

Incentives backfire; rather than ameliorate tension, they convince rogues that bad behavior pays. Both Iran and North Korea, for example, modulate tension to collect incentives while developing nuclear and missile capabilities without interruption. As Kim Il Sung's 1991 outreach or Muammar Qadhafi's 2003 nuclear about-face shows, a demonstration of force is more effective than diplomatic niceties. The State Department once understood this, but its culture changed over the decades. Since the Cold War's end, Western officials operate under the assumption that they should sequence diplomacy and coercion, rather than combine them. The sum of the parts seldom equals the whole, however. Combining diplomacy, sanctions, military strategies, and an effective information strategy to broadcast the American perspective directly into foreign lands can amplify diplomacy's effect.

Seldom anymore do diplomats set the right circumstances for success. Neither Pakistan nor the Taliban have incentive to seek peace when the United States releases Taliban prisoners before talks start, or announces a timeline for withdrawal. Nor does Iran believe that it must compromise on its nuclear program when it regards American power as being in retreat. Leverage has become a dirty word. The State Department regularly opposes new sanctions, and presidents waive those at their disposal.

Complicating the mix is the bizarre attraction that Islamism holds for many Western progressives. On its surface, the embrace is illogical: Islamism is the antithesis of liberalism when it comes to feminism, gay rights, tolerance, and individual rights. Yet leftists find Islamism's rhetoric of social justice and its fierce anti-Americanism attractive. Radical chic is alive and well.

Diplomats may see negotiation as a means to resolve conflict, but rogues do not share that view. After decades of watching how Washington operates, ayatollahs, commissars, and fedayeen all understand that once diplomats begin engaging, they seldom stop. When diplomats become invested in high-profile engagement, they refuse to admit failure. Too often, a rogue's pledge to act substitutes for results.

The State Department avoids metrics to judge diplomacy's effect, and therefore seldom cuts its losses when its policy fails. Soldiers spend less time in the field than in the classroom poring over after-action reports and identifying errors, but diplomats seldom acknowledge or reflect on failure. When Obama offered Iran an outstretched hand, he never considered why similar efforts by Jimmy Carter and George H. W. Bush had failed, nor did the State Department ever consider why Clinton's negotiations with the Taliban went nowhere but Obama's talks with the same figures should succeed. "It is always an error to concentrate on negotiations rather than real progress on the ground," observed Elliott Abrams, a former National Security Council official, in reflecting upon George W. Bush's failed Middle East peacemaking.[1]

Compounding the problem is a tendency at the State Department to shop around for partners. The most compliant partners, however, are seldom those who can deliver. Partner shopping allows rogues to play good cop / bad cop, collecting incentives while pursuing goals through terror. Diplomats see hope in political rivalries that they might exploit, but seldom do internal factions within rogues matter on the issues of greatest concern to U.S. national security. Great optimism accompanied the election of the "reformer" Mohammad Khatami to the Iranian presidency in 1997, but he was no liberal. As minister of culture and Islamic guidance, he had banned hundreds of books and films, such as *Bashu, the Little Stranger*, censored both for its depiction of war in a negative light and for a story revolving around a strong, independent woman.[2] Iranian reformers are just as committed to the nuclear program as hardliners. Similarly, members of Fatah often embrace the same attitudes toward Jews and Americans as do Hamas militants. Sometimes the White House is blind to this pattern; a desire to let diplomacy succeed can corrupt analysis and politicize intelligence.

Personal ambition also pushes engagement further than is strategically wise. Richard Holbrooke and Bill Richardson each sought to leverage rogue outreach into top State Department slots, and diplomats like Christopher Hill, David Welch, and Dennis Ross built careers on outreach to rogues despite a record of failure. Even if their motives were pure and uncorrupted by personal ambition, their upward career trajectories—rapid promotion, jet-setting, Oval Office attention—can inspire junior diplomats to replicate their path, often at the expense of U.S. national security. The State Department hands out meritorious service awards for breaking new ground or weathering crises, not for quiet management of the status quo. Sometimes, however, silence is a virtue.

The maxim that "it never hurts to talk" has cost lives. Diplomacy imbues rogue leaders with respectability and rewards both bluster and terror. Rogue rulers are not idiots; they understand that they can delay retaliation for months or even years by feigning sincerity. Iranian authorities have become masterful at taking ten steps forward toward their nuclear goal, so long as they mollify diplomats by occasionally taking one step back.

Once diplomats shatter a rogue's stigma, it is nearly impossible to restore. Ariel Sharon's complaints about American outreach to Yasir Arafat fell on deaf ears because the Israeli prime minister himself had maintained indirect contacts.[3] Likewise, the efforts by Recep Tayyip Erdoğan, Turkey's prime minister, to isolate the Kurdistan Workers' Party ended forever when he launched talks with the terror group.

When it comes to diplomacy with democracies, rogues also have the advantage of time: they know that every four or eight years, they can seek a better deal. The tendency of new American presidents to blame predecessors for the failure of diplomacy remains a serious handicap. Meanwhile, rogues realize that they can create false baselines. The Palestinians often claim fictitious understandings to create a new baseline for talks. The "grand bargain" peddled to U.S. journalists by an Iranian agent of influence in 2003 should be seen in the same light.

False sincerity threatens U.S. national security in other ways. While diplomats swore that North Korean behavior improved with the Agreed Framework, the opposite was true: It was during this period that North Korea sent nuclear blueprints and other technology to Pakistan and Iran.[4] As President Clinton corralled international partners to condemn

Pyongyang at the United Nations, North Korea destroyed evidence of its nuclear cheating. The same pattern gave Saddam Hussein time to plan the insurgency, and it repeats with Iran.

Defiance also inspires other rogues. When North Korea conducted a nuclear test, it was not only the Dear Leader who celebrated. "By carrying out a nuclear test," the Pakistani newspaper *Nawa-i-Waqt* declared, "North Korea has slapped the United States in the face." The paper urged Pakistani authorities to learn the North Korean lesson and defy the West.[5]

The fallout from outreach to rogues affects not only America, but also its allies. Scores of South Koreans and Israelis have died as a result of poorly timed and naïve American outreach to North Korea and to Palestinian groups. The greatest numbers of victims, however, are among the citizens subject to rogue despots and roaming terror militias. Iranian respect for human rights declined and executions doubled alongside engagement. Persecution of religious minorities increased.[6] Saddam's regime filled mass graves while diplomats sipped wine, and the Taliban terrorized women while their representatives met American diplomats thousands of miles away.

Deal making undermines moral clarity. Such concerns are often dismissed by diplomats. Charles Pritchard, a State Department official in the George W. Bush era, described as "maddening" the tendency of political appointees to invoke moral clarity as reason to avoid compromise.[7] Sometimes, however, national security and an antidote to suffering are best found in regime change rather than regime subsidy. Because diplomats are averse to considering regime change as an option, however, they entrench partners. Lost is the big picture: Every initiative to embrace rogue regimes risks repeating the moral and strategic error of George H. W. Bush's "Chicken Kiev" speech.

Choosing to preserve rogues rather than undermine them is dangerous. The most quiescent rogue leader will exploit American distraction when a crisis erupts elsewhere. In the 1960s and 1970s, North Korea exploited American involvement in Vietnam, and in the 2000s it exploited

American involvement in the Middle East. Iran has become adroit at provoking crises to distract Americans.

Diplomacy is a potent tool, but no tool can solve every problem. It is true that war carries a tremendous cost, and sanctions are not foolproof either. But just because strategies A and B are not perfect does not make strategy C a panacea. The evidence from repeated diplomatic outreach to rogue regimes is overwhelming: When presidents embrace dialogue and incentives as the solution to rogue behavior—when hope trumps change—the United States does not win peace, but instead hastens conflict.

ACKNOWLEDGMENTS

The idea to explore the cost of U.S. diplomacy toward rogue regimes began with a Council on Foreign Relations International Affairs Fellowship more than a decade ago. That opportunity, which placed me in the Pentagon working on the Iran and Iraq desk, provided an education in the formulation of policy concerning Saddam Hussein's Iraq and the Islamic Republic of Iran. The generosity of the Smith Richardson Foundation and the American Enterprise Institute (AEI) enabled me to conduct the broader research that underpins *Dancing with the Devil.*

I benefited from the assistance of many people: AEI interns—Nicholas Pugliese, Rochelle Lipsky, Soon Lee, Patrick Knapp, Emily Kangas, Tamir Haddad, Robert Fragnito, Aaron Epstein, Timothy Cramton, and Niklas Anzinger—helped track down and sift through documents and proofread drafts. Research assistants Suzanne Gershowitz and Jeffrey Azarva ably helped in the early stages. Many AEI colleagues—including Tom Donnelly, Gary Schmitt, Marc Thiessen, Ali Alfoneh, and Danielle Pletka—offered thoughtful advice on issues relating to diplomacy and intelligence. Nicholas Eberstadt provided numerous introductions and assisted me greatly with Korea issues, and Ahmad Khalid Majidyar did likewise with Afghanistan and Pakistan.

Jon Alterman, Samantha Ravich, and Ambassador John Bolton read various chapters with a critical eye, improving them considerably. The late Ambassador William L. Eagleton was patient with my numerous questions about his observations and experiences. Admiral (Ret'd) James "Ace" Lyons Jr. was likewise generous with his time. Stephen Rademaker, Abe Shulsky, Tim Morrison, Chuck Downs, Andrew Natsios, John Hannah, Vance Serchuk, Paul Wolfowitz, John Tirman, and Daniel Brumberg all participated in group discussions to flesh out ideas presented in the text. Valuable insights came from three retired generals: William Crouch, former vice chief of staff, U.S. Army; Dan Petrovsky, former commander, U.S. 8th Army; and Stephen Bradner, special advisor to the commander, United Nations Command / Combined Forces Command / U.S. Forces Korea. At the Smith-Richardson Foundation, I am grateful for the advice of Nadia Schadlow, Marin Strmecki, and Allan Song.

I am grateful to many other officials who freely offered advice and hospitality. In Afghanistan: Amrullah Saleh, former director of the National Directorate of Security; Davood Moradian of the American University in Afghanistan; Haji Din Mohammad, former governor of Kabul; and Ahmad Shah Ahmadzai, former prime minister. In Pakistan: Tanver Ahmad Khan, director of the Institute of Strategic Studies; Khalid Rahman, director of the Institute for Policy Studies; Brig. Bashir Ahmad, president of the Institute of Regional Studies, and his colleagues Arshi Saleem Hashmi and Shaheen Akhtar; and Asad Durrani, the former head of Inter-Services Intelligence. In Korea: Han Seung-soo, former prime minister, foreign minister and UN ambassador; Kim Jong-ro, director, Ministry of Unification; Hyun Hong-cho, former ambassador to the United States; Lee Chung-min, dean of Yonsei University; and Lee Guen, professor at Seoul National University. Mohamed Eljahmi lent his expertise with regard to Libya.

I am most grateful to Carol Staswick for her keen editorial eye and her remarkable ability to bring order to chaos, and to Roger Kimball for his encouragement and interest in this topic, as well as the other fine staff at Encounter Books for their efficiency and professionalism.

Finally, I am grateful for the patience and support of my wife, Anna Borshchevskaya, who stood with me every step of the way.

NOTES

Introduction: Pariahs to Partners: Bringing Rogues to the Table

1. Madeleine Albright, remarks at the Council on Foreign Relations, September 30, 1997.

2. "Remarks by Secretary of Defense William Perry on Nuclear Proliferation," Federal News Service, April 25, 1996; William S. Cohen, "Rogue States Cannot Hope to Blackmail America or Her Allies," *Times* (London), March 1, 2000.

3. Richard K. Betts, "Pygmies, Pariahs, and Nonproliferation," *Foreign Policy*, Spring 1977, pp. 165–67; Robert E. Harkavy, "Pariah States and Nuclear Proliferation," *International Organization*, Winter 1981.

4. Richard Burt, "Fear of Nuclear 'Outcasts' Intensifies Control Debate," *New York Times*, October 28, 1979.

5. "Rogue Regime," Editorial, *Washington Post*, April 5, 1979.

6. Ronald Reagan, remarks at the Annual Convention of the American Bar Association, July 8, 1985.

7. Michael T. Klare, *Rogue States and Nuclear Outlaws: America's Search for a New Foreign Policy* (New York: Hill & Wang, 1995), p. 27.

8. Jim Abrams, "Aspin Announces Program to Counter Weapons of Mass Destruction," Associated Press, December 7, 1993.

9. President Bill Clinton, remarks to a Multinational Audience of Future Leaders of Europe, Hotel De Ville, Brussels, January 10, 1994.

10. Warren Christopher, "Maintaining the Momentum for Peace in the Middle East," Georgetown University, Washington, D.C., October 24, 1994.

11. Anthony Lake, "Confronting Backlash States," *Foreign Affairs*, March–April 1994.

12. Robert S. Litwak, *Rogue States and U.S. Foreign Policy: Containment after the Cold War* (Washington: Woodrow Wilson Center Press, 2000), pp. 47–48.

13. Noam Chomsky, *Rogue States: The Rule of Force in World Affairs* (Cambridge, Mass.: South End Press, 2000); Clyde V. Prestowitz Jr., *Rogue Nation: American Unilateralism and the Failure of Good Intentions* (New York: Basic Books, 2004).

14. Litwak, *Rogue States and U.S. Foreign Policy*, p. 48.

15. Leslie Stahl interview with Madeleine Albright, *Sixty Minutes*, CBS, May 12, 1996.

16. Nicholas Burns, statement before the Senate Committee on Foreign Relations, May 6, 2009.

17. "Why Not Talk?" *Time*, May 14, 2006.

18. James B. Foley, Daily Press Briefing, U.S. Department of State, August 25, 1999.

19. Joel S. Wit, "Don't Sink Diplomacy," *New York Times*, May 19, 2010.

20. James A. Kelly, "Two for Now," *National Interest*, November–December 2008.

21. Karim Sadjadpour, "Should the U.S. Negotiate Directly with Iran?" Council on Foreign Relations, May 15, 2006.

22. Arlen Specter, "Trip to Europe and the Mideast," U.S. Senate, January 30, 2003, S1775.

23. "Q&A: Charles Hunter, Chargé d'Affaires, US Embassy in Syria," *Syria Today* (Damascus), November 2010.

24. Joe Biden, "Enhancing Our Diplomatic Readiness—A Critical Test of American Leadership," U.S. Senate, May 21, 1997, S4911.

25. Joe Biden, "North Korea and Iraq," U.S. Senate, January 17, 2003.

26. News Conference of the Senate Democratic Leadership and National Security Advisory Group to the Senate Democratic Leadership, March 5, 2003.

27. Nicholas Burns, statement before the Senate Committee on Foreign Relations, May 6, 2009.

28. Leon V. Sigal, *Disarming Strangers: Nuclear Diplomacy with North Korea* (Princeton, N.J.: Princeton University Press, 1998), p. 12.

29. Henry Kissinger, *Diplomacy* (New York: Simon & Schuster, 1994), p. 599.

30. Henry A. Kissinger, "A Nuclear Test for Diplomacy," *Washington Post*, May 16, 2006.

31. Daniel C. Kurtzer and Scott B. Lasensky, *Negotiating Arab-Israeli Peace: American Leadership in the Middle East* (Washington: United States Institute of Peace Press, 2008), p. 34.

32. Chuck Hagel, Speech on U.S.-Iran Relations at the Jewish Public Affairs Council, Washington, D.C., February 26, 2007.

33. Philip J. Crowley, Daily Press Briefing, U.S. Department of State, March 3, 2010.

34. Ryan C. Crocker, testimony at the Hearing on Hezbollah, Senate Committee on Foreign Relations, June 8, 2010.

35. Nicholas Burns, statement before the Senate Committee on Foreign Relations, May 6, 2009.

36. Joe Biden, "Secretary Baker's Mission to Beijing: The Realities of Chinese Intransigence," U.S. Senate, November 19, 1991, S17038.

37. "Text of President Bush's Speech to the Israeli Parliament," Associated Press, May 15, 2008.

38. Joe Biden, "Sarajevo on the Abyss: The Fatal Moment before Bosnia's Tragedy and the West's Shame Are Complete," U.S. Senate, August 3, 1993.

39. Joe Biden, "The Situation in Kosovo," U.S. Senate, October 14, 1998.

40. Kissinger, *Diplomacy*, p. 332.

Chapter 1: From Machiavelli to Muammar

1 Harold Nicolson, *The Evolution of Diplomatic Method* (London: Constable, 1954), p. 2.

2. David Reynolds, *Summits: Six Meetings That Shaped the Twentieth Century* (New York: Basic Books, 2007), p. 11.

3. Sun Tzu, *The Art of War*, trans. Samuel B. Griffith (New York: Oxford University Press, 1971), p. 77.

4. Nicolson, *The Evolution of Diplomatic Method*, p. 12.

5. Ibid., p. 17; Brian Campbell, "Diplomacy in the Roman World (c. 500 BC–AD 235)," *Diplomacy and Statecraft*, March 2001, p. 19.

6. Nizam al-Mulk, *The Book of Government or Rules for Kings*, trans. Hubert Drake (London: Routledge & Kegan Paul, 1978), p. 95.

7. U.S. Embassy Tehran, "Negotiations," August 13, 1979, Tehran 8980.

8. G. R. Berridge, Maurice Keens-Oper, and T. G. Otte, *Diplomatic Theory from Machiavelli to Kissinger* (New York: Palgrave, 2001), p. 8; Nicolson, *The Evolution of Diplomatic Method*, pp. 31–32.

9. Niccolò Machiavelli, *The Discourses*, II.13, as quoted in Berridge, Keens-Oper, and Otte, *Diplomatic Theory from Machiavelli to Kissinger*, p. 11.

10. Machiavelli, *The Discourses*, II.1, as quoted in ibid., p. 11.

11. Niccolò Machiavelli, *The Prince* (New York: Penguin, 1952), p. 92.

12. Berridge et al., *Diplomatic Theory from Machiavelli to Kissinger*, p. 40.

13. Armand Jean du Plessis, duc de Richelieu, *Testament politique*, as quoted in ibid., p. 80.

14. Ibid., p. 81.

15. Ibid., pp. 55–56.

16. Sir Ernest Satow to Sir Edward Grey (private), March 31, 1906, Grey MSS, PRO, FO 800/44; Satow diary, July 3, 1900, PRO 30/33/16/3; as quoted in Berridge, Keens-Oper, and Otte, p. 142.

17. Woodrow Wilson, "Fourteen Points," Address to a Joint Session of Congress, January 8, 1918.

18. Reynolds, *Summits*, p. 34.

19. Berridge et al., *Diplomatic Theory from Machiavelli to Kissinger*, p. 158.

20. Ibid., p. 184.

21. Kissinger, *Diplomacy*, p. 26.

22. Henry Kissinger, *White House Years* (New York: Little, Brown & Co., 1979), p. 54.

23. Joshua Muravchik, "Obama's 'Talking' Cure," *Commentary*, September 2008.

24. "Appeasement Policy Compromises Good Delivery of Services," *Talk of the Town* (Port Alfred, South Africa), October 15, 2010; "Andrew Leigh and Kelly O'Dwyer Talk Politics," *Lateline*, Australian Broadcasting Corporation, October 22, 2010.

25. Stephen F. Hayes, "Hollywood Takes On the Left," *Weekly Standard*, August 11, 2008.

26. Paul Kennedy, "A Time to Appease," *National Interest*, June 28, 2010.

27. Pryor Jordan, "Ex-Cabinet Member Tells LR Crowd U.S. Must Know Its Limits," *Arkansas Democrat-Gazette*, November 9, 2007.

28. Muravchik, "Obama's 'Talking' Cure."

29. Reynolds, *Summits*, p. 174.

30. See, for example, Stuart H. Loory, "Summit Talk Set Today in New Jersey," *Los Angeles Times*, June 23, 1967.

31. Muravchik, "Obama's 'Talking' Cure."

32. Ronald Reagan, Speech on the Geneva Summit, Joint Session of the U.S. Congress, November 21, 1985.

33. Muravchik, "Obama's 'Talking' Cure."

34. Haynes Johnson, "Vision on the World Stage," *Washington Post*, December 9, 1988.

35. CNN/YouTube Democratic Presidential Debate, July 23, 2007.

36. Charles A. Kupchan, "Enemies into Friends: How the United States Can Court Its Adversaries," *Foreign Affairs*, March–April 2010.

37. Peter H. Langer, *Transatlantic Discord and NATO's Crisis of Cohesion* (Washington: Pergamon-Brassey's, 1986), p. 30.

38. "Snow Right and Europe," *Economist*, February 27, 1982.

39. Gallup Political Index no. 270, February 1983, p. 18, as quoted in David Watt, "The Conduct of American Foreign Policy: As a European Saw It," *Foreign Affairs*, 1983.

40. Watt, "The Conduct of American Foreign Policy: As a European Saw It."

41. Henry Kissinger, *Years of Upheaval* (New York: Little, Brown & Co., 1982), p. 625.

42. Dianne E. Rennack and Robert D. Shuey, "Economic Sanctions to Achieve U.S. Foreign Policy Goals: Discussion and Guide to Current Law," CRS Report for Congress, November 1, 1999.

43. Gary Clyde Hufbauer et al., *Economic Sanctions Reconsidered*, 3rd ed. (Washington: Peterson Institute for International Economics, 2007), pp. 23–29.

44. Steven Kull, "Seeking a New Balance: A Study of American and European Public Attitudes on Transatlantic Issues," Program on International Policy Attitudes, June 1998, p. 48.

45. Ibid., p. 49.

46. Ibid., p. 53.

47. Jörg Monar, "Political Dialogue with Third Countries and Regional Political Groupings: The Fifteen as an Attractive Interlocutor," in *Foreign Policy of the European Union*, ed. Elfriede Regelsberger, Philippe de Schoutheete de Tervarent, and Wolfgang Wessels (Boulder, Col.: Lynne Rienner Publishers, 1997), pp. 263–64.

48. Ibid., p. 266.

49. Ibid., p. 269.

50. Wilbur G. Landrey, "France Tries to Fill Void Left by U.S.," *St. Petersburg Times*, August 4, 1996.

51. Michael Gordon, "As West Shuns Iran, Russia Pulls Closer," *New York Times*, April 12, 1997.

52. "Iranian Foreign Minister Visit Sparks EU Parliament Outcry," Deutsche Presse-Agentur, June 1, 2010.

Chapter 2: Great Satan vs. Mad Mullahs

1. See also, for example, James Hider and Tom Baldwin, "America Prepares to Talk with Iran after 28 Years of Silence," *Times* (London), April 30, 2007.

2. Tim Weiner, *Legacy of Ashes: The History of the CIA* (New York: Anchor, 2008), p. 426.

3. Cyrus Vance, *Hard Choices: Critical Years in America's Foreign Policy* (New York: Simon & Schuster, 1983), pp. 316–17.

4. According to William G. Miller, as interviewed by John W. Limbert, *Negotiating with Iran: Wrestling the Ghosts of History* (Washington: United States Institute of Peace Press, 2009), p. 89 n.2.

5. Zbigniew Brzezinski, *Power and Principle: Memoirs of the National Security Advisor, 1977–1981* (New York: Farrar, Straus & Giroux, 1983), p. 355.

6. Limbert, *Negotiating with Iran*, p. 91.

7. Richard Falk, "Trusting Khomeini," *New York Times*, February 16, 1979.

8. Secretary of State to U.S. Embassy Tehran, January 7, 1979, State 4510.

9. Vance, *Hard Choices*, p. 343.

10. Limbert, *Negotiating with Iran*, p. 92.

11. Secretary of State to U.S. Embassy Ankara, August 28, 1979, State 226730.

12. Steven Erlanger, "Iran's Shaky Theocracy," *New Republic*, November 10, 1979.

13. U.S. Embassy Tehran, "Moderation: Does It Have a Chance?" October 26, 1979, Tehran 11319.

14. Limbert, *Negotiating with Iran*, pp. 92–93.

15. Vance, *Hard Choices*, p. 373.

16. Brzezinski, *Power and Principle*, pp. 475–76.

17. Harold H. Saunders, "The Crisis Begins," in *American Hostages in Iran*, ed. Warren Christopher (New Haven: Yale University Press, 1985), p. 43.

18. Associated Press, November 5, 1979.

19. Massoumeh Ebtekar, *Takeover in Tehran: The Inside Story of the 1979 U.S. Embassy Capture* (Vancouver, B.C.: Talon Books, 2000), pp. 58, 86.

20. Saunders, "The Crisis Begins," p. 47.

21. Harold H. Saunders, "Diplomacy and Pressure, November 1979–May 1980," in *American Hostages in Iran*, ed. Christopher, p. 73.

22. John M. Goshko and J. P. Smith, "Bazargan Government Resigns; Carter, Security Aides Meet Twice," *Washington Post*, November 7, 1979. Gary Sick, a National Security Council staffer, later described the meeting in "Military Options and Constraints," in *American Hostages in Iran*, ed. Christopher, pp. 144–47.

23. Bernard Gwertzman, "U.S. Rejects Demand of Students in Iran to Send Shah Back," *New York Times*, November 6, 1979.

24. Peter W. Rodman, "The Hostage Crisis: How Not to Negotiate," *Washington Quarterly*, Summer 1981, p. 12.

25. Barry Rubin, *Paved with Good Intentions: The American Experience in Iran* (New York: Oxford University Press, 1980), p. 304.

26. Ebtekar, *Takeover in Tehran*, p. 97.

27. Ibid., p. 75.

28. William Beecher, "Peaceful Outcome Is Thought Possible," *Boston Globe*, November 24, 1979.

29. Vance, *Hard Choices*, p. 375.

30. "U.S. Emissaries in Iranian Crisis," *Washington Post*, November 8, 1979; Ronald Koven, "Head of Iranian Regency Council Resigns in Paris," *Washington Post*, January 23, 1979.

31. Vance, *Hard Choices*, p. 376; Robert Spencer, "Kerry: Carter II?" *Human Events Online*, August 19, 2004.

32. Ebtekar, *Takeover in Tehran*, p. 119.

33. UN Security Council Resolution 457 (December 4, 1979); UN Security Council Resolution 461 (December 31, 1979).

34. John Bausman, "International News—United Nations," Associated Press, January 13, 1980.

35. *United States Diplomatic and Consular Staff in Tehran* (*United States of America v. Iran*), International Court of Justice, May 24, 1980.

36. Rodman, "The Hostage Crisis: How Not to Negotiate," p. 14.

37. Vance, *Hard Choices*, p. 376.

38. Ibid., p. 379.

39. Saunders, "Diplomacy and Pressure, November 1979–May 1980," pp. 74–84.

40. Ibid., pp. 96, 119–20.

41. Ibid., p. 81.

42. Ibid., p. 82.

43. Ibid., pp. 96–97.

44. Ibid., pp. 97, 100; Vance, *Hard Choices*, p. 378; Jimmy Carter, *White House Diary* (New York: Farrar, Straus & Giroux, 2010), p. 415.

45. Saunders, "Diplomacy and Pressure, November 1979–May 1980," pp. 99–100; Rodman, "The Hostage Crisis: How Not to Negotiate," p. 16.

46. Rodman, "The Hostage Crisis: How Not to Negotiate," p. 15.

47. Notes on Meeting of Soviet Foreign Minister Gromyko and Afghan Foreign Minister Shah-Valih, New York, September 27, 1979, Cold War International History Project, Woodrow Wilson International Center for Scholars.

48. Saunders, "Diplomacy and Pressure, November 1979–May 1980," p. 135.

49. Harold H. Saunders, "Beginning of the End," in *American Hostages in Iran*, ed. Christopher, p. 285.

50. Ibid., p. 286.

51. Don Oberdorfer, "Vance Formally Resigns, Citing Raid Opposition," *Washington Post*, April 29, 1980.

52. Roberts B. Owen, "The Final Negotiation and Release in Algiers," in *American Hostages in Iran*, ed. Christopher, p. 297.

53. Ibid., p. 298.

54. *Department of State Bulletin*, vol. 81, no. 2048 (March 1981), p. 17, as quoted in Owen, "The Final Negotiation and Release in Algiers," p. 298.

55. Owen, "The Final Negotiation and Release in Algiers," pp. 298–99.

56. Ibid., p. 299.

57. Ibid., p. 306.

58. Rodman, "The Hostage Crisis: How Not to Negotiate," p. 22.

59. Owen, "The Final Negotiation and Release in Algiers," pp. 306, 310.

60. William Luers, Thomas R. Pickering, and Jim Walsh, "How to Deal with Iran," *New York Review of Books*, February 12, 2009.

61. Rodman, "The Hostage Crisis: How Not to Negotiate," p. 19.

62. "Transcript of Carter's Speech in Plains, Georgia," Associated Press, January 21, 1981; A. M. Rosenthal, "America in Captivity: Points of Decision in the Hostage Crisis," *New York Times Magazine*, May 17, 1981.

63. Jimmy Carter, *White House Diary* (New York: Farrar, Straus & Giroux, 2010), pp. 368, 371.

64. See James Fallows, "The Passionless Presidency," *Atlantic*, May 1979; Burton I. Kaufman and Scott Kaufman, *The Presidency of James Earl Carter, Jr.* (Lawrence: University Press of Kansas, 2006), pp. 249–50.

65. Rodman, "The Hostage Crisis: How Not to Negotiate," pp. 10, 22.

66. John Tower et al., *The Tower Commission Report* (New York: Times Books, 1987), p. 36.

67. Ibid., p. 20.

68. James Gerstenzang, "Reagan Urges Tougher U.S. Stand in Iranian Hostage Crisis," Associated Press, March 28, 1980.

69. "Obama harf-e Bush mizenad," *Agahsazi* (Tehran), December 9, 2008.

70. *The Tower Commission Report*, p. 45.

71. Ibid., p. 47.

72. Ibid., pp. 47–48.

73. Bernard Gwertzman, "Why President Ended Silence on Iran Policy," *New York Times*, November 14, 1986.

74. See, for example, "Militant Clergy Association Issues Statement Calling on People to Take Part Extensively in the Second Round of Majlis Elections," *Iran* (Tehran), April 10, 1996; "Hajj Pilgrims Protest against Israel, USA during Symbolic Ceremony," Islamic Republic News Agency, April 30, 1996.

75. Bahman Baktiari, *Parliamentary Politics in Revolutionary Iran: The Institutionalization of Factional Politics* (Gainesville: University Press of Florida, 1996), p. 135.

76. Nora Boustany, "Beirut Magazine Says McFarlane Secretly Visited Tehran," *Washington Post*, November 4, 1986; Stanley Reed, "'Beirut Rag': *Al Shiraa* Magazine," *Nation*, December 20, 1986.

77. *The Tower Commission Report*, p. 51.

78. Bootle Cosgrove-Mather, "A Look Back at the Polls," CBS News, June 7, 2004.

79. David B. Ottaway, "Bush Seems to Appeal to Iran on Hostage Issue," *Washington Post*, January 21, 1989.

80. "Bush Says Iran Could Help Free Hostages," Associated Press, January 27, 1989.

81. Ibid.

82. See, for example, Bill Hewitt, "Burying the Passions Khomeini Inflamed," *Newsweek*, June 19, 1989.

83. Limbert, *Negotiating with Iran*, p. 141.

84. "Subject: U.S. Policy Toward the Persian Gulf," National Security Directive 26, The White House, October 2, 1989.

85. Giandomenico Picco, *Man Without a Gun* (New York: Times Books, 1999), p. 111.

86. Ibid., pp. 113–14.

87. For example, see Lucia Mouat, "Signs of U.S.-Iran Thaw Appear," *Christian Science Monitor*, December 18, 1989.

88. Picco, *Man Without a Gun*, p. 115; Donald M. Rothberg, "Bush's Deal: Better Iran Relations in Return for Hostages," Associated Press, April 24, 1990.

89. Picco, *Man Without a Gun*, p. 118.

90. "Ravayeh fa'li siyasat-I kharaji motalib nist" [The current practice is not good foreign policy], *Diplomasi-ye Irani*, July 13, 2011.

91. Martin Indyk, "The Clinton Administration's Approach to the Middle East," The Washington Institute for Near East Policy, May 18, 1993.

92. Ibid.

93. Executive Order 12957 (March 15, 1995); Executive Order 12959 (May 6, 1995).

94. Executive Order 13059 (August 19, 1997).

95. Zbigniew Brzezinski, Brent Scowcroft, and Richard Murphy, "Differentiated Containment," *Foreign Affairs*, May–June 1997.

96. Kianouche Dorranie, "Khatami Sworn In, Calls for 'Détente' in Iran's Foreign Relations," Agence France-Presse, August 4, 1997.

97. Louis J. Freeh, "Remember Khobar Towers," *Wall Street Journal*, May 20, 2003.

98. Gary Sick, "U.S. Can Exploit Peaceful Iran Revolution," *Newsday*, June 11, 1997.

99. Graham Fuller, "U.S.-Iran Relations: A Road Map for Normalization," The Atlantic Council of the United States, March 19, 1998.

100. "Washington and Its One-Sided View of Diplomacy," *Akhbar* (Tehran), August 30, 1997, translation provided by the Open Source Center.

101. "Sources: U.S. Sought a Government Dialogue with Iran," CNN.com, January 9, 1998.

102. Douglas Jehl, "Iranian President Calls for Opening Dialog with U.S.," *New York Times*, December 15, 1997.

103. Mohammad Khatami interview with Christiane Amanpour, CNN.com, January 7, 1998.

104. Secretary of State Madeleine K. Albright, remarks at the Asia Society Dinner, Waldorf-Astoria Hotel, New York, June 17, 1998.

105. Robin Wright, "Diplomatic Exit; For Iran's Javad Zarif, a Curtain Call Behind the Scenes," *Washington Post*, April 15, 2007.

106. "Why Is America After Dialogue with Iran?" *Emruz* (Tehran), April 18, 1999, translation provided by the Open Source Center.

107. Lee H. Hamilton, James Schlesinger, and Brent Scowcroft, *Thinking Beyond the Stalemate in U.S.-Iranian Relations*, vol. 1, *Policy Review* (Washington: The Atlantic Council of the United States, May 2001), p. 2.

108. "Compromise with America, War with Friends?" *Misaq* (Tabriz), October 11, 1999, translation provided by the Open Source Center.

109. "Khemene'i Says Détente Policy Excludes U.S.," Islamic Republic of Iran Broadcasting (Tehran), August 16, 1999, translation provided by the Open Source Center.

110. "Abdollah Ramezanzadeh: Siast pish pirdeh dawlat-i Khatami adamayeh-i fa'aliyatha-ye hasteha-ye bud," Fars News Agency, June 14, 2008.

111. Ali Akbar Dareini, "Iran Cleric Wants 'Special Weapons' to Deter Enemy," Associated Press, June 14, 2010.

112. "To Compensate for the Disappointment," *Resalat* (Tehran), December 2, 1999, translation provided by the Open Source Center.

113. Hamilton, Schlesinger, and Scowcroft, *Thinking Beyond the Stalemate in U.S.-Iranian Relations*, vol. 1, *Policy Review*, p. 3.

114. "Talk of Reestablishing Iran-U.S. Relations an 'Insult': Khamenei," Agence France-Presse, July 27, 2000.

115. Voice of the Islamic Republic of Iran Radio 1 (Tehran), August 15, 2000, translation provided by the Open Source Center.

116. Hamilton, Schlesinger, and Scowcroft, *Thinking Beyond the Stalemate in U.S.-Iranian Relations*, vol. 1, *Policy Review*, p. 3.

117. Ibid., p. 3; "New Reassessment of Iran's File at the White House," *Afarinesh* (Tehran), February 12, 2001, translation provided by the Open Source Center.

118. Hamilton, Schlesinger, and Scowcroft, *Thinking Beyond the Stalemate in U.S.-Iranian Relations*, vol. 1, *Policy Review*, pp. ix, 10.

119. "State Department Replaces Term 'Rogue States' with 'States of Concern,'" *All Things Considered*, NPR, June 19, 2000.

120. Christopher Marquis, "U.S. Declares 'Rogue Nations' Are Now 'States of Concern,'" *New York Times*, June 20, 2000.

121. "More American than Americans," *Jomhuri-ye Eslami* (Tehran), June 25, 2000, translation provided by the Open Source Center.

122. Ayatollah Ruhollah Khomeini, "The Granting of Capitulatory Rights to the U.S.," October 27, 1964, in *Imam Khomeini: Islam and Revolution*, ed. and trans. Hamid Algar (London: KPI, 1981), p. 185.

123. Reuters, "Shah Nephew Killed in 'Purge of Pawns,'" *Globe and Mail* (Toronto), December 8, 1979.

124. *No Safe Haven: Iran's Global Assassination Campaign*, Iran Human Rights Documentation Center, May 2008, pp. 16–17.

125. Youssef M. Ibrahim, "Trial of Accused Mastermind in Bombings Begins in Paris," New York Times, January 30, 1990.

126. Paul Lewis, "France Breaks Iran Ties and Isolates Embassy," *New York Times*, July 18, 1987.

127. Steven Greenhouse, "Bold Iranian Raid on French Craft Heightens Gulf Tensions," *New York Times*, July 19, 1987.

128. "Anything Else, Mr. Khomeini?" *Economist*, December 12, 1987.

129. Ayatollah Ruhollah Khomeini, *Hukumat-i Islami*, in *Imam Khomeini: Islam and Revolution*, ed. and trans. Algar, p. 139.

130. See Peter Rudolf, "The European Union and Iran," in *Trans-Atlantic Tensions: The United States, Europe, and Problem Countries*, ed. Richard Haass (Washington: Brookings Institution Press, 1999), p. 73; Anthony Parsons, "Iran and Western Europe," *Middle East Journal*, Spring 1989, p. 228.

131. European Council in Edinburgh, December 11–12, 1992, *Conclusions of the Presidency*, Part D: External Relations: Iran, ¶ 15 (p. 96).

132. Rick Atkinson, "Killing of Iranian Dissenters: 'Bloody Trail Back to Tehran'; Trial in Berlin Follows Deaths across Europe," *Washington Post*, November 21, 1993.

133. "Bonn 'Role' in Spy Deal," *Herald Sun*, November 2, 1993; Igal Avidan, "Bonn Aiding Iran Secret Service," *Jerusalem Post*, November 1, 1993.

134. *Murder at Mykonos: Anatomy of a Political Assassination*, Iran Human Rights Documentation Center, March 2007, pp. 2–20.

135. "Fury in Iran over German Accusations," Agence France-Presse, April 11, 1997.

136. "Declaration by the European Union on Iran," European Council in Luxembourg, April 29, 1997, PESC/97/41, as cited in V. Matthias Struwe, *The Policy of "Critical Dialogue": An Analysis of European Human Rights Policy Towards Iran from 1992 to 1997*, Durham Middle East Papers (School of Government and International Affairs, University of Durham, UK, 1998), p. 2.

137. Dr. Klaus Kinkel, Federal Minister for Foreign Affairs, speech in the Bundestag debate on policy toward Iran, Bonn, April 17, 1997.

138. "Europe: Choose Between Iran and the United States," *Abrar* (Tehran), October 2, 1997; "Europe Oil Deal Shows US Policy Failure," Voice of the Islamic Republic of Iran Radio (Tehran), March 2, 1999; translations provided by the Open Source Center.

139. Kinkel, speech in the Bundestag debate on policy toward Iran.

140. Foreign Minister Klaus Kinkel, news conference with Secretary of State Madeleine Albright, U.S. Department of State, November 5, 1997.

141. Michael Gahler, "Report on the Communication from the Commission to the European Parliament and the Council on EU Relations with the Islamic Republic of Iran," European Parliament, Committee on Foreign Affairs, Human Rights, Common Security and Defense Policy, November 26, 2001, A5-0418/2001.

142. Mohamed ElBaradei, "Introductory Statement to the IAEA Board of Governors," Vienna, November 20, 2003; "Implementation of the NPT Safeguards Agreement in the Islamic Republic of Iran," IAEA Board of Governors, November 10, 2003, GOV/2003/75.

143. Ian Traynor, "Iran's Nuclear Secrets Split EU and US," *Guardian* (London), November 21, 2003.

144. Brian Murphy, "Iran Claims Victory in EU Nuke Deal," Associated Press, October 22, 2003.

145. "Agreed Statement at the End of a Visit to the Islamic Republic of Iran by the Foreign Ministers of Britain, France, and Germany," UK Foreign and Commonwealth Office, October 21, 2003.

146. "Iran Agrees to Key Nuclear Demands," BBC News, October 21, 2003.

147. "Nagoftaha-ye Hassan Rouhani as diplomasi hasteh-ye dureh eslahat az europa qol vatave tareh-i Amrika ra gerefteh budam," *Etemaad* (Tehran), October 24, 2011.

148. Michael Adler, "Soft European Line on Iran Seen Undermining U.S. Stance," Agence France-Presse, February 25, 2004.

149. "Sardar Safavi: Hezbollah-e luban az Basijiyan-e Iran alegu gereft," *Asr-i Iran*, November 27, 2010.

150. "Iran Agrees to Suspend Enrichment," CNN.com, November 15, 2004.

151. Steven Everts, "Engaging Iran: A Test Case for EU Foreign Policy," Centre for European Reform, March 2004, p. 18.

152. "Khatami Praises U.S.; Says Protests in Iran Part of Normal Process," Associated Press, November 12, 2001.

153. Senator Joe Biden, "Prospects for Progress: America and Iran after 9-11," remarks to the Iranian American Council, March 13, 2002; Zalmay Khalilzad, speech to the American Iranian Council, March 13, 2002.

154. *9-11 Commission Report* (Washington: The National Commission on Terrorist Attacks upon the United States, July 22, 2004), pp. 240–41.

155. "Terror in America (17): Conservatives and Reformists in Iran: Divided in Condemning the Attacks; United in Opposition to the American Response," MEMRI, Special Dispatch 286, October 15, 2001; Alireza Malekian, "Public Opinion Based on a Fabricated Scenario," *Kayhan* (Tehran), September 18, 2001, translation provided by the Open Source Center.

156. S. Nawabzadeh, "How Frail Is the Spider's Web!" *Kayhan International* (Tehran), September 13, 2001.

157. Biden, "Prospects for Progress: America and Iran after 9-11."

158. "A Letter to the US Congress and the Responsibility of the Foreign Ministry," *Entekhab* (Tehran), June 30, 2001, translation provided by the Open Source Center.

159. "Those Who Benefit from Trade with America Have Become Advocates of Negotiations," *Kayhan* (Tehran), July 15, 2001, translation provided by the Open Source Center.

160. James Dobbins, "Moral Clarity and the Middle East," speech to the New America Foundation, August 24, 2006.

161. Ibid.

162. Michael Ware, "Iran's Man in Iraq: 'We Do Not Take Orders from the Americans,'" *Time*, April 12, 2006; "Iraqi Governing Council Member Says Iran Playing 'Decisive Role' in Unrest," *Al-Hayat* (London), April 6, 2004, translation by BBC Summary of World Broadcasts.

163. Bill Samii, "Herat and Iran Strengthen Ties," *RFE/RL Iran Report*, July 8, 2002.

164. Douglas Jehl, "A Nation Challenged: Outside Influences," *New York Times*, March 9, 2002.

165. Zalmay Khalilzad, speech to the American Iranian Council, March 13, 2002.

166. Ibid.

167. Laura Secor, "The Fugitives," *New Yorker*, November 21, 2005.

168. Zalmay Khalilzad, "Where Is Iran—and U.S. Iran Policy—Heading?" remarks to the Washington Institute for Near East Policy, August 2, 2002.

169. George W. Bush, "State of the Union," January 29, 2002.

170. Siamek Behbudi, "The Role of Military Monopolies in America's Regional Diplomacy," *Sobh-e Emruz* (Tehran), April 9, 2000, translation provided by the Open Source Center.

171. George W. Bush, *Decision Points* (New York: Crown, 2010), p. 415.

172. "Interview with Mohsen Mir-Damadi, Chairman of the Majlis Foreign Affairs and Security Committee," Islamic Republic News Agency, April 21, 2002.

173. "Iran: Daily Reports on Secret Contacts with US," *Entekhab* (Tehran), April 22, 2002, translation by BBC Summary of World Broadcasts; "Recent Talks and Meetings between Iran and the United States," *Iran* (Tehran), April 22, 2002.

174. "Iran: Daily Reports on Secret Contacts with US."

175. "Powell Backs Off Intervention in Iranian Politics," *New York Times*, July 2, 2003.

176. Robin Wright, "U.S. Now Views Iran in More Favorable Light," *Los Angeles Times*, February 14, 2003.

177. Peter Galbraith, "The Victor?" *New York Review of Books*, October 11, 2007.

178. Iranian UN Ambassador Javad Zarif to Trita Parsi, email, March 30, 2006, 7:34 a.m.

179. See, for example, Barbara Slavin, *Bitter Friends, Bosom Enemies: Iran, the U.S., and the Twisted Path to Confrontation* (New York: St. Martin's Press, 2007), p. 212; William Luers, Thomas R. Pickering, and Jim Walsh, "How to Deal with Iran," *New York Review of Books*, February 12, 2009; Chuck Hagel, "Iran," U.S. Senate, December 4, 2007, S14729.

180. John W. Limbert, "Negotiating with the Islamic Republic of Iran," United States Institute of Peace, Special Report 199, January 2008.

181. Seyed Hossein Mousavian and Mohammad Ali Shabani, "How to Talk to Tehran," *New York Times*, January 3, 2013.

182. Ali Reza Nourizadeh, "Iranian Sources Say Revolutionary Guards Elements Entered Iraq with SCIRI," *Asharq al-Awsat*, April 25, 2003, translation provided by the Open Source Center.

183. "Daily Views Importance of US Request for Iran's Help in Iraq," *Tose'ah* (Tehran), April 15, 2004, translation by BBC Worldwide Monitoring; see also "Iranian Editorial Says US Request on Iraq a 'Turning Point,'" *Mardom Salari* (Tehran), April 18, 2004, translation by BBC Worldwide Monitoring.

184. "Implementation of the NPT Safeguards Agreement in the Islamic Republic of Iran," IAEA Board of Governors, June 6, 2003, GOV/2003/40.

185. "Nearly 400 Al-Qaeda Members and Other Terror Suspects in Iran: Newspaper," Agence France-Presse, July 15, 2004.

186. "Powell Backs Off Intervention in Iranian Politics."

187. Carol Giacomo and Arshad Mohammed, interview with Condoleezza Rice, Reuters, March 11, 2005.

188. "Iran Says U.S. Incentives Offer 'Insignificant,'" Reuters, March 11, 2005.

189. Islamic Republic News Agency, April 21, 2004; Mark John, "EU Promises 'Generous' Offer to Iran," Reuters, May 15, 2006.

190. "Nagoftaha-ye Hassan Rouhani as diplomasi hasteh-ye dureh eslahat az europa qol vatave tareh-I Amrika ra gerefteh budam," *Etemaad* (Tehran), October 24, 2011.

191. Sue Pleming, "Rice Open to Bilateral Talks with Iran at Meeting," Reuters, April 5, 2007.

192. Secretary of State Condoleezza Rice, U.S. Department of State, May 31, 2006.

193. Dieter Bednarz, Ralf Beste, Konstantin von Hammerstein, and Marcel Rosenbach, "EU Diplomacy Takes a Beating: The Failure of Europe's Iran Policy," *Spiegel Online International,* April 16, 2007.

194. Daniel Dombey, "Solana Sees Hope of Deal with Iran on Nuclear Enrichment," *Financial Times,* September 16, 2006.

195. Ibid.

196. Daniel Dombey and Fidelius Schmid, "Iran on Course for Nuclear Bomb, EU Told," *Financial Times,* February 12, 2007.

197. Nicholas Burns, statement before the Senate Committee on Foreign Relations, May 6, 2009.

198. Elaine Sciolino, "Iranian Pushes Nuclear Talks Back to Square 1," *New York Times,* December 2, 2007.

199. "Iran: Terrorist Freed in Germany Is Welcomed by Tehran," Radio Farda (Prague), December 11, 2007.

200. Yang Jiechi, Bernard Koucher, Frank-Walter Steinmeier, et al., letter to Manuchehr Mottaki, June 12, 2008.

201. Robin Wright, "Iranian Flow of Weapons Increasing, Officials Say," *Washington Post,* June 3, 2007; Allison Lampert, "Iran Aiding Taliban: Mackay; Minister Says Arms Crossing Border to Insurgents," *National Post* (Toronto), November 26, 2007.

202. Press briefing by Major-General William Caldwell, Spokesman, Multi-National Force–Iraq, and Major Marty Webber, Explosive Ordnance Disposal Expert, Combined Press Information Center, Baghdad, February 14, 2007.

203. William Luers, Thomas R. Pickering, and Jim Walsh, "How to Deal with Iran," *New York Review of Books,* February 12, 2009.

204. Kim Murphy, "Iran Holds Foes in Complex Balance; Tehran Is Finding New Ways to Assert Itself in Mideast Conflict," *Los Angeles Times,* August 14, 2007.

205. Michael R. Gordon and Jeff Zeleny, "Obama Envisions New Iran Approach," *New York Times,* November 2, 2007.

206. Nicholas Burns, statement before the Senate Committee on Foreign Relations, May 6, 2009.

207. Roger Cohen, "Iran Is Job One," *New York Times,* October 22, 2008.

208. Seyed Hossein Mousavian, *The Iranian Nuclear Crisis: A Memoir* (Washington: Carnegie Endowment for International Peace, 2012), p. 325.

209. Nazila Fathi, "In Rare Turn, Iran's Leader Sends Letter to Obama," *New York Times*, November 7, 2008.

210. "Iran-U.S.-Soltanieh," Islamic Republic News Agency, December 1, 2008.

211. "Obama Tells Al Arabiya Peace Talks Should Resume," Al Arabiya, January 27, 2009.

212. Jay Solomon, "Senior Democrat Snubbed by Iran in Outreach Bid," *Wall Street Journal*, February 2, 2009.

213. Voice of the Islamic Republic of Iran Radio 1 (Tehran) in Persian, 0855 GMT, February 6, 2009.

214. Sheryl Gay Stolberg and Helene Cooper, "Obama Makes Case as Stimulus Bill Clears Hurdle," *New York Times*, February 10, 2009.

215. Luers, Pickering, and Walsh, "How to Deal with Iran."

216. Naser Piran, "What Do New White House Efforts Indicate?" *Iran* (Tehran), October 20, 1999, translation provided by the Open Source Center.

217. Islamic Republic News Agency, March 21, 2009; "Iran Rejects Idea of U.S. Talks at Moscow Meeting on Afghanistan," RIA Novosti (Moscow), March 27, 2009.

218. "Warnings on Iran," *Wall Street Journal*, April 6, 2009.

219. "Analyst: Enemies Admit Defeat in Iran's N. Issue," Fars News Agency, April 9, 2009.

220. Donna Miles, "Gates Assures Arab Friends: No 'Secret Bargain' in Works with Iran," American Forces Press Service, May 5, 2009; Makram Muhammad Ahmad, "Dhaminat muhimeh fi al-'aliqat al-arabiya al-iraniya la tastati'a Washington taqdimaha" [Important guarantees for Arab-Iranian relations that Washington cannot provide], *Al-Ahram*, May 9, 2009; U.S. Embassy Riyadh, "Saudi King Abdullah and Senior Princes on Saudi Policy toward Iraq," April 20, 2008, Riyadh 649; Jason Koutsoukis, "Iran Buying Time, Says Israel," *Sydney Morning Herald*, March 10, 2009.

221. Alan Cowell and Helene Cooper, "Obama Plays Down Divide with Israel," *New York Times*, June 3, 2009.

222. "'This Week' Transcript: Iranian President Mahmoud Ahmadinejad," ABC News, April 26, 2009.

223. "US Willing to Hold Face-to-Face Talks with Iran, State Department," Islamic Republic News Agency, April 9, 2009; "Towze'ah bazgasht beh nezam-e jehane beh me'ane taslem-e moqabel qodratha-ye zurgu ast," *Abrar* (Tehran), April 16, 2009.

224. Mark Landler, "A New Iran Overture, with Hot Dogs," *New York Times*, June 1, 2009.

225. President Barack Obama interview, CBS, June 19, 2009.

226. Seyed Hossein Mousavian, *The Iranian Nuclear Crisis: A Memoir* (Washington: Carnegie Endowment for International Peace, 2012), p. 339.

227. President Barack Obama interview, Associated Press, July 2, 2009.

228. Thomas Erdbrink, "Iran Read for Talks, Says Nuclear Negotiator," *Washington Post*, September 2, 2009.

229. Herb Keinon, "Defiant Ahmadinejad Rules Out Nuclear Concessions," *Jerusalem Post*, September 8, 2009.

230. David Gollust, "U.S. to Send Senior Diplomat to Talks with Iran," Voice of America News, September 14, 2009.

231. "Lawmaker: Iran Specifies Location for 10 New N. Sites," Fars News Agency, January 9, 2010.

232. Ian Kelly, Daily Press Briefing, U.S. Department of State, October 1, 2009.

233. Bobby Ghosh, "CIA Knew about Iran's Secret Nuclear Plant Long before Disclosure," *Time*, October 7, 2009.

234. Mark Landler and Steven Erlanger, "On the Eve of Nuclear Talks, Iran's Foreign Minister Makes a Washington Visit," *New York Times*, October 1, 2009.

235. Yaakov Katz, "Iran Tests Long-Range Missiles as Nuclear Crisis Deepens," *Jerusalem Post*, September 29, 2009.

236. "Iran Agrees to Allow UN Visit to Nuclear Plant," Agence France-Presse, October 2, 2009.

237. See comments in Eric Etheridge, "Did Iran Blink?" Opinionator, *New York Times* Blogs, October 5, 2009. "Pwned" is slang for "dominated."

238. "Iran to Seek Guaranteed Supply of Nuclear Fuel at Vienna," NOW Lebanon (Beirut) in English, 1038 GMT, October 18, 2009.

239. David E. Sanger, "Iran Said to Ignore Effort to Salvage Nuclear Deal," *New York Times*, November 9, 2009; "Obama on Tehran's Democrats: 'We Do Not Interfere in Iran's Internal Affairs,'" *Wall Street Journal*, November 5, 2009.

240. "Former Hostage's Advice for Iran Negotiations," NPR, September 19, 2009.

241. "The Road Ahead for U.S.-Iran Relations," *Tehran Times*, October 7, 2009.

242. "Supreme Leader: Iranian Nation Will Not Be Deceived by US Gov't," Islamic Republic News Agency, November 3, 2009.

243. "Text of Obama's Interview," Reuters, November 9, 2009.

244. "Construction of New Nuclear Plants, Strong Response to G5+1: Salehi," Islamic Republic News Agency, November 30, 2009.

245. "FM Spokesman: US Talks Not on the Table," Islamic Republic News Agency, December 8, 2009.

246. Parisa Hafezi and Reza Derakhshi, "Iran Says Launches Satellite Rocket," Reuters, February 3, 2010.

247. Secretary of State Hillary Clinton, news conference with Qatar Prime Minister Sheikh Hamad Bin Jassim Jabar al-Thani, U.S. Department of State, January 4, 2010.

248. Nasser Karimi, "Iran Accepts Clinton Non-Deadline on Nuclear Talks," Associated Press, January 5, 2010.

249. "Iran Has Material for 1–2 Atom Bombs: Ex-IAEA Aide," Reuters, August 26, 2010.

250. See, for example, Trita Parsi, *A Single Roll of the Dice: Obama's Diplomacy with Iran* (New Haven: Yale University Press, 2012).

251. Louis Charbonneau, "China: Big Powers Should Talk with Iran, Not Punish," Reuters, February 5, 2010.

252. "Agar mikhahid az goftogu natijeh begardid akhlaq taghavati ra kenar begozarid," ILNA (Tehran), December 1, 2010.

253. Josh Rogin, "Cat and Mouse: Iranian Foreign Minister Shakes Hands with Senior U.S. Official but Dodges Hillary Clinton," *Foreign Policy*, December 4, 2010; "Iziharat-i Clinton mamalu az tunaqaz / zaman bar rivabateh ba amrika narasideh ast," Mehr News Agency (Tehran), October 29, 2011.

254. "Empty Nuclear Talks with Iran," *Washington Post*, December 8, 2010.

255. Jay Solomon, "Iran Agrees to New Round of Talks in Turkey," *Wall Street Journal*, December 8, 2010.

256. Suzanne Maloney and Ray Takeyh, "Ahmadinejad's Fall, America's Loss," *New York Times*, June 16, 2011.

257. "In fakr ghalat ast keh agar ba Amrika maravdeh dasteh bashim, keshavarman tusa'yeh peda mikonad," Farda News (Tehran), November 16, 2011; "Jaryan Anharafi beh Donbal Shakast-e Nizam-e Suriya," *Daneshjoo* [Student News Agency, SNN.ir] (Tehran), September 28, 2012.

258. Hassan Rouhani, "Why Iran Seeks Constructive Engagement," *Washington Post*, September 19, 2013.

259. Barack Obama, Statement by the President, The White House, September 27, 2013.

260. "Sokhanrani Hojjat ol-Islam va al-Musulmin Doktor Hassan Rouhani dar Jame'ah Nakhbagan Firdowsi Mashhad," February 9, 2005.

261. Voice of the Islamic Republic Radio 1 (Tehran), October 2, 2013.

262. Thomas Erdbrink, "Iran's Leaders Signal New Effort at Thaw," *New York Times*, September 18, 2013; "Salehi Strongly Rejects Rumors of Fordo Close Down," Islamic Republic News Agency, September 18, 2013.

263. "Estratezhi 'Narmesh Qaharnamaneh' Haman Estratezhi Kali Nizam Ast ba Taktiki Mutafavat," *Bashgah-e Khabarnagaran* (Tehran), September 20, 2013.

264. "Dr. Rouhani's 1st TV Report to the People," Presidency of the Islamic Republic of Iran webpage, September 12, 2013.

265. Paul Richter, "State Dept. Official Urges Congress to Delay New Iran Sanctions," *Los Angeles Times*, October 3, 2013.

266. U.S. Embassy Tehran, "Negotiations," August 13, 1979, Tehran 8980.

267. "'We Are Ordered to Crush You': Expanding Repression of Dissent in Iran," Amnesty International, 2012.

268. Joby Warrick, "Iran's Nuclear Program Suffering New Setbacks, Diplomats and Experts Say," *Washington Post*, October 18, 2011.

269. *Kayhan*, May 11, 2008.

270. Thomas Erdbrink, "Iran Sees Success in Its Atom Strategy," *International Herald Tribune*, May 16, 2012,

271. David Crawford, Richard Boudreaux, Joe Lauria, and Jay Solomon, "U.S. Softens Sanction Plan against Iran," *Wall Street Journal*, March 25, 2010.

272. Hassan Nasrallah interview, New TV (Beirut), August 27, 2006.

273. Neil MacFarquhar, "U.S. Walks Out as Iran Leader Speaks," *New York Times*, September 23, 2010.

274. "Iran Cancels Aid Ship to Gaza," Reuters, June 28, 2010.

Chapter 3: Team America and the Hermit Kingdom

1. Chuck Downs, *Over the Line: North Korea's Negotiating Strategy* (Washington: American Enterprise Institute, 1999), p. 94.

2. Ibid., p. 95.

3. Ibid., p. 96.

4. Ibid., pp. 118–19.

5. Ibid., p. 127.

6. Ibid., pp. 143–44.

7. Narushige Michishita, *North Korea's Military-Diplomatic Campaigns, 1966–2008* (New York: Routledge, 2010), pp. 38–39.

8. Talking Points, National Security Council, April 16, 1969: Korea.

9. Downs, *Over the Line*, p. 146.

10. Ibid., p. 151.

11. Michishita, *North Korea's Military-Diplomatic Campaigns*, p. 70.

12. Don Oberdorfer, *The Two Koreas: A Contemporary History* (New York: Basic Books, 2001), p. 61.

13. Ibid., p. 95.

14. Michishita, *North Korea's Military-Diplomatic Campaigns*, pp. 52–54.

15. Ibid., pp. 58–59.

16. Downs, *Over the Line*, pp. 153–54.

17. T. Jefferson Coolidge Jr., "Korea: The Case against Withdrawal," *Asian Affairs*, November–December 1976, p. 71.

18. "Democratic Party Platform of 1976," July 12, 1976.

19. Cyrus Vance, *Hard Choices: Critical Years in America's Foreign Policy* (New York: Simon & Schuster, 1983), p. 128; Donald Brandon, "Carter and Asia: The Wages of Inexperience," *Asian Affairs*, May–June 1978.

20. Chalmers Johnson, "Carter in Asia: McGovernism without McGovern," *Commentary*, January 1978.

21. Frank Gibney, "The Ripple Effect in Korea," *Foreign Affairs*, October 1977. Gibney was also vice president of *Encyclopedia Britannica*.

22. Oberdorfer, *The Two Koreas*, p. 101.

23. Ibid., p. 95.

24. Michishita, *North Korea's Military-Diplomatic Campaigns*, p. 9.

25. Oberdorfer, *The Two Koreas*, p. 103.

26. Ibid., p. 104.

27. Ibid., p. 108.

28. Ibid., p. 142; Daryl M. Plunk, "North Korea: Exporting Terrorism?" The Heritage Foundation, February 25, 1988.

29. Downs, *Over the Line*, p. 201.

30. Morley Myers, "Seoul Surprises Nagoya for Olympic Bid," UPI, September 30, 1981.

31. Tracy Dahlby, "Award of 1988 Olympics Boosts S. Korea's Effort for Political Security," *Washington Post*, October 4, 1981.

32. George P. Shultz, *Turmoil and Triumph: My Years as Secretary of State* (New York: Touchstone, 1993), p. 981.

33. Oberdorfer, *The Two Koreas*, p. 194.

34. Don Oberdorfer and Fred Hiatt, "S. Korean President Urges End to Isolation of North," *Washington Post*, July 2, 1988.

35. Oberdorfer, *The Two Koreas*, p. 193.

36. Benjamin A. Gilman, "U.S. Policy toward North Korea," testimony before the House Committee on International Relations, September 24, 1998.

37. Oberdorfer, *The Two Koreas*, p. 196.

38. Ibid., p. 196.

39. Ibid., p. 250.

40. Joel S. Wit, Daniel B. Poneman, and Robert L. Gallucci, *Going Critical: The First North Korean Nuclear Crisis* (Washington: Brookings Institution Press, 2004), p. 3.

41. Ibid., p. 4; Downs, *Over the Line*, p. 214.

42. Wit, Poneman, and Gallucci, *Going Critical*, p. 6.

43. James A. Baker III, with Thomas M. DeFrank, *The Politics of Diplomacy: Revolution, War, and Peace, 1989–1992* (New York: Putnam, 1995), p. 595.

44. Terence Roehrig, *From Deterrence to Engagement: The U.S. Defense Commitment to South Korea* (Lanham, Md.: Lexington Books, 2007), p. 203.

45. Wit, Poneman, and Gallucci, *Going Critical*, p. 7.

46. Ibid., p. 8.

47. Baker, *The Politics of Diplomacy*, p. 595.

48. Oberdorfer, *The Two Koreas*, p. 257.

49. Wit, Poneman, and Gallucci, *Going Critical*, p. 7.

50. "Iran Rejects Tough Atomic Inspections, Citing 'Double Standard,'" Reuters, May 5, 2008; "Senior Cleric Rejects Compromise on Nuclear Rights," Fars News Agency (Tehran), November 6, 2009.

51. Baker, *The Politics of Diplomacy*, pp. 596–97.

52. "Agreement on Reconciliation, Nonaggression, and Exchanges and Cooperation between South and North Korea," February 19, 1992.

53. Baker, *The Politics of Diplomacy*, p. 597.

54. Downs, *Over the Line*, pp. 216–17.

55. Elaine Sciolino, "C.I.A. Chief Says North Koreans Are Hiding Nuclear Arms Projects," *New York Times*, February 26, 2002.

56. Oberdorfer, *The Two Koreas*, p. 260.

57. Baker, *The Politics of Diplomacy*, p. 596.

58. Wit, Poneman, and Gallucci, *Going Critical*, p. 12.

59. Ibid., p. 13.

60. Ibid., p. xiv.

61. Ibid., p. 13.

62. Baker, *The Politics of Diplomacy*, p. 597; Leon V. Sigal, *Disarming Strangers: Nuclear Diplomacy with North Korea* (Princeton, N.J.: Princeton University Press, 1998), p. 5.

63. Downs, *Over the Line*, p. 212.

64. Oberdorfer, *The Two Koreas*, pp. 273–75; Michishita, *North Korea's Military-Diplomatic Campaigns*, p. 93.

65. Michishita, *North Korea's Military-Diplomatic Campaigns*, p. 13.

66. Ibid., p. 94.

67. Wit, Poneman, and Gallucci, *Going Critical*, p. xiv.

68. Downs, *Over the Line*, p. 227.

69. Wit, Poneman, and Gallucci, *Going Critical*, p. xiv.

70. Downs, *Over the Line*, p. 228.

71. Wit, Poneman, and Gallucci, *Going Critical*, p. 30.

72. Ibid., p. 31; Oberdorfer, *The Two Koreas*, p. 286.

73. UN Security Council Resolution 825 (May 11, 1993).

74. Kim Chi-yong, "'Patience' and Flexibility,' DPRK's Dialogue Strategy Predicting Offensive," *Choson Sinbo* (Tokyo), May 12, 2004.

75. Downs, *Over the Line*, p. 225.

76. Wit, Poneman, and Gallucci, *Going Critical*, pp. 53–54.

77. Ibid., p. 57.

78. Joe Snyder, Daily Press Briefing, U.S. Department of State, June 14, 1993.

79. Downs, *Over the Line*, p. 231.

80. David E. Sanger, "Seoul's Leader Says North Is Manipulating U.S. on Nuclear Issue," *New York Times*, July 2, 1993.

81. Wit, Poneman, and Gallucci, *Going Critical*, pp. 71–72.

82. Ibid., p. 77.

83. Oberdorfer, *The Two Koreas*, p. 291; Wit, Poneman, and Gallucci, *Going Critical*, p. 55.

84. Wit, Poneman, and Gallucci, *Going Critical*, p. 75.

85. Ibid., p. 85.

86. James Sterngold, "North Korea Assails Atomic Unit, Asks U.S. Talks," *New York Times*, October 13, 1993.

87. Wit, Poneman, and Gallucci, *Going Critical*, p. 96.

88. Bill Clinton interview with Timothy Russert and Tom Brokaw, *Meet the Press*, NBC, November 7, 1993.

89. Wit, Poneman, and Gallucci, *Going Critical*, p. 100.

90. Downs, *Over the Line*, p. 239.

91. Wit, Poneman, and Gallucci, *Going Critical*, p. 107.

92. "U.S., North Korea to Meet Again; Military Exercise Suspended," U.S. Department of State, March 3, 1994; Wit, Poneman, and Gallucci, *Going Critical*, p. 114.

93. Wit, Poneman, and Gallucci, *Going Critical*, p. 124.

94. Oberdorfer, *The Two Koreas*, p. 302.

95. Wit, Poneman, and Gallucci, *Going Critical*, pp. 116–17.

96. Ibid., p. 137.

97. Bradley K. Martin, *Under the Loving Care of the Fatherly Leader* (New York: Thomas Dunne, 2006), p. 487.

98. Michishita, *North Korea's Military-Diplomatic Campaigns*, p. 100.

99. Ibid., p. 108.

100. Christine Shelly, "North Korea Still Discharging Fuel from Reactor," U.S. Department of State, June 1, 1994.

101. Michishita, *North Korea's Military-Diplomatic Campaigns*, p. 100.

102. "Interview of the President by the 'Today Show,'" Office of the Press Secretary, The White House, June 20, 1994.

103. Wit, Poneman, and Gallucci, *Going Critical*, p. 225.

104. Oberdorfer, *The Two Koreas*, pp. 330–33.

105. Robert Gallucci, Press Briefing, The White House, June 19, 1994.

106. *Nightline*, ABC News, May 18, 1994.

107. Oberdorfer, *The Two Koreas*, p. 352.

108. President Clinton and Robert Gallucci, Press Briefing, The White House, October 18, 1994.

109. William Safire, "Clinton's Concessions," *New York Times*, October 24, 1994.

110. Terrence Roehrig, *From Deterrence to Engagement: The U.S. Defense Commitment to South Korea* (Lanham, Md.: Lexington Books, 2007), p. 208.

111. James Sterngold, "South Korea President Lashes Out at U.S.," *New York Times*, October 8, 1994.

112. Wit, Poneman, and Gallucci, *Going Critical*, p. 331.

113. Downs, *Over the Line*, p. 214.

114. Ibid., pp. 247–49.

115. Sterngold, "South Korea President Lashes Out at U.S."

116. Daniel Goodkind and Loraine West, "The North Korean Famine and Its Demographic Impact," *Population and Development Review*, 2001, p. 221.

117. James Sterngold, "North Korea Assails Atomic Unit, Asks U.S. Talks," *New York Times*, October 13, 1993.

118. Andrew Pollack, "Escaped Family of 5 Tells of Starvation in North Korea," *New York Times*, May 3, 1994.

119. Andrew Natsios, "The Politics of Famine in North Korea," United States Institute of Peace, Special Report, August 2, 1999, p. 2.

120. Mark E. Manyin and Ryun Jun, "U.S. Assistance to North Korea," CRS Report for Congress, March 17, 2003, p. 2.

121. Natsios, "The Politics of Famine in North Korea," p. 13.

122. Safire, "Clinton's Concessions."

123. Wit, Poneman, and Gallucci, *Going Critical*, p. 336.

124. "Fed Up in North Korea," *Washington Post*, April 9, 2000.

125. Martin, *Under the Loving Care of the Fatherly Leader*, p. 531.

126. "Agreement on the Establishment of the Korean Peninsula Energy Development Organization," March 9, 1995. The European Union joined KEDO's executive board on September 17, 1997. Australia, New Zealand, Canada, Indonesia, Chile, Argentina, Poland, the Czech Republic, and Uzbekistan also serve as KEDO members.

127. Leon V. Sigal, *Disarming Strangers: Nuclear Diplomacy with North Korea* (Princeton, N.J.: Princeton University Press, 1998), p. 200.

128. Wit, Poneman, and Gallucci, *Going Critical*, p. 359.

129. Ibid., p. 356.

130. Thomas C. Hubbard, Deputy Assistant Secretary of State for East Asian and Pacific Affairs, transcript, U.S. Information Agency, Television and Film Service, March 14, 1995.

131. "Gallucci: US Prepared to Meet North Koreans Again in Geneva," U.S. Department of State Briefing, April 21, 1995.

132. "Gallucci: Agreed Framework 'Back on Track,'" Foreign Press Center, U.S. Information Agency, June 22, 1995.

133. Max Ruston, "Nuclear Agreements Signed," Voice of America, January 8, 1997.

134. "President Clinton Welcomes U.S.-D.P.R.K. Agreement Statement," Office of the Press Secretary, The White House, June 13, 1995; President Clinton, President Kim Young Sam, "R.O.K.-U.S. Joint Announcement Proposal to Hold a Four Party Meeting to Promote Peace on the Korean Peninsula," April 16, 1996; Michishita, *North Korea's Military-Diplomatic Campaigns*, pp. 118–19.

135. Nicholas Burns, Daily Press Briefing, U.S. Department of State, April 8, 1997.

136. Nicholas Burns, Daily Press Briefing, U.S. Department of State, April 22, 1997; Michishita, *North Korea's Military-Diplomatic Campaigns*, p. 119.

137. Briefing by State Department Official on U.S.-DPRK Bilateral Meeting, U.S. Mission to the United Nations, March 7, 1997.

138. Nicholas Burns, Daily Press Briefing, U.S. Department of State, March 12, 1997.

139. Nicholas Burns, Daily Press Briefing, U.S. Department of State, April 22, 1997.

140. Michishita, *North Korea's Military-Diplomatic Campaigns*, p. 119.

141. James P. Rubin, Daily Press Briefing, U.S. Department of State, August 27, 1997.

142. "Nobody Can Slander DPRK's Missile Policy—KCNA Commentary," KCNA (Pyongyang), June 16, 1998, as quoted in Michishita, *North Korea's Military-Diplomatic Campaigns*, p. 120.

143. James P. Rubin, Daily Press Briefing, U.S. Department of State, August 27, 1997.

144. Downs, *Over the Line*, p. 270.

145. Ibid., pp. 275–76.

146. James P. Rubin, Daily Press Briefing, U.S. Department of State, July 15, 1998.

147. Mark E. Manyin and Ryun Jun, "U.S. Assistance to North Korea," CRS Report for Congress, March 17, 2003, p. 1.

148. James P. Rubin, Daily Press Briefing, U.S. Department of State, November 19, 1998; Philip Shenon, "Suspected North Korean Atom Site Is Empty, U.S. Finds," *New York Times*, May 28, 1999; Fred Cooper, "U.S./North Korea Missile Talks," Voice of America, March 29, 1999.

149. "US 'Insulting' DPRK Honor; KPA Anger 'Reached Its Limit,'" KCNA (Pyongyang), December 12, 1998.

150. Secretary of State Madeleine K. Albright, U.S. Department of State, March 16, 1999.

151. "DPRK Party Organ Reviews 10 Years of Military-First Politics, DPRK-US Nuclear Confrontation," *Rodong Sinmum* (Pyongyang), July 20, 2005, translation provided by the Open Source Center.

152. Michishita, *North Korea's Military-Diplomatic Campaigns*, p. 125.

153. James P. Rubin, Daily Press Briefings, U.S. Department of State, September 10, 1998; September 18, 1998.

154. Michishita, *North Korea's Military-Diplomatic Campaigns*, p. 135.

155. Mitchell B. Reiss, Robert Gallucci, et al., "Red-Handed," *Foreign Affairs*, March–April 2005; Benjamin Gilman, letter to Dennis Hastert, October 29, 1999.

156. Michishita, *North Korea's Military-Diplomatic Campaigns*, p. 122.

157. Ibid., p. 123.

158. Ibid., p. 146.

159. Hyun-Sung Khang, "Correspondent Report," Voice of America, August 18, 1999.

160. Jim Randle, "Korea Missile Talks," Voice of America, July 29, 1999.

161. William J. Perry, *Review of United States Policy toward North Korea: Findings and Recommendations*, Office of the North Korea Policy Coordinator, U.S. Department of State, October 12, 1999.

162. Sheena Chestnut, "Illicit Activity and Proliferation: North Korean Smuggling Networks," *International Security*, Summer 2007.

163. Statement by the Press Secretary, The White House, September 17, 1999.

164. Roehrig, *From Deterrence to Engagement*, p. 212.

165. Selig S. Harrison, "Time to Leave Korea?" *Foreign Affairs*, March–April 2001.

166. James B. Foley, Daily Press Briefing, U.S. Department of State, September 29, 1999; "Foreign Ministry Spokesman on 'Timetable' for Deployment of U.S. Forces," KCNA (Pyongyang), December 1, 1999.

167. Richard Boucher, Daily Press Briefing, U.S. Department of State, June 15, 2000.

168. Don Kirk, "Seoul Leader Pressed on Funds Sent to North," *New York Times*, February 1, 2003.

169. Sung-Yoon Lee, "Engaging North Korea: The Clouded Legacy of South Korea's Sunshine Policy," *AEI Asian Outlook*, April 2010.

170. U.S. Department of State, Transcript: Albright October 24 news conference in North Korea, Koryo Hotel, Pyongyang, October 24, 2000.

171. David Gollust, "Clinton/Korea," Voice of America, October 10, 2000.

172. Joe Biden, "Testing North Korea's Commitment to Peace," U.S. Senate, October 19, 2000.

173. Jane Perlez, "North Korea's Missile Pledge Paves the Way for New Talks," *New York Times*, June 22, 2000.

174. Reiss, Gallucci, et al., "Red-Handed."

175. Charles L. Pritchard, *Failed Diplomacy: The Tragic Story of How North Korea Got the Bomb* (Washington: Brookings Institution Press, 2007), pp. 4–5.

176. U.S. Department of State, Transcript: Colin Powell's media availability with the Swedish Foreign Minister and EU Representatives, March 6, 2001.

177. Fred Kaplan, "Rolling Blunder: How the Bush Administration Let North Korea Get Nukes," *Washington Monthly*, May 1, 2004.

178. Pritchard, *Failed Diplomacy*, p. 12.

179. Ibid., p. 6.

180. Ibid., p. 12

181. "DPRK Blasts New U.S. Govt for Hardline Policy," Xinhua (Beijing), February 22, 2001; "DPRK's KCNA: U.S. Anachronistic Policy Towards DPRK Denounced," KCNA (Pyongyang), April 1, 2001; "Media Suggest P'yongyang Posturing Conclusion of US North Korean Policy Review," Open Source Center, April 18, 2001. Translations provided by the Open Source Center.

182. Pritchard, *Failed Diplomacy*, p. 15.

183. Ibid., pp. 8–9; see also, for example, Jocelyn Ford, "North Korea/G-8," Voice of America, June 21, 1999.

184. "Bush's 'Evil Axis' Comment Stirs Critics," BBC News, February 2, 2002.

185. "Memorandum of DPRK Foreign Ministry," KCNA (Pyongyang), March 3, 2005, translation provided by the Open Source Center.

186. "Bush Remark Assailed," *Rodong Shinmun* (Pyongyang), October 29, 2001.

187. "Brunei Forum at One on Terrorism, Korea," RIA Novosti (Moscow), July 31, 2002.

188. Pritchard, *Failed Diplomacy*, p. 32.

189. Reiss, Gallucci, et al., "Red-Handed"; Henry Sokolski, "Implementing the DPRK Nuclear Deal: What US Law Requires," *Nonproliferation Review*, Fall–Winter 2000.

190. Michishita, *North Korea's Military-Diplomatic Campaigns*, p. 163.

191. Mark E. Manyin and Ryun Jun, "U.S. Assistance to North Korea," CRS Report for Congress, March 17, 2003, p. 4.

192. "KCNA Urges U.S. to Have Right Option for Peace," KCNA (Pyongyang), November 4, 2002.

193. "President George Bush Discusses Iraq in National Press Conference," The White House, March 6, 2003.

194. See, for example, "U.S. Official Downplays Rocket Test," *Washington Times*, July 7, 2001.

195. "KCNA Ridicules Western Media's Talk about DPRK's 'Brinkmanship Tactics,'" KCNA (Pyongyang), February 22, 2003.

196. Leon V. Sigal, "North Korea Is No Iraq: Pyongyang's Negotiating Strategy," *Arms Control Today*, December 2002.

197. "U.S. Has No Reason to Avoid Conclusion of Non-Aggression Treaty," KCNA (Pyongyang), November 17, 2002, translation provided by Open Source Center; Manyin and Jun, "U.S. Assistance to North Korea," p. 4.

198. Joel S. Wit, "New Rules of Engagement with North Korea," *New York Times*, October 19, 2002.

199. Joshua D. Pollack, "The United States, North Korea, and the End of the Agreed Framework," *Naval War College Review*, Summer 2003, pp. 13–14.

200. Ibid., p. 37.

201. Manyin and Jun, "U.S. Assistance to North Korea," p. 4.

202. "Worldwide Threats to U.S. Security," Senate Committee on Armed Services, February 12, 2003.

203. "DPRK 'Editorial Bureau Special Article': Military-First Politics Brings 'Invincibility,'" Korean Central Broadcasting Station (Pyongyang), April 2, 2003.

204. "Rodong Sinmun on U.S. Policy of Pressure," KCNA (Pyongyang), June 29, 2003. The same theme was enunciated in "United States Accused of Letting Loose War Outcries," KCNA, February 24, 2007. Translations courtesy of the Open Source Center.

205. Reiss, Gallucci, et al., "Red-Handed."

206. Pritchard, *Failed Diplomacy*, p. 65.

207. Ibid., p. 103.

208. Ibid.

209. Jack [*sic*] Pritchard, "What I Saw in North Korea," *New York Times*, January 21, 2004.

210. Richard Boucher, Daily Press Briefing, U.S. Department of State, March 4, 2004.

211. Pritchard, *Failed Diplomacy*, p. 108.

212. Ibid., p. 113.

213. U.S. Department of State, "Joint Statement of the Fourth Round of the Six-Party Talks," Beijing, September 19, 2005.

214. Catherine Armitage, "N Korea Abandons Its Nukes," *Australian*, September 20, 2005.

215. Mark E. Manyin, "U.S. Assistance to North Korea," CRS Report for Congress, April 26, 2005, p. 1.

216. "Spokesman for DPRK Foreign Ministry on Six-Party Talks," KCNA (Pyongyang), September 20, 2005.

217. Sonni Efron, "A Tilt Toward N. Korea," *Los Angeles Times*, September 21, 2005.

218. Laurence Brahm, "In from the Cold?" *South China Morning Post*, October 24, 2006.

219. Devika Bhat, "Rice Tells Japan: 'We Will Defend You,'" *Times* (London), October 18, 2006.

220. Mark Mazzetti and William J. Broad, "The Right Confronts Rice over North Korea Policy," *New York Times*, October 25, 2007.

221. As quoted in Sung Chull Kim and David C. Kang, "Engagement as a Viable Alternative to Coercion," in *Engagement with North Korea: A Viable Alternative*, ed. Sung Chull Kim and David C. Kang (Albany: State University of New York Press, 2009), p. 2.

222. Michael Abramowitz and Colum Lynch, "U.S. Urges Sanctions on North Korea," *Washington Post*, October 10, 2006.

223. UN Security Council Resolution 1718 (October 14, 2006).

224. Larry A. Niksch, "North Korea: Terrorism List Removal?" CRS Report for Congress, July 10, 2008, p. 3.

225. Ibid., pp. 8–9.

226. Michishita, *North Korea's Military-Diplomatic Campaigns*, p. 173.

227. Jim Yardley, "North Korea to Close Reactor in Exchange for Raft of Aid," *New York Times*, February 13, 2007.

228. "What Would a Diplomat Do?" *New York Times*, July 23, 2007.

229. James A. Kelly, "Two for Now," *National Interest*, November–December 2008.

230. Yardley, "North Korea to Close Reactor in Exchange for Raft of Aid."

231. "Pyongyang's Accomplice," *Wall Street Journal*, December 7, 2010.

232. "DPRK Party Organ Decries 'Imperialists' for 'Crafty' Methods, Use of 'Aid,'" KCNA (Pyongyang), April 5, 2007.

233. Glenn Kessler, "U.S. Ready to Ease Sanctions on N. Korea," *Washington Post*, April 11, 2008.

234. Winston Lord and Leslie H. Gelb, "Yielding to N. Korea Too Often," *Washington Post*, April 26, 2008.

235. "North Korea Given Time to Send Data," Reuters, January 8, 2008.

236. Larry A. Niksch, "North Korea's Nuclear Weapons Development and Diplomacy," CRS Report for Congress, March 30, 2009, pp. 3–4.

237. U.S. Embassy Seoul, "Mongolia's Consultation with DPRK Vice Foreign Minister Kim," August 13, 2009, Ulaanbator 234.

238. Jin Dae-woong, "Obama Must Be Bold on N.K. Policy," *Korea Herald*, December 3, 2008.

239. "Nuclear Disarmament Would Follow U.S. Diplomatic Ties, North Korea Says," Global Security Newswire, January 12, 2009.

240. Secretary Robert Gates interview with Fox News, U.S. Department of Defense, News Transcript, March 29, 2009.

241. Stephen W. Bosworth, "U.S. Policy Regarding North Korea," U.S. Department of State, April 3, 2009.

242. "N. Korea Using Clinton Visit 'to Promote Kim's Son,'" Agence France-Presse, August 9, 2009.

243. U.S. Embassy Seoul, "Mongolia's Consultation with DPRK Vice Foreign Minister Kim," August 13, 2009, Ulaanbator 234.

244. Twitter/StateDept, May 20, 2010, 3:01 p.m.

245. Joel S. Wit, "Don't Sink Diplomacy," *New York Times*, May 19, 2010.

246. Matthew Lee, "US: North Korean War Damages Claim 'Preposterous,'" Associated Press, June 25, 2010.

247. "North Korea Threatens Harsher Punishment for US Detainee," *AsiaOne* (Singapore), June 24, 2010.

248. Mark Landler, "U.S. Considers Possibility of Engaging North Korea," *New York Times*, August 28, 2010.

249. Jimmy Carter, "North Korea Wants to Make a Deal," *New York Times*, September 15, 2010.

250. Jimmy Carter, "North Korea's Consistent Message to the U.S.," *Washington Post*, November 24, 2010.

251. "U.S. Urged to Make Switchover to Dialogue and Fence Mending," KCNA (Pyongyang), January 19, 2011.

252. Chico Harlan, "South Korean President Hardens Stance," *Washington Post*, December 29, 2010.

253. "U.S. Officials Made Secret Visit to Pyongyang in August," *Chosun Ilbo* (Seoul), October 10, 2013.

254. Josh Rogin, "Exclusive: U.S. and North Korea Held Secret Meeting in March," *Foreign Policy*, April 9, 2013.

255. "S. Korea's Spy Agency Confirms N. Korea Restarted Yongbyon Reactor," *Yonhap* (Seoul), October 8, 2013.

256. *Meet the Press*, NBC, July 9, 2006.

257. Korean Central Broadcasting Station (Pyongyang), 0900 GMT, August 24, 2010, as provided by BBC Worldwide Monitoring.

258. U.S. Embassy Seoul, "A/S Campbell Discusses DPRK Future with Experts," February 18, 2010, Seoul 248.

259. U.S. Department of State, "Post Requested to Follow Up on Ongoing Matters of Proliferation Concern Raised at APEC by President Bush," November 3, 2007, State 152317.

260. U.S. Embassy Beijing, "PRC/DPRK: Chinese Scholars on UNSCR 1874 and Possible Next Steps for China and Washington," June 26, 2009, Beijing 1761.

Chapter 4: Lying Down with Libyans

1. Final Report of the Commission on the Intelligence Capabilities of the United States Regarding Weapons of Mass Destruction, April 1, 2005, p. 252.

2. Mahmoud G. ElWarfally, *Imagery and Ideology in U.S. Policy Toward Libya, 1969–1982* (Pittsburgh: University of Pittsburgh Press, 1988), pp. 75–76, 86–88.

3. Mohamed Eljahmi, "Libya and the U.S.: Qadhafi Unrepentant," *Middle East Quarterly*, Winter 2006.

4. Col. Muammar Qadhafi, "A Message to the American People," Arab-American People-to-People Dialogue Conference, Tripoli, October 9, 1978.

5. ElWarfally, *Imagery and Ideology in U.S. Policy Toward Libya*, pp. 63–66.

6. Ibid., p. 106.

7. Jimmy Carter, *White House Diary* (New York: Farrar, Straus & Giroux, 2010), pp. 438–39.

8. "Cables from Libya: Billy Carter's Visit 'a Positive Event,'" *Washington Post*, August 1, 1980.

9. Bob Woodward, "Intelligence 'Coup' Tied Libya to Blast; Berlin Messages Read," *Washington Post*, April 22, 1986.

10. Sandy Grady, "Go Ahead, Make My Departure! The Reagan-Gadhafi Show's Big Finish," *Miami Herald*, January 6, 1989; James McCartney, "Sending a Message to Terrorists," *Miami Herald*, February 16, 1989.

11. "Mu'ammar al-Qadhafi's Speech on September 4, 1986," Voice of the Greater Arab Homeland (Harare), September 4, 1986, translation by BBC Summary of World Broadcasts; "Libya Deplores Alleged Gorbachev Invitations to Reagan and Thatcher," JANA (Tripoli) in Arabic, 1850 GMT, August 25, 1986, translation by BBC Summary of World Broadcasts.

12. Gideon Rose, "The United States and Libya," in *Trans-Atlantic Tensions: The United States, Europe, and Problem Countries*, ed. Richard Haass (Washington: Brookings Institution Press, 1999), p. 143.

13. Ibid., p. 145.

14. Willy Tuohy, "U.S. Pressing Allies on Libya Chemical Plant," *Los Angeles Times*, January 3, 1989.

15. U.S. Embassy Tripoli, "U.K. Visit to Rabta Chemical Weapons Production Facility," July 14, 2008, Tripoli 574.

16. Jonathan Schwartz, "Dealing with a 'Rogue State': The Libya Precedent," *American Journal of International Law*, 2007, p. 560.

17. Ronald Bruce St. John, "'Libya Is Not Iraq': Preemptive Strikes, WMD, and Diplomacy," *Middle East Journal*, Summer 2004.

18. Michael Ross, "Libya Plant 'Tour' Only Fuels Doubt; Foreign Press Gets View from Bus after Dark," *Los Angeles Times*, January 8, 1989.

19. Gary Hart, "My Secret Talks with Libya, and Why They Went Nowhere," *Washington Post*, January 18, 2004.

20. Ibid.

21. "Implementation of the NPT Safeguards Agreement of the Socialist People's Libyan Arab Jamahiriya," IAEA Board of Governors, February 20, 2004, GOV/2004/12.

22. Milton Viorst, "The Colonel in His Labyrinth," *Foreign Affairs*, March–April 1999.

23. *Patterns of Global Terrorism: 1998*, U.S. Department of State, April 1999.

24. "With Eye on U.S., Libya Denounces Terrorism," Associated Press, December 3, 1999.

25. Schwartz, "Dealing with a 'Rogue State': The Libya Precedent," p. 567.

26. "Libyan Leader Urges Aid for US Victims," JANA (Tripoli) in Arabic, 2030 GMT, September 11, 2001, as provided by the Open Source Center.

27. Jessica Berry, "Expelled Libyan Spy Chief Returns for Talks with MI6," *Sunday Telegraph* (London), October 7, 2001.

28. Richard Boucher, Daily Press Briefing, U.S. Department of State, October 12, 2001.

29. "Libya 'Ready to Pay' for Lockerbie," CNN.com, August 8, 2002.

30. Schwartz, "Dealing with a 'Rogue State': The Libya Precedent," pp. 569–70.

31. Scott MacLeod, "Behind Gaddafi's Diplomatic Turnaround," *Time*, May 18, 2006.

32. Douglas Frantz and Josh Meyer, "The Deal to Disarm Kadafi," *Los Angeles Times*, March 13, 2005.

33. Robert G. Joseph, *Countering WMD: The Libyan Experience* (Fairfax, Va.: National Institute Press, 2009), p. 15.

34. Ibid.

35. Frantz and Meyer, "The Deal to Disarm Kadafi."

36. Robin Wright, "State Dept. Official Meets with Gaddafi on Relations," *Washington Post*, March 24, 2004.

37. "Libya Seeks U.S. Compensation for 1986 Airstrikes," Deutsche Presse-Agentur, August 11, 2004.

38. "Libyan Official Criticizes US State Department Spokesman on Compensation," Great Jamahiriyah TV (Tripoli) in Arabic, 1930 GMT, August 11, 2004, translation provided by the Open Source Center.

39. LBC Satellite TV, Beirut, 0500 GMT, May 16, 2004, as provided by BBC Monitoring International Reports.

40. "Saddam's Defense Committee Funded by Arab Countries," Associated Press, July 6, 2004.

41. U.S. Embassy Tripoli, "Libya Enforces Travel Restrictions Against U.S. Officials," July 21, 2008, Tripoli 588.

42. Curt Weldon, "Time's Up, Qadhafi," *New York Times*, April 5, 2011.

43. "Rescission of Libya's Designation as a State Sponsor of Terrorism," Office of the Spokesman, U.S. Department of State, May 15, 2006.

44. Matt Roper, "Cobblers to You, Tony," *Mirror* (London), March 27, 2004.

45. John Mintz and Peter Slevin, "Alleged Plot to Kill Saudi Ruler Detailed; Libyan Leader Behind It, Detainee Says," *Washington Post*, June 11, 2004; Libya TV, Tripoli, 1600 GMT, June 10, 2004, as provided by BBC Monitoring International Reports; Al-Watan website (Abha), June 13, 2004, as provided by BBC Monitoring International Reports.

46. Matthew L. Wald, "U.S. Drops Libya from List of Terrorist Countries," *New York Times*, July 7, 2006.

47. Christopher M. Blanchard, "Libya: Background and U.S. Relations," CRS Report for Congress, March 16, 2010.

48. Tom Barkley, "U.S., Libya Sign Trade and Investment Pact to Improve Ties," *Wall Street Journal*, May 20, 2010.

49. Patrick E. Tyler, "Libyan Stagnation a Big Factor in Qaddafi Surprise," *New York Times*, January 8, 2004.

50. Timothy J. Burger, "Qadhafi's 9/11 Fears," *Time*, April 4, 2006. This point was reinforced by interviews that a Norwegian scholar conducted with Libyan officials; see Målfrid Braut-Hegghammer, "Libya's Nuclear Turnaround: Perspectives from Tripoli," *Middle East Journal*, Winter 2008.

51. George Tenet, "DCI's Worldwide Threat Briefing," Senate Select Committee on Intelligence, February 11, 2003.

52. Joseph, *Countering WMD*, p. 3.

53. John Bolton, Under Secretary of State for Arms Control and International Security Affairs, interview with Radio Sawa, April 16, 2003.

54. Charles Krauthammer, "Aftershocks of War," *Washington Post*, December 26, 2003.

55. Joseph, *Countering WMD*, pp. 12–13.

56. "Dans un entretien au 'Figaro', le numéro un libyen estime que le président français doit 'tenir bon'; Kadhafi : 'La victoire de Bush ne serait que provisoire'," *Le Figaro* (Paris), March 11, 2003.

57. Braut-Hegghammer, "Libya's Nuclear Turnaround: Perspectives from Tripoli."

58. Ronald Bruce St. John, "'Libya Is Not Iraq': Preemptive Strikes, WMD, and Diplomacy," *Middle East Journal*, Summer 2004.

59. Bruce W. Jentleson and Christopher A. Whytock, "Who 'Won' Libya?" *International Security*, Winter 2005–6, p. 80.

60. "President Bush: Libya Pledges to Dismantle WMD Programs," The White House, December 19, 2003.

61. Joseph, *Countering WMD*, p. 15.

62. Final Report of the Commission on the Intelligence Capabilities of the United States Regarding Weapons of Mass Destruction, April 1, 2005, pp. 252–53; Joby Warrick, "U.S. Displays Nuclear Parts Given by Libya," *Washington Post*, March 16, 2004; Prime Minister Tony Blair, press conference, Tripoli, March 29, 2004.

63. Colin Powell, Speech to the United States Institute of Peace, Washington, D.C., July 15, 2004.

64. Libyan Jamahiriya Broadcasting Corporation, July 17, 2004.

65. Ari Fleischer, Press Briefing, The White House, January 23, 2003.

66. Socialist People's Libyan Arab Jamahiriya, Department of the Americas, "Reply of the Socialist People's Arab Jamahiriya to the Report Issued by the Office of Democracy, Human Rights and Labour at the US State Department, on February 28, 2005."

67. "Libya's Qadhafi Urges Backers to 'Kill' Enemies," Reuters, September 1, 2006.

68. Chester A. Crocker, chairman, and C. Richard Nelson, rapporteur, *U.S.-Libyan Relations: Toward Cautious Reengagement* (Washington: The Atlantic Council of the United States, April 2003), p. xi.

69. Sudarsan Raghavan, "Saif al-Islam al-Gaddafi, a Proponent of Change, May One Day Lead Libya," *Washington Post*, May 26, 2010; Landon Thomas Jr., "Unknotting Father's Reins in Hope of 'Reinventing' Libya," *New York Times*, February 28, 2010. For other examples, see Omri Ceren, "Middle East Experts Got Saif Qaddafi Exactly Backward, Didn't They?" *Commentary*, February 21, 2011.

70. "President, Mrs. Bush Mark Progress in Global Women's Human Rights," Remarks by the First Lady and the President on Efforts to Globally Promote Women's Human Rights, The White House, March 12, 2004.

71. U.S. Embassy Tripoli, "Scenesetter for Secretary Rice's Visit to Libya," August 29, 2008, Tripoli 680.

72. U.S. Embassy Tripoli, "Regime-Orchestrated Attacks Against Berbers in Yefren," January 13, 2009, Tripoli 22.

73. Eli Lake, "Ex-Envoy, Bechtel Gain from Revolving Door," *Washington Times*, February 20, 2009.

74. Dana Moss, *Reforming the Rogue: Lessons from the U.S.-Libya Rapprochement* (Washington: The Washington Institute for Near East Policy, 2010), p. 48.

75. U.S. Embassy Tripoli, "Libya: 2009 Country Reports on Terrorism Ref: State 109980," December 22, 2009, Tripoli 1030; U.S. Embassy Tripoli,

"Scenesetter for the Visit of General William Ward to Libya," March 5, 2009, Tripoli 201.

76. Moss, *Reforming the Rogue*, p. 35.

77. U.S. Embassy Tripoli, "Libya Seeks to Purchase 130,000 Kalashnikovs for Unknown End-Users," August 18, 2008, Tripoli 650.

78. "Qadhafi: Don't Make Me Kill Again," Associated Press, April 27, 2004; Judy Dempsey, "Gadaffi Threatens to Support 'Freedom Fighters' if West Rejects Offer of Peace," *Financial Times*, April 28, 2004.

79. "Gadhafi Son Allegedly Linked to Iraq Bomb Blast," Associated Press, January 26, 2008.

80. "Libya Defends Syria against WMD Accusation," *Khaleej Times* (Dubai), May 15, 2004.

81. Alex Bollfrass, "Libya Backs Out of CW Destruction Agreement," *Arms Control Today*, July–August 2007; U.S. Embassy Tripoli, "Libya's Chemical Weapons Destruction Chief Defends Extension Request Ref: A) State 100809; B) Tripoli 490," October 5, 2009, Tripoli 795.

82. Bollfrass, "Libya Backs Out of CW Destruction Agreement."

83. Moss, *Reforming the Rogue*, p. 4.

84. "Libyan Leader Calls for UN Reform, Says Swine Flu 'Manufactured,'" Al Jamahiriya TV in Arabic, 1500 GMT, September 23, 2009, translation provided by the Open Source Center.

85. U.S. Embassy Tripoli, "Libyan Atomic Energy Establishment Confirms Desire to Sell Uranium Yellowcake," January 15, 2009, Tripoli 32; U.S. Embassy Tripoli, "Libyans Seek Renewed Commitment from U.S. in Return for Progress on HEU Shipment," November 30, 2009, Tripoli 941.

86. James Risen and Eric Lichtblau, "Hoard of Cash Lets Qaddafi Extend Fight against Rebels," *New York Times*, March 10, 2011.

Chapter 5: Tea with the Taliban

1. U.S. Embassy Islamabad, "Meeting with the Taliban in Kandahar: More Questions than Answers," February 15, 1995, Islamabad 01686.

2. U.S. Embassy Islamabad, "Finally, a Talkative Talib: Origins and Membership of the Religious Students' Movement," February 20, 1995, Islamabad 1792.

3. U.S. Embassy Islamabad, "A/S Raphel Discusses Afghanistan," April 22, 1996, Islamabad 3466.

4. Warren Christopher, U.S. Department of State, "Dealing with the Taliban in Kabul," September 28, 1996, State 203322.

5. U.S. Embassy Islamabad, "Afghanistan: Taliban Deny They Are Sheltering HUA Militants, Usama Bin Laden," November 12, 1996, Islamabad 9517.

6. Christina B. Rocca, U.S. Department of State, "U.S. Engagement with the Taliban on Usama Bin Laden," p. 2.

7. U.S. Department of State, "Afghanistan: Taliban Rep Won't Seek UN Seat for Now," December 13, 1996, State 254682.

8. Rocca, "U.S. Engagement with the Taliban on Usama Bin Laden," p. 2.

9. U.S. Embassy Islamabad, "Afghanistan: Raising Bin Ladin with the Taliban," March 28, 1997, Islamabad 2533.

10. Ibid.

11. U.S. Embassy Islamabad, "Afghanistan: Raising Bin Ladin with the Taliban," March 4, 1997, Islamabad 1750.

12. U.S. Embassy Islamabad, "Official Informal for SA Assistant Secretary Robin Raphel and SA/PAB," March 10, 1997, Islamabad 1873.

13. Thomas W. Lippman, "U.N. Ambassador Will Deliver Message to Afghan Faction," *Washington Post*, April 9, 1998.

14. Judy Woodruff, "Bill Richardson Brokers Truce Between Afghanistan's Rival Factions," CNN WorldView, April 17, 1998.

15. Karl Inderfurth, "Afghanistan: Meeting with the Taliban," December 11, 1997, State 231842.

16. Strobe Talbott, "Afghanistan: Meeting with the Taliban," December 11, 1997, State 231842.

17. Madeleine Albright, "Afghanistan: Taliban's Mullah Omar's 8/22 Contact with State Department," August 23, 1998, State 154712.

18. "Taleban Chief Denies Protecting Taliban," AFP (Hong Kong), August 29, 1998; Aimal Khan, "Report: Taliban Bans All Contacts with Bin Ladin," *Frontier Post* (Peshawar), February 11, 1999.

19. Alan Eastham, "Afghanistan: Demarche to the Taliban on New Bin Laden Threat," September 14, 1998, Islamabad 6863.

20. Madeleine Albright, "Message to Mullah Omar," October 1, 1998, State 181837.

21. William B. Milam, "Usama Bin Laden: High-Level Taliban Official Gives the Standard Line on Bin Laden with a Couple of Nuances," October 12, 1998, Islamabad 7665.

22. Madeleine Albright, "Afghanistan: Message to Taliban on Usama Bin Laden," November 11, 1998, State 210367.

23. Abdul Salam Zaeef, *My Life with the Taliban* (New York: Columbia University Press, 2010), p. 137.

24. Assistant Secretary Karl F. Indefurth to Secretary of State Madeleine Albright, "Your Meeting on Usama Bin Laden," Talking Points, November 24, 1998.

25. Karl F. Inderfurth, "A Taliban 'Rope-a-Dope' Strategy?" *Foreign Policy*, January 25, 2012.

26. U.S. Embassy Islamabad, "Osama bin Laden: Taliban Spokesman Seeks New Proposal for Resolving bin Laden Problem," November 28, 1998, State 220495.

27. U.S. Embassy Islamabad, "Usama bin Ladin: Charge Reiterates U.S. Concern to Key Taliban Official, Who Sticks to Well-Known Taliban Positions," December 19, 1998, Islamabad 9222.

28. U.S. Embassy Islamabad, "Usama bin Ladin: Charge Underscores U.S. Concerns on Interviews; Taliban Envoy Says Bin Ladin Hoodwinked Them and It Will Not Happen Again," December 30, 1998, Islamabad 9488.

29. UN Security Council Resolution 1267 (October 15, 1999); UN Security Council Resolution 1333 (December 19, 1999).

30. Jessica Stern, *Terror in the Name of God: Why Religious Militants Kill* (New York: HarperCollins, 1993), p. 193.

31. U.S. Embassy Islamabad, "A/S Inderfurth and S/CT Sheehan Meet Taliban Representatives," February 1, 2000, Islamabad 567.

32. Zaeef, *My Life with the Taliban*, p. 138.

33. Ibid., p. 139.

34. U.S. Department of State, "Taliban Deliver Letter from Muttawakil; Say They Will Comply with Office Closing in New York," February 15, 2001.

35. Zaeef, *My Life with the Taliban*, pp. 137–38.

36. Ibid., p. 138.

37. Hafeez Malik, *U.S. Relations with Afghanistan and Pakistan* (Karachi: Oxford University Press, 2009), p. 174.

38. Dudley Althaus, "U.S. Intensifies Air Attack; Powell: Taliban May Have Place in Future," *Houston Chronicle*, October 17, 2001.

39. Fareed Zakaria, "A Turnaround Strategy," *Newsweek*, February 9, 2009.

40. Ashley J. Tellis, *Reconciling with the Taliban? Toward an Alternative Grand Strategy in Afghanistan* (Washington: Carnegie Endowment for International Peace, 2009), pp. 13, 25.

41. Ibid., p. 10.

42. Mike Mount, "Gates: U.S. Would Support Afghan Peace Talks with Taliban," CNN International, October 10, 2008, as quoted in Tellis, *Reconciling with the Taliban*, p. 9.

43. *Asharq al-Awsat* (London), March 15, 2009, as translated by MEMRI, Special Dispatch 2353, May 12, 2009.

44. *Al-Hayat* (London), March 25, 2009, as translated by MEMRI, Special Dispatch 2353, May 12, 2009.

45. Hizb-e-Islami website, March 11, 2009, translation courtesy of MEMRI.

46. Syed Saleem Shahzad, "Afghanistan: Taliban Leader Rejects Prospect of Truce," ADNKronos International, November 25, 2008, as quoted in Tellis, *Reconciling with the Taliban*, p. 13.

47. Dexter Filkins and Carlotta Gall, "Taliban Leader in Secret Talks Was an Impostor," *New York Times*, November 22, 2010.

48. "Afghan Taliban Comments on Imposter Mullah Akhtar Muhammad," SITE Intelligence Group, November 30, 2010.

49. "Counterterrorism Activities (Neo-Taliban)," Issue Paper for Vice President Cheney, December 9, 2005.

50. Fotini Christia and Michael Semple, "Flipping the Taliban," *Foreign Affairs*, July–August 2009.

51. Davood Moradian, "Reconciliation with the Taliban: The View from Kabul," International Institute for Strategic Studies, October 15, 2009.

52. Ibid.

53. "Browne: The Taliban Must Take a Role in the Afghan Peace Process," *Daily Mail* (London), September 25, 2007.

54. Karen DeYoung, "British Official Urges Afghan Leaders to Negotiate with Taliban," *Washington Post*, March 11, 2010.

55. Kim Sengupta, "Exclusive: Army Chief: 'We Must Tackle Taliban Grievances," *Independent* (London), September 18, 2009.

56. *News* (Karachi), January 26, 2010, as distributed by MEMRI, Special Dispatch 2770, January 26, 2010.

57. Moradian, "Reconciliation with the Taliban: The View from Kabul."

58. Helene Cooper and Sheryl Gay Stolberg, "Obama Ponders Outreach to Elements of Taliban," *New York Times*, March 7, 2009.

59. President Barack Obama, Address to the Nation at the United States Military Academy at West Point, December 1, 2009.

60. Rob Crilly, Ben Farmer, and Dean Nelson, "US Seeks Direct Talks with Taliban's Mullah Omar," *Telegraph* (London), June 5, 2011.

61. Mark Landler and Alissa J. Rubin, "War Plan for Karzai: Reach Out to Taliban," *New York Times*, January 29, 2010.

62. General David Petraeus interview with David Gregory, *Meet the Press,* NBC, August 15, 2010.

63. Christoph Reuter, Gregor Peter Schmitz, and Holger Stark, "How German Diplomats Opened Channel to Taliban," *Spiegel Online International,* January 10, 2012.

64. Steven Lee Myers, Matthew Rosenberg, and Eric Schmitt, "Against Odds, Path Opens Up for U.S.-Taliban Talks," *New York Times*, January 11, 2012.

65. *Meet the Press*, NBC, March 14, 2011.

66. "Colonel Imam Offers to Facilitate Contact between United States, Mullah Omar," *Jinnah* (Islamabad), January 28, 2010, translation provided by the Open Source Center.

67. Missy Ryan, Warren Strobel, and Mark Hosenball, "Exclusive: Secret U.S., Taliban Talks Reach Turning Point," Reuters, December 19, 2011.

68. Ben Farmer, "Taliban Diplomats Arrive in Qatar," *Telegraph* (London), January 26, 2012.

69. Ali M. Latifi, "Taliban Talks in Doha Drag On Endlessly," Al Jazeera, February 26, 2013.

70. Salman Siddiqui, "Taliban 'Waiting for Baradar to Reopen Peace Talks in Doha,'" *Gulf Times* (Doha), September 23, 2013.

71. Crilly et al., "US Seeks Direct Talks with Taliban's Mullah Omar."

72. "U.S. Withdrawal Date Has Boosted Morale of Taliban, Says General," Reuters, August 24, 2010.

73. Indira A. R. Lakshmanan, "Clinton Says U.S. Met with Militants Who Later Attacked Embassy in Kabul," Bloomberg, October 21, 2011.

Chapter 6: Double Dealing in the Land of the Pure

1. See James H. Noyes, Deputy Assistant Secretary of Defense for Near East Affairs, statement before the Subcommittee on the Near East and South Asia, House Committee on Foreign Affairs, March 20, 1973.

2. Craig Baxter et al., "Modernization and Development," in *Government and Politics in South Asia*, 2nd ed. (Boulder, Col.: Westview Press, 1991), p. 246.

3. See U.S. response to Pakistan's request for $2 billion in military and financial aid conveyed to Laik Ali, Special Emissary of Jinnah, by State Department officials, October 30, 1947, in Rashmi Jain, "Political Relations, 1947–2006," in *The United States and Pakistan, 1947–2006: A Documentary Study*, ed. Rashmi Jain (New Delhi: Radiant Publishers, 2007), p. 4.

4. Hamid H. Kizilbash, "Anti-Americanism in Pakistan," in *Anti-Americanism: Origins and Context*, ed. Thomas Perry Thornton (Thousand Oaks, Calif.: Sage Publications, 1988), p. 61.

5. United Press, "Anti-American Sentiment Grows," *New York Times*, September 5, 1947.

6. "Pakistan Troops to Aid Arabs," Associated Press, May 26, 1948; "Pakistan Plans Palestine Force," Associated Press, July 6, 1948.

7. Air Marshal (Ret'd) Ayaz Ahmed Khan, "Pak-US Ties in Historical Perspective," *Nation* (Pakistan), February 18, 2007.

8. Latif Ahmed Sherwani, *Pakistan, China, and America* (Karachi: Council for Pakistan Studies, 1980), pp. 37–40.

9. "Truman Greets Liaquat Ali as Pakistani's Tour Begins," *New York Times*, May 4, 1950.

10. Harold A. Gould, *The South Asia Story* (New Delhi: Sage Publications, 2010), pp. 32–33.

11. Ibid., p. 34.

12. Walter H. Waggoner, "President Grants Arms Aid to Pakistan, Assures India," *New York Times*, February 26, 1954.

13. "Pakistan-U.S. Pact Signed: Aid for Internal Security," *Times* (London), May 20, 1954.

14. "Britain Will Aid Turkey and Iraq," *Washington Post*, April 5, 1955; Hanson W. Baldwin, "SEATO's Impact Now Mainly Psychological," *New York Times*, September 12, 1954.

15. Norman D. Palmer, *The New Regionalism in Asia and the Pacific* (Lanham, Md.: Lexington Books, 1991), p. 159.

16. See President Lyndon Johnson's report to Congress on the Foreign Assistance Program for FY 1966, January 1967. Also, see statement by Arthur J. Goldberg, U.S. Ambassador to the United Nations, in the Security Council, September 17, 1965.

17. Statement by the Foreign Minister of Pakistan, April 17, 1967, in *The United States and Pakistan, 1947–2006*, ed. Jain, p. 310.

18. President Ayub, letter to President Johnson, Rawalpindi, July 19, 1968, in Johnson Library, National Security File, Head of State Correspondence File, Pakistan, vol. 3, President Ayub Correspondence, 12/31/67–[*sic*], delivered to the White House by the Pakistani embassy on July 31.

19. Adolph Dubs, Deputy Assistant Secretary of State for Near East Affairs, statement before the Subcommittee on Asian and Pacific Affairs, House Committee on Foreign Affairs, March 22, 1977.

20. Gould, *The South Asia Story*, pp. 56–57.

21. "United States Interests and Policies toward South Asia," Subcommittee on the Near East and South Asia, House Committee on Foreign Affairs, 1973.

22. Gould, *The South Asia Story*, pp. 57–59.

23. Kamila Hyat, "No Room for Doubt and Division," *News International* (Karachi), September 25, 2008; Hafeez Malik, *U.S. Relations with Afghanistan and Pakistan* (Karachi: Oxford University Press, 2009), p. 179; U.S. Embassy Islamabad, "Ambassador's Condolence Call on Asif Zardari," January 28, 2008, Islamabad 405.

24. See Henry Kissinger's news conference, February 25, 1975.

25. Zulfiqar Ali Bhutto interview, *Spectator* (London), September 11, 1976.

26. General K. M. Arif, *Khaki Shadows: Pakistan 1947–1997* (Karachi: Oxford University Press, 2001), pp. 305–6, as quoted in Howard B. Schaffer and Teresita C. Schaffer, *How Pakistan Negotiates with the United States* (Washington: United States Institute of Peace Press, 2011), pp. 1–2.

27. Associated Press, November 21, 1979.

28. Gould, *The South Asia Story*, pp. 72–73.

29. *Dawn*, April 18, 1983, quoted in A. Z. Hilali, "Motives Behind the U.S.-Pakistan Relationship," in *U.S.-Pakistan Relationship: Soviet Invasion of Afghanistan* (Farnham, UK: Ashgate Publishing, 2005), p. 84.

30. Pakistan and United States, Agreement for Cooperation Concerning Civil Uses of Atomic Energy, signed in Washington on August 11, 1955.

31. Syed Ali Zafar, "A National Asset," *Nation* (Lahore), October 9, 2007.

32. "Who Has the Bomb," *Time*, June 3, 1985.

33. David Binders, "Pakistan Sees India as Nuclear Threat," *New York Times*, May 21, 1974.

34. Bernard Weinraub, "Pakistani Presses U.S. for Arms," *New York Times*, October 14, 1974.

35. Angus Deming, with Lloyd H. Norman and James Bishop Jr., "Diplomacy: Bombs Away?" *Newsweek*, March 8, 1976.

36. Bernard Gwertzman, "Kissinger Meets Pakistani Leader on Nuclear Issue," *New York Times*, August 9, 1976.

37. Fred Iklé, Director of the U.S. Arms Control and Disarmament Agency, statement before the Subcommittee on Arms Control, Senate Committee on Foreign Relations, February 23, 1976. See also Deming et al., "Diplomacy: Bombs Away?"

38. Zulfiqar Ali Bhutto, press conference in Ottawa, February 26, 1976; Rashmi Jain, "Nuclear Relations, 1947–2006," in *The United States and Pakistan 1947–2006*, ed. Jain, p. 371.

39. Symington Amendment of 1976; Glenn Amendment of 1977.

40. Douglas Frantz and Catherine Collins, "Those Nuclear Flashpoints Are Made in Pakistan," *Washington Post*, November 11, 2007.

41. "Nukes: What the US Can Do," *Christian Science Monitor*, June 22, 1981.

42. International Security and Development Cooperation Act of 1981 (P.L. 97-113), waiving application of Section 669 (Symington Amendment) to Pakistan for six years, December 29, 1981.

43. "Afghan War Gave Space to Pak to Prepare N-Bomb: Khan," *India Post* (New York), September 9, 2009.

44. General Mohammed Zia ul-Haq, President of Pakistan, interview in *U.S. News and World Report*, September 21, 1981.

45. "Pakistan Could Have Exploded Bomb in 1984: Disgraced Nuclear Scientist," *Kyodo News International*, May 28, 2010; "Exclusive Interview with Dr. Abdul Qadeer Khan," *Nawa-i-Waqt* (Lahore), February 9, 1984.

46. The Pressler Amendment and Pakistan's Nuclear Weapons Program, U.S. Senate, July 31, 1992.

47. Munir Ahmed Khan, Chairman of the Pakistan Atomic Energy Commission, press conference in Lahore, January 30, 1991.

48. "Bhutto Threatens to Match Indian 'Nuclear Escalation,'" Agence France-Presse, October 3, 1996.

49. Khalid Akhtar, "Partnership with US—a Tricky Road," *Muslim* (Islamabad), April 22, 1998.

50. Ibid.

51. Karl F. Inderfurth, Under Secretary of State for South Asian Affairs, statement before the Subcommittee on Near Eastern and South Asian Affairs, Senate Committee on Foreign Relations, May 13, 1998; Secretary of State Madeleine Albright, statement at the U.S. Coast Guard Academy, May 20, 1998.

52. Robert T. Grey Jr., statement at the Conference on Disarmament, Geneva, June 2, 1998.

53. Fahd Husain, "Sailing across a Sea of Mistrust," *Nation* (Lahore), November 12, 1998.

54. "Pakistan Blasts U.S. for Imposing New Sanctions," *Kyodo News International*, September 3, 2001.

55. "Pakistan Ambassador Calls US Sanctions 'Discriminatory,'" Radio Pakistan (Islamabad), May 31, 1998.

56. "Chief Nuclear Scientist Interviewed," *Al-Majallah* (London), June 10, 1998; "Fresh US Sanctions on China and Pakistan," *Jang* (Rawalpindi), September 3, 2001.

57. Prime Minister Mohammad Nawaz Sharif, press conference in Islamabad on 28th May, Pakistan TV, Islamabad, in English, 1843 GMT, May 28, 1998.

58. Pervez Musharraf, "Nuclear Proliferation," *In the Line of Fire: A Memoir* (New York: Free Press, 2006), p. 287.

59. Ibid., p. 285.

60. Husain, "Sailing across a Sea of Mistrust."

61. Musharraf, "Nuclear Proliferation," p. 286.

62. U.S. Embassy Islamabad, "Senator Kerry Meets with Pakistani President Zardari," February 23, 2010, Islamabad 428.

63. Hafeez Malik, *U.S. Relations with Afghanistan and Pakistan* (Karachi: Oxford University Press, 2009), p. 176.

64. Ibid., p. 177.

65. Shamshad Ahmad, "Where Is U.S. Public Diplomacy?" *News* (Karachi), January 13, 2010.

66. Alan Sipress and Steven Mufson, "America Lines Up Support for Strike; Pakistan Pressured to Aid Any Reprisal," *Washington Post*, September 13, 2001.

67. Colin Powell, "Memorandum for the President: Your Meeting with Pakistan President Musharraf," U.S. Department of State, November 5, 2001.

68. U.S. Embassy Islamabad, "Scene-Setter for the Visit of Senators Levin and Warner," November 16, 2001, Islamabad 6322.

69. "Afghanistan: Pakistani Foreign Minister Admits Contacting Taliban," Islamic Republic News Agency, September 15, 2001, transcript provided by the Open Source Center.

70. Interview by author with Lt. General Assad Durrani, Islamabad, Pakistan, October 1, 2010.

71. Inayatullah, "Weakness Attracts Aggression," *Nation* (Karachi), October 1, 2010.

72. U.S. Department of State to U.S. Embassy Islamabad et al., "Deputy Secretary Armitage–Mahmoud Phone Call," September 18, 2001, State 161279.

73. U.S. Embassy Islamabad, "Mahmud Plans and 2nd Mission to Afghanistan," September 24, 2001, Islamabad 5337.

74. Pervez Musharraf speech, Pakistan TV, September 19, 2001.

75. President George W. Bush, Address to a Joint Session of Congress and the American People, September 20, 2001.

76. "U.S. 'Threatened to Bomb' Pakistan," BBC News, September 22, 2006.

77. U.S. Embassy Islamabad, "Pakistan Afghan Policy: Anyone but Rabbani/Massoud—Even the Taliban," October 18, 1995, Islamabad 09675.

78. U.S. Department of State, "Discussing Afghan Policy with the Pakistanis," December 22, 1995, State 291940.

79. Ahmed Rashid, *Descent into Chaos: The United States and the Failure of Nation Building in Pakistan, Afghanistan, and Central Asia* (New York: Viking, 2008), p. 30.

80. Mushahid Hussain, "Can Pakistan's Leader Hold On?" *New York Times*, October 11, 2001.

81. Pervez Musharraf speech, Pakistan TV, Islamabad, 0517 GMT, October 8, 2001, translation provided by BBC World Monitoring.

82. "Hamid Gul Supports Musharraf's Policy against Terrorism," *Pakistan Newswire*, September 27, 2001; "Hameed Gul Endorses Call for Jihad," *Pakistan Newswire*, October 14, 2001; "Taliban Withdrawal from Kabul a Strategic Step: Gul," *Nation* (Lahore), November 16, 2001.

83. Colin Powell, "Memorandum for the President: Your Meeting with Pakistan President Musharraf," U.S. Department of State, November 5, 2001.

84. Naveed Miraj, "Mutawakil Seeks Respite in US Attacks; Holds Parleys with DG ISI," *Frontier Post* (Peshawar), October 16, 2001.

85. "Powell, Musharraf Agree on Officials," Associated Press, October 16, 2001.

86. "America Strikes Back: Interview with Madeleine Albright," CNN, October 23, 2001.

87. *Face the Nation*, CBS News, October 21, 2001.

88. "Future Government Has 'No Place' for Taliban: Opposition," Agence France-Presse, October 17, 2001.

89. "A Nation Challenged: Islamabad; Powell Suggests Role for Taliban," *New York Times*, October 17, 2001.

90. Tyler Marshall, "Response to Terror: Diplomacy; Warlord's Politics Could Prove Problematic," *Los Angeles Times*, October 24, 2001.

91. "Taleban Foreign Minister Met Pakistani Spy Chief in Islamabad," *Frontier Post* (Peshawar), October 16, 2001.

92. Deborah Orin, "U.S. Skeptical of Afghan Defector," *New York Post*, October 17, 2001.

93. "A Nation Challenged: Diplomacy; Pakistani Leader Seeks 'Gestures' for Backing U.S.," *New York Times*, November 10, 2001.

94. Bob Woodward, *Bush at War* (New York: Simon & Schuster, 2002), p. 303; "Northern Alliance Should Not Take Kabul: Bush," Agence France-Presse, November 11, 2001.

95. "A Nation Challenged: The Big Picture; Rebels In Control in Kabul as Taliban Troops Retreat; Bin Laden Hunt Intensifies," *New York Times*, November 14, 2001.

96. Rashid, *Descent into Chaos*, p. 87.

97. Ibid.

98. "Envoy to UN Says Alliance Entered Kabul with US Advice, Support," *Jang* (Rawalpindi), November 18, 2001.

99. David E. Sanger, "In North Korea and Pakistan, Deep Roots of Nuclear Barter," *New York Times*, November 24, 2002.

100. David E. Sanger, "A Nation at War: Asian Front: U.S. Rebukes Pakistanis for Lab's Aid to Pyongyang," *New York Times,* April 1, 2003.

101. Colin Powell's media availability en route to Mexico City, transcript, U.S. Department of State, November 25, 2002.

102. Masood Haider, "N-Material Not Supplied to N. Korea, Powell Assured," *Dawn* (Karachi), October 21, 2002.

103. "Pakistani Leader Suspected Moves by Atomic Expert," *New York Times*, February 10, 2004.

104. "U.S. Image Up Slightly, but Still Negative," Pew Global Attitudes Project, June 23, 2005.

105. Shamshad Ahmad, "Where Is U.S. Public Diplomacy?" *News* (Karachi), January 13, 2010.

106. "Pakistani Minister Says US Sanction Waiver Sign of 'Warm Relations,'" *News* (Islamabad), March 15, 2003.

107. "Pakistan Clerics Reject Sanctions Waiver, Urge Use of Nukes against U.S., India," *News* (Islamabad), March 17, 2003.

108. John Lancaster and Kamran Khan, "Musharraf Named in Nuclear Probe," *Washington Post*, February 3, 2004.

109. "Comments and Explanatory Notes by the Islamic Republic of Iran on the Report of the IAEA Director General (GOV/2004/11)," in "Communication

of 5 March 2004 from the Permanent Mission of the Islamic Republic of Iran Concerning the Report of the Director General Contained in GOV/2004/11," IAEA Information Circular, March 5, 2004, INFCIRC 628.

110. *World*, Pakistan TV, Islamabad, October 6, 2003, transcript provided by the Open Source Center.

111. "Joint Declaration Says Pakistan, China Cooperation 'Indispensable' for Asia," *News* (Islamabad), November 6, 2003.

112. "Pakistani Senators Demand Probe into Reported Arrest of Nuclear Scientists," *News* (Islamabad), December 11, 2003.

113. Gordon Corera, *Shopping for Bombs: Nuclear Proliferation, Global Insecurity, and the Rise and Fall of the A. Q. Kahn Network* (New York: Oxford University Press, 2006), p. 207.

114. "Pakistan to Prosecute for Anti-State Crimes Any Scientists Who Sold Nuclear Secrets: Musharraf," *Pakistan Newswire*, January 23, 2004.

115. "Iran's Nuclear Programme," BBC TV, May 3, 2005.

116. "The A. Q. Khan Network: Case Closed?" Subcommittee on International Terrorism and Nonproliferation, House Committee on International Relations, May 25, 2006.

117. "Hamid Gul," *India Abroad* (New York), February 13, 2004.

118. "Colin Powell's Arrival," *Nawa-i-Waqt* (Rawalpindi), March 16, 2004.

119. "District Multan: Strong Reaction on Arrest of Scientists," *Pakistan Newswire*, January 19, 2004.

120. U.S. Embassy Islamabad, "President Zardari Discusses AQ Khan Release," February 9, 2009, Islamabad 284.

121. "Pakistan Editorial Urges US to Provide Civilian Nuclear Technology," *Jang* (Rawalpindi), June 26, 2006, translation provided by BBC Monitoring International Reports.

122. "US-India Nuclear Deal Opens Way for Similar Deal with Pakistan: PM Gilani," Pakistan Press International (Multan), October 3, 2008.

123. David E. Sanger and William J. Broad, "U.S. Secretly Aids Pakistan in Guarding Nuclear Arms," *New York Times*, November 18, 2007.

124. Joby Warrick, "Pakistan Expanding Nuclear Program," *Washington Post*, July 24, 2006; David E. Sanger, "Pakistan Is Rapidly Adding Nuclear Arms, US Says," *New York Times*, May 17, 2009; Saeed Shah, "Pakistan 'Developing' Advanced Nuclear Technology," *Telegraph* (London), September 3, 2009.

125. Sanger and Broad, "U.S. Secretly Aids Pakistan in Guarding Nuclear Arms."

126. Mohammad Yaqub Shahiq, "Has Pakistan's Turn Arrived?" *Nawa-i-Waqt*, August 29, 2007.

127. U.S. Embassy Islamabad, "Scenesetter for CJCS Admiral Mullen," February 5, 2008, Islamabad 525.

128. Francesca Caferri, "It Is Time to Make a Break with the United States, or Terrorism Will Spread Like Wildfire," interview with Hamid Gul, *La Repubblica* (Rome), August 19, 2008, translation provided by the Open Source Center.

129. "POL: Washington Trying to Access Nukes through Aid: Warns –JI," Pakistan Press International (Lahore), April 19, 2008.

130. U.S. Embassy Islamabad, "U.S. Removal of Pakistan's Research Reactor Fuel on Hold," May 27, 2009, Islamabad 1152.

131. "No Question of Nuclear Assets Falling into Wrong Hands," *Balochistan Times* (Quetta), January 27, 2008.

132. "FO: Pakistan Rejects IAEA Statement Regarding Nuclear Assets," Pakistan Press International (Islamabad), January 10, 2008.

133. "Fazal Demands Release of Dr A Q Khan," Pakistan Press International (Hyderabad), April 27, 2008.

134. U.S. Embassy Islamabad, "Corrected Copy: Pakistan: Fixing Coalition Support Funding," December 15, 2007, Islamabad 5288; "About Those Billions," *Newsweek*, October 21, 2009.

135. Maqbool Arshad, "US's Ghastly Plans against Pakistan," *Fact* (Lahore), September 30, 2009, translation provided by the Open Source Center.

136. Secretary Hillary Clinton, Town Hall at Government College University, Lahore, October 29, 2009.

137. Ben Arnoldy, "Why Pakistanis Would Reject $7.5 Billion in US Aid," *Christian Science Monitor*, October 14, 2009.

138. Secretary Hillary Clinton, Roundtable with Senior Pakistani Editors, Lahore, October 30, 2009.

139. "Do Not Make Richard Holbrooke 'Viceroy,'" *Nawa-i-Waqt* (Rawalpindi), June 5, 2009.

140. "Rally Demands Release of Dr. Aafia," *News Online* (Islamabad), August 12, 2008.

141. Mumtaz Alvi, "Senate Urges US to Repatriate Dr. Aafia," *News Online* (Islamabad), January 30, 2009; "Pak to Make Every Possible Effort for Dr. Aafia's Release: FO," *News Online* (Islamabad), February 4, 2010; "Protest against Aafia's Detention," *News Online* (Islamabad), January 20, 2010.

142. "Aafia Case: Protest Demonstrations Across Country; Afghan Taliban Threaten to Kill US Hostage Troops," *Mashriq* (Peshawar), February 5, 2010; "Govt Should End NATO Supply; US Will Be Forced to Release Aafia: Citizens," *Jinnah* (Islamabad), February 6, 2010. Translations provided by the Open Source Center.

143. Ayaz Amir, "Spy vs. Spy," *Newsline* (Karachi), March 2011.

144. Jam Sajjad Hussain, "Davis Enjoys Lavish Life as Inmate," *Nation Online* (Islamabad), March 14, 2011.

145. "US Terrorist's Release Is Joke with National Honor; JUI Punjab," *Islam* (Karachi), March 18, 2011, translation provided by the Open Source Center.

146. "Revolution Will Start from Mosque and Seminary; Revolutionary Leaders Like Imam Khomeini and Mullah Omar Will Emerge," interview with Imtiaz Ali Taji Khokhar, *Islam* (Karachi), March 4, 2011, translation provided by the Open Source Center.

147. Farrukh Saleem, "Pak-US 'War on Terror' Talks Not Going Well," *News Online* (Islamabad), April 19, 2011.

148. Shamim Bano, "Davis's Release Sparks Protests," *News Online* (Islamabad), March 17, 2011.

149. Saifur Rahman, "Release of US Killer Unmasked True Face of Rulers; Nation's Heads Lowered with Sahme: Khabrain Survey," *Khabrain* (Islamabad), March 18, 2011, translation provided by the Open Source Center.

150. "Davis' Release Slurred Pakistan's Prestige: Mufti Saifuddin," *Islam* (Karachi), March 19, 2011, translation provided by the Open Source Center.

151. "Punjab Government Ready to Give Blood Money for Dr. Aafia Siddiqui: Law Minister," *Jinnah* (Islamabad), March 19, 2011, translation courtesy of the Open Source Center.

152. U.S. Embassy Islamabad, "Musharraf Tells Deputy Secretary Pakistan Is Committed to Fight Al Qaeda, Taliban," September 27, 2007, Islamabad 4085.

153. U.S. Embassy Islamabad, "Codel Biden's Meeting with COAS Kayani and ISI Pasha," February 6, 2009, Islamabad 270; U.S. Embassy Islamabad, "Scenesetter for General Kayani's Visit to Washington," February 19, 2009, Islamabad 365.

154. U.S. Embassy Islamabad, "GOP Denies Agreement to Transfer Beradar to Afghanistan; Lahore High Court Intervenes," February 26, 2010, Islamabad 461.

155. U.S. Embassy Islamabad, "President Musharraf Meets Speaker Pelosi and 110th Congressional Delegation," January 31, 2007, Islamabad 521.

156. U.S. Embassy Islamabad, "Scenesetter for General Kayani's Visit to Washington," February 19, 2009, Islamabad 2524.

157. U.S. Embassy Islamabad, "Ambassador's Condolence Call on Asif Zardari," January 28, 2008, Islamabad 365.

158. U.S. Embassy Islamabad, "Focusing the U.S.-Pakistan Strategic Dialogue," February 21, 2009, Islamabad 386.

159. "Newseye Analyzes Clinton's Visit to Pakistan, Foreign Militants in S. Waziristan," *Dawn* (Karachi), October 29, 2009.

160. Anwar Iqbad, "Pakistan's Vulnerability Exploited by US," *News* (Islamabad), December 9, 1998.

161. Nahal Toosi, "No End in Sight to Pakistan-NATO Supply Standoff," Associated Press, October 2, 2010.

162. U.S. Embassy Islamabad, "Scenesetter for PM Gilani's Visit to Washington," July 25, 2008, Islamabad 2524.

163. Howard B. Schaffer and Teresita C. Schaffer, *How Pakistan Negotiates with the United States* (Washington: United States Institute of Peace, 2011), p. 32.

164. Hussain Haqqani, "An Ally of Necessity," *Wall Street Journal*, July 27, 2010.

165. Francesca Caferri, "It Is Time to Make a Break with the United States, or Terrorism Will Spread Like Wildfire," interview with Hamid Gul, *La Repubblica* (Rome), August 19, 2008, translation provided by the Open Source Center.

166. Haqqani, "An Ally of Necessity."

Chapter 7: Sitting with Saddam

1. Secretary of State Kissinger, chairman, "In Attendance," April 28, 1975, provided through George Washington University National Security Archives.

2. Henry A. Kissinger, "Memorandum of Conversation," U.S. Department of State, December 17, 1975.

3. Henry Kissinger, *Years of Renewal* (New York: Simon & Schuster, 1999), pp. 576, 582–85.

4. J. P. Smith, "Oil Wealth Causing a Shift in Iraq's Foreign Policy; Iraq Adopting More Pragmatic Foreign Policy," *Washington Post*, August 8, 1978.

5. Jonathan C. Randal, "Iraq Rebuffs U.S. on Formal Links," *Washington Post*, May 12, 1980.

6. *Patterns of International Terrorism: 1980*, National Foreign Assessment Center, June 1981.

7. Bernard D. Nossiter, "Muskie Confers with Iraqi Aide; Gets Assurances," *New York Times*, October 1, 1980.

8. Alexander M. Haig Jr. to United States Interests Section in Iraq, "Secretary's Message to Iraqi Foreign Minister," April 8, 1981.

9. Don Oberdorfer, "Haig Sends Envoy to Explore Ties with Iraq," *Washington Post*, April 11, 1981.

10. David B. Ottaway, "Visiting U.S. Envoy Sees Resumption of Ties with Iraq Unlikely Soon," *Washington Post*, April 14, 1981.

11. William L. Eagleton Jr., United States Interests Section in Iraq, to U.S. Department of State, "Meeting with Tariq Aziz," May 28, 1981, Baghdad 1446.

12. Bernard D. Nossiter, "U.S. Consults Iraqis on Israeli Raid," *New York Times*, June 18, 1981.

13. Milt Freudenheim, Barbara Slavin, and William C. Rhoden, "The World in Summary: Readjustments in the Mideast," *New York Times*, February 28, 1982.

14. Bruce W. Jentleson, *With Friends Like These: Reagan, Bush, and Saddam, 1982–1990* (New York: Norton, 1994), pp. 33, 42.

15. David B. Ottaway, "Iraq Gives Haven to Key Terrorist," *Washington Post*, November 9, 1982.

16. U.S. Department of State, "Background on Iraqi Use of Chemical Weapons," November 10, 1983, included in Action Memorandum from Jonathan T. Howe to Lawrence S. Eagleburger, "Iraqi Use of Chemical Weapons," Office of the Assistant Secretary for Near Eastern and South Asian Affairs, U.S. Department of State; John M. Goshko and Ward Sinclair, "U.S. Offering Iraq Credits on Food Commodity Sales," *Washington Post*, February 16, 1983.

17. "Iraq Foreign Ministry Official Visits Washington for Talks," *New York Times*, September 8, 1983.

18. Jonathan T. Howe to the Secretary of State, Information Memorandum, U.S. Department of State, November 1, 1983.

19. U.S. Embassy London, to the Secretary of State, "Rumsfeld Mission: December 20 Meeting with Iraqi President Saddam Hussein," December 21, 1983, London 26572.

20. Donald Rumsfeld, *Known and Unknown* (New York: Sentinel, 2011), p. 7.

21. Bernard Gwertzman, "Iraq Gets Reports from U.S. for Use in War with Iran," *New York Times*, December 16, 1986.

22. Bill Eagleton, "Ismet Kittani's Reaction to US Chemical Weapons Statement and Next Steps in US-Iraq Relations," March 7, 1984, Baghdad 525.

23. George Shultz, "Kittani Call on Under Secretary Eagleburger," March 18, 1984, State 79782.

24. George Shultz, "Briefing Notes for Rumsfeld Visit to Baghdad," March 24, 1984, State 86663.

25. George P. Shultz to U.S. Embassy Lebanon [et al.], "Department Press Briefing, March 30, 1984," March 31, 1984; George P. Shultz to U.S. Embassy Jordan, "Chemical Weapons: Meeting with Iraqi Chargé," April 6, 1984.

26. "Interview with Iraqi President: The War with Iran," Iraqi News Agency, 1610 GMT, October 11, 1984, translation by BBC Summary of World Broadcasts.

27. Bernard Gwertzman, "U.S. Restores Full Ties with Iraq but Cites Neutrality in Gulf War," *New York Times*, November 27, 1984.

28. Jentleson, *With Friends Like These*, p. 51; "Defense Estimative Brief: Prospects for Iraq," Defense Intelligence Agency, September 25, 1984, DEB8584.

29. Jane Wallach, "The Artful Ambassador," *Washington Post Magazine*, December 8, 1985.

30. "Talking Points: At Iraqi Embassy, Table's Set for Jeane Kirkpatrick," *Washington Post*, April 25, 1986.

31. Elaine Sciolino, "Shultz to See Iraqi on Reported Gassing of Kurds," *New York Times*, September 8, 1988.

32. Jentleson, *With Friends Like These*, pp. 77–78.

33. April Glaspie, "Minister of Industry Blasts Senate Action," September 13, 1988, Baghdad 5023.

34. "Why Did This Happen?" *Time*, June 1, 1987.

35. Elaine Sciolino, "U.S. Seeks Iraqi Payment for Kin of Dead Sailors," *New York Times*, January 31, 1988.

36. Elaine Sciolino, "U.S. Delegation to Press Iraq on Reparations in *Stark* Case," *New York Times*, March 22, 1989.

37. Elaine Sciolino, "Kurdish Chief Gains Support in U.S. Visit," *New York Times*, June 22, 1988.

38. David B. Ottaway, "Iraq Said to Have Expelled High-Level U.S. Diplomat," *Washington Post*, November 17, 1988.

39. "Subject: U.S. Policy Toward the Persian Gulf," National Security Directive 26, The White House, October 2, 1989.

40. Jentleson, *With Friends Like These*, p. 95.

41. Bruce W. Jentleson, "Iraq: The Failure of a Strategy," in *Reversing Relations with Former Adversaries*, ed. C. Richard Nelson and Kenneth Weisbrode (Gainesville: University Press of Florida, 1998), p. 147.

42. Donald Trelford, "Executed by Saddam Hussein: The Death of *Observer* Reporter Farzad Bazoft, 20 Years On," *Observer* (London), March 14, 2010.

43. Youssef M. Ibrahim, "Iraq, in Retaliation, Ousts an American Envoy," *New York Times*, April 10, 1990.

44. Joan Mower, "Some Lawmakers Back Sanctions Against Iraq," Associated Press, April 10, 1990.

45. Arlen Specter, "U.S.-Iraq Relations," Senate Committee on Foreign Relations, June 15, 1990.

46. "Interview with Arlen Specter," *Middle East Quarterly*, March 1997.

47. Michael R. Gordon, "Pentagon Objected to Bush's Message to Iraq," *New York Times*, October 25, 1992.

48. Elaine Sciolino with Michael R. Gordon, "Confrontation in the Gulf: U.S. Gave Iraq Little Reason Not to Mount Kuwait Assault," *New York Times*, September 23, 1990; U.S. Embassy Baghdad, "Saddam's Message of Friendship to President Bush," July 25, 1990, Baghdad 4237.

49. Don Oberdorfer, "Glaspie Says Saddam Is Guilty of Deception; Ex-Envoy Breaks Silence, Answers Critics," *Washington Post*, March 21, 1991.

50. Gordon, "Pentagon Objected to Bush's Message to Iraq."

51. Ibid.

52. U.S. Embassy Baghdad, "Saddam's Message of Friendship to President Bush," July 25, 1990, Baghdad 4237.

53. UN Security Council Resolution 678 (November 29, 1990).

54. Stephen Kurkjian, "Bush Offers Direct Talks with Iraq," *Boston Globe*, December 1, 1990.

55. "Excerpts from Iraqi Statement on Bush's Invitation to Talk," *New York Times*, December 2, 1990.

56. Thomas L. Friedman, "Standoff in the Gulf," *New York Times*, December 10, 1990.

57. FBI Interview with Saddam Hussein, Baghdad Operations Center, March 5, 2004.

58. Al Gore, Center for National Policy, September 29, 1992.

59. Joe Biden, "President Bush's Policy toward Iraq," U.S. Senate, October 2, 1992.

60. Tim Weiner, *Legacy of Ashes: The History of the CIA* (New York: Anchor, 2008), p. 496.

61. Julian Borger, "Inside Story: The Anthrax Hunter," *Guardian*, April 10, 2002.

62. FBI interview of Saddam Hussein, Baghdad Operations Center, February 13, 2004.

63. Thomas L. Friedman, "The New Presidency: Clinton Backs Raid but Muses about a New Start," *New York Times*, January 14, 1993.

64. Mary Curtius, "No Policy Switch on Iraq, Clinton Says; Denies He Intends to Normalize Ties," *Boston Globe*, January 15, 1993.

65. "Iraqi Leader Appeals to Clinton for New Relations," *New York Times*, February 15, 2003.

66. R. Jeffrey Smith and Julia Preston, "U.S. Relents on Removal of Saddam; Other Conditions to Be Spelled Out for Ending Sanctions on Iraq," *Washington Post*, March 27, 1993.

67. David Brown, "Christopher Says Saddam Has 'Been Put on Notice,'" *Washington Post*, October 17, 1994.

68. John Lancaster, "Saddam Frees 2 Americans after Congressman's Pleas," *Washington Post*, July 17, 1995.

69. Joe Biden, U.S. Senate, February 12, 1998, S708–S716.

70. Foreign Minister Muhammad Said al-Sahhaf, letter to Sir Jeremy Greenstock, October 19, 1998, Iraq News Agency (Baghdad), October 20, 1998, translation provided by the Open Source Center.

71. Iraq News Agency (Baghdad), February 10, 1999, translation provided by the Open Source Center.

72. Hani Wuhayyib, "The Escalation of Aggression and the Failed Tours," *Al-Qadisiyah* (Baghdad), March 8, 1999, translation provided by the Open Source Center.

73. Lee H. Hamilton, James Schlesinger, and Brent Scowcroft, *Thinking Beyond the Stalemate in U.S.-Iranian Relations*, vol. 2, *Issues and Analysis* (Washington: The Atlantic Council of the United States, July 2001), pp. 54–55.

74. "Saddam's Iraq: Sanctions and U.S. Policy," Subcommittee on Near Eastern and South Asian Affairs, Senate Committee on Foreign Relations, March 22, 2000.

75. FBI interviews of Saddam Hussein, Baghdad Operations Center, June 28, 2004, and June 11, 2004.

76. Kelly Wallace, "Bush Administration Cool to Saddam Speech," CNN. com, August 8, 2002.

77. Michael Kramer, "Now, the Heat Is on Saddam," *New York Daily News*, December 12, 2001.

78. "Saddam: 'I Am Ready to Dialogue with Bush,'" *Guardian*, February 27, 2003.

79. Kevin Woods, James Lacey, and Williamson Murray, "Saddam's Delusions: The View from the Inside," *Foreign Affairs*, May–June 2006.

Chapter 8: Hijackers into Peacemakers

1. Dennis Roddy, "On Arafat's Death, a Cold River of Memory," *Pittsburgh Post-Gazette*, November 13, 2004.

2. Henry Kissinger, *Years of Upheaval* (New York: Little, Brown & Co., 1982), p. 625.

3. Ibid., pp. 627–29.

4. William B. Quandt, *Peace Process: American Diplomacy and the Arab-Israeli Conflict since 1967* (Washington: Brookings Institution Press, 1993), p. 368.

5. Speech by Yasser Arafat to the United Nations General Assembly, November 13, 1974.

6. Aaron David Miller, "The False Religion of Mideast Peace," *Foreign Policy*, May–June 2010.

7. P.L. 98-473, §535, October 12, 1984.

8. "Interview with Mr. Edward G. Abington," The Foreign Affairs Oral History Collection of the Association for Diplomatic Studies and Training, April 17, 2000.

9. Secretary of State to All Diplomatic and Consular Posts, "Applications by PLO Members," November 25, 1976, State 289668.

10. Quandt, *Peace Process*, p. 327.

11. Jimmy Carter, *White House Diary* (New York: Farrar, Straus & Giroux, 2010), p. 351.

12. Cyrus Vance, *Hard Choices: Critical Years in America's Foreign Policy* (New York: Simon & Schuster, 1983), p. 378.

13. Clyde Mark, "Palestinians and Middle East Peace: Issues for the United States," CRS Issue Brief, October 10, 2003.

14. Allan Gerson, *The Kirkpatrick Mission: Diplomacy without Apology—America at the United Nations, 1981–1985* (New York: Free Press, 1991), pp. 26, 42.

15. Alfonso Chardy, "PLO Has Lost Lofty Status as Third World's Darling," *Miami Herald*, October 25, 1985.

16. Dennis Ross, *The Missing Peace: The Inside Story of the Fight for Middle East Peace* (New York: Farrar, Straus & Giroux, 2004), p. 47.

17. Mohamed Rabie, *U.S.-PLO Dialogue: Secret Diplomacy and Conflict Resolution* (Gainesville: University Press of Florida, 1995), p. 14.

18. Ibid., p. 15.

19. Secretary of State George Shultz, "The Reagan Administration's Approach to Middle East Peacemaking," remarks before the Washington Institute for Near East Policy, September 16, 1988.

20. Rabie, *U.S.-PLO Dialogue*, p. 64.

21. Ibid., p. 79.

22. Ibid., p. 81.

23. "Text of Arafat's Statement to News Conference in Geneva," in ibid., p. 180.

24. Rabie, *U.S.-PLO Dialogue*, p. 85.

25. "U.S. Opens Dialogue with PLO; Ronald Reagan, George Shultz Statements; Transcript," *Department of State Bulletin*, February 1, 1989.

26. Ross, *The Missing Peace*, pp. 54–55; Rabie, *U.S.-PLO Dialogue*, p. 104.

27. Rabie, *U.S.-PLO Dialogue*, p. 104.

28. Ross, *The Missing Peace*, p. 57.

29. Title VIII, P.L. 101-246, February 16, 1990.

30. Ross, *The Missing Peace*, p. 65.

31. Ibid., p. 82.

32. "Text of Arafat's Remarks," Associated Press, September 14, 1993.

33. The Middle East Peace Facilitation Act of 1993, P.L. 103-125, October 28, 1993.

34. Mark, "Palestinians and Middle East Peace: Issues for the United States."

35. Ross, *The Missing Peace*, p. 123.

36. Ibid., p. 125.

37. Ibid.

38. Ibid., p. 135.

39. Ibid., p. 190.

40. Foreign Operations, Export Financing, and Related Programs Appropriations Act, 1995, P.L. 103-306.

41. "Interview with Arlen Specter," *Middle East Quarterly*, March 1997.

42. Mark, "Palestinians and Middle East Peace."

43. Jonathan Broder, "The American Diplomat in Arafat's Corner," *Jerusalem Report*, April 10, 2000.

44. Ibid.

45. Steven Plaut, "Continue the Peace Process? No, It's Heading for Disaster," *Middle East Quarterly*, September 1995.

46. Ross, *The Missing Peace*, p. 256.

47. Ibid., p. 259.

48. Ibid., p. 261.

49. Ibid., p. 265.

50. Ibid., p. 267.

51. Ibid., pp. 290–91.

52. Ibid., p. 305.

53. Mark, "Palestinians and Middle East Peace."

54. Ross, *The Missing Peace*, p. 338.

55. Ibid.

56. Ibid., p. 371.

57. Ibid., pp. 371–72.

58. Ibid., p. 407.

59. Ibid., p. 410.

60. Mark, "Palestinians and Middle East Peace."

61. Ross, *The Missing Peace*, p. 418.

62. Ibid., p. 450.

63. "Interview with Arlen Specter," *Middle East Quarterly*, March 1997.

64. Mark, "Palestinians and Middle East Peace."

65. "The Peace Process and the Wye Memorandum, Elections for the President and Vice President, and Political Affiliation," Palestinian Center for Policy and Survey Research, Ramallah, November 12–14, 1998.

66. Ross, *The Missing Peace*, p. 477.

67. Ibid., p. 479.

68. Ibid., pp. 483–84.

69. Ibid., p. 489.

70. Jeffrey Boutwell, "The Wild West Bank," *Bulletin of Atomic Scientists*, January–February 1999.

71. Lachlan Carmichael, "Arabs More Cautious than West about Peace Prospects under Barak," Agence France-Presse, March 19, 1999; Ross, *The Missing Peace*, p. 495.

72. Ross, *The Missing Peace*, p. 592.

73. Ibid., p. 597.

74. Ibid., p. 605.

75. Ibid., pp. 606–7.

76. Ibid., pp. 617–18.

77. Ibid., p. 620.

78. Ibid., p. 624.

79. Ibid., p. 637.

80. Ibid., p. 643.

81. Ibid., p. 644.

82. Ibid., p. 645

83. Ibid., p. 668.

84. Ibid., p. 676.

85. Ibid., p. 689.

86. Ibid., p. 705.

87. President Clinton, Press Briefing, The White House, July 25, 2000.

88. Suleyman Demirel, Thorbjoern Jaglan, Warren B. Rudman, Javier Solana, and George J. Mitchell, "Sharm El-Sheikh Fact-Finding Committee Report," April 30, 2001.

89. "Palestinian Cabinet Minister Says Palestinian Uprising Was Planned," Associated Press, March 2, 2001; Suha Arafat on Dubai TV, December 16, 2012.

90. Mark, "Palestinians and Middle East Peace."

91. Fahd al-Fanik, "The Intifada and Timely Words," *Al-Ra'y* (Amman), February 20, 2001.

92. Aaron David Miller, "The False Religion of Mideast Peace," *Foreign Policy*, May–June 2010.

93. Nitzan Horowitz, "Arafat Hires a Former U.S. Consul to East Jerusalem as PA Lobbyist," *Haaretz*, January 16, 2000.

94. Hope Keller, "On the Palestinians' PR Front," *Baltimore Sun*, August 27, 2001; Shlomo Gazit and Edward Abington, "The Palestinian-Israeli Conflict," *Middle East Policy*, March 2001.

95. Elliott Abrams, *Tested by Zion: The Bush Administration and the Israeli-Palestinian Conflict* (New York: Cambridge University Press, 2013), p. 8.

96. Alan Sipress, "Powell Urges Cooperation in Ending Mideast Violence; Sharon, Arafat Hold to Hard Lines in Meetings with Secretary," *Washington Post*, February 26, 2001; Negotiations Support Unit memorandum to Gen. Hajj Isma'il Jabr, head of public security, West Bank, "'Internationalizing' the US Monitoring Mechanism," July 25, 2001; Negotiations Support Unit memorandum to Minister Yasser Abed Rabbo, "Necessary Improvements to U.S. Monitoring Proposal," July 26, 2001.

97. Alan Sipress, "Bush Blames Arafat for Problems in Mideast Talks," *Washington Post*, December 15, 2001.

98. P.L. 107-115, January 10, 2002.

99. Amos Harel, "Hezbollah Paid for *Karine A*; PA Paid for Arms—Army Source," *Haaretz*, February 1, 2002.

100. David Makovsky, "The Seizure of Gaza-Bound Arms: Political Implications," Peacewatch no. 358, The Washington Institute for Near East Policy, January 8, 2002.

101. Jennifer Griffen, "Prison Interview with Palestinian Ship Captain Smuggling 50 Tons of Weapons," Fox News, Jerusalem, January 7, 2002.

102. "Arafat Takes Blame for Arms Shipment," BBC News, February 14, 2002.

103. George W. Bush, "President to Send Secretary Powell to Middle East," The White House Rose Garden, April 4, 2002.

104. Arlen Specter, "The Mideast," U.S. Senate, April 10, 2002, S2443.

105. "Bush Outlines Middle East Peace Plan," CNN.com, June 24, 2002.

106. Tony Karon, "Clinton Saves Last Dance for Arafat," *Time*, January 2, 2001.

107. Condoleezza Rice, *No Higher Honor: A Memoir of My Years in Washington* (New York: Crown, 2011), p. 145.

108. Joel Greenberg, "Israeli Pullback Ends 10-Day Siege of Arafat's Base," *New York Times*, September 30, 2002.

109. Mark, "Palestinians and Middle East Peace."

110. John S. Wolf, letter to Sa'eb Erekat, October 17, 2003.

111. "Breakfast with George Mitchell," "Meeting with Former Secretary of State, Madeleine Albright," and "Meeting with Martin Indyk," in Meeting Notes on Minister Mohammad Dahlan's (MD) Visit to Washington, D.C., April 6, 2005, as leaked to Al Jazeera.

112. Abrams, *Tested by Zion*, pp. 71–76.

113. "Mr. Abbas Goes to Washington," *New York Times*, May 26, 2005; George W. Bush, "President Welcomes Palestinian President Abbas to the White House," The White House, October 20, 2005.

114. Meeting Notes: Saeb Erekat, Habib Hazzan, Liz Dibble, David Pearce, Jim Bever, Marc Melenger, May 4, 2005, as released by Al Jazeera in the "Palestine Papers."

115. Meeting Minutes: Minister Mohamad Dahlan and Minister Condi Rice, Al-Muqata, Ramallah, July 23, 2005.

116. Joel Brinkley, "Rice, on Tour, Finds Egypt Unreceptive to Hamas Aid Cutoff," *New York Times*, February 22, 2006.

117. Saeb Erekat, letter to Consul General Walles and Consul General Jenkins, March 16, 2006.

118. Thom Shanker and Greg Myre, "Rice, Meeting Abbas, Promised U.S. Push on Mideast Peace," *New York Times*, January 15, 2007.

119. Helene Cooper, "Rice Tries to Hold Together Plan for Mideast Talks," *New York Times*, February 19, 2007; Abrams, *Tested by Zion*, pp. 219–28.

120. Steven Erlanger, "In Gesture to Abbas, Israel Releases 255 Palestinian Prisoners," *New York Times*, July 21, 2007.

121. Meeting Summary: Saeb Erekat and Keith Dayton, July 24, 2007, as released by Al Jazeera in the "Palestine Papers."

122. Glenn Kessler, "Aid Request Emphasizes U.S. Support of Palestinian Authority Leadership," *Washington Post*, October 31, 2007.

123. Meeting Summary: Condoleezza Rice with Ahmed Qurei, Saeb Erekat, Zeinah Salahi, U.S. Department of State, July 29, 2008, 2:15 p.m.

124. "2008 Summary—Data and Trends in Palestinian Terror," Israel Security Agency (Shabak), December 2008.

125. Meeting Minutes: Saeb Erekat and David Welch, Washington, D.C., December 2, 2008, 12:00–1:30 p.m.

126. Ethan Bronner, "Housing Plan, with U.S. Aid, May Aid Abbas in West Bank," *New York Times*, April 15, 2008.

127. "The U.S. Will Contribute Another $85 Million for Humanitarian Assistance to Palestinian Refugees," Office of the Spokesman, U.S. Department of State, December 30, 2008.

128. Ethan Bronner, "State Dept. Reinstates Gaza Fulbright Grants," *New York Times*, June 2, 2008.

129. Mahmoud Abbas, letter to Barack Obama, October 1, 2008, as released by Al Jazeera in the "Palestine Papers."

130. Aaron David Miller, "The False Religion of Mideast Peace," *Foreign Policy*, May–June 2010.

131. Mahmoud Abbas, letter to Barack Obama, February n.d. 2009; Salam Fayyad, letter to John Kerry, March 13, 2009; as released by Al Jazeera in the "Palestine Papers."

132. Helene Cooper, "Obama Urges Progress in Middle East, as Officials Confront Israel on Settlements," *New York Times*, May 29, 2009.

133. "Remarks by the President on a New Beginning, Cairo University," Office of the Press Secretary, The White House, June 4, 2009.

134. Itamar Marcus and Barbara Crook, "Will the US Follow Its Laws and Suspend Funding to Abbas?" *Jerusalem Post*, May 25, 2009.

135. Meeting Minutes: Saeb Erekat and George Mitchell, U.S. Mission to the United Nations, September 24, 2009; "Abbas: We Will Not Recognize Israel as a Jewish State," *Jerusalem Post*, July 9, 2010.

136. Miller, "The False Religion of Mideast Peace."

137. Jake Tapper, "Hot Mic Catches Obama, Sarko, Griping about Netanyahu," ABC News, November 8, 2011.

Chapter 9: Is It Time to Talk to Terrorists?

1. "U.S. Wants to Build Up Moderate Hezbollah: Adviser," Reuters, May 18, 2010.

2. Michael Slackman, "Disentangling Layers of a Loaded Term in Search of a Threat of Peace," *New York Times*, February 26, 2009.

3. Chris Patten, "Time to Judge Palestine on Its Results," *Financial Times*, March 13, 2007.

4. Bobby S. Sayyid, *A Fundamental Fear: Eurocentrism and the Emergence of Islamism* (London: Zed Books, 2003), p. xi.

5. Joseph J. Eason and Alex P. Schmid, "250-plus Academic, Governmental, and Intergovernmental Definitions of Terrorism," in *The Routledge Handbook of Terrorism Research*, ed. Alex P. Schmid (New York: Routledge, 2011), Appendix 2.1, pp. 99–157.

6. Peter R. Neumann, "Negotiating with Terrorists," *Foreign Affairs*, January–February 2007.

7. Nancy Soderberg, *The Superpower Myth: The Use and Misuse of American Might* (New York: John Wiley & Sons, 2005), pp. 70–72.

8. R. William Ayres, "No Peace at Any Price: The Effectiveness of Spoilers in Interstate Conflicts," paper presented to the Annual Meeting of the International Studies Association, San Diego, March 22–25, 2006.

9. Andrew H. Kydd and Barbara F. Walter, "The Strategies of Terrorism," *International Security*, Summer 2006, pp. 72–74; Andrew H. Kydd and Barbara F. Walter, "Sabotaging the Peace: The Politics of Extremist Violence," *International Organization*, Spring 2002, p. 264.

10. Tony Karon, "Clinton Saves Last Dance for Arafat," *Time*, January 2, 2001.

11. "Terrorism: The Current Threat," panel discussion, The Brookings Institution, February 10, 2000.

12. Neumann, "Negotiating with Terrorists."

13. Oliver McTernan, speech at the Institute for Public Policy Research, April 27, 2009.

14. Robert Malley, "U.S. Policy toward Islamists: Engagement versus Isolation," Weinberg Founders Conference, The Washington Institute for Near East Policy, September 24, 2005.

15. *NewsHour with Jim Lehrer*, PBS, June 12, 2003.

16. George W. Bush, "Rose Garden Speech on Israel-Palestine Two-State Solution," The White House, June 24, 2002.

17. Peter Beinart, "Hamas: U.S. Diplomacy's Final Frontier," *Time*, May 1, 2009.

18. George Mitchell, News Briefing, U.S. Department of State, August 20, 2010.

19. Jackson Diehl, "Is George Mitchell in the Middle East, or Northern Ireland?" PostPartisan, *Washington Post* Blogs, September 16, 2010.

20. Melanie Phillips, "Sir Jeremy Greenstock Says Hamas Is Only about 'Resistance,'" *Spectator*, January 13, 2009.

21. Michael Herzog, "Can Hamas Be Tamed?" *Foreign Affairs*, March–April 2006.

22. Zion Evrony, "Hamas Is Not the IRA," *New York Times*, August 31, 2007.

23. Article VII, "The Covenant of the Islamic Resistance Movement," August 18, 1988, translated by the Avalon Project, Yale Law School.

24. Michael Weiss, "Hamas Isn't the IRA," *Slate*, September 17, 2010.

25. Steven Simon and Jonathan Stevenson, "Disarming Hezbollah," *Foreign Affairs*, January 11, 2010.

26. Mark Perry, *Talking to Terrorists: Why America Must Engage with Its Enemies* (New York: Basic Books, 2010), p. 123.

27. Ibid., p. 130.

28. Ibrahim Humaydi, "Mish'al to 'Al-Hayat': Pullout from Gaza Is Beginning of End for Israel and Resistance Is Strategic Option," *Al-Hayat* (London), August 16, 2005.

29. Jimmy Carter, "Preliminary Report on the Middle East," Jerusalem, April 21, 2008.

30. Karin Laub, "Hamas Wants Acceptance without Changing Ideology," Associated Press, May 18, 2009.

31. Jimmy Carter interview with Meredith Vieira, NBC News, January 26, 2009.

32. Richard Haass, "The New Middle East," *Foreign Affairs*, November–December 2006.

33. "Bilwara Mahwar jadid dhad Iran," *Al-Quds al-Arabi*, December 18, 2008.

34. Claude Salhani, "Politics and Policies: U.S. Must Engage Hamas," United Press International, January 23, 2006.

35. Marina Ottaway, "Islamists and Democracy: Keep the Faith," *New Republic*, June 6, 2005.

36. Chris Patten, "Time to Judge Palestine on Its Results," *Financial Times*, March 13, 2007.

37. Herzog, "Can Hamas Be Tamed?"

38. David Welch, Assistant Secretary of State for Near Eastern Affairs, testimony before the Senate Committee on Foreign Relations, September 25, 2008.

39. Mark Heller, "Should the European Union Talk to Hamas?" Transatlantic Issues no. 32, Transatlantic Institute, June 25, 2008.

40. Maurizio Caprara, "Non Regaliamo Hamas ad Al Qaeda," *Corriere della Sera* (Milan), July 17, 2007.

41. Carolin Goerzig, "Engaging Hamas: Rethinking the Quartet Principles," *ISS Opinion*, March 2010.

42. "Peace Will Be Achieved Only by Talking to Hamas," *Times* (London), February 26, 2009.

43. Natasha Lennard, "'Hamas Is a Reality on the Ground': Gaza-Born Journalist Taghreed El-Khodary on What Israel's Blockade Has Really Meant for Life in Palestine," *Salon*, June 2, 2010; Joe Klein, "Why the U.S. Should Start Talking to Hamas," *Time*, June 11, 2009; Charles Grant, "Let's Talk to Hamas," *Guardian*, July 19, 2007.

44. Charles Levinson, "U.S. Ex-Officials Engage with Hamas," *Wall Street Journal*, April 2, 2010.

45. Ibid.

46. "Mustashir lihukumat Hamas: Altaqina mustashiran lal Obama sara fi Ghaza," *Ad-Dastur* (Amman), November 12, 2008.

47. Laub, "Hamas Wants Acceptance without Changing Ideology."

48. Taghreed El-Khodary, "Congressmen and Kerry Visit Gaza," *New York Times*, February 20, 2009; Levinson, "U.S. Ex-Officials Engage with Hamas."

49. David Hearst, "Hamas Leader Says American Envoys Making Contact, but Not Openly," *Guardian*, May 30, 2010.

50. "Hamas Letters to Obama Unanswered," Agence France-Presse, May 9, 2010.

51. Paul Scham and Osama Abu-Irshaid, "Hamas: Ideological Rigidity and Political Flexibility," United States Institute of Peace, Special Report 224, June 1, 2009, p. 17.

52. Denis MacEoin, "Tactical Hudna and Islamist Intolerance," *Middle East Quarterly*, Summer 2008.

53. "Interview with Mark Malloch Brown," *Financial Times*, August 1, 2006.

54. Augustus Richard Norton, *Hezbollah: A Short History* (Princeton, N.J.: Princeton University Press, 2007), pp. 98–99.

55. Ken Silverstein, "Augustus Norton on Hezbollah's Social Services," *Harpers*, March 14, 2007.

56. John F. Burns, "Hezbollah and Britain to Resume Contacts," *New York Times*, March 6, 2009.

57. "Hezbollah Says No Longer Considered Pariah by West," Agence France-Presse, April 15, 2009.

58. Tom Baldwin and Catherine Philp, "America Angered by 'Secret' Talks with Hezbollah," *Times* (London), March 14, 2009.

59. "Al-Mussawi: Yuntiqad Istimrar Tawaqif al-Dhabat," *Al-Mustaqbal* (Beirut), March 12, 2009.

60. Frances Guy, "The Passing of Decent Men," *Guardian*, July 9, 2010.

61. Steven Simon and Jonathan Stevenson, "Disarming Hezbollah," *Foreign Affairs*, January 11, 2010.

62. Ryan C. Crocker, testimony at the Hearing on Hezbollah, Senate Committee on Foreign Relations, June 8, 2010.

63. Intelligence Review, February 14, 1946, no. 1.

64. Lawrence Wright, *The Looming Tower: Al Qaeda and the Road to 9/11* (New York: Vintage, 2006), p. 29.

65. Edward Djerejian, "The U.S. and the Middle East in a Changing World," speech at Meridian House International, U.S. Department of State *Dispatch*, June 2, 1992.

66. Recep Tayyip Erdoğan interview with Nilgun Cerrahoğlu, *Milliyet* (Istanbul), July 14, 1996.

67. Robert S. Leiken and Steven Brooke, "The Moderate Muslim Brotherhood," *Foreign Affairs*, March–April 2007.

68. Eli Lake, "Look Who's Talking," *New Republic*, March 3, 2011.

69. "Muslim Brotherhood Website: Jihad against Non-Muslims Is Obligatory," MEMRI, Special Dispatch 2085, October 17, 2008.

70. Neil J. Kressel, *Bad Faith: The Danger of Religious Extremism* (New York: Prometheus Books, 2007), p. 67.

71. Radwan A. Masmoudi et al., Open Letter to Barack Obama, Center for the Study of Islam and Democracy, March 10, 2009.

72. Scott Shane, "As Islamist Group Rises, Its Intentions Are Unclear," *New York Times*, February 3, 2011.

73. Al Jazeera, December 9, 2001.

74. "We Can Read Arabic, Too!" *Al-Ahram* (Cairo), September 13, 2012.

75. Noah Feldman, "Morsi Turns Tyrant to Save Democracy," Bloomberg, November 26, 2012.

76. John Hudson, "Knives Come Out for U.S. Ambassador to Egypt Anne Patterson," *Foreign Policy*, July 3, 2013.

77. Vikram Dodd, "Time to Talk to Al Qaida, Senior Police Chief Urges," *Guardian*, May 29, 2008.

78. "Positive and Negative Developments in Palestinian Thinking," The Israel Project, November 19, 2010.

Chapter 10: Playing Poker with Pariahs

1. David Watt, "The Conduct of American Foreign Policy: As a European Saw It," *Foreign Affairs*, Essay Special, 1983.

2. Caspar W. Weinberger, *Fighting for Peace: Seven Critical Years in the Pentagon* (New York: Warner Books, 1991), pp. 177–78.

3. Joe Biden, "Iraq," U.S. Senate, February 12, 1998.

4. "French President Sees Iran as 'Major Partner,'" Islamic Republic News Agency, April 22, 2004.

5. Dennis Ross, *The Missing Peace: The Inside Story of the Fight for Middle East Peace* (New York: Farrar, Straus & Giroux, 2004), p. 53.

6. Ibid., p. 636.

7. "Senator Specter Speaks on the Senate Floor Regarding Iran and North Korea," website of Arlen Specter, June 16, 2006.

8. Arlen Specter, "The Mideast," U.S. Senate, April 10, 2002, S2443.

9. "Senator Specter Speaks on the Senate Floor Regarding Iran and North Korea."

10. Ross, *The Missing Peace*, p. 301.

11. Carl Levin and Hillary Clinton, "North Korea's Rising Urgency; Not Engaging Is Not an Alternative," *Washington Post*, July 5, 2005.

12. Warren Christopher, "Ensuring Peace and Stability on the Korean Peninsula," remarks to the Korea-America Friendship Society, Seoul, November 9, 1994.

13. David E. Sanger, "Threats and Responses: Nuclear Anxiety; U.S. Eases Threat on Nuclear Arms for North Korea," *New York Times*, December 30, 2002.

14. Victor Davis Hanson, "Should We Fix Gaza, Iran and N. Korea?" *Chicago Tribune*, August 19, 2005.

15. Jim Yardley and David E. Sanger, "In Shift, a Deal Is Being Weighed by North Korea," *New York Times*, February 13, 2007.

16. David E. Sanger, "North Korea Takes No Apparent Action as Deadline Passes," *New York Times*, April 15, 2007.

17. John Ward Anderson, "N. Korea Agrees to Nuclear Deadline," *Washington Post*, September 3, 2007.

18. "Powell Presses Syria to Change Its Middle East Policies," *New York Times*, May 3, 2003.

19. Aaron David Miller, "The False Religion of Mideast Peace," *Foreign Policy*, May–June 2010.

20. Scott Sullivan and Nicholas Proffitt, "A Time for Peace," *Newsweek*, October 17, 1977.

21. Arlen Specter, "Iran's Nuclear Ambitions," Subcommittee on Federal Financial Management, Government Information, Federal Services, and International Security, Senate Committee on Homeland Security and Governmental Affairs, April 24, 2008.

22. Ross, *The Missing Peace*, p. 338.

23. Jane Wallach, "The Artful Ambassador," *Washington Post Magazine*, December 8, 1985.

24. Arlen Specter, "Trip to Europe and the Mideast," U.S. Senate, January 30, 2003.

25. Ross, *The Missing Peace*, p. 48.

26. Jonathan B. Schwartz, "Dealing with a 'Rogue State': The Libya Precedent," *American Journal of International Law*, vol. 101, no. 3 (July 2007), p. 565.

27. Jonathan Broder, "Clinton's Last Stand," *Jerusalem Report*, December 4, 2000.

28. Stephanie Mann, "U.S./North Korea," Voice of America, October 12, 2000.

29. Daniel C. Kurtzer and Scott B. Lasensky, *Negotiating Arab-Israeli Peace: American Leadership in the Middle East* (Washington: United States Institute of Peace Press, 2008), p. 34.

30. Caspar W. Weinberger, *Fighting for Peace: Seven Critical Years in the Pentagon* (New York: Warner Books, 1991), p. 357.

31. Joel S. Wit, "New Rules of Engagement with North Korea," *New York Times*, October 19, 2002.

32. Kurtzer and Lasensky, *Negotiating Arab-Israeli Peace*, p. 34.

33. Lee H. Hamilton, James Schlesinger, and Brent Scowcroft, *Thinking Beyond the Stalemate in U.S.-Iranian Relations*, vol. 2, *Issues and Analysis* (Washington: The Atlantic Council of the United States, July 2001), p. 42.

34. Ibid., pp. 44–48.

35. William Luers, Thomas R. Pickering, and Jim Walsh, "How to Deal with Iran," *New York Review of Books*, February 12, 2009.

36. See, for example, Barry Blechman and Daniel Brumberg, *Engagement, Coercion, and Iran's Nuclear Challenge*, Report of a Joint Study Group on U.S.-Iran Relations (Washington: United States Institute of Peace and the Stimson Center, 2010).

37. Helen Dewar and Tom Kenworthy, "Congress Opens Debate on Using Force in Gulf," *Washington Post*, January 11, 1991.

38. Memorandum to the Director, Federal Bureau of Investigation, Bufile 105185148, from Sac. WFO (10045302) (P), May 4, 1970, pp. 1–2.

39. "Manhattan U.S. Attorney Files Civil Action Seeking Forfeiture of Alavi Foundation's Interest in Fifth Avenue Office Tower Controlled by Iran," Federal Bureau of Investigation, November 12, 2009.

40. "U.S. Forces Losing War in Afghanistan: Taliban," *Express Tribune* (Karachi), December 16, 2011; "Taliban Talk: No Longer Our Enemy?" *New Hampshire Union Leader*, December 20, 2011.

41. Warren Christopher, *In the Stream of History: Shaping Foreign Policy for a New Era* (Stanford, Calif.: Stanford University Press, 1997), p. 373.

42. James A. Baker III, with Thomas M. DeFrank, *The Politics of Diplomacy: Revolution, War, and Peace, 1989–1992* (New York: Putnam, 1995), p. 596.

43. Michael McCurry, Daily Press Briefing, U.S. Department of State, September 9, 1993.

44. Warren Christopher, "Maintaining the Momentum for Peace in the Middle East," Georgetown University, Washington, D.C., October 24, 1994.

45. Shlomo Ben-Ami, "So Close and Yet So Far: Lessons from the Israeli-Palestinian Peace Process," *Israel Studies*, vol. 10, no. 2 (2005), p. 76.

46. Philip J. Crowley, Daily Press Briefing, U.S. Department of State, September 14, 2010.

47. Philip J. Crowley, Daily Press Briefing, U.S. Department of State, October 27, 2010.

48. Philip J. Crowley, Daily Press Briefing, U.S. Department of State, June 9, 2010.

49. Jeane J. Kirkpatrick, *Making War to Keep Peace* (New York: HarperCollins, 2007), pp. 293–94.

50. Robert Blackwill, "America Must Give the South to the Taliban," *Financial Times*, July 21, 2010.

51. Ronald Reagan, remarks at the American Bar Association's Annual Convention, July 8, 1985.

52. Sharon A. Squassoni, "Weapons of Mass Destruction: Trade Between North Korea and Pakistan," CRS Report for Congress, March 11, 2004.

53. "Lankan Muslims in Dubai Supplied Nuclear Materials to Pak: Khan," *Times of India*, September 9, 2009.

54. Larry A. Niksch, "North Korea: Terrorism List Removal?" CRS Report for Congress, July 10, 2008, pp. 25–26.

55. Douglas Frantz, "Iran Closes In on Ability to Build a Nuclear Bomb," *Los Angeles Times*, August 4, 2003, as quoted in Niksch, "North Korea: Terrorism List Removal?" p. 26.

56. Robin Wright, "N. Koreans Taped at Syrian Reactor," *Washington Post*, April 24, 2008; Larry A. Niksch, "North Korea's Nuclear Weapons Development and Diplomacy," CRS Report for Congress, March 30, 2009, p. 11.

57. U.S. Department of State, "Flight of Proliferation Concern Between DPRK and Iran," July 23, 2008, State 79112.

58. William J. Broad, James Glanz, and David E. Sanger, "Iran Fortifies Its Arsenal with the Aid of North Korea," *New York Times*, November 28, 2010.

59. Edward Djerejian, Special Briefing, U.S. Department of State, December 18, 1992.

60. Michael McCurry, Daily Press Briefing, U.S. Department of State, February 3, 1994.

61. Michael McCurry, Daily Press Briefing, U.S. Department of State, February 25, 1994.

62. Thomas Hubbard and Christine Shelly, Daily Press Briefing, U.S. Department of State, December 9, 1994.

63. Michael McCurry, written statement on the Repatriation of Chief Warrant Officer Bobby Hall, U.S. Department of State, December 30, 1994.

64. Nicholas Burns, Daily Press Briefing, U.S. Department of State, March 12, 1997.

65. Max Ruston, "Korea Talks, First Day," Voice of America, April 16, 1997.

66. James P. Rubin, Daily Press Briefing, U.S. Department of State, April 27, 1999.

67. Winston Lord, Special Briefing, U.S. Department of State, September 1, 1993.

68. Zalman Shoval, "The Trouble with Wye," *Washington Times*, January 6, 1999.

69. James P. Rubin, Daily Press Briefing, U.S. Department of State, January 6, 1999.

70. See, for example, Nicholas Burns, Daily Press Briefing, U.S. Department of State, January 5, 1996.

71. Ibid.

72. Nicholas Burns, Daily Press Briefing, U.S. Department of State, October 24, 1996.

73. Nicholas Burns, Daily Press Briefings, U.S. Department of State, October 15, 1996; October 21, 1996; October 22, 1996.

74. James P. Rubin, Daily Press Briefing, U.S. Department of State, October 14, 1998.

75. James P. Rubin, Daily Press Briefing, U.S. Department of State, June 18, 1998.

76. Richard Boucher, Daily Press Briefing, U.S. Department of State, September 20, 2000.

77. Patrick Clawson, *The Red Line: How to Assess Progress in U.S. Iran Policy*, A Washington Institute Strategic Report (The Washington Institute for Near East Policy, 2010).

78. Negotiations Support Unit memorandum to Prime Minister Mahmoud Abbas, "U.S. Coordination and Monitoring Mission," July 15, 2003.

79. Richard Boucher, Daily Press Briefing, U.S. Department of State, March 4, 2004.

80. U.S. Troop Readiness, Veterans' Care, Katrina Recovery, and Iraq Accountability Appropriations Act, 2007, P.L. 110-28.

81. European Council in Edinburgh, December 11–12, 1992, *Conclusions of the Presidency*, Part D: External Relations: Iran, ¶ 15 (p. 96).

82. Karl F. Inderfurth, "A Taliban 'Rope-a-Dope' Strategy?" *Foreign Policy*, January 25, 2012.

83. Michael McCurry, Daily Press Briefing, U.S. Department of State, August 30, 1993.

84. Michael McCurry, Daily Press Briefing, U.S. Department of State, September 7, 1993.

85. "U.S.-Libya Relations," Senate Committee on Foreign Relations, February 26, 2004.

86. Richard Boucher, Daily Press Briefing, U.S. Department of State, April 20, 2004.

87. Denis MacShane, Minister for Europe, UK Foreign and Commonwealth Office, August 15, 2003.

Chapter 11: Corrupting Intelligence or Corrupted Intelligence?

1. Robert Jervis, "Why Intelligence and Policymakers Clash," *Political Science Quarterly*, Summer 2010.

2. Robert Dreyfuss, "The Yes-Man," *American Prospect*, May 8, 2006.

3. Jervis, "Why Intelligence and Policymakers Clash."

4. Abram N. Shulsky and Gary Schmitt, *Silent Warfare: Understanding the World of Intelligence* (Washington: Potomac Books, 2002), pp. 57–58.

5. Ibid., pp. 134–36.

6. Robert Gates, "An Opportunity Unfulfilled: The Use and Perceptions of Intelligence at the White House," *Washington Quarterly*, Winter 1989, p. 42.

7. Thomas Graham Jr., former Acting Director of the Arms Control and Disarmament Agency, statement to the Subcommittee on Oversight of Government Management, the Federal Workforce, and the District of Columbia, Senate Committee on Homeland Security and Governmental Affairs, May 15, 2008.

8. Barry M. Blechman and Janne E. Nolan, "Reorganizing for More Effective Arms Negotiations," *Foreign Affairs*, Summer 1983.

9. Hal Brands, "Progress Unseen: U.S. Arms Control Policy and the Origins of Détente, 1963–1968," *Diplomatic History*, April 2006.

10. Thomas Graham Jr. statement, May 15, 2008.

11. Robert Jastrow, "Reagan vs. the Scientists: Why the President Is Right about Missile Defense," *Commentary*, January 1984.

12. Robin Ranger and Dov S. Zakheim, "Arms Control Demands Compliance," *Orbis*, Spring 1990.

13. Jervis, "Why Intelligence and Policymakers Clash."

14. Albert Wohlstetter, "Is There a Strategic Arms Race?" *Foreign Policy*, Summer 1974.

15. Donald Rumsfeld, *Known and Unknown* (New York: Penguin, 2011), pp. 229–31.

16. "Intelligence Community Experiment in Competitive Analysis: Soviet Strategic Objectives, an Alternative View," Report of Team B, Central Intelligence Agency, December 1976, pp. 1, 43.

17. Anne Hessing Cahn, "Team B: The Trillion Dollar Experiment," *Bulletin of the Atomic Scientists*, April 1993.

18. Rumsfeld, *Known and Unknown*, p. 239.

19. Gerhard Wettig, "The Last Soviet Offensive in the Cold War: Emergence and Development of the Campaign against NATO Euromissiles, 1979–1983," *Cold War History*, February 2009, p. 85.

20. President Jimmy Carter, television address, October 1, 1979.

21. Rumsfeld, *Known and Unknown*, p. 259.

22. Alexander M. Haig Jr., "A Certain Idea of Man: The Democratic Revolution and Its Future," *Current Policy*, September 13, 1981.

23. Jonathan B. Tucker, "The 'Yellow Rain' Controversy: Lessons for Arms Control Compliance," *Nonproliferation Review*, Spring 2001, pp. 25–26.

24. Ibid., p. 29.

25. Ibid., pp. 31–32; Elisa D. Harris, "Sverdlovsk and Yellow Rain: Two Cases of Soviet Noncompliance?" *International Security*, Spring 1987, pp. 70–75.

26. Harris, "Sverdlovsk and Yellow Rain," p. 92.

27. Tucker, "The 'Yellow Rain' Controversy," pp. 32–33; Philip M. Boffey, "Washington Talk: Chemical Warfare; Declassified Cables Add to Doubts about U.S. Disclosures on 'Yellow Rain,'" *New York Times*, August 31, 1987.

28. Harris, "Sverdlovsk and Yellow Rain," p. 67.

29. Craig Whitney, "Moscow Rejects Germ-Warfare Report as 'Slander,'" *New York Times*, March 20, 1980.

30. Harris, "Sverdlovsk and Yellow Rain," pp. 46–48.

31. Ibid., pp. 53–55.

32. Rebecca Katz and Burton Singer, "Can an Attribution Assessment Be Made for Yellow Rain?" *Politics and the Life Sciences*, August 24, 2007.

33. Jan T. Knoph and Kristina S. Westerdahl, "Re-Evaluating Russia's Biological Weapons Policy, as Reflected in the Criminal Code and Official Admissions: Insubordination Leading to a President's Subordination," *Critical Reviews in Microbiology*, vol. 32 (1996), p. 2.

34. Tucker, "The 'Yellow Rain' Controversy," pp. 38–39.

35. Ranger and Zakheim, "Arms Control Demands Compliance."

36. Gary L. Guertner, "Three Images of Soviet Arms Control Compliance," *Political Science Quarterly*, November 1988.

37. Jastrow, "Reagan vs. the Scientists."

38. McGeorge Bundy, George F. Kennan, Robert S. McNamara, and Gerard Smith, "The President's Choice: Star Wars or Arms Control," *Foreign Affairs*, Winter 1984–85.

39. Ronald Reagan, letter to the Speaker of the House and the President of the Senate, and the President's Report, December 2, 1987.

40. Guertner, "Three Images of Soviet Arms Control Compliance."

41. William D. Jackson, "Verification in Arms Control: Beyond NTM," *Journal of Peace Research*, vol. 19 (1982), p. 345.

42. See, for example, Gloria Duffy, "Explaining Soviet Compliance," *Society*, July–August 1987.

43. Guertner, "Three Images of Soviet Arms Control Compliance."

44. Raymond L. Garthoff, "Case of the Wandering Radar," *Bulletin of Atomic Scientists*, July–August 1991.

45. Ranger and Zakheim, "Arms Control Demands Compliance."

46. William T. Lee, "The ABM Treaty Was Dead on Arrival," *Comparative Strategy*, April–June 2000.

47. Max Hollan, "Private Sources of U.S. Foreign Policy," *Journal of Cold War Studies*, Fall 2005, pp. 36–37.

48. Margaret O'Brien Steinfels, "Death and Lies in El Salvador," *Commonweal*, October 26, 2001.

49. Robert Jervis, "Why Intelligence and Policymakers Clash," *Political Science Quarterly*, Summer 2010.

50. Steven Mufson, "A 'Rogue' Is a 'Rogue' Is a 'State of Concern': U.S. Alters Terminology for Certain Countries," *Washington Post*, June 20, 2000.

51. Ibid.

52. Lee H. Hamilton, James Schlesinger, and Brent Scowcroft, *Thinking Beyond the Stalemate in U.S.-Iranian Relations*, vol. 2, *Issues and Analysis* (Washington: The Atlantic Council of the United States, July 2001), pp. 52–53, 102.

53. Ibid., pp. 47–51, 101–2.

54. Matt Apuzzo, "Not All Terrorism: Obama Tries to Change the Subject," Associated Press, April 7, 2010.

55. Interview with Homeland Security Secretary Janet Napolitano, "Away from the Politics of Fear," *Spiegel Online International*, March 16, 2009.

56. Don Oberdorfer, *The Two Koreas: A Contemporary History* (New York: Basic Books, 2001), p. 103.

57. Cyrus Vance, *Hard Choices: Critical Years in America's Foreign Policy* (New York: Simon & Schuster, 1983), p. 128.

58. Oberdorfer, *The Two Koreas*, p. 251; Joel S. Wit, Daniel B. Poneman, and Robert L. Gallucci, *Going Critical: The First North Korean Nuclear Crisis* (Washington: Brookings Institution Press, 2004), p. 6.

59. Wit, Poneman, and Gallucci, *Going Critical*, p. 81.

60. David E. Sanger, "Seoul's Leader Says North Is Manipulating U.S. on Nuclear Issue," *New York Times*, July 2, 1993; Oberdorfer, *The Two Koreas*, p. 287.

61. Wit, Poneman, and Gallucci, *Going Critical*, pp. 314–15.

62. Jim Hoagland, "The Selling of the Korea Deal," *Washington Post*, December 6, 1994.

63. Nicholas Burns, Daily Press Briefing, January 24, 1996.

64. Nicholas Burns, Daily Press Briefing, June 9, 1997.

65. "US Envoy Says Four-Way Preferable to Six-Way Talks on Korean Peace," Yonhap News Agency (Seoul), October 20, 1998.

66. "Foreign Assistance: North Korea Restricts Food Aid Monitoring," General Accounting Office, October 1999, GAO/NSIAD0035.

67. Bert T. Edwards, letter to Henry L. Hinton Jr., Assistant Comptroller General, General Accounting Office, September 27, 1999.

68. "Nuclear Nonproliferation: Status of Heavy Fuel Oil Delivered to North Korea Under the Agreed Framework," General Accounting Office, September 1999, GAO/RCED99276.

69. Wit, Poneman, and Gallucci, *Going Critical*, p. 357.

70. James B. Foley, Daily Press Briefing, U.S. Department of State, August 25, 1999.

71. Sung-Yoon Lee, "Engaging North Korea: The Clouded Legacy of South Korea's Sunshine Policy," *AEI Asian Outlook*, April 2010.

72. Joshua D. Pollack, "The United States, North Korea, and the End of the Agreed Framework," *Naval War College Review*, Summer 2003, p. 13.

73. Christopher R. Hill, Assistant Secretary for East Asian and Pacific Affairs, "The Six Party Process: Progress and Perils in North Korea's Denuclearization," testimony before the Subcommittee on Asia, the Pacific, and the Global Environment, and Subcommittee on Terrorism, Nonproliferation, and Trade, House Committee on Foreign Affairs, October 25, 2007.

74. Larry A. Niksch, "North Korea: Terrorism List Removal?" CRS Report for Congress, July 10, 2008.

75. Larry A. Niksch, "North Korea: Terrorism List Removal," CRS Report for Congress, April 15, 2009, p. 20.

76. Ibid., p. 21.

77. Ibid., p. 23.

78. David E. Sanger, "A Nation at War: Asian Front: U.S. Rebukes Pakistanis for Lab's Aid to Pyongyang," *New York Times*, April 1, 2003.

79. "An Israeli Strike on Syria Kindles Debate in the U.S.," *New York Times*, October 10, 2007.

80. Kenneth G. Weiss, "Space Dragon: Long March, Missile Proliferation, and Sanctions," *Comparative Strategy*, October 1999, p. 342.

81. Greg Stohr and Phil Mattingly, "Geithner Delays Currency Report, Urges Flexible Yuan for China," Bloomberg, April 4, 2010.

82. Peter Baker, "Despite Arrests, Working to Rebuild Russia Ties," *New York Times*, June 30, 2010.

83. Bill Gertz, "Spy Swap Puts Halt to Fact Finding," *Washington Times*, July 13, 2010.

84. Bruce W. Jentleson, *With Friends Like These: Reagan, Bush, and Saddam, 1982–1990* (New York: Norton, 1994), p. 33.

85. George Shultz, letter to Howard Berman, June 20, 1985, as quoted in ibid., p. 54.

86. Defense Department memorandum, "Subject: High Technology Dual Use Exports to Iraq," July 1, 1985, as quoted in Jentleson, *With Friends Like These*, p. 51.

87. Joost R. Hiltermann, *A Poisonous Affair: America, Iraq, and the Gassing of Halabja* (New York: Cambridge University Press, 2007), pp. 37–46.

88. Joe Biden, "President Bush's Policy toward Iraq," U.S. Senate, October 2, 1992.

89. Robert Jervis, *Why Intelligence Fails: Lessons from the Iranian Revolution and the Iraq War* (Ithaca, N.Y.: Cornell University Press, 2010), pp. 126–27.

90. Ibid., pp. 131–33.

91. Ibid., p. 133.

92. Joseph C. Wilson IV, "What I Didn't Find in Africa," *New York Times*, July 6, 2003.

93. David Crist, *The Twilight War: The Secret History of America's Thirty-Year Conflict with Iran* (New York: Penguin, 2012), pp. 17–18.

94. Jervis, *Why Intelligence Fails*, pp. 34–122.

95. Staff Report on the Khobar Towers Attack, Senate Select Committee on Intelligence, September 12, 1996, pp. 5, 8–10.

96. Caspar Weinberger, Joint Hearing on Terrorism, Senate Select Committee on Intelligence, August 1, 1996.

97. Secretary of State Madeleine K. Albright, remarks at the Asia Society Dinner, Waldorf-Astoria Hotel, New York, June 17, 1998.

98. Robin Wright, "U.S. Now Views Iran in More Favorable Light," *Los Angeles Times*, February 14, 2003.

99. Adam Ereli, Daily Press Briefing, U.S. Department of State, April 9, 2004.

100. Gary Thomas, "No Evidence of Iranian Role in Iraq Unrest, Says US State Department," Voice of America, April 9, 2004.

101. "Iran: Nuclear Intentions and Capabilities," National Intelligence Council, November 2007.

102. "'High Confidence' Games," *Wall Street Journal*, December 5, 2007.

103. "Iran: Nuclear Intentions and Capabilities."

104. Edward Jay Epstein, "How the CIA Got It Wrong on Iran's Nukes," *Wall Street Journal,* July 29, 2010.

105. "Iran: Where We Are Today," Senate Committee on Foreign Relations, May 4, 2009.

106. *Proceedings of the 111th Annual Convention of the Veterans of Foreign Wars of the United States,* Indianapolis, August 21–26, 2010.

107. Arlen Specter with Chris Bradish, "Dialogue with Adversaries," *Washington Quarterly,* Winter 2007.

108. Mark Phythian, "The Illicit Arms Trade: Cold War and Post–Cold War," *Crime, Law, and Social Change,* March 2000, p. 42.

109. Jason Allardyce, "Lockerbie Bomber 'Set Free for Oil,'" *Sunday Times* (London), August 30, 2009; Steven Mufson, "Libyan Controversy Adds to BP's Woes," *Washington Post,* July 16, 2010.

110. "U.S. Renews Diplomatic Relations with Libya," Associated Press, June 28, 2004.

111. Adam Ereli, Daily Press Briefing, U.S. Department of State, June 28, 2004.

112. Dennis Ross, *The Missing Peace: The Inside Story of the Fight for Middle East Peace* (New York: Farrar, Straus & Giroux, 2004), p. 58.

113. Madeleine Albright, Special Briefing, U.S. Department of State, July 25, 2000.

114. Philip Reeker, Daily Press Briefings, U.S. Department of State, July 27, 2000; August 1, 2000; August 29, 2000.

115. PLO Compliance Report (December 15, 2000–June 15, 2001), Pursuant to Title VIII of Public Law 101-246, Foreign Relations Authorization Act for Fiscal Year 2000–2001, As Amended.

116. Ambassador Francis X. Taylor, Coordinator for Counterterrorism, On-the-Record Briefing on Release of *Patterns of Global Terrorism 2001* Annual Report, Washington, D.C., May 21, 2002.

117. PLO Commitment Compliance Act, May 7, 2002.

118. Matthew Levitt, "PLOCCA 2002: Empty Words," PeaceWatch no. 384, The Washington Institute for Near East Policy, May 24, 2002.

119. Sean McCormack, Daily Press Briefing, U.S. Department of State, October 14, 2008.

120. P. S. Suryanarayana, "No Assurance That A.Q. Khan Network Is Dismantled," *Hindu,* June 7, 2004; Condoleezza Rice interview, *Late Edition with Wolf Blitzer,* CNN, October 3, 2004.

121. Mark Mazzetti, Jane Perlez, Eric Schmitt, and Andrew W. Lehren, "Pakistan Aids Insurgency in Afghanistan, Reports Assert," *New York Times,* July 25, 2010.

122. Hillary Rodham Clinton, opening remarks at U.S.-Pakistan Strategic Dialogue, Foreign Ministry, Islamabad, July 19, 2010.

123. Richard Holbrooke, "Briefing by Special Representative Holbrooke on His Recent Trip to Afghanistan, Pakistan, Central Asia, Georgia, and Germany," U.S. Department of State, March 2, 2010; "India Rejects Holbrooke's Opinion, Menon Heads to Kabul," *Zee News* (New Delhi), March 4, 2010.

124. Mazzetti et al., "Pakistan Aids Insurgency in Afghanistan, Reports Assert."

125. Leon Panetta on *This Week*, ABC, June 27, 2010.

126. Spencer S. Hsu and Greg Miller, "U.S. Charges Pakistani Taliban Leader in CIA Attack," *Washington Post*, September 2, 2010.

Chapter 12: Blessed Are the Peacemakers?

1. Scott Atran and Robert Axelrod, "Why We Talk to Terrorists," *New York Times*, June 29, 2010.

2. Mohamed Rabie, *U.S.-PLO Dialogue: Secret Diplomacy and Conflict Resolution* (Gainesville: University Press of Florida, 1995), pp. 66–75.

3. Shlomo Ben-Ami, "So Close and Yet So Far: Lessons from the Israeli-Palestinian Peace Process," *Israel Studies*, vol. 10, no. 2 (2005), p. 72.

4. Don Oberdorfer, *The Two Koreas: A Contemporary History* (New York: Basic Books, 2001), p. 14.

5. Ben-Ami, "So Close and Yet So Far," p. 73.

6. M. J. Zuckerman, "Can 'Unofficial' Talks Avert Disaster?" *Carnegie Reporter*, Fall 2005.

7. Ibid.

8. Farah Stockman, "Blogs Bridge Iran-U.S. Gulf," *Boston Globe*, December 3, 2008.

9. Joel S. Wit, Daniel B. Poneman, and Robert L. Gallucci, *Going Critical: The First North Korean Nuclear Crisis* (Washington: Brookings Institution Press, 2004), p. 52.

10. Zuckerman, "Can 'Unofficial' Talks Avert Disaster?"

11. Leon V. Sigal, *Disarming Strangers: Nuclear Diplomacy with North Korea* (Princeton, N.J.: Princeton University Press, 1998), p. 134.

12. Michelle Higgins, "For a Few Weeks, North Korea Joins Axis of Tourism," *New York Times*, May 7, 2006; Matt Shiraki, "A Glimpse of North Korea: We Have Seen It, but Where Do We Go from Here?" *Citizen* (Cambridge, Mass.), September 20, 2010.

13. Victoria Nuland, Daily Press Briefing, U.S. Department of State, January 3, 2013.

14. Senator Ted Stevens (R-Alaska), news conference with Senators Thad Cochran (R-Mississippi), Daniel Inouye (D-Hawaii), Pete Domenici (R-New Mexico), and Pat Roberts (R-Kansas), U.S. Capitol, April 11, 1997.

15. "U.S. Congressman Offers Peace Plan to Taliban," *Gulf Times* (Doha), April 12, 2001.

16. William H. Sullivan, *Mission to Iran* (New York: Norton, 1981), pp. 193–94.

17. Harold H. Saunders, "Diplomacy and Pressure," in *American Hostages in Iran: The Conduct of a Crisis*, ed. Warren Christopher (New Haven: Yale University Press, 1985), pp. 84–85.

18. Ibid., p. 90.

19. George Bush and Brent Scowcroft, *A World Transformed* (New York: Knopf, 1998), pp. 413–14.

20. John W. Limbert, "Negotiating with the Islamic Republic of Iran," United States Institute of Peace, Special Report 199, January 1, 2008.

21. "Hooshang Amirahmadi: Ahmadinezhad bish az har kasi dar sudad shakstin qafil rabiteh ba amrikast," *Asr-i Iran*, March 15, 2008.

22. Lee H. Hamilton, James Schlesinger, and Brent Scowcroft, *Thinking Beyond the Stalemate in U.S.-Iranian Relations*, vol. 2, *Issues and Analysis* (Washington: The Atlantic Council of the United States, July 2001), pp. 69–72.

23. See, for example, Nicholas D. Kristof, "Diplomacy at Its Worst," *New York Times*, April 29, 2007.

24. Robin Wright, "Diplomatic Exit: For Iran's Javad Zarif, a Curtain Call Behind the Scenes," *Washington Post*, April 15, 2007.

25. Amitai Etzioni, "Time to Make a Deal with Iran," *USA Today*, May 2, 2006.

26. Wit, Poneman, and Gallucci, *Going Critical*, p. 66; Sigal, *Disarming Strangers*, pp. 236–37.

27. Wit, Poneman, and Gallucci, *Going Critical*, pp. 131, 148.

28. Ibid., p. 95.

29. Ibid., p. 201.

30. Jimmy Carter, "Introduction," in Marion V. Creekmore, *A Moment of Crisis: Jimmy Carter, the Power of a Peacemaker, and North Korea's Nuclear Ambitions* (New York: PublicAffairs, 2006), pp. xxii–xxv.

31. Wit, Poneman, and Gallucci, *Going Critical*, p. 235.

32. Sigal, *Disarming Strangers*, p. 135.

33. Ibid., p. 142.

34. Senator Joe Biden, "Prospects for Progress: America and Iran after 9-11," remarks to the Iranian American Council, March 13, 2002.

35. "Iran Will Not Issue Permission for AIC," Press TV, October 21, 2008.

36. Carl Marziali, "National Academies Visit Iran," USC Dornsife, December 1, 2007.

37. Glenn E. Schweitzer, *U.S.-Iran Engagement in Science, Engineering, and Health (2000–2009)* (Washington: The National Academies Press, 2010), p. 6.

38. Ibid., p. 7.

39. Marziali, "National Academies Visit Iran."

40. "Iran Makes Science Part of Revolution," Fars News Agency, June 12, 2008.

41. Jeremy Goldberg, "Sporting Diplomacy: Boosting the Size of the Diplomatic Corps," *Washington Quarterly*, Autumn 2000.

42. Robert Levey and Richard H. Stewart, "Should We Boycott the Olympics?" *Boston Globe*, January 12, 1980; James Riordan, "Olympics' Flame Yes, but Smudgepot, No," *New York Times*, June 29, 1980.

43. Levey and Stewart, "Should We Boycott the Olympics?"

44. Henry Kissinger, *White House Years* (New York: Little, Brown & Co., 1979), pp. 685–711.

45. "Sporting Initiatives with Iran: Wrestling Diplomacy Finds a Common Voice," Bureau of Educational and Cultural Affairs, U.S. Department of State, n.d.

46. *International Iran Times*, June 26, 1998, as quoted in Houshang Chehabi, "Sport Diplomacy between the United States and Iran," *Diplomacy and Statecraft*, vol. 12, no. 1 (2001).

47. Fereydun Hajipur, "Football Diplomacy, a Trap for Subservience?" *Javan* (Tehran), January 5, 2000, translation provided by the Open Source Center.

48. Rosa Prince, "Iran 'Carried Out Surveillance of New York City,'" *Telegraph* (London), March 22, 2012.

49. "Majira-ye dar khvast Seyyed Hossein Nasr az rahbar-i inqilab," *Asr-i Iran*, October 17, 2009.

Conclusion: Is Talking the Shortest Path to War?

1. Elliott Abrams, *Tested by Zion: The Bush Administration and the Israeli-Palestinian Conflict* (New York: Cambridge University Press, 2013), p. 309.

2. Judith Miller, "Film: Movies of Iran Struggle for Acceptance," *New York Times*, July 19, 1992.

3. Abrams, *Tested by Zion*, p. 24.

4. Chuck Downs, *Over the Line: North Korea's Negotiating Strategy* (Washington: American Enterprise Institute, 1999), p. 277.

5. "Pakistani Paper Lauds North Korea Test, Urges US to Review 'Biased' Policies," *Nawa-i-Waqt* (Rawalpindi), October 10, 2006, translation provided by BBC Worldwide Monitoring. See also, "Pakistan May Reportedly Relax Restrictions on A.Q. Khan," *Nawa-i-Waqt*, October 12, 2006.

6. "Situation of Human Rights in the Islamic Republic," United Nations General Assembly, October 15, 1997, A/52/472.

7. Charles L. Pritchard, *Failed Diplomacy: The Tragic Story of How North Korea Got the Bomb* (Washington: Brookings Institution Press, 2007), p. 50.

INDEX